MONOGRAPHS OF THE
SOCIETY FOR RESEARCH IN
CHILD DEVELOPMENT

Serial No. 244, Vol. 60, Nos. 2–3, 1995

CAREGIVING, CULTURAL, AND COGNITIVE PERSPECTIVES ON SECURE-BASE BEHAVIOR AND WORKING MODELS: NEW GROWING POINTS OF ATTACHMENT THEORY AND RESEARCH

EDITED BY

Everett Waters
Brian E. Vaughn
German Posada
Kiyomi Kondo-Ikemura

WITH COMMENTARY BY
Christoph M. Heinicke
Inge Bretherton

MONOGRAPHS OF THE SOCIETY FOR RESEARCH IN CHILD DEVELOPMENT
Serial No. 244, Vol. 60, Nos. 2–3, 1995

CONTENTS

ABSTRACT   vii

EDITORS' INTRODUCTION   ix

PART 1:
ON THE SHAPING OF
ATTACHMENT THEORY
AND RESEARCH

ON THE SHAPING OF ATTACHMENT THEORY AND RESEARCH:
AN INTERVIEW WITH MARY D. S. AINSWORTH (FALL 1994)
Mary D. S. Ainsworth and Robert S. Marvin   3

PART 2:
THE GENERALITY OF SECURE-BASE
BEHAVIOR AND SECURE-BASE
INDIVIDUAL DIFFERENCES

INTRODUCTION TO PART 2   25

THE SECURE-BASE PHENOMENON ACROSS CULTURES:
CHILDREN'S BEHAVIOR, MOTHERS' PREFERENCES,
AND EXPERTS' CONCEPTS
German Posada, Yuan Gao, Fang Wu, Roberto Posada, Margarita Tascon,
Axel Schöelmerich, Abraham Sagi, Kiyomi Kondo-Ikemura,
Wenche Haaland, and Berit Synnevaag   27

A QUANTITATIVE APPROACH
TO THE DESCRIPTION AND CLASSIFICATION
OF PRIMARY SOCIAL RELATIONSHIPS
F. Francis Strayer, Manuela Verissimo,
Brian E. Vaughn, and Carollee Howes   49

ATTACHMENTS IN A MULTIPLE-CAREGIVER
AND MULTIPLE-INFANT ENVIRONMENT:
THE CASE OF THE ISRAELI KIBBUTZIM
Abraham Sagi, Marinus H. van IJzendoorn, Ora Aviezer, Frank Donnell,
Nina Koren-Karie, Tirtsa Joels, and Yael Harel   71

PART 3:
CONCURRENT MATERNAL SUPPORT
FOR SECURE-BASE BEHAVIOR

INTRODUCTION TO PART 3   95

MATERNAL BEHAVIOR AND INFANT
SECURITY IN OLD WORLD MONKEYS:
CONCEPTUAL ISSUES AND A METHODOLOGICAL BRIDGE
BETWEEN HUMAN AND NONHUMAN PRIMATE RESEARCH
Kiyomi Kondo-Ikemura and Everett Waters   **97**

A CATEGORICAL DESCRIPTION OF
INFANT-MOTHER RELATIONSHIPS IN THE HOME
AND ITS RELATION TO Q-SORT MEASURES OF
INFANT-MOTHER INTERACTION
David R. Pederson and Greg Moran   **111**

IS IT EASIER TO USE A SECURE MOTHER AS A SECURE BASE?
ATTACHMENT Q-SORT CORRELATES OF
THE ADULT ATTACHMENT INTERVIEW
German Posada, Everett Waters, Judith A. Crowell, and Keng-Ling Lay   **133**

THE ROLE OF PARENTING SENSITIVITY,
INFANT TEMPERAMENT, AND DYADIC INTERACTION
IN ATTACHMENT THEORY AND ASSESSMENT
Ronald Seifer and Masha Schiller   **146**

PART 4:
**LINKING SECURE-BASE PHENOMENA
TO ATTACHMENT REPRESENTATION**

INTRODUCTION TO PART 4   **177**

ATTACHMENT SECURITY, AFFECT REGULATION, AND
DEFENSIVE RESPONSES TO MOOD INDUCTION
Keng-Ling Lay, Everett Waters, German Posada, and Doreen Ridgeway   **179**

NARRATIVE PROCESSES
AND ATTACHMENT REPRESENTATIONS:
ISSUES OF DEVELOPMENT AND ASSESSMENT
David Oppenheim and Harriet Salatas Waters   **197**

THE PROTOTYPE HYPOTHESIS AND
THE ORIGINS OF ATTACHMENT WORKING MODELS:
ADULT RELATIONSHIPS WITH PARENTS AND ROMANTIC PARTNERS
*Gretchen Owens, Judith A. Crowell, Helen Pan, Dominique Treboux,
Elizabeth O'Connor, and Everett Waters*   **216**

APPENDIX A:
THE ATTACHMENT Q-SET (VERSION 3.0)
Developed by Everett Waters   **234**

APPENDIX B:
MATERNAL BEHAVIOR Q-SET
Developed by David R. Pederson and Greg Moran   **247**

APPENDIX C:
BACKGROUND AND SORTING INSTRUCTIONS FOR
THE ATTACHMENT Q-SET FOR INFANT MACAQUES AND
THE MATERNAL Q-SET FOR MACAQUES
Developed by Kiyomi Kondo-Ikemura and Everett Waters 255

APPENDIX D:
SCORING KEY FOR Q-SORT CRITERIA AND DERIVED SCALES
IN THE ATTACHMENT Q-SET AND THE ATTACHMENT Q-SET
FOR INFANT MACAQUES ITEM SETS 280

REFERENCES 283

COMMENTARY

EXPANDING THE STUDY OF THE FORMATION OF
THE CHILD'S RELATIONSHIPS
Christoph M. Heinicke 300

A COMMUNICATION PERSPECTIVE ON ATTACHMENT RELATIONSHIPS
AND INTERNAL WORKING MODELS
Inge Bretherton 310

CONTRIBUTORS 330

STATEMENT OF
EDITORIAL POLICY 336

ABSTRACT

WATERS, EVERETT; VAUGHN, BRIAN E.; POSADA, GERMAN; and KONDO-IKEMURA, KIYOMI (Eds.). Caregiving, Cultural, and Cognitive Perspectives on Secure-Base Behavior and Working Models: New Growing Points of Attachment Theory and Research. With Commentary by CHRISTOPH M. HEINICKE and INGE BRETHERTON. *Monographs of the Society for Research in Child Development*, 1995, **60**(2–3, Serial No. 244).

In 1985 the SRCD *Monographs* series broke with tradition to publish a collection of papers exploring the new growth and directions of attachment theory and research. In the ensuing decade, many of the questions that were posed in that collection—such as, for instance, those concerning cognitive representations of attachment—as well as the methods and analytic approaches used by some of the authors to address these questions (e.g., Q-techniques) are no longer novelties but rather stand as paradigmatic examples of mainstream attachment research.

In the present collection, several of the issues raised in the 1985 *Monograph* are revisited; these include the meaning and implications of attachment in cultures other than the United States and Western Europe (Posada, Gao, et al.), the nature of relations between attachment and temperament constructs (Seifer & Schiller), the links between quality of attachment and the mother's concurrent sensitivity (Pederson & Moran), and the association seen in children between attachment and mood (Lay, Waters, Posada, & Ridgeway). New approaches to traditional questions are explored by examining the relations among a child's different attachment relationships (Sagi et al.) and by constructing strategies for classification of infant-mother attachments on the basis of observations made in the home (Strayer, Verissimo, Vaughn, & Howes); the study of the relation between infant secure-base behavior and maternal support is extended to the investigation of macaque pairs (Kondo-Ikemura & Waters).

New questions about links between attachment and other intimate relationships are considered; these include the relation between adults' attachment history and both the quality of their relationship with an intimate partner (Owens et al.) and the organization of secure-base behavior that their child shows in the home (Posada, Waters, Crowell, & Lay). Focusing on recent advances in research on cognitive development, consideration is also given to methodological issues relating to the assessment of young children's mental representations of relationships (Oppenheim & Waters).

In all, the aim of the *Monograph* is both to consolidate our understanding of the empirical advances that have occurred in this domain of research over the last decade and to stimulate investigators to move beyond current understandings as well as current empiricism.

EDITORS' INTRODUCTION

In 1987 the American Psychological Association recognized Mary Ainsworth's contributions to developmental psychology with its award for distinguished professional contribution. The award statement speaks of her contributions as eloquently today as it did then:

> For her insights into the nature and development of human security. Her exquisite observational studies of infant-mother relationships in Uganda and Baltimore, her conceptual analyses of attachment and dependency, and her contributions to the methodology of infant assessment are the cornerstones of modern attachment theory and research. The patterns of attachment she identified in her work have proven robust and significant in research across diverse cultures and across the human life span. Her theoretical, methodological, and empirical contributions, as well as her teaching, colleagueship, and grace are a secure base from whom generations of students can explore.

The 1985 SRCD *Monograph* "Growing Points in Attachment Theory and Research" testified to the robustness of three key concepts closely identified with Mary Ainsworth, the secure-base phenomenon, patterns of attachment, and the relevance of these concepts throughout the life span. The 1985 essays also highlighted new directions in attachment theory and research, in a sense giving researchers "permission" to branch out from infant studies into older ages, new methods of assessment, and cognitive representations.

As did the first "Growing Points" *Monograph,* this new set of reports reflects the continuing vitality of Mary Ainsworth's insights and inspiration. It reflects also the enthusiasm and success with which issues raised in the 1985 *Monograph* have been pursued. Current attachment theory and research face several challenges. The first is to keep moving forward. The second is to revisit old issues—to make sure that unfinished business is properly completed and the foundations of attachment theory thoroughly evaluated and documented. Quite a few of the issues addressed in the early phases of attachment research deserve additional work. These include the onset of attachment, the origin of individual differences, the conditions that promote stability or change, and numerous issues related to multiple attachments. Although no longer at center stage, such issues are important to the coherence of attachment theory. Such work will also enrich our understanding of the secure-base concept.

A third challenge is to maintain the coherence of attachment theory as we pursue increasingly diverse research directions. Here the secure-base concept is irreplaceable. The notion that infant attachment is similar in kind to adult-adult love relationships was one of Freud's most startling insights. It is among the insights that John Bowlby sought to preserve in his control systems theory of attachment. The secure-base concept suggests a particular interpretation of this insight, a particular way in which infant-mother and close adult-adult relationships can be construed as similar. The coherent developmental perspective afforded by the secure base distinguishes attachment theory from formulations that view close relationships in terms of constructs such as reinforcement, dominance, equity, or exchange. It is critically important, therefore, that we keep the secure-base concept at the center of attachment theory for as long as possible. This involves (a) continuing work on secure-base behavior in infancy and (b) highlighting the secure-base experiences associated with attachment representations.

The reports in this *Monograph* illustrate the continuing relevance of the secure base as the key concept in attachment theory. They also illustrate how well this concept can integrate research from different domains. Finally, they make clear that Mary's contributions will be recognizable in attachment study well into the twenty-first century. We are delighted to dedicate this issue of the *Monographs* to Mary Ainsworth, as always, a secure base from whom generations of attachment researchers can explore.

We have organized this *Monograph* into four parts. Part 1 prints an interview with Mary Ainsworth conducted by Bob Marvin in the fall of 1994. Part 2 includes reports on the generalizability of attachment concepts and data. Posada, Gao, et al. use parents' and experts' reports to examine the generalizability and cross-cultural relevance of the secure-base concept in Western, Oriental, and Latin American countries. Strayer, Verissimo, Vaughn, and Howes investigate the generalizability of secure-base patterns derived from laboratory observation to home observational data. Finally, Sagi et al. examine the consistency of infants' secure-base patterns across several caregivers and also similarities in the secure-base patterns of infants who share a particular caregiver.

Part 3 addresses both normative and individual differences questions regarding the manner in which mothers' behaviors/interactions and children's characteristics interact to support the organization of secure-base behavior in the home. Pederson and Moran revisit the issue of maternal sensitivity and infant security, using new measures and a return to the observationally intensive methods pioneered by Mary Ainsworth. Kondo-Ikemura and Waters examine the role of maternal behavior in support of infant macaques' ability to use her as a secure base well after attachment is formed. Posada, Waters, Crowell, and Lay examine the relation between maternal attachment representations and the ability to serve as a secure base for 3-year-olds. Finally, Seifer and Schiller review and address the current status of arguments concerning the nature of relations between the domains of maternal sensitivity, infant temperament, and the organization of secure-base behavior.

The three reports that constitute Part 4 address issues relevant to mental representations of secure-base relationships. Lay, Waters, Posada, and Ridgeway examine the relation between attachment security and defensive responses to mood induction in $3\frac{1}{2}$-year-olds. The issue here is whether two processes central to attachment theory, secure-base behavior and defensive processes, can be linked empirically. At stake is whether the core phenomena of current attachment theory can be comprehended by a single theory. Oppenheim and Waters examine the extent to which dyadic child-mother interactions are necessary for the child to construct attachment-related mental representations. The co-construction process that they highlight has much in common with the maternal support of secure-base behavior described by Kondo-Ikemura and Waters earlier in this *Monograph*. In addition, Oppenheim and Waters review developmental literature on mental representations and draw a number of important distinctions related to the variety of possible attachment representations that a child might construct. Their conclusions have important implications for both theory and assessment. Finally, Owens et al. examine relations between attachment representations involving one's parents and comparable representations involving an adult romantic partner. A key issue is whether parent-related representations (presumably based in part on early experience) determine models formulated in subsequent relationships. A second issue concerns the effect of a person's parent-related and adult partner–related representations on marital behavior and on the adult partner's representation of the relationship.

Throughout the preparation of this *Monograph*, the editors and authors have taken advantage of many helping hands. In addition to interactions among the editors, suggestions and plain hard work by Wanda Bronson shaped the selection of content and the presentation of each report. Editors and authors alike also benefited from the thorough and thoughtful input from four consulting reviewers, Inge Bretherton, Mark T. Greenberg, Dale Hay, and F. F. Strayer. Finally, very special thanks are due to Bob Marvin, whose lengthy conversations with Mary Ainsworth are the basis for this *Monograph*'s lead article.

PART 1:
ON THE SHAPING OF
ATTACHMENT THEORY
AND RESEARCH

Mary D. Ainsworth

Photograph © Daniel Grogan

ON THE SHAPING OF ATTACHMENT THEORY AND RESEARCH: AN INTERVIEW WITH MARY D. S. AINSWORTH (FALL 1994)

Mary D. S. Ainsworth and Robert S. Marvin

I. ON THE ORIGINS OF THE CONCEPT OF THE SECURE BASE

Robert Marvin.—Your doctoral dissertation, written at the University of Toronto, focused on the security of adult relationships and was supervised by William Blatz—what was the core of Blatz's position, and was he influential in shaping your own thinking about the concept of security?

Mary D. S. Ainsworth.—Very much so. Blatz focused on the warmth and comfort that a parent can give to the baby and on the importance of starting off by making the child feel secure. He believed that, given a background of feeling secure, the infant would interest himself in what goes on around

Editors' note.—This interview with Mary Ainsworth was conducted by Robert Marvin at our request. We are deeply grateful to Bob for making it possible to elicit the memories and thoughts of one who has been so fundamentally influential in shaping the direction of attachment theory and research; without Bob's readiness to collaborate, these comments would have remained unrecorded. To Mary Ainsworth, who acquiesced to our request with the generosity and grace that have always marked her behavior toward colleagues— and particularly toward her "extended family" of attachment researchers—our gratitude remains unbounded. The transcript of the conversation was cut and edited to fit the requirements of this written presentation; however, all Ainsworth's points are reflected faithfully in what follows, and we have tried to preserve as much of her conversational style as possible.

him and want to move out to explore his world. And, should such exploration get him into more than that infant was ready to cope with, it was crucially important that the parent be accessible—that the baby be able to retreat to his "secure base" for comfort and be, as it were, "recharged" before going off again on his own. I first encountered Blatz's thinking—which was brand new, quite original as far as I know, and certainly not like anything that Freud wrote—in a course that I took from him in my fourth undergraduate year, and it was his notion of this nice "back-and-forthing" of the baby, the idea of building a secure base from which one can explore, that struck me most and attracted me to his thinking.

RM.—Did your early exposure to Blatz's ideas influence your subsequent receptiveness to Bowlby's ideas?

MDSA.—Yes, I saw the thinking of both as going in very similar directions. Blatz and Bowlby had no opportunity to influence each other—they were each working quite independently on how early relationships get established and how this then affects the child's further development, and I think they both happened to be observing the same kind of phenomena and that this led to their theories being so compatible.

RM.—When was it that you first became aware of John Bowlby's thinking, and when and how did you come to know him?

MDSA.—I wasn't aware of any of his thinking before I met him. That happened in 1950: I arrived in London in the fall of that year without a job (despite previous efforts to obtain one through correspondence) and looked up a friend, Edith Mercer, whom I got to know during the war when we were serving as "opposite numbers" in our respective armed services. She soon phoned me about a position that was being advertised in the *London Times* and that she thought might interest me. The ad sought someone who was an expert in child development and in projective techniques to work on a project investigating the effects of a young child's prolonged separations from the mother on personality development. I applied, and I was promptly interviewed by John Bowlby for that position. [*With a hearty laugh.*] What can I say? . . . We liked each other! We both liked the same researchers and clinicians who were working on similar issues at the time, and we found we were thinking along the same lines. I got the job, and, as in fairy tales, "they lived happily ever after!" Over the 3 years that I worked there, I continued to be struck by how much Bowlby's and my thinking moved in the same directions.

RM.—What kind of work did this job involve?

MDSA.—At first, John had me read all the existing literature on separation—I spent about year doing that and also becoming familiar with the two projects that he had going on at the time. One of these was a follow-up study of school-aged children who, when they were quite young, had spent long periods separated from their parents in a TB sanatorium, and the other was Jimmy Robertson's study of a particular group of young tubercular children. This was an intensive, clinical study that involved frequent visits to the homes—and it turned out to be just *my* sort of stuff!

I was placed on Jimmy's project after that first year to use my talents in looking for individual differences; originally, John had wanted me to do Rorschachs on this group, but that turned out not to be practical. The materials with which I worked were social workers' handwritten reports of the home visits they had conducted, and I began to notice several patterns in the way in which these children's "personalities" were organized that seemed pertinent to the experiences they had had.

So, as you can see, the approach and methods that I went on to use in Uganda and in Baltimore really had their beginnings in my work with Blatz and then with John Bowlby and Jimmy Robertson . . . though, as I think about it, what is really more correct to say is that the interaction among John, Jimmy, and myself completely changed John's original research project and eventually led to *Infancy in Uganda* as well as all three volumes of *Attachment and Loss*.

RM.—You told me once that, when you went to Uganda, you were not as yet convinced of the validity of Bowlby's thinking, that it was your observations of the Ugandan infants and mothers that you found so compelling. First, was it Bowlby who encouraged you to do direct observation (perhaps as Leaky had encouraged Jane Goodall), or was your focus on naturalistic observation inspired by some other source?

MDSA.—Actually, it came from having familiarized myself so thoroughly with the work of Jimmy Robertson. All of his data on mother-child interactions and relationships—which were very compelling in indexing the effects of prolonged early separations—came from visiting the children in their homes and separation environments and observing as well as listening to what transpired. The power of his observations in reflecting what was going on and communicating it effectively to others impressed me very much, so I took direct observation as my own model.

RM.—Was there any particular observation, or set of observations, that you made in your Ugandan work that became particularly influential in your subsequent thinking?

MDSA.—In seeing these babies on numerous occasions as they interacted with their mothers within the home, I think the thing that struck me most was how *active* babies are and how much it is *they* who take the initiative. They are not passive little things to whom you do things; in fact, in many ways they are the initiators of what happens to them. The picture that you got in those days from the literature was one of a passive infant who merely reacted to whatever the environment did to him, and that was the notion with which I first arrived in Uganda.

Another common belief that I had learned from reading Freud, as well as various other writers, was that what underlies the baby's tie to his mother is the fact that it is she who feeds him—the infant's pleasure in being fed gives preeminence to the figure of the food provider and becomes the basis for forming an attachment bond. The idea that infants' attachments could develop for any other reason was almost unheard of. It took the writings of Bowlby—who had been influenced by the work of ethologists, particularly Lorenz's work on imprinting—to open up people's minds to the notion that other mechanisms might in fact be responsible. My observations in Uganda gave me firsthand evidence that what I had been taught could not be supported—that feeding could *not* be properly conceived as being the "prime mover" of attachment bonds.

RM.—What particular observations were most fundamental in originally shaping your distinction between secure and insecure patterns of attachment?

MDSA.—My observation protocols took special note of instances of crying and of the conditions under which it occurred, and it became evident to me as I went on that both the amount of crying and the circumstances in which the crying took place provided a central behavioral distinction. Babies who would be identified as securely attached did relatively little crying *except,* for instance, if they woke up and the mother wasn't there or if the circumstances were such that they had reason to believe that mother was going to leave them. The ones that seemed insecure in their attachment fussed a lot of the time; anything could set them off, and there wasn't this clear picture that it was the distance from the caregiver that was responsible for the crying.

RM.—These are patterns you could never have discerned had it not been for repeated observations?

MDSA.—Oh, you're absolutely right—you can't really learn much about the relationship between a baby and the mother if you only see them once. You might say here, "Well, how about the Strange Situation, which is designed to elicit artificially what it might take a long period of observation in the home to notice?" Yes, you can indeed learn a lot from brief observation under such conditions, but, if the assessment hadn't been built on the basis of a lot of expectations derived from observations in the natural environment, there would have been no validity to the laboratory situation.

RM.—I understand that you were not much in touch with Bowlby during your stay in Uganda but that, when he visited you after your return to Baltimore and became aware of your views concerning the secure-base phenomenon, he described the similarities to his thinking that he saw in yours as "a pleasing and encouraging convergence of ideas." Is that so?

MDSA.—Yes, he did say it, I think in one of his talks. [*With a chuckle.*] I do remember that, at one point during my stay in Uganda, I became quite concerned that John's use of Lorenz's work to support arguments against the preeminence of feeding as a mechanism for forming attachments might come to hurt him—that using baby chicks' behavior to argue against an entrenched psychoanalytic position might *ruin* his reputation! I even wrote him a gently worded letter in this regard—but, as it turned out, I needn't have worried.

RM.—It seems as if the concept of secure base as you first conceived it in your Ugandan work has proved robust enough to serve virtually un-changed throughout your career. Is this correct, or have your ideas in fact changed in some significant way?

MDSA.—The core concept of using the mother as a secure base from which to explore the world has not changed; what has evolved are elabora-tions of how different patterns of relationships are built in the course of the child's particular experiences in seeking to use the mother as this secure base. At least as a starting point for observation and research, I have never seen any need to change what was already partly incorporated in the theo-ries of Blatz and Bowlby.

RM.—You once told me that, while doing the observational work in Uganda, you experienced a real paradigm shift. Can you say something about it here?

MDSA.—The transition I made from thinking in psychoanalytic terms to thinking in terms of ethology felt very much like what I later read Kuhn describe as a "paradigm shift." It was a sudden, total, and permanent change in perspective—I simply couldn't conceive of viewing what I observed in any other way. [*With a chuckle.*] In my many disagreements with behaviorists, I finally came to realize that, since they had never experienced this new way of looking at things, I really couldn't expect them to understand what I was talking about—and, although it made our quarrels useless, it did enable me to feel vastly superior!

II. ON UNIVERSALITY AND CROSS-CULTURAL DIFFERENCES

RM.—Turning to another topic, attachment theory conceives of the attachment control system as being part of our evolutionary endowment.

Does this mean we should expect to see infants organize their secure-base behavior in a similar fashion across all cultures, or should we expect to see this organization differ somewhat in different ecological settings?

MDSA.—Both. At the most fundamental level, there is a biological basis that determines the emergence and general shape of the behavioral organization—I think that environmental influences play no significant role in the infant's basic need for an attachment figure who can be trusted. But culture-related differences in ecologies and expectations will certainly affect how some specific aspects of that organization are expressed under particular conditions—I am thinking here, for instance, of proximity seeking.

RM.—As an example of what you are saying, are you thinking of the work that the Levines and I did with the Hausa, where living huts contained open fire pits as well as potentially dangerous tools and animals and babies did not explore under their own locomotion but were always carried around and handed from person to person—and yet we found that, despite this constant physical contact with numerous people, a distressed baby would want contact with an attachment figure, and a *very* distressed one would want only his or her primary attachment figure?

MDSA.—Yes, that's a very good example of part of what I mean. But I'm also thinking here of the atypically high incidence of insecure attachments that characterized Karin Grossmann's sample drawn in north (as opposed to south) Germany. Here, after behaving in ways resembling the typical interactions of securely attached mother-child pairs, cultural mores seemed to dictate that, some 3 months earlier than in other samples, the mother say, "This is enough—it's time that my child learn to be independent, to look after himself, and not to need me anymore." Even if done gently, this is very rough on a baby who has learned the definite expectation that "of course mother will pick me up! I've given her all the signals, she knows that I want her . . . and, hey, she's not doing it! and deliberately not doing it, by God!"

Some of the mothers evidently behaved in ways that fostered insecurity from the outset, but I do believe that this sudden and (from the baby's point of view) totally unexplainable shift in maternal behavior acted to make some previously secure attachments change into insecure ones. I do think that the two patterns of insecurity—those of babies who had an earlier "security-fostering" relationship and those of babies who did not—are likely to differ, but I am not sure exactly how, and I certainly think it's something very worthwhile pursuing.

My intuition is that mothers who come to reject their child's proximity bids as a matter of principle—"because this is the way to do things, it's the way my mother taught me"—may not be as consistent in rejecting the baby's requests and desires. That surely must have some effect, but I don't have a sense in exactly what direction. In any event, I have always believed that it was essential that we observe infants in more than one culture—that's what took me to Uganda. There are probably far, far more similarities across cultures during this early period than has ever been acknowledged.

RM.—Extending this line of thinking, let me ask you about work on species other than humans. First, how influential do you think this kind of work was on Bowlby's thinking, and, second, how much has it influenced your own formulations?

MDSA.—I think that Lorenz's work on imprinting was very important to John Bowlby in pointing out the direction that his thinking would take. And Harlow's studies, as well as Robert Hinde's work, were very influential in extending his perception of the similarities between humans' and other species' behavior—in a sense, he saw it as verification of the validity of his evolutionary perspective on human development. As for me . . . many of my best friends have been primatologists and ethologists, and I have always been fascinated by their work. In fact, I have been reading a lot about wolves lately, and learning about their complex social organization certainly enriches one's life as well as enables one to empathize with their behavior. Mainly, however, findings obtained with other species have made me feel that I have been on the right track rather than helping me understand the specifics of human babies' behavior.

RM.—It seems that, in whatever form, cross-fertilization between attachment researchers and those working on nonhuman species has fallen off in recent years. Do you think this is indeed true, and, if so, why did it come about?

MDSA.—I do think it's true, but I'm not sure why it happened. And I do think it's too bad—contact between these two very different branches of science was good for the young scientists on both sides. Perhaps it has been partly because most, if not all, attachment research has focused on procedures aimed at distinguishing between secure and insecure patterns as well as among different patterns of both security and insecurity—and I don't think that most primatologists are interested in this kind of thing. I think they are far more concerned with getting more and better field data and in proposing cause-and-effect relations in an observational way. Research on human mothers and babies has extended in so many different directions: the age at which the attachment relationship—or its representation—is assessed, the figures in the relationship, etc. I think that this has moved attachment researchers much further than primatologists in studying individual differences . . . but, then, I think that's in the nature of the beast.

RM.—What do you mean?

MDSA.—Well, it's obviously so much more difficult to observe the development of interactional patterns between, say, a mother bear and her cub than it is to follow a human mother and infant. And when I think of what it takes to study porpoises and their offspring! . . . In any event, I think that interest in fieldwork—which is one of the things that had connected the two fields—has been largely lost among human attachment researchers. And this is something that I do regret—the fact that our emphasis has increasingly focused on measurement rather than assessment.

III. ON CONSTRUCTING ASSESSMENTS AND RESEARCH DESIGNS

RM.—What is this distinction you make between *measurement* and *assessment*?

MDSA.—To me, measurement implies assigning numbers that reflect a precise amount or an equal interval ordering. In my own work I have focused on classifications of patterns or on matching to behavioral descriptions—and that gives you *assessments.*

RM.—Let me ask some questions about how your systems of assessment came into being. First, I have heard it said that the interactive scales we use to rate Strange Situation observations were developed by cutting up actual transcripts and ranking the relevant pieces—is that true?

MDSA.—My first reaction is to say, "Preposterous!" But in fact I do dimly recall something of this sort. Remember that at the time we had no technologies that could allow us to move information around, so shuffling about printed excerpts of specific behavioral observations was a very effective way to get good definitions of scale points. In fact, it's very similar to what one still does when using a Q-sort deck!

RM.—How about the scales of maternal behavior? How did these develop?

MDSA.—Our narrative transcripts of the home visits were very lengthy, and they didn't focus on detailed descriptions of specific sequences of behavior, so the "chop them up" approach would not have helped. No, here I started as I had in Uganda, by asking, "What is there about the behavior of this mother that is important in making a difference in how the baby behaves?" And that led to the scale of maternal sensitivity, to differences in how observant and responsive the mother is in dealing with the baby. In some cases, I started with the negative pole of what became a scale because the effect of negative qualities on the interaction often can be seen more clearly. For instance, you see the mother sort of buffet the baby around, interfere with what he is doing—and it's very clear that the baby doesn't like it. So I felt this was another dimension we should explore, and, after looking at the whole range of observations we had made, I decided that *cooperation* was the most appropriate opposite end on this particular continuum. At one point I struggled hard to devise a scale of maternal warmth, but that never worked out.

RM.—Why didn't it, do you think?

MDSA.—Various reasons. For one, it is very difficult to be precise in defining behaviors that could be criterial in rating maternal warmth. Russel Tracy tried to explore this in our narratives by doing a very detailed analysis of all affectionate behaviors, and it became clear that something as obviously a candidate for "warmth" as kissing could in fact be a very unaffectionate peck on the cheek or forehead. In a similar way, the Ugandan mothers' habit of sitting the baby in their laps facing out rather than *en face* can look like lack of warmth, but in fact it has to do with their concern to create opportunities for exploration for the child, and the physical contact between the bodies does create an affectional warmth—think of how many 3-year-olds like to sit on a parent's lap!

Another reason I gave up is that maternal warmth did not seem to make much difference in itself—two mothers can be equally warm and yet have very different effects on their babies. There is a great difference between maternal warmth and maternal sensitivity, and it took me a long time to appreciate it.

RM.—Is it perhaps that sensitivity is a response to the baby's initiative and warmth is more of a general characteristic of the mother?

MDSA.—Absolutely—and this focus on how the attachment figure supports or interferes with what the *baby* initiates has served me well all along.

RM.—So, in characterizing maternal sensitivity, we should make sure not to forget that it is sensitivity to the *baby's* initiative that is at issue. In this context, what do you think enabled you to find such robust relations between maternal sensitivity and infant security in your Baltimore study?

MDSA.—The lengthy and repeated home observations on which we based our maternal ratings certainly had a lot to do with it. But I think it was also due to the fact that such a wide range of secure and insecure patterns was represented in the sample—quite a few studies report an absence of C classifications in their groups. It could have been luck, or it could have been that the pediatricians who recruited potential participants for us tended to select women who interested them—"this one is a charmer, that one puzzles me, I wonder how motherhood will work out for this one"—and that this led to our getting a particularly diverse group.

RM.—Moving on to your classificatory system, why is it that you built the system for classification of attachment patterns around behavior observed in the laboratory rather than in the home?

MDSA.—Although the classifications are made from behavior in the Strange Situation, the rationale for assigning particular meanings to these specific behaviors and their patterning was developed from the significance of the different interactional patterns that we had observed in the home—so, in the most fundamental sense, the classification *is* based on what we learned in the home. In fact, I have been quite disappointed that so many attachment researchers have gone on to do research with the Strange Situation rather than looking at what happens in the home or in other natural settings—like I said before, it marks a turning away from "fieldwork," and I don't think it's wise.

RM.—What is it, do you think, that has led to this focus on Strange Situation data rather than on home observation?

MDSA.—Partly it's the problem of getting funding—doing observational work takes an enormous amount of time, especially when it involves repeated visits to the home. Partly it has to do with the responsibilities one feels to one's students—getting them involved in research that can be completed within the time that *they* have available to them. And in part it has to do with the "publish or perish" realities of academic life!

RM.—Can you say a bit more about just how you went about constructing the Strange Situation and the classifications?

MDSA.—I had seen a lot of separations and reunions in the homes, a lot of exploration, a lot of proximity seeking, and a lot of differences in how the baby and the mother behaved in these situations. So constructing the episodes of the Strange Situation wasn't hard at all; as I recall, it took just about half an hour of talking with Barbara Wittig to decide on the episodes and their sequence—it just came naturally. I was very interested to see how the baby would handle these various situations that he encountered in the lab, and the thing that made me feel that I was *really* on the right track was that I turned out to be so good at anticipating what each specific baby would do—that it all was so predictable, it hung together.

RM.—Was it the separations and reunions that you saw at home and in the lab that hung so well together?

MDSA.—They did—but it was also a matter of how the mother behaved at home in many other situations; how she responded to cries, to other bids, to feeding times.

RM.—Do you think that you drew a lot on the observations you made at the end of the year, when the babies could crawl and you saw them move away and back to the mother and using her as a secure base, just as you had seen it in Uganda?

MDSA.—Yes, these were certainly important. They also made me realize that you have to be very careful to think about the child's age, his developmental status—we had some 12-month-olds who couldn't creep, so they might just sit there, cry, and hold out their hands.

RM.—Might such underdeveloped locomotion shift a baby's classification, perhaps even in some major way?

MDSA.—Oh, I think that's a real concern—there has been so much variation in the ages of different samples that sometimes they are not babies anymore. At this point, all you can do is extrapolate; you go by principles you have devised or acquired without being quite sure how, but you don't follow the actual rules of the system. I've done a lot of extrapolating myself in my life, and it doesn't trouble me too much—but then, do other people do it in the same way as I? Of course, never for a minute do I think that *I* could be wrong! [*Laughter.*]

RM.—Turning to another topic, that of research strategies, why do you think there has been so little work examining patterns of maternal behavior and infant secure-base behavior as they co-occur in actual interaction? Most research seems to focus on prediction from one of these two to the other.

MDSA.—I think this is partly because many researchers think that asking, "When mother does this, what does baby do?" gets you nothing but normative description and that that's not very exciting. It's wrong, of course: all the different patterns of attachment behaviors that we established in the Baltimore study, and then the concept that these patterns represent the baby's "strategies"—all these proved to be theoretically *very* exciting, and all came about from looking at, "When baby does this, his mother does that," over and over again. But it takes a lot of time before this kind of work comes together, and it's surely easier to publish a lot of papers if you just look for "significant" correlations! Of course, we did also use the data for some "predictive" analyses—like Silvia Bell's work on how maternal response to crying in an earlier quarter of the baby's first year related to the baby's crying in a later quarter—and this also was very useful in supporting the ideas we were developing about how different patterns of attachment emerge.

RM.—So are you saying that some attachment research—not all, of course, but some significant portion—has shifted from a focus on description and understanding toward simple prediction?

MDSA.—I am sorry to say it, but I do think this has been the case.

IV. ON INDIVIDUAL DIFFERENCES AND MATERNAL SUPPORT

RM.—The idea that attachment has evolutionary underpinnings suggests that there must be some limits on how it is organized behaviorally. Suppose that someone observed some pattern of Strange Situation behavior that departs radically from that of the secure, B babies and also demonstrated that, in terms of all other significant data, babies classified in this "new" pattern behave just as those who are currently classified as secure. Would that pose a problem for attachment theory?

MDSA.—Yes, I'd say it would. But finding that everything in the mother-child interaction indicates security *except* for the child's behavior in the Strange Situation seems so very, very unlikely given all the masses of data we have accumulated that the question strikes me as being somewhat nonsensical.

RM.—What if someone discovered a new pattern of insecure behavior?

MDSA.—That would not be all that surprising; there are many more possible ways of organizing behavioral strategies for coping with an insecure relationship.

RM.—It seems that infants become attached to their primary caregiver almost regardless of the care they receive, as long as the relationship doesn't involve multiple major separations or grave threats to the child's health. Does this surprise you?

MDSA.—Not at all. It's the *presence* of the caregiving figure rather than the caregiving behavior that is essential for the attachment to develop. It's a bit like Lorenz's work with ducklings—it didn't really matter whether the mother duck fussed with the little creatures or just did her own thing; if she would start swimming away, the ducklings would follow. It was her presence that was the essential thing, and I think this phenomenon of imprinting was really important to Bowlby's original formulation of human attachment.

RM.—So does this imply that the development of human attachment is a fairly close analogue to imprinting?

MDSA.—To a certain extent, yes. It differs in the human case in that it needs more time to become effective—it's not that the newborn comes out of the womb, senses the mother, and hah! that's it! It's something that stretches out over a much longer period of time.

RM.—Do you think that there may be some particular period in the first year of life—maybe one in which a lot of different developmental milestones in locomotion and communication are being achieved—that may be particularly important in the consolidation of attachment?

MDSA.—I have a sense that the consolidation is more likely to be more evenly spread out, but it may well be that, if we did some intensive research on this extended early period, we would find evidence that some particular time is particularly crucial. At this point we just don't know.

RM.—It seems nearly paradoxical that, even though you focused so much of your work on maternal sensitivity, you are saying that it is not the mother's sensitivity but just her presence that determines whether the baby becomes attached.

MDSA.—It is not attachment but the *security* of attachment that is affected by the mother's sensitivity.

RM.—I wonder whether this is widely understood—whether some people may not think that your work had always implied that babies become attached to the person who is the most sensitive to them and that sensitivity is more important than presence.

MDSA.—If two potential attachment figures are concurrently involved, I can't help but think that their relative sensitivity to the baby might well affect the growth of the child's attachment—that it would indeed be the more sensitive of the two who first starts the attachment process going. But I'm not sure that this would necessarily be the case.

RM.—Given what you've been saying, what do you think of what is so often said to parents—that it's the quality of the time you spend with your child, not the quantity, that is important?

MDSA.—There are two issues here. One has to do with the nature of the relationship, and here you would expect that devoting "high-quality time" to the child would tend to evolve into a secure relationship. The mere continued presence of the adult figure has little, if anything, to do with the *quality* of the relationship—only with the emergence of *some* form of bond.

RM.—In a related vein, if a child is placed in day care for the full day and from a very early age (say 6 weeks) and is with the mother only in the evenings and over the weekends, do you think that baby's mother is still likely to be his primary attachment figure?

MDSA.—Yes. Group-care situations nearly always include multiple caregivers, and it is much more difficult to form an attachment with one individual out of the several who look after the baby and whose presence is likely to vary day by day. But, if there should be a long-continuing, uninterrupted relationship with some caregiver other than the mother, then, yes indeed, I think you could see the same kind of relationship emerge with that figure as you ordinarily see with the mother. The crucial point is that the relationship be continuing and pretty much uninterrupted—under such conditions, the nonmaternal caregiver can well become an attachment figure closely resembling that which usually evolves in the relationship with the mother.

RM.—In the early stages of your work—like when you first went to Uganda—were you primarily interested in normative questions as opposed to questions of individual differences?

MDSA.—I think my primary interests were normative. I was very interested in what "popped in" in terms of behavior, what new acquisitions emerged at what ages, and how well the normative patterns that I saw replicated what had been observed in the United States and England—I was very sure that normative similarities would be there. But that doesn't mean that I didn't expect to see individual differences as well. . . . I wasn't surprised by them, and I was very curious to see what circumstances made for these differences, for the departures from normative patterns.

RM.—The first reports of Strange Situation behavior that emerged from the Baltimore study focused on the "average" baby's typical responses to a new environment and to brief separations. What made you then shift the focus to individual differences—was it differences among babies or among mothers that caught your eye?

MDSA.—As I said earlier, the home visits led me to have very definite expectations about how individual babies would respond to the Strange Situation, so obviously differences in babies' behavior did catch my eye. But these expectations were built not only on the baby's behavior but also on the mother's—it was the qualities of the many *interactions* that I had seen between the two that were behind my perceptions of differences.

RM.—So, as it has at various points in our conversation, it appears that it was the repeated home visits, the gathering of a *lot* of information over a number of months of observation—that this was the key to understanding what was going on in both your Uganda and in your Baltimore samples.

MDSA.—Indeed it was.

RM.—To move on to debates concerning the determinants of individual differences: arguments concerning effects of maternal sensitivity versus those of temperament have occupied the field for a long time. Do you think there is something particular about these two constructs that has made them so difficult to work with for so long?

MDSA.—I think that what has made them difficult is that we have tried to force them into an either/or dichotomy, whereas I believe that in fact there are effects from both. I happened to have focused on maternal sensitivity, on how babies react to the adult's responsiveness, because to assume that how the baby is treated, that how sensitive or insensitive the mother is in responding to her child, has no effect—that's impossible, especially if you have seen a lot of different interactions. But that's not to say that temperamental differences have no influence on behavior. I think they do, but, since I also think that the kinds of differences that emerge as a result of mother-child interaction have more to do with shaping the nature of the child's later relationships than the child's temperamental qualities, I have given them more emphasis.

RM.—It seems that, when Bowlby and you first started talking about attachment theory, you were perceived as being radically biologically deterministic; that, of course, was in the context of the sway that social learning theory held at that time. Now you are being seen by some as placing too much emphasis on environmental determinants by focusing so much on maternal sensitivity. My own impression is that you have in fact stood stock still over the years and that it's the field that has been swinging like a pendulum around you. [*A hearty laugh from Mary.*] But to return to the notion of temperament—what do *you* perceive it to be?

MDSA.—Well, I remember reading Sheldon's book on the varieties of temperament many years ago and finding it very interesting. I did know some people who seemed to absolutely personify some of Sheldon's types. For instance, I had a professor once who was tall and very skinny, had a very soft voice, made practically no noise in moving about, and was highly intellectual—he seemed to have all the qualities that Sheldon ascribed to an ectomorph and that he thought were genetically determined. And it may well be that such aspects of personality may have a significant effect on a person's behavior in many circumstances, but I don't think that they have any truly basic influence on the kind of relationships that the person will construct with other people.

RM.—So you think that, although temperamental differences can have a big impact on how a baby behaves, they are not the major determinant of whether the child becomes securely or insecurely attached?

MDSA.—Yes, I think it is how the mother responds to the particular kind of behavior shown by her baby that plays by far the major role.

V. ON CONTINUITIES INTO LATER YEARS

RM.—The notion that early relationships serve as prototypes for later ones is viewed by some as being the key concept in attachment theory. What are your thoughts on this matter?

MDSA.—I don't know that I would call it *the* key concept because I see a number of the ideas that I talked about at the beginning of our conversation as also being "key" in defining what attachment theory is all about. I'm also not sure that I like the term *prototype*. It can be taken to imply that we expect a persistence of the same behavioral patterns, and that's clearly nonsense: a securely attached baby will cry when mother leaves him alone in the Strange Situation, but we don't necessarily expect him to do so when he is a preschooler, let alone a teenager!

RM.—But what if we take it in another sense—as perhaps setting a pathway for later relationships or predicting what they are likely to be?

MDSA.—In that sense, yes. But I think we should limit it to *intimate* relationships. We do have some evidence that securely attached youngsters tend to interact more easily with other children and with adults than insecurely attached children, but such differences in social behavior that doesn't involve close ties can come about for a variety of reasons. The differences may well be related to differences in how sensitive a mother is in introducing her baby to unfamiliar people or to how secure she makes the child feel in exploring his environment, but I don't think that they are in any way a *necessary* consequence of differences in the mother-child attachment bond. Work on continuities in the structure of attachment bonds, on figuring out the "rules" by which transformations to qualities of later relationships come about, should focus on relationships that are close—those in which the other can be assumed to serve as some form of an attachment figure.

RM.—How about within the period of infancy? Suppose a baby is attached to one figure, and another caregiver is then added to his life. Do you think that the quality of the second relationship would be much influenced by the experience of the original caregiver?

MDSA.—I think it would certainly be influenced at its beginning because the child's expectations of a caregiver will have been shaped by his interactions with the first figure. But, if the new relationship remains continuous over a long period of time, I don't think this would remain a lasting effect on the nature of the attachment bond formed with the new figure.

RM.—So you think that, to the extent that the child's interactions with the new figure are different, the baby can develop a working model of the attachment relationship that differs from the one he had constructed before?

MDSA.—I keep thinking here of some Adult Attachment Interview [AAI] transcripts where it becomes clear that the child's relationship with the parents was essentially insecure but that a secure relationship with some other important figure—a grandparent, a teacher, a coach, someone who was close and understanding—had functioned to make up for the life of insecurity with the parents. It's hard to point to such instances within infancy itself, but having adults look back on their experiences makes you realize it is possible.

RM.—It sounds like you are saying that two processes—actual interactions and working models—are involved here: the baby initially comes to interaction with the new figure with the same attachment-related expectations that he had developed with the first figure, but, to the extent that the second relationship develops along different lines, the earlier working model will gradually change to become something perhaps quite radically different?

MDSA.—Yes, that's very much what I am implying.

RM.—Thinking about work that has been relevant to this issue, do you think that the maternal deprivation literature can be taken to demonstrate the existence of at least a predictive relation between early attachment and later relationships?

MDSA.—One of the things it certainly demonstrates is that the attachment bond is not simply God given but—as I have said before—that it has to have an opportunity to develop. In Jimmy Robertson's observations of tubercular children who had to spend many months in a sanatorium, the indifference with which the child treated the parent when the mother or father came to visit was remarkable. It was as if the child simply didn't care; it wasn't at all important. And I think it is fair to say that this is by far the most likely way these children would later treat other people—that what is set under such conditions is indeed a prototype for all subsequent affective relationships.

RM.—One of the most important findings in recent attachment research has been Mary Main's demonstration that classifications obtained by mothers on the Adult Attachment Interview are strongly related to their infants' Strange Situation classifications. What do you think has made this finding so influential?

MDSA.—Because it establishes a significant step in what is needed to show that there is a meaningful developmental link between the attachment-related experiences of the child and how that child behaves in attachment relationships when he grows up to be an adult.

RM.—Do you think that studies comparing infants' early Strange Situation classifications with their own subsequent AAI classifications will support this even further by showing a similar predictability?

MDSA.—I do. And, taken all together, it will be eloquent evidence of meaningful developmental links—that just as attachment theory postulates, development follows a logical course and is not just a matter of happenstance.

RM.—Let me push this even further by asking a hypothetical question: What if these data had started by showing the opposite, that is, a lack of continuities?

MDSA.—I think that, as developmentalists, it is safer for us to cling . . . yes, I'll stick by that word . . . *cling* to the belief that the processes of development are patterned. And, even though we have an incomplete understanding of what rules underlie these patternings—what processes they involve and how these processes involve behavior—it is more sensible to believe that such rules exist than to believe that they don't. So I would look very carefully at such contradictory data, try to see what might account for the anomaly, and then try to get the study replicated using an intelligent and impeccable methodology. And, since we're in a hypothetical mode anyway, I'll bet you anything that the results would turn out to support presence of logical continuities!

RM.—Have you ever been surprised by the nature of any of the continuities that you saw in your Baltimore data or that have been reported by Main?

MDSA.—I had anticipated most of what turned out from the Baltimore study, with one exception. What came as a real surprise was to see that mothers who ignored their infants had babies who we thought were clearly ignoring their mothers. This finding has now also been supported by Mary Main's finding that infants of mothers classified on the AAI as dismissing of attachment are classified as avoidant in the Strange Situation. But, originally, I had expected that babies whom mother ignores would demand her attention more and more in trying to get her involved and wind up being fussy babies. I expected to see something more openly grieving, and maybe these babies did go briefly through some such phase. But in the end they wound up becoming avoidant.

RM.—So they ended up looking like the deprived child who is beyond the phase of protest?

MDSA.—Yes. Although not as dramatically as the children described in the literature, these babies *were* deprived: the mother did live in the same house, but the baby was severed from her by the closed nursery door and by the mother's indifference to sounds that emanated from behind that door.

RM.—As researchers have moved to study attachment beyond infancy, there seems to have been a tendency to focus more and more on cognition—working models, thoughts, internal events—and less on observable interactions between the individual and his loved ones. How do you feel about this trend?

MDSA.—As I think I've already stressed at various points in our conversation, I believe that we must continue to rely on direct observation—on what I've called "fieldwork"—in gathering more information on what actually happens in different contexts and in different relationships. But moving to *also* study internal attachment-related events is certainly appropriate and necessary to get at the "rules" and processes I mentioned earlier. As long as this trend doesn't become an "either/or" thing—either you observe, or you probe for internal events—but remains rather a matter of balance between the two, I think it will serve us well.

RM.—Well, we've ranged over many topics in this conversation, and now the time has come to bring it to a close. Is there anything—maybe something personal—that you may wish to add?

MDSA.—Perhaps the most extraordinary thing in my life has been seeing so many people become interested in the concept of attachment and dedicating themselves to developing it further. They've done so much to contribute to its growth. . . . I think of them all as my "extended family," and I send them my love, my thanks, and my very best wishes.

PART 2:
THE GENERALITY OF SECURE-BASE BEHAVIOR AND SECURE-BASE INDIVIDUAL DIFFERENCES

INTRODUCTION TO PART 2

Mary Ainsworth recognized the significance of the secure-base phenomenon as the primary indicator of the presence of an attachment relationship from the perspective of the infant in both the Uganda (Ainsworth, 1967) and the Baltimore (Ainsworth, Blehar, Waters, & Wall, 1978) studies. That is, an infant could be presumed to be attached to an adult if she organized her attachment behavior around said adult as though using the adult as a secure base for exploration and as a haven of safety in times of stress. Furthermore, Ainsworth understood early on that individual differences in the patterning of secure-base behavior reflected the effectiveness of the attachment as a source of security for the infant (Ainsworth, 1973). These fundamental insights led to the classificatory system used to describe patterns of behavior seen in the Strange Situation and have guided research on attachment antecedents and consequences for nearly three decades.

Despite the importance and ubiquity of secure-base behavior and the secure-base concept, questions have been raised repeatedly to the effect that the phenomena may not adequately characterize the attachments of children from different ecological settings or with different regimens of child-rearing experiences. The reports in this section address the generality of secure-base behavior, preferences for patterns indicative of "security," and the generality of patterns across caregivers and infants. In each report, the data summarized span non-Western and/or non-English-speaking sociocultural groups. The data reported attest to the broad generality of the secure-base phenomenon. Although it is clear that the "security prototype" is not necessarily the norm in all sociocultural groups, this prototype is found to be desirable in all groups studied. Furthermore, patterns of secure-base behavior observed in the home and in child-care facilities bear an analogous relation to the patterns of behavioral organization observed in the context of the Strange Situation. Finally, the findings reported by Sagi et al. suggest that both caregivers and infants play important roles in the assembly of secure-base behavior during the early months of life.

While no single approach to studying secure-base behavior and no single sample can answer the many questions that have been raised concerning the interpretation of secure-base behavior in attachment theory, these reports suggest that the questions will be answerable from within the attachment framework. In no culture studied here do the data suggest that secure-base phenomena carry a fundamentally different meaning—for the infant or for the mother—that depends on the unique socioecological features of the culture.

THE SECURE-BASE PHENOMENON ACROSS CULTURES: CHILDREN'S BEHAVIOR, MOTHERS' PREFERENCES, AND EXPERTS' CONCEPTS

German Posada, Yuan Gao, Fang Wu, Roberto Posada, Margarita Tascon,
Axel Schöelmerich, Abraham Sagi, Kiyomi Kondo-Ikemura,
Wenche Haaland, and Berit Synnevaag

In replacing Freud's motivational theory, Bowlby (1969/1982) and Ainsworth (1973) formulated an alternative theory to explain child-mother attachment relationships. They placed the secure-base phenomenon at the center of their analysis and defined as an *attachment figure* a person whom a child uses as a secure base across time and situations. The hallmark of the secure-base phenomenon is the apparently purposeful balance between proximity seeking and exploration at different times and across contexts.

Bowlby (1969/1982) suggested that secure-base behavior was regulated by a neurally represented control system that coordinated diverse input (e.g., mother's location and availability) with a *set goal*—defined first in terms of distance and later as felt security (Sroufe & Waters, 1977)—to initiate behavior such as signaling, greeting, crying, proximity seeking (attachment behaviors), and exploration. To account for the existence of such an attachment control system, Bowlby turned to the Darwinian theory of evolution by natural selection. He argued that the control system governing attachment behavior was a product of the natural selection process in the phylogenetic lineage leading to the human species. That is to say, by virtue of their primate heritage, human infants are endowed with neural structures and

This project was made possible thanks to the collaboration of all authors who collected pertinent information in the different countries presented here. Countries and authors are listed alphabetically: China: Yuan Gao and Fang Wu; Colombia: Roberto Posada and Margarita Tascon; Germany: Axel Schöelmerich; Israel: Abraham Sagi; Japan: Kiyomi Kondo-Ikemura; Norway: Wenche Haaland and Berit Synnevaag; and the United States: German Posada.

biases in their learning abilities that make it possible for them to assemble an attachment control system when exposed to ordinary parental care. According to Bowlby, the neural and behavioral foundations of an attachment control system evolved because of the survival advantages afforded to offspring who maintained proximity to adult caregivers.

Thus, Bowlby postulated attachment behavior as a species-specific behavior, an evolutionary product that becomes organized in all children reared within the range of our species' environment of evolutionary adaptedness. Furthermore, the attachment behavioral system develops (or is assembled) within the context of child-caregiver interactions, and, as a consequence of these interactions, the child and caregiver will construct an attachment relationship. A direct and testable implication of Bowlby's argument is that infants in all cultures should exhibit secure-base behavior and that infants in all cultures will become attached to (i.e., will develop an attachment relationship with) their primary caregivers.[1] This is not to say that the form and patterning of secure-base behavior across cultures are the same or that the variations in the patterning of secure-base relationships are themselves products of natural selection; rather, we suggest that what has been selected for in the course of human evolution can be better understood in terms of a propensity to organize an attachment behavioral system within the context of child-caregiver interactions. The specific patterning of attachment behaviors and the outcomes contingent on those patterns are expected to vary according to the unique history of interactions characterizing a particular child-caregiver pair.

There has been surprisingly little empirical work regarding the generality of secure-base behavior. Most studies in different cultures have employed the Strange Situation to assess attachment security rather than focusing on attachment behaviors per se (e.g., Grossmann, Grossmann, Spangler, Suess, & Unzner, 1985; Miyake, Chen, & Campos, 1985; Sagi et al., 1985; Takahashi, 1990), and while results suggest that secure-base behavior is at least common in other countries, the data are not decisive in addressing Bowlby's hypothesis for a number of reasons. First, the Strange Situation is not an appropriate method to determine whether an attachment relationship exists—in fact, the existence of such a relationship is a precondition for coding and interpreting the behavior of the child being observed. Second, the procedure has been validated against external criteria (either concurrent or predictive) in only a few sociocultural settings, most of which

[1] Note that the universality suggested by attachment theory is due, not to some kind of child-care practices or other social experience common across peoples, but rather to evolutionary considerations about the development of the attachment behavioral system that suggest an interplay between biological tendencies and child-care experience. It is in this sense that we use the term *universality*.

represent Western societies. Similar validation studies in other sociocultural contexts are required to ensure that children's behavior in these settings supports the kind of interpretations that have been drawn from studies conducted in the United States and other Western societies. Finally, an important limitation of the Strange Situation data is that the phenomenon of using the mother as a secure base may reflect demands and constraints imposed by the laboratory setting rather than by an underlying control system.

Thus, although the cross-cultural data generated by the Strange Situation lend support to the proposed universality of secure-base behavior, they cannot settle the issue. To do this we need data on secure-base behavior as seen over longer observations and in the diverse conditions of naturalistic settings (e.g., Ainsworth, 1967); furthermore, we need to obtain such information in a greater diversity of cultures and social contexts.

The most influential naturalistic studies of children's secure-base behavior at home have been Ainsworth's Uganda longitudinal study (Ainsworth, 1967) and her Baltimore longitudinal study of 26 infants and their mothers (Ainsworth, Blehar, Waters, & Wall, 1978). It was her observation of attachment behavior as it occurs in the home that allowed Ainsworth to define the secure-base phenomenon and to develop a procedure for its assessment; further studies of secure-base behavior in naturalistic settings, however, have been rare. This is due in part to the difficulty of conceptualizing and developing measures that allow researchers to capture the underlying construct (Waters, Kondo-Ikemura, Posada, & Richters, 1990) and in part to the expense of conducting such studies. Yet if we are to achieve a better understanding of the phenomenon—specifically, if we are to address such issues as the universality of secure-base behavior, its optimality as perceived in different cultural contexts, and the validity of assessment procedures—it is necessary to gather information in naturalistic settings.

Although the goals of gathering ecologically valid information and controlling the expenses of data collection may seem incompatible, they need not be so. One tactic that has been used in this effort is to enlist mothers as expert informants/observers for their own children (see Teti & McGourty, in press). Although maternal report has been criticized, using mothers as observers has several advantages over other data-acquisition approaches since mothers often have access to information about secure-base behavior that is not available to any other observer (see Waters & Deane, 1985) and because in certain cultural settings it may not be feasible for trained observers to obtain access to the home.

Understanding attachment behavior in diverse cultural contexts also requires data on mothers' preferences regarding how the child should behave during child-mother interactions. This is important for both theoretical and methodological reasons. If attachment behavior is the product of mother-child interactions and relationship history, we need to determine what the commonalities and differences in mothers' preferences (i.e., the "ideal" child behavior that mothers would like to see) may be across cultures and whether (or to what degree) the mother's preferences regarding the form of the secure-base phenomenon are related to a child's secure-base behavior since—as Hinde (1987) has argued—parents frequently work to create parent-child relationships that conform to the norms considered desirable in their culture. From a methodological point of view, collecting information about the mother's preferences concerning secure-base behavior is important in order to determine whether a mother's description of her child's actual behavior is simply a reflection of such preferences. Insofar as notions about "ideal" child behavior can be assumed to reflect cultural prescriptions for behavior, mothers' preferences can be used to index the influence of social desirability on their characterizations of their own child's behavior.

The notion of what reflects optimality in a child's use of her or his mother as a secure base also requires consideration of how professional experts within a given culture view secure-base behavior. A child's attachment behaviors are typically assessed against experts' conceptualizations and definitions of the secure-base phenomenon, and what is considered to be an optimal organization of such behaviors in one culture may differ in another. Hence, we need to determine whether such conceptualizations are culturally biased or similar across cultures.

To address these issues, we undertook a collaborative study to investigate whether children's behavior with their mothers—as seen at home in everyday life circumstances—is organized in a way that indicates that the child uses the mother as a secure base and whether mothers' preferences regarding secure-base behavior and experts' definitions of the secure-base phenomenon are similar across cultures or whether they are culture specific. Seven different labs participated in this collaborative effort. The countries we sampled were China, Colombia, Germany, Israel, Japan, Norway, and the United States. It is important to note that the data about children's secure-base behavior and about mothers' preferences were being collected, or already had been collected, as part of independent research projects; consequently, research goals, targeted variables, and demographic characteristics of the families varied across sites. Information about mothers' preferences regarding secure-base behavior was gathered in all countries but Norway; experts' definitions of the optimal organization of secure-base behavior were obtained in each participating country.

To collect all three types of information we relied on the 90-item version of the Attachment Q-Set (AQS; Waters, 1987; see also App. A, in this volume). The AQS was developed as an economical alternative to Ains-

worth's observational methodology, one that covers essentially the same behavioral content as her narratives yet allows studying larger samples in
naturalistic settings, keeps the observers blind to the constructs that are
being assessed, and lends itself to an array of quantitative analyses (Block,
1961/1978; Waters & Deane, 1985). The AQS was developed to describe
the behavior of children aged between 1 and 5 years, who are observed at
home. As with all Q-methods, the AQS has the advantage of characterizing
all subjects in terms of a common, well-defined language that is provided
by the Q-items and according to a standard distribution of item placements,
thus facilitating comparisons among groups (for further discussion of the
advantages of Q-methodology, see Block, 1961/1978; and Waters & Deane,
1985). The AQS item set includes numerous behaviors relevant to indexing
the secure-base phenomenon; however, it is the organization of these behaviors—as shown by the Q-sort profile—that indicates the degree to which
secure-base behavior is featured in a given child's repertoire when interacting with the mother. Existence of the secure-base phenomenon is not
presumed by the technique; rather, its presence or absence is inferred from
the profile.

A significant advantage of the AQS is that it permits summarizing the
profile of behavior for a given child in terms of the similarity it bears to the
profile of a prototypical "optimally secure" child whose secure-base behavior
is smoothly organized, with an appropriate balance being maintained between proximity seeking and exploration away from the caregiver (this criterion profile is shown in App. A). Constructed as a composite of sorts provided by experts who were instructed to describe the "optimally secure"
child, the correlation between this criterion and an individual's sort indexes
the extent to which that child's behavioral profile reflects use of the mother
as a secure base for comfort and exploration. The most frequent application
of these correlation indices has been to interpret them as "security scores"
that fall along a linear continuum of attachment security and can be used
in research on individual differences (e.g., Vaughn & Waters, 1990; Waters
& Deane, 1985). Because our focus here is on the generality of the secure-
base phenomenon rather than on individual differences in attachment security, it should be kept in mind that, when we use the term *security score*, we
are referring to an index of congruence between a given child's profile and
the U.S. experts' profile.

The goals of our study were to provide descriptive information about
the following sets of questions. First, since Q-sort descriptions of the child's
secure-base behavior were provided by the mothers, we needed to determine whether the mothers may have responded simply in terms of social
desirability. Hence, our first question was whether mothers' descriptions of
their preferences regarding secure-base behavior—that is, their sorts of the

"ideal" child—differed from what they reported about their own child. Second, with respect to the children's behavior, we posed the following two questions: in terms of behavior covered by the AQS and reported by mothers, do children in all the countries sampled organize their behavior in ways that indicate that they are using their mother as a secure base? If so, are descriptions of the secure-base phenomenon more similar within cultures than they are across cultures? The universality of the phenomenon implicit in attachment theory leads to a prediction of no differences; that is, children's use of their mother as a secure base from which to explore is expected to be common in all cultures (van IJzendoorn & Kroonenberg, 1988). Third, regarding mothers' preferences, we asked whether descriptions of the secure-base behavior of the "ideal" child are more similar within than across cultures. Finally, with respect to issues of optimality of child behavior when using the mother as a secure base, we asked whether child professionals from different cultures define *optimal secure-base behavior* similarly, or whether this definition varies depending on the culture, and whether child professionals' definitions of *optimal secure-base behavior* resemble mothers' notions of "ideal" child behavior within and across cultures.

METHOD

Subjects

Across the seven countries that we sampled, a total of 228 mothers provided AQS descriptions of their child's behavior at home, and 132 mothers provided sorts of the hypothetical "ideal" child. A total of 104 child professionals used the Q-set to describe their conception of the *optimally secure child*. A brief demographic characterization of informants used in each of the countries follows.

Mothers

In each country, the mothers who described their own child shared the same sample characteristics as those who provided sorts of their "ideal" child; hence, the two subsamples are characterized jointly. The same mothers in the samples from Israel and Japan (see below) provided the two types of Q-descriptions. All but the Colombian mothers (see below) were married and living with the child's father. Descriptions of "own" child involved roughly similar numbers of sons and daughters—except in the United States, where they applied only to boys. Across all subsamples ($N = 301$), the mothers' average age was 31 years (range = 20–47 years), and they had achieved a mean of 12.5 years of education (range = 0–22 years). On average, they had 1.9

children; the "own" children whom the mothers described (N = 228) ranged in age from 12 to 55 months (M = 28.7 months).

Chinese samples.—The average age of the 41 mothers who described their own child and of the 14 who provided sorts of their "ideal" child was 33.2 years (range = 28–41 years). All of them lived in the city of Beijing. Except for one family with twins, all had only one child; these children's ages ranged from 13 to 44 months (M = 30.7 months). The mothers averaged 13.9 years of education (range = 9–22 years); along with the Norwegian, German, and U.S. samples, this group included some of the most extensively educated among the mothers sampled. Both parents in the Chinese families worked full-time outside the home, with the care of the child being entrusted to grandparents and child-care centers; their socioeconomic circumstances can be fairly described as comfortable within the context of Chinese culture.

Colombian samples.—In contrast to all the other mothers sampled, the 31 mothers who provided "own" child sorts and the 15 who described their "ideal" child came from an impoverished educational as well as socioeconomic stratum. Ranging in age from 22 to 47 years (M = 30.7 years), they had an average of only 5.2 years of schooling (range = 0–11 years). Only 21 of the 46 were legally married and living with their children's father; 19 lived with the father but were not married to him, and six more were separated or living alone. Inhabitants of the city of Bogota, all lived in one of its poorest sections, typically in two-room residences that, on average, housed 5.6 people. The family income came from very low-paying jobs (mothers working as maids, their partners as security guards or construction workers). The mothers had on average 2.5 children; 32 described themselves as the main child caretaker, and 12 reported being helped by other persons in providing care for their children—by the father (two), other mothers (four), a grandmother (two), older siblings (three), or sitter and day care (two). The children averaged 43.8 months of age (range = 30–55 months).

German samples.—Informants were recruited from around two urban centers, Osnabrück and Munich. The average age of the 31 mothers who described their own child and of the 17 who provided sorts of their "ideal" child was 30.3 years (range = 20–39 years). These mothers averaged 12.3 years of education (range = 10–17 years), and they were the principal caregivers for their children. These mothers had on average 1.6 children, and their occupations were diverse (skilled worker, clerk, federal employee, engineer, schoolteacher, designer, lawyer, dentist, and homemaker). The children they described ranged in age from 12 to 36 months (M = 24.8 months). These families' socioeconomic circumstances can be described as good.

Israeli sample.—Mothers were recruited in the city of Haifa, and all 30 of them provided sorts both of their own child and of the "ideal" child they would like to have. Their average age was 29 years (range = 22–39 years). The informants had on average 13 years of education (range = 9–16 years), and all their children were described at 12 months of age. The average number of children per family was 2.2; 15 mothers were the principal caregiver, eight sent their children to infant day care (more than eight children in the group), four to family day care (up to eight children), and three used a caregiver at home. These informants came from a middle-class background.

Japanese samples.—Forty-two Japanese mothers were recruited in the city of Osaka. Forty-one provided descriptions of the "ideal" child, and 29 also described their own child. One additional informant provided information only about her own child. Mothers' ages ranged from 21 to 33 years (*M* = 28.9 years), and on average they had 14.3 years of education (range = 9–16 years). Informants described the "ideal" child when their own children were 4 months of age, and later, when their children were 12 months old, 30 mothers described their own child. The mothers had 1.6 children on average, and most (27) took care of their child themselves. In six cases a grandmother was the child's main caretaker, three children were cared for by a neighbor, three others were in day care, and two children were cared for by a sitter or a relative. As with most other participating samples, the socioeconomic status of these families can be described as good.

Norwegian sample.—The 20 mothers providing descriptions of their own child lived in the city of Bergen. They averaged 30 years of age (range = 21–33 years), and their level of education ranged from 13 to 18 years (*M* = 15.5 years). Children were described when they were 36 months of age. No information about the "ideal" child was gathered in Norway. The majority of the Norwegian mothers and fathers were graduate students, and both of them shared the daily responsibilities of child care. Their living conditions could be described as very good.

U.S. samples.—Recruited around Stony Brook (a suburban town on Long Island, New York), the average age of the 45 mothers who described their own child and of the 15 who provided sorts of their "ideal" child was 32.5 years (range = 22–43 years). Children's ages ranged from 34 to 45 months (*M* = 38.1 months). Mothers averaged 14.5 years of education (range = 12–21 years). Most fathers worked full-time outside the home, and mothers were the principal child caregiver; parents had 2.4 children on average, and their socioeconomic conditions can be described as comfortable.

Child Professionals

Of the 104 professionals who provided descriptions of the hypothetical "most securely attached" child, the 44 Chinese experts were all professors of psychology and early childhood education working in diverse fields (social development, personality development, cognitive development, general psychology, and education), and none were familiar with attachment theory. The six Colombian experts were all psychologists (except for one language therapist) who dealt with different aspects of child development and whose familiarity with attachment theory was typically slight. Eleven German experts (all developmental psychologists except for one, an educator who worked in the area of early care) contributed Q-sorts; they had moderate to extensive knowledge of attachment theory. The 10 Israeli professionals were psychologists and social workers with experience in clinical or counseling work with children and with moderate to extensive knowledge of attachment theory. All the 18 Japanese experts were psychologists who had had some experience observing child-mother interactions, and all were familiar with attachment theory. The nine Norwegian experts worked in the field of developmental and clinical psychology, and they too were all familiar with attachment theory. All six U.S. professionals had worked in the field of child development, and all of them are recognized as experts with respect to attachment theory.

Measure

The AQS was used to gather the data. The AQS descriptions provided by both subsamples of mothers were summarized by deriving a security score (i.e., an index of congruence with the security criterion sort) for each informant's Q-sort description. In all instances, the composite of sorts provided by the U.S. experts to describe the "optimally secure child" served as the criterion. We used the U.S. criterion sort to derive the security scores because it is the only criterion that has established reliability and because its validity has been demonstrated in diverse studies (e.g., Park & Waters, 1989; Pederson et al., 1990; Vaughn & Waters, 1990; Waters & Deane, 1985); also, using the same criterion allows us to make interpretable comparisons across samples. It is also important to note that, according to the theory, the criterion description of the optimally attached child should not vary substantially from culture to culture (a proposition that we also investigated empirically; see below).

Procedures

Most mothers who were to describe their own child's behavior were first visited at home by the authors and/or their research assistants and instructed in how to use the AQS. They were first asked to read the 90 items and then shown how to sort them into nine piles. Any questions they had concerning the meaning of an item or about the sorting task were answered; they were additionally told to call the investigators if any further questions arose as they proceeded with their Q-sort descriptions. They were then asked to keep the Q-set items, observe their child for 3–4 days with the Q-items in mind, and then describe their observations in the language of the Q-sort.

These procedures were followed individually with all mothers in each country except in Colombia; because the Colombian sample had a very low level of education, these mothers were brought in small subgroups to a health community center in their neighborhood where each item was read and explained to them; this precaution was intended to motivate participation and ensure that the mothers understood their task. The sorting procedure was also explained on these occasions, and the mothers were then asked to observe their child's behavior for the next 3 or 4 days before proceeding with the sorting task. An investigator was always present when Colombian mothers did their Q-sort descriptions to ensure correct completion of the task and to answer questions about either their child's behavior or the Q-items that these mothers may have had after they completed their observations. The investigator's presence was important for reminding several of these mothers how to proceed when forming the nine piles. Colombian mothers were paid when they finished the sorting task.

Except for the request that mothers observe their child for a few days, the same procedures were used with both the mothers who described the "ideal" child's behavior and the child professionals who described the "optimally attached" child. Mothers were instructed to "describe with these 90 items the ideal or best child you would like to have," and the child professionals were instructed to "describe the hypothetical 'most secure' child with these 90 items."

RESULTS

Social Desirability as a Response Bias

Since we obtained Q-descriptions of children's behavior from their mothers, we assessed the possible effect of a social desirability bias on mothers' reports by conducting within-subjects analyses using all Israeli mothers ($N = 30$) and 29 of 41 Japanese mothers who provided Q-sort descriptions for both their own and the "ideal" child. First, a Pearson correlation between the two types of descriptions was computed, and this yielded a moderate but significant value ($r = .37$, $p < .01$). Second, we compared the mean security scores derived from each mother's two descriptions. The mean security score derived from sorts of their own children was .35 (SD = .20);

the comparable mean security score calculated from the "ideal" sorts was .55 (SD = .20) and significantly higher ($t[58]$ = 6.62, p < .001). This difference was in the same direction and statistically significant in both countries (by t test for dependent samples; see Table 1). Finally, we evaluated the possible effect of a social desirability bias in the remainder of the sample, by similar comparison of sorts of "own" (M = .35, SD = .20) and "ideal" (M = .59, SD = .13) child; the latter was significantly higher ($F[1, 207]$ = 79.28, p < .001) across all samples as well as in each of the individual samples (see Table 1). Although the between-subjects comparisons cannot be taken as definitive, the conjunction of all these results suggests that the "own" child data cannot be construed simply as information about culturally determined social desirability response biases.

Mothers' Descriptions of Their Own Child

As articulated by Bowlby and Ainsworth, attachment theory suggests two hypotheses about our cross-cultural data. First, insofar as secure-base behavior is universal, the secure-base patterns summarized by the AQS criterion sort should characterize children in each culture; that is, there should be few negative or zero security scores. We examined this hypothesis by plotting individual security scores for each sample; as seen in Figure 1, the range of scores proved to be almost entirely within the positive range in

TABLE 1

WITHIN-COUNTRY PLANNED COMPARISONS OF SECURITY SCORES DERIVED FROM MOTHERS' AQS DESCRIPTIONS OF THE "IDEAL" CHILD AND THEIR OWN CHILD

	SECURITY SCORES								
	Ideal Child			Own Child					
	N	M	SD	N	M	SD	t	df	p
Within subjects:[a]									
Israel	30	.47	.23	30	.34	.17	3.82	29	< .001
Japan	29	.63	.11	29	.37	.23	5.69	28	< .001
							F	df	p
Between subjects:[b]									
China	14	.51	.10	41	.30	.19	15.83	1, 53	< .001
Colombia	15	.59	.07	31	.24	.19	49.72	1, 44	< .001
Germany	17	.58	.15	31	.42	.16	11.30	1, 46	< .01
Norway[c]				20	.58	.11			
United States...	15	.67	.13	45	.42	.11	24.18	1, 58	< .001

[a] t tests for dependent samples were used in both instances.
[b] The Tukey test for unequal samples was used in each within-country comparison.
[c] "Ideal" child sorts were not collected in Norway.

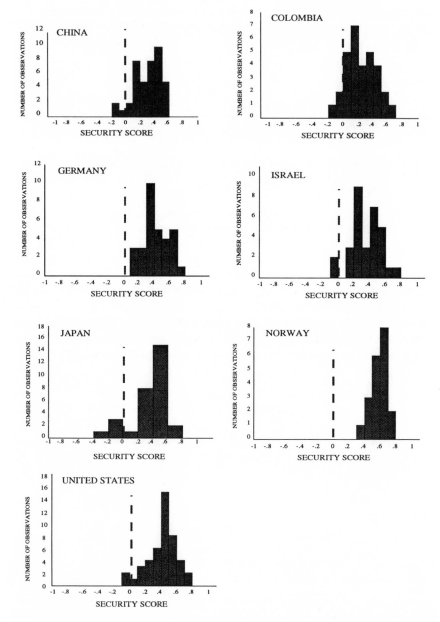

FIG. 1.—Distribution of security scores derived from mothers' descriptions of their own child's secure-base behavior in each of the seven countries; the dashed lines indicate the potential midpoint on the scale that would have been obtained had the full range of scores been reported.

each of the seven cultures. Thus, overall, mothers' Q-descriptions indicate that children use their mothers as a secure base in a variety of sociocultural contexts.

Second, we investigated whether characteristic patterns of secure-base behavior were similar across cultures rather than specific to particular cultures. We computed correlations between all pairs of mothers' AQS descriptions both within and across samples; viewing each sort as a 90-item profile of secure-base behavior, these correlations provide an index of similarity among profiles. The resultant correlations were converted to Fisher's z, averaged within and across samples, and then converted back to correlation coefficients; the within- and across-sample means of these converted values are presented in Table 2.

As predicted, the similarity of secure-base patterns seen within samples ($M = .31$, range $= .24–.37$) is close to that obtained across cultures ($M = .23$, range $= .15–.32$); in no instance did children in any culture appear highly similar to one another and yet very unlike children in other cultures. Despite this evidence of cross-cultural consistency, the absolute levels of similarity both within and across cultures were rather low. Determining whether this reflects openness of the secure-base system to ecological influences or psychometric characteristics of the AQS will entail supplementing AQS data with the kinds of narrative reports that Ainsworth collected in her Baltimore study.

Mothers' Descriptions of the "Ideal" Child

Our next analysis examined whether mothers' preferences regarding patterns of secure-base behavior are more similar within than across cultures. As in the previous analysis, we computed correlations between all

TABLE 2

MEAN CORRELATIONS AMONG MOTHERS' Q-SORT DESCRIPTIONS OF THEIR OWN CHILD
BOTH WITHIN AND ACROSS CULTURES

	China (N = 41)	Colombia (N = 31)	Germany (N = 31)	Israel (N = 30)	Japan (N = 30)	Norway (N = 20)	United States (N = 45)
China	**.25**						
Colombia	.16	**.24**					
Germany	.24	.19	**.33**				
Israel	.21	.16	.25	**.31**			
Japan	.23	.17	.26	.27	**.31**		
Norway	.24	.15	.32	.24	.26	**.37**	
United States . . .	.23	.19	.30	.23	.24	.32	**.35**

NOTE.—Within-culture correlations are highlighted in boldface type on the diagonal of the correlation matrix.

pairs of mothers' AQS descriptions both within and across samples; the resultant correlations were converted to Fisher's z, averaged within and across samples, and then converted back to correlation coefficients. The within- and across-sample means of these converted values are presented in Table 3.

The similarity of mothers' preferences regarding patterns of secure-base behavior within cultures ($M = .53$, range $= .38–.64$) was close to that of mothers' preferences across samples ($M = .44$, range $= .33–.58$). As was the case for "own child" descriptions, in no case did mothers' preferences in one culture turn out to be highly similar and yet very unlike mothers' preferences in other cultures—the only possible exception being the Japanese sample, in which a somewhat higher within- than between-country profile similarity was obtained. Both the average ($r = .47$) and the range of correlations indicate a relatively high degree of similarity among mothers' preferences regarding secure-base behavior across these countries.

Since this degree of similarity still permits presence of cultural differences in what mothers stress when describing the "ideal" child, we investigated in an exploratory fashion possible differences in mothers' preferences regarding more specific domains of the secure-base phenomenon that are assessed by the AQS. The four Q-sort-derived scales that we used to compare the samples were "Smooth interactions with mother," "Proximity to mother," "Physical contact with mother," and "Interactions with other adults," each of which refers to specific and interrelated aspects of the secure-base phenomenon (for a more detailed description of these scales, see Posada, Waters, Crowell, & Lay, in this volume; the items making up these scales are listed in App. D).

The results, presented in Table 4, indicated significant among-sample differences on all four scales; Tukey tests for unequal sample sizes were used for post hoc comparisons to investigate the sources of those differ-

TABLE 3

MEAN CORRELATIONS AMONG MOTHERS' Q-SORT DESCRIPTIONS OF THE "IDEAL" CHILD
BOTH WITHIN AND ACROSS CULTURES

	China (N = 14)	Colombia (N = 15)	Germany (N = 17)	Israel (N = 30)	Japan (N = 41)	United States (N = 15)
China	**.47**					
Colombia	.40	**.55**				
Germany	.38	.43	**.44**			
Israel	.33	.33	.35	**.38**		
Japan	.48	.48	.47	.42	**.64**	
United States	.46	.51	.51	.42	.58	**.64**

NOTE.—"Ideal" child Q-sorts were not obtained from mothers in Norway. Within-culture correlations are highlighted in boldface type on the diagonal of the correlation matrix.

TABLE 4

Comparison of Mean AQS Scale Scores Obtained from Mothers' Descriptions of the "Ideal" Child

	China	Colombia	Germany	Israel	Japan	United States	F^a	p
Smooth interactions with mother:								
M	7.4	7.5	7.0	6.7	7.4	7.7	4.60	< .001
SD	1.2	.53	1.0	.99	.53	.57		
Range	4.9–9.0	6.4–8.2	4.4–8.3	4.6–8.3	5.8–8.4	6.5–8.4		
Proximity to mother:								
M	5.9	6.8	5.9	5.6	5.5	5.4	6.37	< .001
SD	1.4	.57	.85	.55	.81	.85		
Range	3.5–8.9	5.9–7.7	4.3–7.4	4.6–7.2	3.9–7.0	3.5–6.9		
Physical contact with mother:								
M	5.9	6.5	6.8	6.7	6.5	6.7	2.54	< .05
SD	.81	.94	.92	.86	.71	.79		
Range	4.9–7.3	4.6–8.1	5.4–8.1	4.6–8.1	5.0–7.6	5.4–8.9		
Interactions with other adults:								
M	6.5	5.4	5.1	5.5	6.2	5.9	7.05	< .001
SD	1.2	.90	.74	.99	.54	.93		
Range	4.3–8.5	4.0–7.2	3.7–6.3	3.4–7.3	4.8–7.5	4.3–7.2		

[a] $df = 5$ for all analyses.

ences. On the "Smooth interactions with mother" scale, the scores of Israeli mothers were significantly lower than those of U.S. and Japanese mothers; on the "Proximity to mother" scale, the scores of Colombian mothers were significantly higher than those of mothers in all other samples; and, on the "Physical contact with mother" scale, the Chinese sample yielded significantly lower scores than the German sample and marginally significantly lower scores than the Israeli sample ($p < .07$). Finally, on the "Interactions with other adults" scale, descriptions made by Chinese mothers yielded significantly higher scores than those made by German, Colombian, and Israeli mothers, and the scores of Japanese mothers were significantly higher than those of both German and Israeli mothers.

In summary, mothers' preferences regarding secure-base behavior expressed in their descriptions of the "ideal" child were similar across cultures; nevertheless, some significant differences among countries at the level of more specific behavioral domains that are components of the secure-base phenomenon were established as well.

Experts' Descriptions of the Hypothetical ''Most Secure Child''

Our final set of questions asked first whether child professionals from different cultures define optimal secure-base behavior in a similar fashion. Composite sorts of the hypothetically most securely attached child were created for each country from the descriptions provided by the experts and then intercorrelated; the resultant r's (presented in Table 5) ranged from .74 to .93, indicating that notions of optimality are very similar across cultures.

Second, we asked whether child professionals' definitions of optimal secure-base behavior and mothers' notions of the "ideal" child's behavior are similar within and across cultures. Experts' composite sorts of the hypothetically most securely attached child for each country were correlated with mothers' composite sorts of the "ideal" child in each sample; results of these

TABLE 5

PEARSON CORRELATION COEFFICIENTS AMONG COMPOSITE SORTS OF THE HYPOTHETICAL "MOST SECURE" CHILD PROVIDED BY CHILD PROFESSIONALS IN EACH COUNTRY

	China (N = 44)	Colombia (N = 6)	Germany (N = 11)	Israel (N = 10)	Japan (N = 18)	Norway (N = 9)	United States (N = 6)
Colombia	.87						
Germany	.78	.76					
Israel	.80	.74	.89				
Japan	.88	.78	.87	.89			
Norway	.82	.78	.90	.90	.91		
United States . . .	.83	.80	.93	.92	.90	.91	

TABLE 6

PEARSON CORRELATION COEFFICIENTS AMONG COMPOSITE SORTS OF THE "MOST SECURE"
CHILD PROVIDED BY CHILD PROFESSIONALS AND COMPOSITE SORTS OF THE "IDEAL" CHILD
PROVIDED BY MOTHERS IN EACH COUNTRY

| CHILD PROFESSIONALS | MOTHERS' "IDEAL" CHILD | | | | | |
	China	Colombia	Germany	Israel	Japan	United States
China	**.85**	.77	.86	.77	.88	.89
Colombia	.81	**.80**	.88	.72	.86	.91
Germany.	.68	.74	**.85**	.76	.75	.80
Israel.	.70	.67	.78	**.79**	.76	.80
Japan	.76	.71	.79	.77	**.86**	.84
United States	.72	.78	.85	.76	.77	**.84**

NOTE.—Within-culture correlations are highlighted in boldface type on the diagonal of the correlation matrix.

analyses are presented in Table 6. Correlation coefficients ranged from .67 to .91, indicating that, as described with the AQS, experts' definitions of optimality and mothers' notions of ideal child behavior are very similar. This similarity between experts and mothers does not appear to be culturally specific (i.e., higher within than across countries): mothers' definitions of their ideal child were highly correlated with experts' notions of optimality regardless of culture; likewise, experts' notions of optimal secure-base behavior were highly correlated with mothers' definitions of the "ideal" child across countries.

DISCUSSION

Bowlby and Ainsworth's theory postulates that attachment behavior is common to all members of the species. Using the AQS, we investigated three perspectives on secure-base behavior across seven countries: mothers' characterizations of the behavior of their own child, mothers' characterizations of their notion of the "ideal" child, and experts' descriptions of the hypothetically most securely attached child. Each of these sources of data provided support for the Bowlby/Ainsworth conjecture regarding the generality of secure-base behavior.

As a preliminary step, we examined the discriminant validity of mothers' reports concerning the secure-base behavior of their child by comparing them to mothers' descriptions of how an "ideal" child would behave, under the assumption that these latter reflect personal and cultural preferences for desirable behavior. Since response sets are known to influence many types of psychological and behavioral ratings (see Edwards, 1990; Paulhus, 1984), it was important to establish that mothers' characterizations of their child did not simply reflect their understanding of what is socially desirable within their culture. A within-subjects analysis indicated that mothers' sorts of their own child were only moderately correlated with mothers' sorts of the "ideal" child they would like to have. In addition, mothers who described their child's actual behavior achieved far lower security scores (as indexed by similarity to the U.S. criterion of optimality) than those who were instructed to describe their notion of an "ideal" child, in all countries.

These findings support the proposition that mothers' AQS descriptions of their child cannot be construed merely as reports of how mothers would like their children to behave and hence dismissed as noninterpretable owing to social desirability biases in any of the samples. Our findings in this regard conform with other evidence that, when mothers or other care providers are properly instructed, they can provide valid descriptions of a child's behavior (e.g., Bosso, Corter, & Abramovitch, 1995; Sagi et al., in this volume; Teti & McGourty, 1994).

These differences between descriptions of the "ideal" child's and their own children's secure-base behavior suggest that mothers' preferences do not necessarily translate directly into child behavior (see Gao, Posada, & Waters, 1995); that is, children's secure-base behavior does not simply reflect mothers' preferences regarding the secure-base phenomenon. This was so in each sample we studied, perhaps most persuasively for the samples from Israel and Japan, in which the same mothers provided both types of descriptions. Because mothers' preferences should be associated with their cognitions and expectations concerning children's behavior, we would expect those preferences to be implicated in determining parenting practices that influence those patterns of behavior. The lack of match between mothers' preferences and actual child behavior indicated by our data needs to be explored further, for it is a crucial point for research investigating cognitive aspects of parents' behavior and their associations with children's secure-base behavior.

Children's Secure-Base Behavior at Home

The first line of evidence to support the universality of secure-base behavior was found in the analyses of mothers' characterizations of the behavior of their own children. The security scores that we derived indicated that, on average, children in all samples were characterized as behaving more like (than unlike) the hypothetical child, whose AQS profile indexes an optimal pattern of secure-base behavior. The fact that in all countries these security scores were skewed toward the positive side of the distribution (see Fig. 1) indicates that secure-base behavior is not a phenomenon exclusive to middle-class children in the United States but is observed and described by mothers from various sociocultural contexts.

Note that the strong positive skew of the distribution that we obtained cannot be dismissed as a mere artifact of the procedures used to derive the security scores, for two reasons. First, when another criterion sort—that of a prototypically dependent child (Waters, 1987)—was scored in the same fashion from our data, correlations between the individual sorts provided by mothers and the dependency criterion ranged between $-.49$ and $.45$ ($M = .03$); that is, dependency scores were as likely to fall below the theoretical midpoint of the scale as above it. Second, the distribution of security scores reported by Howes, Hamilton, and Allhusen (1995) in their study of relationships between children and their nonfamilial caregivers—in which many of the relationships lacked the history of long-term consistency that is requisite for the development of an attachment bond and the child's consequent use of the adult as a secure base—extended across both positive and negative values and included a substantial number of the latter.

A second line of support for conjectures regarding universality of the secure-base phenomenon arises from examining the within- and between-sample similarity among mothers' Q-sort descriptions. Consistent with predictions from the theory, the similarity in descriptions of secure-base behavior within countries was not markedly greater than similarities between countries. Had the samples proved to be markedly more similar within than between groups, an inference that cultural stereotypes were influencing mothers' descriptions of their children could be justified. In fact, our results (see Table 2 above) indicate that the similarity of Q-sort profiles was not much greater within each of the sociocultural groups than between groups, suggesting that culturally specific biases regarding the behavior of young children are unlikely to be obscuring individual differences either within or between groups.

We note, however, that the extent of the sociocultural similarity among the Q-sort profiles—be it within or between samples—was modest, indicating that there is considerable diversity in the ways that children organize their secure-base behavior. Additional research is needed to establish the functional value that such diversity may have in different sociocultural milieus and to discover whether relatively homogeneous clusters of children can be identified and discriminated in terms of the characteristic organization of secure-base behavior (for a program of research along such lines, see Strayer, Verissimo, Vaughn, & Howes, in this volume).

To the extent that such homogeneous groups can in fact be identified, it becomes relevant to identify the ecologies in which such clusters emerge and to determine whether these contextual characteristics are associated with similar groupings across varied socioeconomic and sociocultural settings. At the very least, the evidence of diversity with respect to the organization of secure-base behavior provided by our data suggests the importance of studying attachment relationships in naturalistic settings. Although the Strange Situation and other laboratory procedures have proved their value as indicators of different strategies for adaptation in affectively toned relationships, relying solely on such techniques may restrict our view of secure-base phenomena in ways that are potentially important but presently unknown.

Mothers' Preferences: Characterizing the Behavior of the "Ideal" Child

Mothers' preferences regarding the form and organization of secure-base behavior also proved to be similar across countries. Furthermore, the average security score for descriptions of the "ideal" child in each country was relatively high (ranging from .47 to .67), suggesting that, across participating countries, mothers' preferences with respect to behaviors included in the AQS are consistent with behavioral patterns that are considered as indicative of security by U.S. experts. This should not be taken to imply that sociocultural differences in mothers' notions of ideal secure-base behavior do not exist; despite the relatively high degree of correlations among Q-profiles (both within and between samples), there is still room for finding differences among countries.

Indeed, our exploratory analyses of specific behavioral domains of secure-base behavior provided some indications of possible cultural differences in mothers' preferences. For example, we found that U.S. and Japanese mothers placed more emphasis than Israeli mothers on the child's readiness to interact with mother and his or her positive emotional tone during such interactions as well as on issues of compliance. More than mothers from any other country, Colombian mothers valued having children return to mother, check her location, and go back to her when upset, bored, or in need of help. German and Israeli mothers tended to emphasize more than Chinese mothers the child's enjoyment of physical contact and of the comfort derived from it. Finally, Chinese and Japanese mothers preferred that children show readiness to interact, share, and participate in interactions with other adults, more than German and Israeli mothers.

Such differences notwithstanding, the important point is that, overall, mothers' descriptions of the ideal child indicated that they prefer that children behave in ways consistent with what attachment theory defines as adaptive use of the mother as a secure base for exploration and that this is common across a range of sociocultural contexts. The fact that differences of emphasis regarding diverse domains of the secure-base phenomenon can be found among the different samples is a theoretically provocative point that deserves further and systematic investigation.

Experts' Descriptions of Optimal Secure-Base Behavior in a Child

Behavioral profiles of the hypothetical securely attached child provided by experts from different countries were very highly correlated, suggesting a common understanding of what constitutes an optimal organization of secure-base behavior. This was not an obligatory finding since many of these child professionals did not have any in-depth knowledge of attachment theory that could potentially affect their conceptualization of the secure-base phenomenon. In fact, the correlations of composites obtained from experts who were less familiar with Bowlby's theory (i.e., Chinese and Colombian professionals) were somewhat lower than those of professionals who were better versed in the theory; overall, however, experts from all countries showed substantial congruence in their descriptions. This may be due to a basic knowledge of development and of relationships that they acquired in their professional education or from their experiences working with children and families. Whatever the reasons, such similarity of expert descriptions suggests that constructing different security criterion sorts for each culture may not be necessary.

It is also notable that experts' profiles of optimal secure-base behavior were highly correlated with those of the "ideal" child that mothers provided, indicating that both mothers and experts defined optimal child behavior alike when using the AQS. This is interesting since mothers were not told to define the "optimally secure" child and were not aware that this construct was being assessed. Similarity between experts' profiles of the "optimal" child and mothers' profiles of the "ideal" child within each country was not markedly higher than that across countries, suggesting again that, with regard to behavior covered by the AQS, notions of optimality cannot be dismissed as culturally biased.

CONCLUDING COMMENTS

Our findings support the Bowlby/Ainsworth conjecture that secure-base behavior is characteristic of our species. We found that, on average, children in all countries and contexts represented in this study were characterized as using their mothers as a secure base. The fact that the information was collected in different sociocultural contexts and that different research goals were being pursued by each of the participating labs (i.e., information was not being gathered to test the hypothesis of universality of attachment) makes an even stronger case for the findings presented here. However, this commonality does not imply that children in all cultures organize their secure-base behavior with respect to their mothers in the same manner.

Indeed, we found great diversity in the degree to which these children's behavior conformed to the definition of the securely attached child, perhaps more than theoretical statements and laboratory procedures may lead us to anticipate.

It also appears that mothers' notions of "ideal" child behavior overlap considerably with behavior that characterizes the secure-base phenomenon. Regardless of differences in sociocultural context, mothers ideally would like their children to use them as a secure base for exploration. The specific ways in which they would like their children to do so, however, may vary in different contexts; thus, for example, the German and Israeli mothers we sampled preferred children to enjoy physical contact to a greater extent than did the Chinese mothers. In addition, experts' notions of what constitutes optimality in secure-base behavior were similar across the seven countries we studied—the definition of *attachment security* and of *secure-base behavior* did not change appreciably as a function of nationality or of degree of familiarity with attachment theory. Finally, mothers' ideals about secure child behavior were highly convergent with experts' definitions of optimal secure-base behavior across countries, supporting the notion that culture-specific criterion Q-sorts may not be needed.

A QUANTITATIVE APPROACH TO THE DESCRIPTION AND CLASSIFICATION OF PRIMARY SOCIAL RELATIONSHIPS

F. Francis Strayer, Manuela Verissimo, Brian E. Vaughn, and Carollee Howes

Questions about how best to characterize physical, behavioral, or psychological diversity have had a long and complex history in disciplines as diverse as child psychiatry, behavioral ecology, and developmental psychobiology. Variation with respect to specific characteristics can be seen as reflecting either qualitative or quantitative differences in development. Both approaches to individual diversity have intuitive appeal, perhaps because each offers unique analytic possibilities. Identification of categorical or taxonomic differences between children draws attention to homogeneous subgroups of individuals who may share common experiences during development. For example, the early socialization experiences of boys may be quite different from those experienced by girls (e.g., Block, 1983). On the other hand, many individual differences are better characterized in terms of graded dimensions rather than categorical types (e.g., Block & Block, 1980). Since such conceptual continua are not always well reflected in a descriptive account of stylistic variants, quantitative assessments often provide more precise predictions about how individuals adapt across social settings.

When diversity is characterized as variation along a linear dimension, prediction about the location of individuals along similar (linear) continua

This research was supported in part by grants from the Spencer Foundation, Fonds pour la Formation de Chercheurs et Aide a la Recherche, and the Social Science and Humanities Research Council of Canada, as well as National Institute of Child Health and Development grant HD18-296. We are especially grateful to the families in Montréal and Chicago who gave their time to our research. Direct correspondence to F. F. Strayer, Laboratory of Human Ethology, Psychology Department, Université du Québec à Montréal, Postal Box 8888, Station A, Montréal, Québec, Canada H3C 3P8; or to Brian E. Vaughn, Department of Family and Child Development, Auburn University, Auburn, AL 36849.

may be facilitated, but discovery of distinct modes of adaptation becomes difficult. Often, the choice of the points on the continuum at which to divide a population into subgroups appears arbitrary (e.g., "younger" and "older" preschool children), and the identified "types" frequently grade one into the other, especially near category boundaries. Relating such ad hoc classifications to specific experiences or to developmental outcomes may reveal greater heterogeneity within groups than between groups. The qualitative description of developmental diversity in modes of early functioning requires specifying critical features that should be used to isolate specific behavioral styles. These features can be related to specific developmental experiences or to particular developmental outcomes contingent on early experience. In contrast to quantitative approaches stressing the discovery of predictive relations among graded assessments of individual differences, qualitative analyses of social style emphasize the identification of communality in adaptive processes underlying various developmental pathways.

Arguments about representing individual differences as taxonomic distinctions or as quantified distances on conceptual continua are especially relevant to modern research on primary attachment. From Bowlby's (1958) original concern with the impact of loss, to Ainsworth's work in Uganda and Baltimore (Ainsworth, 1967; Ainsworth, Blehar, Waters, & Wall, 1978), to the recent exploration of adults' state of mind regarding attachment (e.g., George, Kaplan, & Main, 1985; Main & Goldwyn, in press-b), attachment theorists have emphasized the value of characterizing individual differences in terms of patterns or modes of behaving and interacting, rather than in terms of rates and frequencies of specific behaviors or latencies of particular responses. Viewing the organization of social activity both at home and in the laboratory in terms of broad profiles of interactions relevant to the functioning of the attachment behavioral system led to the development of a classification taxonomy for attachment during early infancy that remains influential for the field of social and emotional development (Ainsworth et al., 1978; Ainsworth & Wittig, 1969; Sroufe & Waters, 1977).

One of Ainsworth's major insights was her recognition that qualitative differences in the patterning of attachment and caregiving behaviors observed in the home were related to discrete patterns of child behavior in response to brief separations and reunions in the Strange Situation (Ainsworth et al., 1978). Although behavior in the laboratory situation was not isomorphic with activities in the home, the child's behavior was related by common elements evident in the mother-child interaction. Thus, Ainsworth reasoned that the child's use of the mother as a secure base at home can predict her effective use of the mother as a source of comfort when the child is distressed by separation in the Strange Situation because both these aspects of attachment organization share a common history of sensitive and cooperative caregiving. Likewise, the failure (or apparent inability) to use the mother as a secure base at home is associated with distortions of attachment behavior in the Strange Situation, either by failure to acknowledge overtly the separation/reunion (or active avoidance at reunion of interaction offered by the mother), or by a nearly complete loss of emotional control in response to separation. These patterns share common histories of less sensitive and less cooperative caregiving and, for the avoidant cases, less acceptance from and less accessibility to the attachment figure (for an extended discussion of this issue, see Pederson & Moran, in this volume). It has been this interconnection of behavioral profiles on the part of children and their caregivers that gave rise to the wide acceptance of attachment as a construct that characterizes a relationship rather than as a construct that refers primarily to the individual child (see Sagi et al., in this volume; Seifer & Schiller, in this volume).

While recognizing the importance of attachment patterns as organizers of much of the infant's social-emotional experience, some researchers have argued that an exclusive assessment of qualitative differences in mother-child relations limits study of how primary attachment relates to other indices of child development (Water & Deane, 1985). Indeed, in many published reports, the several "patterns" of attachment were collapsed to a dichotomy (i.e., "secure" vs. "insecure") for data analysis. Faced with this limitation, some investigators have attempted to convert the Strange Situation classification system into a linear scale reflecting a continuum of differences in attachment security (e.g., Cassidy & Marvin, 1987; Cummings, 1990; Greenberg, 1984; Main & Cassidy, 1988; Schneider-Rosen, 1990). Studies adopting this strategy often report modest to moderately high associations between the continuum score for security and other unidimensional scales such as ego resiliency or self-esteem (e.g., Arend, Gove, & Sroufe, 1979; Cassidy, 1988), but they have been unable to clarify relations between security and these other indices of adaptation for avoidant, resistant, and disorganized-disoriented types of insecurely attached children.

An alternative, mixed approach was proposed by Richters, Waters, and Vaughn (1988), who employed discriminant analyses of the interactive scales used for the Strange Situation (Ainsworth et al., 1978) to produce two functions for classifying quality of attachment: the first function distinguished secure children from others, while the second separated avoidant from resistant cases. Although such multivariate strategies provide alternative empirical perspectives on how to deal with diversity in early mother-child relations, no single procedure has yet generated a classification taxonomy that precisely reproduces the Strange Situation classifications. Apparently, when shifting from a qualitative to a quantitative approach, the gain in terms of predictive validity is associated with a loss in terms of richness of description.

Q-methods provide an alternative approach to this problem. Historically, Q-sort data have been used both to distinguish individual types and to assess individual differences (Block, 1971; McKeown & Thomas, 1988). From its inception, the Attachment Q-Set (AQS) has been used to provide quantitative indices of attachment security, dependency, and sociability (see Waters & Deane, 1985). However, the AQS can also be used to identify coherent, homogeneous subgroups of children who appear similar on multiple facets of early social behavior. In addition, Q-data offer a variety of possibilities for multivariate analysis (for a thorough discussion of R-type and Q-type approaches, see Cattell, 1944). Q-sort data aggregated across subjects may be scaled, factor analyzed, or clustered in a conventional manner using R-correlations (i.e., correlations between *variables* over a sample of persons) to reveal covariation among items, thus permitting the construction of subscales of homogeneous traits (Block, 1961/1978; Stephenson, 1953). Alternatively, similar analytic procedures with Q-correlations (i.e., correlations between *persons* over a sample of variables) permit the identification of homogeneous subsets of individuals.

While several families of multivariate methods provide mathematically acceptable solutions to the problem of reducing full data matrices to a more manageable number of entities (e.g., components, factors, clusters), hierarchical cluster analysis has particular appeal since objects (be they variables or persons) are assigned to one and only one group at each level in the hierarchical cluster tree or dendrogram (Legendre & Legendre, 1984; Sneath & Sokal, 1973). Furthermore, the dendrograms produced by most computerized clustering algorithms permit a visual examination of the relative similarity among objects. This family of procedures lends itself well to taxonomic analyses since the objects (again, variables or persons) within a cluster are more similar to each other than to the members of other clusters. However, questions concerning the number of clusters to be retained, or the optimal degree of within-cluster similarity versus between-cluster differences, must be addressed by conceptual rather than mathematical criteria. Principal components analysis and common factor analysis, on the other hand, partition the "variance" of items or subjects across several underlying components/factors. While these solutions are often elegant in the sense that considerable between-variable (or between-person) covariation in the zero-order correlation matrix is reduced to a small number of linear dimensions, such data reduction often has the adverse effect of making the assignment of particular elements to a single group somewhat arbitrary when "loadings" are nearly equal in magnitude on two or more orthogonal dimensions.

In a previous study (Vaughn, Strayer, Jacques, Trudel, & Seifer, 1991), we exploited the advantages of Q-analyses to make cross-cultural comparisons of mothers' descriptions of their young children's attachment behavior (see also Posada, Gao, et al., in this volume). In this report, we extend these initial comparisons to descriptions of Québécois and American children's behavior as evaluated in the home setting by trained observers. We were interested in using the AQS as an instrument for identifying subgroups of children with similar patterns of attachment behavior at home, much as Ainsworth and her associates identified subgroups of children in the Baltimore study from their behavior in the Strange Situation (Ainsworth et al., 1978). In comparison with the Strange Situation, the Q-method offers the distinct advantage of a more formal characterization of observed behavior as well as the possibility of providing a more explicit description of subgroups than has been achieved by clinical observation procedures with post hoc decision rules. Finding such identifiable subgroups would be a first step in validating the classification taxonomy obtained from the Strange Situation against the attachment-relevant behavior exhibited by the child in the everyday physical and social environment.

Our specific objectives included (1) definition and refinement of descriptive scales derived from the AQS for assessing diversity in mother-child relationships, (2) evaluation of differences in social functioning within and across sociocultural groups, and (3) use of Q-correlation analyses to isolate homogeneous subgroups of subjects within and across the two research sites. Comparisons between sociocultural contexts were conducted at the level of individual AQS items, derived scale scores, and criterion scores for attachment security, dependency, and sociability. We reasoned that significant differences between the two cultural contexts on the scale or criterion measures could provide evidence for situational specificity in processes of social and emotional development that may have their basis in differing cultural codes and values (e.g., Vaughn et al., 1991). On the other hand, similarity in modal patterns of social functioning across the two cultural sites would provide support for the generality of both the descriptive scales and the underlying developmental constructs derived from attachment theory.

METHOD

Subjects

English-speaking subjects were drawn from a larger sample of mother-child pairs participating in longitudinal research projects taking place in the Chicago metropolitan area. A total of 67 children (30 girls, 37 boys) who met the criterion of being between 24 and 36 months of age when Q-sort observations were completed were selected from the larger sample. On the basis of father's job title, family income, and years of mother's and father's education, the subjects in this sample would be characterized as "middle class" by the standards of the Chicago metropolitan area. Over 95% of the subjects were of European-American ancestry, and all had been born in the United States. The French-speaking, Montréal sample was drawn from a longitudinal research project concerning effects of early socialization environments. A total of 65 cases (35 girls, 30 boys) who were between 18 and 30 months of age when observed at home were included in this latter group. On the basis of years of education and family income, these subjects would be considered "middle class" by Québécois standards at the time data were collected. Over 90% of the families were of European ancestry, and the remaining families were Asian.

Procedure

We used the original AQS composed of 100 items descriptive of specific behavioral attributes or characteristics of children aged between 12 and 48 months (Waters & Deane, 1985).[1] For the Québécois sample, these items were translated into French and then back-translated by fully bilingual speakers to evaluate any connotative differences in the wording of the items. Items whose meaning had changed across translations were retranslated with appropriate changes and back-translated a second time.

Observers were asked to order the 100 items in a quasi-normal distribution ranging from those that were "least like the child" to those "most like the child" (distribution = 5, 8, 12, 16, 18, 16, 12, 8, 5). All Q-sort descriptions were conducted by trained observers who had extensive experience with both the theoretical and the technical aspects of the evaluation. For

---

[1] The original items and criterion sorts for the Security, Dependency, and Sociability constructs, as well as the criterion for social desirability bias, can be found in Waters and Deane (1985). This 100-item Q-set was developed for use by trained observers and researchers familiar with the basic structure of attachment theory and with the behavior of infants and young children. The 100-item Q-set proved to be difficult for less well-trained observers (such as mothers), and a revised 90-item Q-set was developed by Waters (1987), in part in response to the widespread use of mothers as informants in research studies. This Q-set, the AQS (see App. A, in this volume), is now the de facto standard for researchers conducting Q-sort studies of attachment.

In deriving the 90-item Q-set, Waters eliminated items that had very low variances in his development samples, reworded items in such a way that none contained double negatives, and dropped items that might not be seen regularly in 2–4-hour visits to homes (e.g., items referring to the child's behavior in unfamiliar surroundings). Content relevant to the three primary constructs (i.e., Security, Dependency, and Sociability) was retained in the 90-item Q-set. Inclusion of this content suggests that the revision of the Q-set should produce scales for proximity/exploration balance, differential responsiveness to the parent (as opposed to other adults), independence, expression of positive affect, sociability, and social perceptiveness. Our scales measuring endurance and object use may not be reproducible using the 90-item Q-set.

the Chicago sample, the two assistants observed each child at home with the mother on two separate occasions, for a total observation time of 4–6 hours. After the second home visit, they generated a consensus Q-sort description of the child by jointly sorting the items into the required distribution after discussing notes taken during the two visits. For the Montréal sample, two observers described each child after watching between 6 and 8 hours of videotaped interactions in the home setting that were recorded over three or four separate visits by members of the research team.

Design of Analyses

Q-sort data provide a comprehensive description of individual cases, or groups of cases, along the multiple dimensions reflected in the items of the Q-set. However, the information contained in Q-sort data is voluminous and diverse and often difficult to comprehend. For this reason, it is a common practice to summarize Q-sort data with reference to "criterion" or "prototype" scores (see Block, 1961/1978; Waters & Deane, 1985), which are based on the aggregated Q-sorts provided by individuals "expert" with reference to a given construct (e.g., attachment security). A given child's "score" for a particular theoretical construct is the congruence (i.e., correlation) between his or her observer-based Q-sort description and the Q-sort criterion definition of that construct. Waters and Deane (1985) provided criterion sorts for three substantive constructs (attachment security, dependency, and sociability) as well as a criterion sort for social desirability response bias. Although the social desirability criterion was originally intended for use as a control variable that might help adjust for biases of observers, Waters and Deane (1985) noted that it was strongly associated with security; that is, it is desirable to be secure (for a related discussion, see Posada, Gao, et al., in this volume). Therefore, we included scores for each of the four Waters and Deane (1985) constructs in our analyses.

A second method of deriving "scores" from Q-sort data is to extract items from the Q-set that share common themes and to sum across these items to derive a score for that theme. Waters and Deane (1985) identified eight such content themes in the original 100-item Q-set (i.e., attachment/exploration balance, differential responsiveness to caregiver, affect expression, social involvement, object use, independence/dependence, social perceptiveness, and endurance/resilience) and suggested items from the Q-set to reflect those themes. We generated scales for each of these content domains for use in our analyses. Finally, groups can be compared at the level of individual Q-items. In the present study, analyses of group differences involved simple comparison of sample means for scores at each level of measurement. Because such tests are not independent, we increased the alpha for identifying significant between-site differences to $p < .005$ in all contrasts.

To assess between-group similarities in modes of adaptation, we used hierarchical clustering techniques and evaluated between-cluster differences for the criterion scores and the empirical scales. Initial cluster analyses were conducted separately within the two subsamples. We then used the same clustering algorithm in a global analysis that aggregated all subjects to examine the reproducibility of the original cluster groups. Finally, we evaluated the patterns of differences between these final clusters using a two-factor (site × cluster membership) ANOVA design.

RESULTS

Deriving Q-Sort Scales

The derivation of descriptive scales from the AQS required identifying specific items that may serve as indices of the conceptual content areas originally suggested by Waters and Deane (1985): that is, proximity/exploration balance, differential responsiveness to caregiver, social involvement, positive affect, independence, social perceptiveness, endurance, and object use. An initial list of items pertinent to these scales was obtained by asking four colleagues, all of whom were familiar with the AQS procedures, to assign the 100 items to the eight descriptive categories; the 14 items that were not unanimously assigned by them to a single content area were excluded as potential constituents of the derived scales. Examination of the internal consistency (Cronbach's alpha) of the set of descriptors associated with each scale permitted isolation of a limited number of items that could serve as an aggregated index of each content area. In subsequent analyses, items that reduced the observed reliability of each scale were progressively eliminated to arrive at a final set of eight descriptors that optimized the internal coherence of each descriptive dimension. Seven of the eight scales had sufficiently high Cronbach alphas to warrant further analysis; only the Object Use scale proved unreliable. Table 1 provides a summary of the results of these findings for the full sample and for the Montréal and Chicago subsamples (for a listing of the items included in each of the final scales, see the Appendix to this report).

Between-Site Comparisons

Mean Differences for Items, Scales, and Criterion Scores

Comparisons of site differences on the full Q-set showed that 40 of the 100 items distinguished between the two samples (with $p \leq .005$). The Chi-

TABLE 1

RELIABILITY OF THE DERIVED Q-SORT SCALES

DESCRIPTIVE Q-SCALES	NUMBER OF ITEMS		CRONBACH ALPHAS		
	Initial	Final[a]	Full Sample (N = 132)	Montréal (N = 65)	Chicago (N = 67)
Proximity/Exploration Balance	12	8	.83	.89	.78
Differential Responsiveness to Caregiver	12	8	.84	.75	.84
Positive Affect	8	8	.85	.78	.87
Sociability	13	8	.88	.81	.91
Independence	12	8	.84	.76	.87
Social Perceptiveness	12	8	.73	.74	.77
Endurance	10	8	.74	.70	.80
Object Use[b]	7	7	.26	.35	.19

[a] The final set of items for each scale is presented in the Appendix to this report.

[b] Because the reliability for the Object Use scale was unacceptably low, this scale was dropped from further analysis.

cago children received higher scores on 19 of these, while 21 items were seen as more characteristic of the Montréal children. However, despite the relatively high number of item differences, the scale scores derived from the Q-sort data showed that the two samples were quite similar; Table 2 provides a summary of site comparisons for the seven descriptive scales and the four Q-sort criterion scores. Only two scales showed a significant difference between the groups—Chicago children were described as more differentially responsive to their primary caregiver and as less independent. There was a nonsignificant trend for Chicago children to be described as more socially sensitive ($p < .02$) and for Québécois children to have lower scores on the Dependency criterion score ($p < .01$); this latter finding corresponds to the result described on the Independence scale. However, since neither of these latter two effects attained our preestablished level of significance, definitive interpretations of between-site differences in perceptiveness and dependency must await replication of these findings.

Although the item analyses suggested a relatively large number of differences between the two sociocultural groups, most of these item-level effects appear to be counterbalanced when the items are aggregated in the scale and criterion scores. Comparative analyses using higher-order measures revealed considerable similarity in the mean scores of the two samples. However, similarity on either particular items or scale scores does not imply that the AQS profiles are the same for the two groups: analyses of similarity in group means do not deal with the question of similarity in the patterning of relations among the various scores. The next series of analyses were designed to permit a direct comparison of Q-sort profiles obtained for children in each of the two samples.

TABLE 2

Sample Means and Standard Deviations on the Seven Descriptive Scales
and the Four Q-Set Criterion Scores

Q-Sort Measure	Montréal	Chicago	F Value	p Level
Descriptive scales:				
Proximity/Exploration[a]	5.04	5.32	1.94	. . .
	(1.22)	(1.11)		
Differential Responsiveness	5.56	6.27	25.42	.001*
	(.57)	(1.00)		
Positive Affect	6.45	6.12	2.61	. . .
	(.85)	(1.40)		
Sociability	6.03	6.19	.39	. . .
	(1.09)	(1.81)		
Independence	6.57	5.93	8.22	.005*
	(1.04)	(1.43)		
Social Perceptiveness	5.11	5.47	5.38	.02
	(.74)	(.99)		
Endurance	5.68	5.54	.73	. . .
	(.74)	(1.05)		
Criterion scores:				
Security[b]	.39	.43	.55	. . .
	(.20)	(.35)		
Dependency	−.21	−.08	7.38	.01
	(.23)	(.31)		
Sociability	.41	.43	.21	. . .
	(.20)	(.38)		
Social desirability	.43	.41	.13	. . .
	(.23)	(.39)		

Note.—Standard deviations are given in parentheses.

[a] Mean values are averaged values for the eight items included in each scale.

[b] Mean values reflect the congruence (i.e., correlation) between the vector of item scores for subjects and the criterion vector for a given construct.

* Significant at established level of $p < .005$.

Profile Comparisons

To assess the degree of association among our Q-sort descriptors, correlations among the seven scales were calculated separately for each sample. Inspection of the results suggested that the relations among derived scales were quite similar for the two sites, and principal component analyses (PCAs) of these correlation matrices showed identical factor structures for each group. The first component was strongly associated with descriptors of social functioning, while the second bipolar factor involved opposition between the Proximity/Exploration and Differential Responsiveness scales and the Independence scale. These findings, which are depicted in Table 3, suggest that the degree of similarity in association among the Q-sort measures obtained in the two sites is sufficiently strong to justify a two-dimensional representation of assessed individual differences. For both

TABLE 3

Principal Component Analysis of Q-Sort Scale Scores Obtained
in Each Sociocultural Context

| | Component Loadings | | | |
| | Montréal | | Chicago | |
Q-Scales	Social	Attachment	Social	Attachment
Endurance	.87[a]	− .13	.84[a]	− .07
Positive Affect	.85[a]	− .13	.83[a]	− .08
Social Perceptiveness	.83[a]	.13	.70[a]	.19
Sociability	.83[a]	− .13	.70[a]	− .07
Proximity/Exploration	− .24	.89[a]	.01	.90[a]
Differential Responsiveness ...	.49	.69[a]	.25	.84[a]
Independence	.60	− .62[a]	.40	− .79[a]
Eigen value	3.61	1.61	2.65	2.14
Percentage variance	51.6	23.0	37.8	30.5

[a] Indicates principal loading of each Q-sort scale.

samples, the obtained two-component solution accounted for nearly 70% of the total variance; however, in the interest of conserving potentially unique contributions of specific descriptive scales, the intercorrelations between the scales were reexamined using complete linkage cluster analyses.

The cluster analysis results are presented as dendrogram plots in Figure 1. In both subsamples, five distinct subgroupings of scales are readily identified (marked with a bold vertical line in each dendrogram plot). The Positive Affect and Sociability scales are joined quickly in all three analyses, and the Endurance and Social Perceptiveness scales are joined at the next level. At the next level, these two clusters are joined, forming a higher-order cluster resembling the first principal component described above in Table 3. Note, however, that there is substantially more similarity within the cluster pairs than there is in the larger combined cluster. That is to say, the distance between the two clusters is substantially greater than the distance between the two variables composing each cluster. Next, note that the Independence scale score is grouped with the large cluster formed from the Positive Affect–Sociability and Endurance–Social Perceptiveness clusters rather than with the Proximity/Exploration and Differential Responsiveness scales, as was the case in the PCAs. There is also a between-site difference in the similarity between the Proximity/Exploration and the Differential Responsiveness scales. These two scales join very quickly in the analysis of the Montréal data, but they do not form a cluster in the Chicago sample until late in the analysis, after several primary clusters have emerged. Thus, the cluster analyses provide a markedly different picture of the "structure" characterizing the correlation matrix for these scales. At the very least, these analyses indicate that the scale score for Independence should be treated

Dendrogram for Montréal

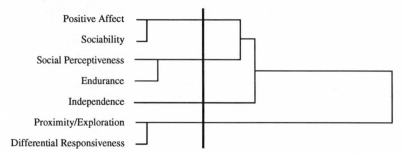

Dendrogram for Chicago

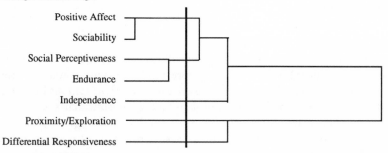

Dendrogram for Combined Sample

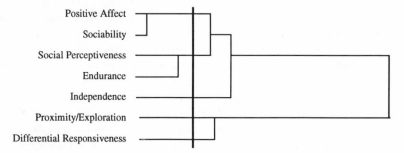

Fig. 1.—Dendrogram plots of the cluster analysis for the descriptive Q-scales for each site separately and for the full sample.

as an unique unit, rather than as associated with either the two attachment scales or the other social measures.

We used the results from the cluster analyses to select a reduced set of descriptors for a multivariate classification of the Q-sort profiles. The Positive Affect and Sociability scales were combined to furnish a composite measure of Prosocial Disposition, and the Endurance and Social Perceptiveness scales were combined to yield a composite measure of Social Sensitivity. In conjunction with the scale scores for Independence, Proximity/Exploration Balance, and Differential Responsiveness, these two composite scales serve as final descriptive criteria in classifying children according to similarities among their Q-sort profiles.

Classification of Q-Sort Profiles at Each Site

To assess similarities among the Q-sort profiles, we used cluster analyses to group the subjects on the basis of the five scores identified above. Clusters were derived separately within the two subsamples and again for the combined sample. Clusters were formed using Ward's method (Norusis, 1990, p. 361), for which squared Euclidean distances serve as indices of dissimilarity; the dendrograms obtained for the Montréal and Chicago samples are shown in Figure 2.

Note that these graphic representations of the clustering history have been rescaled to reveal *relative*, not absolute, distances between clusters for each group. Longer horizontal lines in the dendrogram indicate greater relative distances between the clusters they join; thus, the two large clusters are maximally dissimilar in both subsamples. Each of the two dendrograms is composed of two relatively large subgroups of children, both of which can be subdivided into a number of successively smaller and increasingly homogeneous subgroups. In any attempt to generate an empirical classification system, a central question concerns the number of distinct subgroups to be retained, and the answer requires specifying a set of decision rules that direct analytic choices and ultimately establish the nature of the descriptive taxonomy.

In the present analysis, we used two rules to determine the number of subgroups. First, we decided to keep only clusters containing more than 15% of the sample. The second rule concerned the stability of our classification algorithm: we chose as the final number that set of clusters that showed stable placement of children both in the initial, site-based analysis and in the secondary, combined analysis. This second rule provided a part-whole validation of our classification procedure. At an operational level, we assessed the validity of our classification in terms of the concordance of findings between global and site analyses.

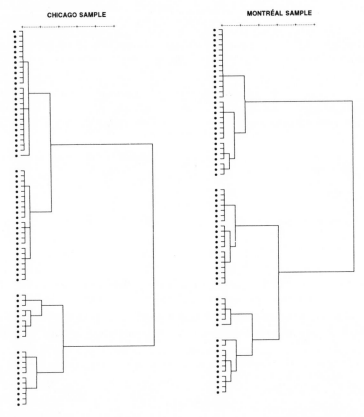

CHICAGO SAMPLE

MONTRÉAL SAMPLE

FIG. 2.—Dendrogram plots of the cluster analysis of cases for the Chicago and Montréal subsamples.

In both of the within-site analyses, a three-cluster solution provided the most economical and interpretable description of subjects. Analyses of variance were conducted for the five final scales and the four criterion scores using cluster membership as an independent variable. The resulting statistics on the effect of cluster membership calculated separately for each data set are presented in Table 4.

Inspection of differences in scale means for each subgroup indicates the relative importance of the final descriptive scales as criteria in describing the three subgroups. For the Chicago sample, all five scales clearly differentiated the three clusters; for the Montréal sample, Social Sensitivity was the only descriptor that failed to distinguish strongly between the subgroups. Analyses of the Q-sort criterion scores add support to the conclusion that the clusters of children from each site share common characteristics. In both samples, the first cluster scored highest on the Security and Sociability

TABLE 4

MEANS, STANDARD DEVIATIONS, AND ANOVA PROBABILITY LEVELS
FOR WITHIN-SITE CLUSTERS

	MONTRÉAL CLUSTERS[a]				CHICAGO CLUSTERS[a]			
	I [19]	II [29]	III [17]	p^b	I [25]	II [22]	III [20]	p^c
Descriptive scales:								
Proximity/Exploration	5.7^d	4.0	6.1^d	.001	5.7^d	4.3	6.0^d	.001
	(.69)	(.68)	(.99)		(.59)	(.66)	(1.26)	
Differential Responsiveness	5.7^d	5.2	5.9^d	.001	6.9	5.9^d	5.9^d	.001
	(.41)	(.33)	(.72)		(.68)	(.55)	(1.32)	
Prosocial Disposition	6.8	6.2^d	5.7^d	.001	7.0^d	6.9^d	4.2	.001
	(.68)	(.81)	(.91)		(.56)	(.75)	(1.36)	
Independence	6.7^d	7.4^e	5.1^f	.001	6.0^d	7.0^e	4.6^f	.001
	(.40)	(.58)	(.64)		(.77)	(.70)	(1.58)	
Social Sensitivity	5.7^d	5.4^{d,e}	5.1^e	.02	6.0^d	5.9^d	4.4	.001
	(.48)	(.59)	(.81)		(.29)	(.55)	(.86)	
Criterion scores:								
Security	.52	.38^d	.27^d	.001	.65^d	.58^d	−.02	.001
	(.11)	(.18)	(.25)		(.08)	(.13)	(.31)	
Dependency	−.20^d	−.40^e	.09^f	.001	−.12^d	−.34^e	.25^f	.001
	(.10)	(.11)	(.15)		(.10)	(.14)	(.32)	
Sociability	.54	.37^d	.31^d	.002	.67^d	.60^d	−.05	.001
	(.13)	(.18)	(.24)		(.11)	(.15)	(.32)	
Social Desirability	.56^d	.46^d	.25	.001	.64^d	.63^d	−.11	.001
	(.13)	(.20)	(.26)		(.10)	(.14)	(.30)	

NOTE.—Cluster means with similar superscripts are *not* different from each other in post hoc analyses using Tukey's HSD test. Values in parentheses are standard deviations.

[a] N's are given in square brackets.

[b] $df = 2, 62$.

[c] $df = 2, 64$.

criteria and lowest on Dependency. Similarly, at each site, the second cluster emerged as the least dependent and intermediate on all of the three remaining scores. Finally, the third cluster contained children with the highest scores on the Dependency criterion.

Global Classification of Q-Sort Profiles

The final step in our classification analysis involved applying the algorithm used in the site analyses to the full sample of 132 subjects. Given the greater number of subjects in the combined analysis, either a three- or a four-cluster solution would be acceptable. However, the four-cluster solution that we obtained did not fulfill our criterion for minimum cluster size for either subsample. In addition, cross-classification analyses comparing the placement of subjects in the global and the site analyses revealed better concordance for the three-cluster model: the percentage of cases classified in the same category increased from 63% for the four-cluster solution (Cohen κ = .473) to 68% in the three-cluster model (Cohen κ = .572). The difference in these agreement indices supports the choice of a three-cluster solution as the most appropriate classification model for these data.

In the global analysis, the patterns of scores characterizing the three clusters were quite similar to those obtained in the separate site analyses. Analysis of variance indicated that there was a significant linear trend for each of the four Q-sort criterion scores to distinguish the three clusters ($F[3, 129] > 16.74, p < .001$). Members of Cluster I had the highest average scores on Security, Sociability, and social desirability, while children in Cluster II were intermediate, and members of Cluster III had the lowest scores on these three criterion variables. In contrast, children in Cluster III had the highest Dependency scores, members of Cluster I were intermediate, while children in Cluster II had the lowest scores for this construct. Although the magnitude of these criterion scores within a given cluster differed somewhat between the sites, the relative patterning of scores for the four criteria is surprisingly similar within a given cluster at each site.

DISCUSSION

Our first objective in this study was to examine the utility of the AQS for comparative studies of mother-child interactions in different cultural contexts. In this regard, the findings indicated that observer-based assessments provide reliable and similar descriptions of young children for the Chicago and the Montréal samples. Although site differences were evident at the level of individual items, analyses of the derived Q-set scales and construct scores suggested an overall pattern of similarity with respect to Q-sort characterizations. The degree of similarity is especially noteworthy in view of the fact that the methods of observation differed across sites (live vs. videotaped assessments) and that the ages represented in the samples were not precisely equivalent (24 and 36 months in the Chicago sample, 18–30 months in the Montréal sample).

To the extent that patterns of mother-child activities are characterized as similar across these settings, the AQS can be seen as a valuable instrument for cross-cultural studies of mother-child relationships. Our findings suggest that interpretations concerning the structure of attachment and other social domains made on the basis of Q-sort descriptions of middle-class, English-speaking children in the United States need not be substantially modified when interpreting Q-sort descriptions made by observers from a different sociocultural context. Both French- and English-speaking observers furnished meaningful descriptions that yielded comparable information about individual differences within each sample, and similar results have been reported by Posada, Gao, et al. (in this volume) and by Vaughn et al. (1991) with respect to Q-sort descriptions provided by mothers from different cultures. Of course, to obtain interpretable scores at either the scale or the construct level, respondents must be given clear instructions about the meaning of specific items and about the procedures for sorting according to the required distribution (see also Teti & McGourty, in press). In cross-cultural studies, it is important that additional care be accorded to the translation/back-translation process so as to assure that item content is rendered equivalently in the language native to the observer.

Our second objective involved using multivariate clustering techniques adopted from numeric ecology (Legendre & Legendre, 1984) to examine qualitatively distinct modes of social activity characterizing mothers and their 2–3-year-old children. The similarities in the cluster solutions obtained for each of the two samples provide strong empirical evidence for the validity of the underlying dimensions derived from the AQS as well as for the utility of the AQS itself for isolating modes of adaptation in different sociocultural contexts. We interpret these results as evidence that the AQS offers researchers a valid tool for conducting cross-cultural research on the nature and impact of child-mother attachment.

Perhaps most interesting from the standpoint of taxonomic classifications of attachment behavior is the suggestive similarity between the qualities that distinguished the three clusters described here and the three more traditional categories derived from behavior observed in the Strange Situation. In both of the samples we analyzed, children in Cluster I have the highest scores for the Security construct, with high or intermediate scores on the Dependency and Sociability constructs. These children describe a type that shares characteristics with the group B (secure) classification in the Strange Situation. Children in Cluster II were seen as not dependent on their mothers (they had the highest scores on the Independence scale and the lowest on the Dependency construct). In Montréal, Cluster II children differed from those in Cluster I by also having lower mean scores for Security and Sociability; however, in Chicago, the corresponding differences were not significant. Nonetheless, inspection of the descriptive scale scores showed that, in both samples, children from Cluster II scored the lowest on Proximity/Exploration Balance and lower than members of Cluster I on the Differential Responsiveness scale. Thus, children in the second clusters seem to share some of the attributes of children classified as avoidant in the Strange Situation. Finally, although Cluster III was the least similar across sites, all these children had the highest scores for the Dependency construct and the lowest scores for Security and Sociability. In both sites, Cluster III children were characterized as the least sensitive to social cues, as the least independent and least prosocial, and yet also as the most concerned with maintaining proximity. These children appear less mature socially and, at least in some sense, resemble the insecure resistant (group C) category of the Strange Situation classification system.

Although we do not intend to argue that the three clusters derived from our Q-sort data correspond directly to Strange Situation classifications in kind or quantity, the analogy between the two taxonomies is striking— and it is made even more impressive by the fact that it arises within each of the two samples of children. Previous research comparing the Security scores derived from the AQS with classifications obtained in the Strange Situation (e.g., Bosso, Corter, & Abramovitch, 1995; Vaughn & Waters, 1990) had not distinguished between the avoidant and the resistant types; since both are insecurely attached, differentiation on the basis of their Q-sort Security scores would not necessarily be expected. Our data suggest that the avoidant versus resistant distinction may be drawn in terms of differential patterns of emerging autonomy and dependence at home. The verification of this interpretation in future research could provide important insights into the nature of insecure attachments as well as directly validating the Strange Situation classificatory system.

A third and somewhat more technical goal of this study involved developing and validating empirical scales for the eight conceptual content areas that Waters and Deane (1985) used in constructing the original AQS. These scales provide an intermediate level of description necessary for the classification of individual Q-sort profiles. The derivation of seven internally consistent scales, each being an aggregate of scores for eight unique items, provides a new and potentially very interesting set of standards for scoring the AQS. In the present study, this descriptive information was useful for distinguishing between the two cultural groups, increasing the descriptive richness of the AQS, and helping isolate organized patterns of social activity as qualitatively distinct modes of social functioning.

A second, less obvious advantage of these descriptive scale scores is that they permit more direct comparison of findings obtained with different versions of the AQS (see n. 1 above). During the past 10 years, we have witnessed the publication of at least three versions of the AQS item set (Stevenson-Hinde, 1985; Waters, 1987; Waters & Deane, 1985), each with its own criterion profiles for calculating construct scores. Without a common standard, it is difficult to ascertain the degree to which these various versions are saturated with secure-base, dependency, and sociability content. By computing scores on empirically validated descriptive scales, we might better situate the sense of Q-sort correlations for constructs like Security, Sociability, and Dependency in a given set of Q-items. The urgency of a common standard is clear when we realize that literally thousands of Q-sorts have been completed with different versions of the AQS and that there is at present no way directly to interpret differences (or similarities) across studies in which different sets of items were sorted.

CONCLUDING REMARKS

Theorists and researchers of early attachment have had an abiding interest in describing how variations in the patterning of early social relationships relate to individual differences in developmental outcome. Rather than measuring quantitative differences in particular underlying constructs such as security or dependency, Ainsworth proposed a classification scheme of primary relationships based on patterns of mother-child interaction. This choice linked her work to a rich conceptual heritage. The notion of qualitatively distinct developmental forms corresponds well with classic conceptions of experiential canalization elaborated by early psychobiologists (Baldwin, 1895; Holt, 1931; Waddington, 1942; Wallon, 1934). Furthermore, interest in modes of adaptation anticipated the interest among current developmental scientists in the early canalization of developmental trajectories (Gottlieb, 1991; Kraemer, 1992; LeBlanc, Cote, & Loeber, 1991; Loeber, 1982; Thelen & Ulrich, 1991).

From this perspective, the course of early development is characterized as an initially diffuse behavioral potential that is progressively structured by experiences unique to the individual (Gottlieb, 1991). Interaction with familiar partners leads children to consolidate particular patterns of social adjustment. In the course of constructing locally adaptive characteristics, alternative modes of functioning become increasingly less available to the child; thus, development proceeds through a progressive loss of potential in the service of optimizing immediate adaptive functions (Baldwin, 1895; Edelman, 1987). The concept of ontogenetic selection implies that past experience constrains the possible range of reactions in future developmental contexts. Particular aspects of past experience, encoded either as physiological or as mental representations, orient children on different developmental pathways that reflect the progressive consolidation of particular modes of social functioning (Strayer, 1989).

Underlying the interest in describing and classifying qualitative differences in primary social bonds is a more fundamental concern with clarifying how variation in patterns of early social experience leads children onto different developmental trajectories. Although the Strange Situation was useful for describing and classifying infant attachments, corresponding procedures for studying diversity in modes of social adaptation during later childhood have only recently begun to receive serious attention. From a psychometric perspective, the aggregated scores from AQS scales offer robust descriptive indices for use in quantifying cross-setting variations in children's early social activity. However, from a developmental psychobiological perspective, qualitative analyses of similarity in AQS profiles provide an alternate basis for investigating how early experiences modulate ontogenetic relations between primary attachment and subsequent modes of social adaptation. Like most biological systems, the behavioral control systems regulating primary attachment must be seen as fundamentally adaptable, albeit within a limited range of external conditions. Such an understanding of how phylogeny constrains the reaction ranges of both partners during the co-construction of a primary relationship leads to the proposition that underlying control systems must be subject to modulation by both ecological and cultural factors. The interplay between phylogenetic and ontogenetic constraints invariably leads to repetitions of variations on a theme. The present comparative findings provide a modest first step in elucidating both the communality and the diversity in primary social relationships. The more important, long-term goal entails clarifying how qualitative differences in primary relationships facilitate the selection of particular social pathways and shape individual developmental trajectories.

APPENDIX: ITEM CONTENTS FOR EACH OF THE SCALES DERIVED FROM THE 100-ITEM ATTACHMENT Q-SET (AQS)[2]

Proximity/Exploration Balance

43. Returns from play/exploration spontaneously at home.
63. Becomes distressed when adult moves away.
80. More tolerant of self-initiated than adult-initiated separation.
94. Returns from play/exploration spontaneously in unfamiliar places.
12. *Play/exploration bouts away from adult are brief.*
34. *Does not approach or follow when adult moves away.*
61. *Is not bolder or more confident to play when adult nearby.*
72. *Does not stay closer to adult in unfamiliar places.*

Differential Responsiveness to Caregiver

4. Easily comforted by mother.
18. Actively solicits comforting from mother when distressed.
22. Easily distracted from distress.
35. Prefers to be comforted by mother.

---

[2] Italicized entries indicate items that were reverse coded prior to calculating internal consistency estimates.

31. *Does not look to adult for reassurance when wary.*
51. *Does not accept adult's assurances when wary in familiar places.*
86. *Does not accept adult's assurances when wary in unfamiliar places.*
98. *Does not prefer physical contact with mother.*

Positive Affect

3. Predominant mood is happy.
8. Laughs easily with observer.
25. Is affectively responsive and expressive.
76. Expresses enjoyment or accomplishment of achieving.
77. Affective sharing occurs during play.
92. Does not become angry with toys.
82. *Easily becomes angry with mother.*
87. *Does not laugh easily with mother.*

Sociability

2. Eager to demonstrate songs, games, etc.
32. Initiates interaction with familiarized adults.
40. Acts to maintain social interaction.
47. Interacts directly with adults.
79. Imitates observer's behavior.
21. *Is indifferent to observer's invitation to play.*
70. *Is indirect or hesitant in making observations/requests.*
95. *Child's observations/requests difficult to understand.*

Independence

42. Is independent with most adults.
69. Is independent with mother.
93. Accepts mother's attention to others.
20. *Distressed by separation at home.*
29. *Cries to prevent separation.*
48. *Lacks self-confidence.*
55. *Cries in response to separation.*
74. *Is demanding when initiating activities with mother.*

Social Perceptiveness

16. Is upset by negative evaluations/disapproval from mother.
30. Is responsive to distress in mother.

39. Hesitates or does not repeat previously prohibited behavior.
41. Is flexible in trying to communicate with adults.
96. Is obedient when mother gives instructions.
11. *Does not recognize distress in mother.*
58. *Is not compliant with mother's control.*
84. *Does not adapt active play to avoid hurting mother.*

Endurance

23. Has good endurance; is not easily tired.
59. Is attracted to novelty.
90. Shows signs of self-control.
 6. *Prefers tasks and activities that are not difficult.*
13. *Becomes bored quickly.*
28. *Is not adaptable when moved from one activity to another.*
62. *Becomes distressed when social activity is blocked or difficult.*
66. *Does not persist when nonsocial goals are blocked.*

ATTACHMENTS IN A MULTIPLE-CAREGIVER AND MULTIPLE-INFANT ENVIRONMENT: THE CASE OF THE ISRAELI KIBBUTZIM

Abraham Sagi, Marinus H. van IJzendoorn, Ora Aviezer, Frank Donnell, Nina Koren-Karie, Tirtsa Joels, and Yael Harel

Most infants are raised in an environment that contains more than one caregiver and more than one child, interacting on a regular basis with their mothers, fathers, grandparents, and siblings as well as with baby-sitters or professional caregivers. Similarly, both parents and nonparental caregivers very often establish attachments with more than one child. Nevertheless, until relatively recently, attachment research has focused mainly on the attachment relationship of only the mother and with only one of her children, and the most widely used assessments of attachment quality—the Strange Situation procedure (Ainsworth, Blehar, Waters, & Wall, 1978) and the security scores derived from the Attachment Q-Set (Vaughn & Waters, 1990; Waters & Deane, 1985)—had been validated only for infant-mother dyads.

During the last decade, infant-father relationships came to be studied more intensively (for a meta-analysis of these studies, see Fox, Kimmerly, & Schafer, 1991), and some observational studies of infant attachments to nonfamilial caregivers have been reported (Anderson, Nagle, Roberts, & Smith, 1981; Goossens & van IJzendoorn, 1990; Howes & Hamilton, 1992a,

This project was supported by the Israel Science Foundation administered by the Israel Academy of Sciences and Humanities (grant 336-93-2) and by a University of Haifa Research Authority grant to Abraham Sagi and a PIONEER grant of the Netherlands Organization for Scientific Research to Marinus H. van IJzendoorn. Thanks are due to Moshe Tuvia for assistance in data collection and to Arza Avrahami, director of the Institute for Research on Kibbutz Education. The cooperation of all kibbutz members and children involved in the study is greatly appreciated. Direct correspondence to Abraham Sagi, Department of Psychology, University of Haifa, Haifa 31905, Israel.

1992b; Howes, Phillips, & Whitebrook, 1992; Krentz, 1983; Sagi et al., 1985). Some work has also focused on the mother's attachment relationships with more than one of her children, be they siblings (Teti & Ablard, 1989; Ward, Vaughn, & Robb, 1988) or twins (Goldberg, Perrotta, Minde, & Corter, 1986; Minde, Corter, Goldberg, & Jeffers, 1990).

Focus on the potential network of attachment relationships that are formed by infants and toddlers has raised important conceptual questions (van IJzendoorn, Sagi, & Lambermon, 1992). For example, Do infants develop attachments to their nonparental, professional caregivers? If so, can the quality of these attachments be described validly using existing procedures? And is the quality of attachment relationships that a nonfamilial caregiver establishes with different children likely to be congruent or incongruent—that is, do caregivers tend to behave in ways that potentiate similar attachment qualities across different children in their care? Finally, are the attachment relationships that the child co-constructs with different caregivers likely to be concordant or nonconcordant with respect to their quality?

Regarding the first of these questions, accumulating evidence suggests that infants do construct attachment relationships with nonparental caregivers who care for them on a regular basis and for a sufficiently long period of time. In a recent analysis (van IJzendoorn, Goldberg, Kroonenberg, & Frenkel, 1992), a number of criteria were specified for evaluating whether a relationship is correctly identified as an attachment relationship; this analysis has suggested that young children are indeed able to develop an attachment relationship with their professional caregiver. For example, using both Strange Situation and Q-sort techniques, an infant's attachment relationships with professional caregivers have been shown to exist and to be independent of the quality of the attachments that the child forms with the parents (Goossens & van IJzendoorn, 1990; Howes & Hamilton, 1992a, 1992b; Sagi et al., 1985). Moreover, the quality (i.e., Strange Situation classification) of the infant-caregiver bond appeared to be related to the caregiver's sensitivity in the same way as it is in the case of infant-parent attachments (Goossens & van IJzendoorn, 1990). Additionally, among children living in Israeli kibbutzim, the quality of the attachments formed between infants and their metaplot (Hebrew for "caregivers"; singular, *metapelet*) was found to predict theoretically relevant aspects of the child's later socioemotional functioning (Oppenheim, Sagi, & Lamb, 1988).

Taking this evidence as sufficient to permit at least provisional assumption of the reality of child-caregiver attachments, we focused in this study on the congruence of the quality of attachments that two children form with the same caregiver and on the concordance of the attachments that two caregivers form with the same child. The research was conducted in Israeli kibbutzim.

Congruence of the quality of attachment of two (or more) children to a single caregiver.—This topic has been an important theoretical issue ever since the introduction of the concept of intergenerational transmission of attachment (Bowlby, 1973; Main, Kaplan, & Cassidy, 1985). Studies in which the Adult Attachment Interview (Main & Goldwyn, 1994) was used to address this concept have reported impressive correspondence between the parent's working model of attachment (or attachment representations) and the infant-parent attachment relationship as assessed in the Strange Situation. Main and Goldwyn (in press-b), for example, reported a correspondence of 75% between measures using the traditional three-way Strange Situation classifications (i.e., anxious-avoidant, secure, and anxious-ambivalent), and this level of correspondence has been replicated in several additional studies (for a review, see van IJzendoorn, 1992; for a meta-analysis, see van IJzendoorn, 1995).

The assumption underlying the concept of intergenerational transmission is that the adult's working model of attachment is expressed in caregiving behaviors and that these then determine the infant's attachment relationship to that adult. Implied by this assumption is the proposition that, as long as rearing conditions and the children's characteristics remain comparable, a caregiver would tend to establish similar attachment relationships with the different children in her or his care. Some evidence to support this hypothesis comes from studies of siblings (Teti & Ablard, 1989; Ward et al., 1988) that have indicated that, in approximately 50%–60% of cases, both children have the same, secure or insecure, relationship with their parent; in three small-scale studies of twins, the reported 30%–50% congruence is of less impressive magnitude (Minde et al., 1990; Szajnberg, Skrinjaric, & Moore, 1989; Vandell, Owen, Wilson, & Henderson, 1988).

The kibbutz provides a unique opportunity to evaluate the congruence hypothesis. The caregiving arrangements, the socioeconomic circumstances, the time frame, and the children's ages are all similar, but the children are not biologically related either to the caregiver or to each other; thus, confounding intergenerational transmission with biological relatedness can be avoided (van IJzendoorn, 1992). Some data supporting the congruence hypothesis under such circumstances were reported by Sagi et al. (1985), who found that, in 12 of 16 cases in which a metapelet cared for different children, congruent Strange Situation classifications of these children's attachment relationships with her were obtained. The authors interpreted this finding as indicating that most caregivers behave in characteristic ways that potentiate either secure or insecure attachments with the infants in their care.

Concordance of a child's attachment relationships with different caregivers.— The possibility that a child would construct nonconcordant relationships with different caregivers—a notion that is implied by the concept of attachment as a characteristic of relationships—raises additional theoretical issues.

Sroufe (1985) has argued that each caregiver relates to a given child in a unique fashion and that it is the given caregiver's behavior, rather than any endogenous trait of the child (such as temperament), that determines the nature of the attachment relationship. Even though some associations between temperamental variability and attachment *behavior* have been documented (Belsky & Rovine, 1987; Vaughn, Lefever, Seifer, & Barglow, 1989), theorists continue to emphasize that the child's attachment *relationship* is shaped by the behavior of the particular caregiver and that quality of attachment to different caregivers might consequently not be concordant (Sroufe, 1985; van IJzendoorn, Goldberg, Kroonenberg, & Frenkel, 1992).

In the case of the child's attachments to both parents, similarity in the parents' caregiving behavior—and a consequent concordance in the quality of the child's attachments to the two—might be explained by the similarity of attachment representations between the spouses. In their meta-analysis of attachment representations in 226 couples, van IJzendoorn and Bakermans-Kranenburg (in press) found that secure women and secure men marry each other more often than chance would indicate, as do insecure men and insecure women. Furthermore, we would like to suggest that parents may implicitly model to each other their caregiving behavior. On a more explicit level, parents may discuss their child and co-construct corrected, joint representations of her or his particular strengths and weaknesses and how to take these into account in their child-rearing behaviors.

However, focusing on results of their meta-analysis of studies of quality of attachment to both parents that indicated that cross-parent symmetry of attachment classifications is not completely random, Fox et al. (1991) suggested that attachment theorists may have prematurely jettisoned temperament explanations of concordance. Of all these alternatives, studies in a kibbutz setting can at least omit the hypothesis of similarity of attachment representations between caregivers because pairs of caregivers are not selected on the basis of their attachment representations. Furthermore, in the kibbutz context, the temperament hypothesis that is based on genetic relatedness between the child and her or his caregivers is not plausible either.

THE KIBBUTZ STUDY

The Israeli kibbutz is no longer new to sociological and psychological research; its characteristics as a social experiment and as a natural child-rearing laboratory have been discussed by Beit-Hallahmi and Rabin (1977), and the setting has been used in previous studies of attachment (Fox, 1977; Maccoby & Feldman, 1972; Sagi et al., 1985). In all kibbutzim, women return to work approximately three months following the birth of their child, and all infants are then placed in the kibbutz "infant house." The size of these infant groups is rather small (with an adult-to-children ratio of 1:3), the level of caregivers' commitment is relatively high, and the infant house has been described as the most optimal group-care facility in Israel (Sagi & Koren-Karie, 1993).

Over the past few years, changes have occurred in the kibbutzim regarding the division of child-rearing responsibilities between infant houses and family homes, and the majority have now abandoned the traditional communal sleeping arrangement in favor of sleeping in the family home. The primary reason for this change in customs was parents' dissatisfaction with the previous arrangement. At the moment, only one of 260 kibbutzim continued to adhere to the old custom (for a review, see Aviezer, van IJzendoorn, Sagi, & Schuengel, 1994); however, when the current study was being conducted (during 1988–1989), it was possible to recruit a substantial number of subjects from kibbutzim that had still retained the communal sleeping arrangements. A group of children who slept in their parents' houses was also recruited; this design permitted us to examine the effects that might be exerted by the two ecological contexts defined by the differing sleeping arrangements.

Previous studies of congruences and concordances in infant-caregiver attachments have relied on a single index of attachment security, typically derived from the Strange Situation. In our study, we additionally used the Attachment Q-Set (AQS; see Vaughn & Waters, 1990; Waters & Deane, 1985) so as to test the substantive hypotheses with multiple measures as well as to determine the extent of association between these two assessments— and hence of their reciprocal validation—within the unique caregiving setting of the kibbutz. In support of the reciprocal validity of the AQS, sorts from trained observers have been found to relate in theoretically predictable ways to Strange Situation attachment classification (Howes & Hamilton, 1992a; Valenzuela & Lara, 1987; Vaughn & Waters, 1990). However, studies of such association that have relied on caregivers as AQS informants are scarce, and van Dam and van IJzendoorn (1988) failed to detect substantial overlap between Q-sort security scores derived from mothers' descriptions and Strange Situation classifications. In this regard, Teti and McGourty (1994) have recently raised various concerns about the veracity of mothers' reports. Nevertheless, and despite these concerns, they have shown that mothers who are carefully trained in using the AQS can provide descriptions of their children's secure-base behavior that moderately correlate with observer-derived security scores. In the current study, the AQS descriptions were provided by the metaplot, and, because metaplot have a wide range of experiences with a large number of infants and substantial training in observational skills, we assumed that their descriptions would tend to be more reliable and valid than those of most parents.

SAMPLE AND DESIGN

Infants

The study involved 108 full-term and developmentally healthy infants aged between 11 and 15 months (M = 12.6 months, SD = 1.24 months); selection of this age range was dictated by the requirement that it be appropriate for conducting Strange Situation assessments. Thirty-three of the subjects were firstborn, 75 had older siblings, and all came from intact families. In terms of family demographics, each kibbutz is a rural cooperative community with an average population of 400–900 people. Every kibbutz member, man or woman, works for the kibbutz economy; the profits of their work belong to the community, which, in turn, provides all with housing, food, clothing, and health and educational services on an equal basis. It is also a selective community in that acceptance of new members is determined by membership vote. Both its selectivity and its socioeconomic organization make it hard to assess socioeconomic status using the traditional indices, but kibbutz members are generally considered as being middle or upper middle class (Tiger & Shepher, 1975).

Subjects were recruited with the assistance of the Institute of Research on Kibbutz Education. Educational coordinators in each kibbutz were contacted by a letter explaining the research and requesting their cooperation and help in the kibbutz; this was followed by a phone call in which they directed us to the relevant families, whose consent was then obtained by phone.

Of the total sample of infants, 54 (28 female and 26 male) were recruited from kibbutzim with communal sleeping arrangements and 54 (27 of each sex) from those where sleeping arrangements were family based. All these infants were participating in a larger research project (see, e.g., Sagi, van IJzendoorn, Aviezer, Donnell, & Mayseless, 1994); the present report focuses only on data concerning infant-metaplot classifications and AQS security scores.

Metaplot

A total of 79 metaplot participated in the study; on average, the infants with whom they were observed had been in their care for a period of 7.84 months (range = 3–20 months). This duration of care is well in excess of the 3 months that we had set as the criterion for participation, and it indicates very low turnover rates as far as our subjects are concerned. Thus, since infants spend the first 3–4 months with their mothers, these infants had been cared for primarily by their mother and their metapelet during their first year of life. The metaplot mean age was 31.0 years (SD = 8.20

years). They had an average of 7.8 years of experience (range = 4 months–27 years) and 4.16 years of experience in infant care (range = 3 months–27 years); 65% were married, and 70% had children (number of children: $M = 1.8$, range = 0–5).

Of these women, 78% had elected to care for the given child on the basis of personal choice rather than assignment by the central administration of the kibbutz, and the women were fairly well satisfied with their work (a mean score of 8.03 on a scale of 10). As regards professional training, 66% had undergone some type of child-care training. Of these, 39% had 1–2 years of professional training in infant care, 6% had a preschool teacher's diploma, and 22% had attended various workshops on infancy issues; the remainder had no formal training in child care.

The Kibbutzim

A total of 37 kibbutzim, located in the northern region of Israel, participated in the study, and, in order to transmit the rationale of the research design adequately, some elaboration of the kibbutz early education system is in order. Infant groups are formed as soon as children are born; in all kibbutzim (whatever their sleeping arrangements), six infants and two caregivers constitute the typical group of an "infant house." The number of infant houses in a given kibbutz varies from year to year and from one kibbutz to another as a function of annual birthrates; it should be noted, therefore, that there is no correspondence between the number of kibbutzim participating in the study (37) and the number of infant houses (54; for further elaboration, see the subsequent section). Most infant houses consist of two bedrooms designed to accommodate three to four infants each, a kitchenette and a dining room, and a playroom and a yard equipped with a large variety of play materials. Infants have their own cribs, toys, and a shelf for other personal belongings; the arrangement of the infant house is such that it provides each child with sufficient private space as well as room for making contact with peers.

Kibbutz infants are exposed to multiple caregiving very early in their lives, regardless of sleeping arrangement (Lavi, 1990). In their first 3 months of life, kibbutz infants are cared for exclusively by their mothers in the family residence. They are brought to the infant house as soon as their mothers return to work part-time, and during the initial period of their stay in the infant house they are cared for jointly by the mother and the metapelet. Mothers are almost exclusively in charge of feeding during this period, and they arrange their work schedule accordingly; metaplot are responsible for the infants between the mothers' visits. During the second half of the infants' first year, metaplot gradually assume increasing responsibility for the children's various needs as the mothers increase their workload. Thus, by their second year, infants come under the full care of the metaplot, who play an increasingly larger role in their socialization with respect to issues such as table manners, sharing, play habits, and knowledge of the environment (Aviezer et al., 1994).

A major ecological difference exists between kibbutzim that adhere to different sleeping arrangements. Under communal sleeping conditions, the child goes to the family's residence in the afternoons and evenings as well as on weekends and holidays; both parents try to be available at these times. However, parents bring their children back to the children's house—which is considered their home—and put them to bed there for the night. During the night, two watchwomen are responsible for all children younger than 12 years; these women, who are assigned on a weekly rotation basis and hence are unfamiliar to the infants, monitor the children's houses from a central location (usually the infant house) by making rounds and via intercoms. Introduction of family-based sleeping arrangements changed the proportion of time that infants spend with their families to a pattern similar to that of nonkibbutz day-care settings: infants are brought to the children's house in the morning and taken home in the late afternoon. The family assumes additional caregiving functions, and the influence of metaplot relative to the family has declined.

Another difference—which had direct consequences in determining our research design—is that, in kibbutzim with family-based sleeping arrangements, the prevailing practice was for infants to remain in the same house with the same group of children and under the care of the same two metaplot until about the age of 3 years; thus, the metaplot's care continued into toddlerhood. In kibbutzim with communal sleeping arrangements, however, the infant typically first entered a house designed for infants only, then moved to a "toddler house" at about the age of 12–15 months—a transition that entailed replacement of at least one of the previous metaplot.

This shift to a new caretaker—which occurred within the age range that we had designated for our assessment—precluded studying the concordance of a child's attachment to two different caretakers because one of them would not have cared for the child for the minimum of 3 months required by our criteria; the alternative of conducting Strange Situation assessments with both metaplot before the transition would have violated the requirement of a minimum of 2 months having elapsed between the two occasions, and delaying the assessment until the child had accrued 3 months of experience with the new metapelet would have exceeded the appropriate age limit for this observation. Consequently, assessment of concordances in quality of attachment to two different caregivers was limited to the sample drawn from kibbutzim with family-based sleeping arrangements.

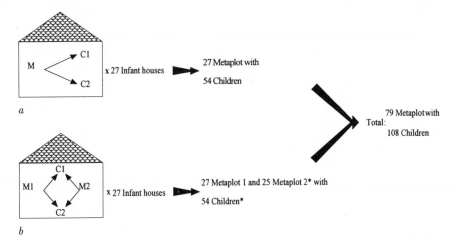

FIG. 1.—*a*, Infant house in kibbutzim with communal sleeping arrangements (designated as [c]). (M = metapelet; C_1 = child 1; C_2 = child 2.) *b*, Infant house in kibbutzim with family-based sleeping arrangements (designated as [f]). (M_1 = metapelet 1; M_2 = metapelet 2; C_1 = child 1; C_2 = child 2.) (* Two pairs of children were tested with the second metapelet.)

Designation of Subgroups of Infant-Metapelet Relationships

Preserving the distinction between communal and family-based living arrangements in our analyses required the designation of six subgroups; the design is illustrated in Figure 1 and elaborated in what follows.

a) Sample drawn from communally sleeping kibbutzim.—In each of the 27 infant houses of these kibbutzim, two children (selected randomly from the group of six infants) were observed with the same metapelet. These two relationships, designated by *[c]* C_1-M ($N = 27$) and *[c]* C_2-M ($N = 27$), permit us (i) to index the effect of the communal sleeping arrangements on two different children's relationships to the same caretaker across 27 different caretakers and (ii) to examine the extent to which a caretaker potentiates the same attachment pattern in different children (the congruence hypothesis).

b) Sample drawn from family-sleeping kibbutzim.—In this sample of 27 infant houses, two randomly selected children were tested in two sessions, once with each of their two metaplot (with an intervening interval of 3 months). These four relationships, designated *[f]* C_1-M_1 ($N = 27$) and *[f]* C_2-M_1 ($N = 27$) for those observed in the first session and *[f]* C_1-M_2 ($N = 25$) and *[f]* C_2-M_2 ($N = 25$)[1] for those seen in the second one, permit us (i)

---

[1] Two pairs of children were not tested with the second metapelet.

to index the effect of family-based sleeping arrangements; (ii) to examine the extent to which two different children are similarly attached to the same caregiver across a total of 27 different caregivers and the extent to which the same children (50 of 54) are similarly attached to the other of their caregivers across a total of 25 different caregivers (the congruence hypothesis), and, finally, (iii) to examine the extent of concordance in the quality of children's attachments to two different caregivers (the concordance hypothesis). In terms of inter-subgroup dependencies, the same metaplot are represented in both groups of children (C_1 and C_2) at each session; while different metaplot are represented at the two sessions, the groups of C_1 and C_2 children remain the same (for pictorial elaboration, see Fig. 1).

Ignoring the distinction between communal and family-based sleeping arrangements (i.e., [c] vs. [f]) permits combining selected subgroups into two larger subsamples that contain no overlapping members, and we do so in some of the analyses to be presented.

PROCEDURES AND MEASURES

The unique nature of the design (and especially the study of the relationships between the metapelet and two different children in each infant house) made it impossible to bring our subjects to the laboratory. Instead, all assessments took place on site in rooms similar to the setting specified by Ainsworth et al. (1978). Camera operators filmed unobtrusively from outside the room through a crack in the curtains; all observations were conducted during the morning hours.

In communally sleeping kibbutzim, conducting this assessment involved two consecutive observations of the same metapelet with first one, then the second of her charges. Immediately following these observations, the children were returned to the infant house, and the metapelet was given the Q-sort deck by the research assistant. She was then asked to complete a sort for each of the two children with whom she had been observed, describing them on the basis of what had characterized her interactions with each during the preceding week and sorting the cards according to the conventions listed in Appendix A (in this volume). The possibility that the immediately preceding experience of what happened during the Strange Situation might have colored the metapelet's description of the child must be considered; however, we suggest that, given the unique nature of the Strange Situation and the specificity and range of AQS items, this does not seem likely.

The same procedure was followed in the family-based kibbutzim; in these, however, it was also repeated 2 months later with the second metapelet of the two children.

The Strange Situation Assessment

Both the observation and the scoring of the videotapes followed the guidelines given in Ainsworth et al. (1978), and the infants were classified into one of the three major categories of the Ainsworth system (i.e., secure [B], avoidant [A], or resistant-ambivalent [C]). All tapes were rated independently by two of the authors (Joels and Koren-Karie); the 37 tapes they found difficult to code were additionally rated by two other of the authors (Sagi and van IJzendoorn). The coders were unaware of the type of kibbutz in which the child was housed (i.e., communal or family based) since none had participated in the data collection, and the sequence in which the tapes were coded was determined by the other authors (who were not engaged in the ratings) so as to ensure a lengthy interval between coding dyads containing the same child or the same metapelet. Given that the coding of the 158 tapes extended over more than a year, it is reasonable to assume that the classifications were independent in this regard. The mean interjudge agreement among these coders was 89% and the mean kappa .62.

The Attachment Q-Sort

The 90-item version of the AQS listed in Appendix A was jointly translated by three of the authors (Aviezer, Joels, and Sagi); all three are fluent in both English and Hebrew as well as well versed in attachment theory. Following Brislin's (1980) guidelines, we used a back-translation procedure; difficult items were discussed jointly, and, if necessary, an additional bilingual expert was consulted (A. Z. Guiora, the editor of *Language Learning*). Security scores were computed via correlations with the criterion sort listed in Appendix A. Note that the criterion is American based; although a criterion sort has recently been developed by Israeli experts (see Posada, Gao, et al., in this volume), it was not available at the time the present study took place. We decided to retain the American criterion sort on the grounds of its established validity (which the Israeli sort would not have had as yet), its comparability to the body of extant studies, and its strong convergence with the Israeli criteria.

RESULTS

Preliminary Analyses

To ensure that any differences between the infant-metaplot relationships of dyads housed in the two different types of kibbutzim (i.e., communal and family based) were not confounded by extraneous factors, all the variables mentioned in describing the full group of metaplot (see the Sample and Design section above) as well as infants' ages were contrasted in a series of t tests. The single statistically significant difference ($p = .02$) to emerge from these analyses indicated that infants in the communal kibbutzim were slightly older than those in the family-based ones ($M = 12.9$ and 12.3 months, respectively); this inexplicable difference is so slight that there is no good reason to assume that it could have any substantive implications. Since all the characteristics of the metaplot working in the two types of arrangements showed no significant differences, and since we showed else-where that the parents in both arrangements also do not differ in terms of basic characteristics (Sagi et al., 1994), the assumption that any differences between the two types of kibbutzim follow from the difference in their ecologies can be properly entertained.

Additionally, the ages of the two members of the pair of children who were cared for by the same metapelet and the number of months that each had been in her care were contrasted; none of the t tests yielded any significant difference. Thus, findings concerning the congruence and concordance of relationships are not influenced by either the child's age or his or her extent of experience with the caretaker. As regards the issue of possible effects of the child's sex, we assumed that, given the absence of evidence of such differences in the parent-child attachment literature as well as their theoretical inexplicability, undertaking such analyses (particularly with small samples) could not yield informative results; hence, none were attempted.

Infant-Metapelet Attachment Relationships

Beginning at a descriptive level, we obtained the distribution of A, B, and C classifications that were assigned to infants in each of the six sub-groups of relationships and contrasted these (via chi square) to the distribution obtained for infant-mother dyads in a metasample composed of 21 different American samples (the latter values were taken from van IJzen-doorn, Goldberg, et al., 1992); these data are displayed in Table 1.

The percentage of secure (B) classifications in the infant-metapelet sub-groups ranged from 44% to 64% (67% was obtained in the metasample), and the difference in the distribution of classifications was significant in four of the six subgroups. The standardized residuals show quite clearly that secure and avoidant classifications were less frequent and resistant-ambivalent ones more prevalent in the infant-metapelet subgroups; these latter represent a considerably larger proportion of insecure relationships in the kibbutz subgroups than in the metasample. Ignoring the distinction between communal and family-based kibbutzim and combining subgroups that do not overlap in membership (i.e., contain different infants and differ-

TABLE 1

DISTRIBUTION OF STRANGE SITUATION CLASSIFICATIONS OBTAINED FOR
INFANT-METAPELET RELATIONSHIPS AS CONTRASTED WITH THE U.S. METASAMPLE OF
INFANT-MOTHER RELATIONSHIPS

	CLASSIFICATION (N)			STANDARDIZED RESIDUALS			
RELATIONSHIP	A	B	C	A	B	C	χ^{2a}
Metasample[b] ($N = 1,584$)	325	1,062	197				
	(21)	(67)	(12)				
[c] $C_1 = M^*$ ($N = 27$)	4	16	7	−1.5	−2.1	3.6	N.S.
	(15)	(59)	(26)				
[c] $C_2 = M$ ($N = 27$)	1	16	10	−4.5	−2.1	6.5	16.5
	(4)	(59)	(37)				
[f] $C_1 = M_1^*$ ($N = 27$)	2	15	10	−3.5	−3.1	6.5	15.3
	(7)	(56)	(37)				
[f] $C_2 = M_1$ ($N = 27$)	5	17	5	−.5	−1.1	1.6	N.S.
	(18.5)	(63)	(18.5)				
[f] $C_1 = M_2$ ($N = 25$)	2	11	12	−3.1	−5.7	8.8	27.8
	(8)	(44)	(48)				
[f] $C_2 = M_2$ ($N = 25$)	3	11	11	−2.1	−5.7	7.8	21.8
	(12)	(44)	(44)				
Subsample I ($N = 79$)	9	42	28	−6.9	−10.4	17.3	34.7
	(11)	(53)	(35)				
Subsample II ($N = 79$)	8	44	27	−7.8	−8.5	16.4	31.9
	(10)	(56)	(34)				

NOTE.—The designation of infant-metapelet relationship subgroups is given in the Sample and Design section; subgroups marked by an asterisk are combined in Subsample I and those unmarked in Subsample II (see the text). Percentages are given in parentheses.

[a] All significant at $p < .001$.

[b] The metasample is derived from Van IJzendoorn, Goldberg, Kroonenberg, & Frenkel (1992).

ent metaplot) into two larger subsamples shows this effect most clearly: of the around 45% insecure classifications obtained in each of these groups, around 35% were categorized as C; in the metasample, by contrast, only 33% of the relationships were classified as insecure, and only 12% of the metasample cases were classified as C (Subsample I results from combining the subgroups marked by an asterisk in Table 1 and Subsample II from those that are not so marked). These results extend previously reported findings (Sagi et al., 1994) concerning the relatively high prevalence of ambivalent classifications among samples of Israeli mothers to metaplot samples as well.

Convergence between Strange Situation Classifications and AQS Security Scores

The mean and range of AQS-derived security scores of children classified as secure (B) as opposed to insecure (A or C) in each subgroup are displayed in Table 2; since the AQS methodology was designed to permit assessing attachment security as a continuous variable but has not as yet been used to establish different patterns of insecure behavior, the two insecure Strange Situation categories were combined for this analysis. Although only one of the six subgroup contrasts shown in Table 2 achieved statistical significance, the increased power of the test gained in combining these into the two larger subsamples indicates that AQS security scores predictably discriminate between secure and insecure subjects as assessed by the Strange Situation procedure. However, because the convergence between Strange Situation and AQS assessments is a theoretically important issue, it should be noted that the AQS failed to discriminate between avoidant and secure subjects: the mean values of the AQS security scores for the avoidant, secure, and ambivalent infants were, respectively, .25 (SD = .21), .24 (SD = .22), and .13 (SD = .21) for Subsample I and .23 (SD = .11), .27 (SD = .18), and .16 (SD = .21) for Subsample II. It is thus evident that the association between the AQS and the Strange Situation indices of security in this sample is due mainly to the behavior of the ambivalent infants.

Congruence in the Attachment Relationships of Two Children with the Same Metapelet

Strange Situation classification.—The classifications assigned to each pair of children observed with the same metapelet were examined. Instances in which the same classification (be it secure or insecure) characterized both members of the pair were deemed "congruent," those in which classifications differed "incongruent." The relative frequency of congruent and in-

TABLE 2

MEAN AQS SCORES OF INFANTS ASSIGNED A SECURE (B) VERSUS AN INSECURE (A or C) CLASSIFICATION IN THE STRANGE SITUATION FOR EACH SUBGROUP

RELATIONSHIPS	SECURE			INSECURE			t	df	p [a]
	M	SD	Range	M	SD	Range			
[c] $C_1 = M*$	.20	.25	$-.25-.55$	.16	.20	$-.10-.46$	.42	25	N.S.
[c] $C_2 = M$	.27	.20	.04$-$.63	.15	.21	$-.28-.43$	1.47	25	N.S.
[f] $C_1 = M_1*$	.31	.19	$-.06-.60$	.23	.20	$-.16-.50$	.96	25	N.S.
[f] $C_2 = M_1$	.34	.17	.05$-$.58	.21	.17	$-.12-.44$	1.90	25	< .05
[f] $C_1 = M_2$	.24	.14	$-.11-.51$	.17	.20	$-.22-.38$	$-.08$	23	N.S.
[f] $C_2 = M_2*$	.22	.20	$-.02-.40$	.10	.22	$-.35-.53$	1.22	23	N.S.
Subsample I	.24	.22	$-.25-.60$	.16	.21	$-.35-.53$	1.69	77	< .05
Subsample II	.27	.18	$-.11-.63$	.18	.19	$-.28-.44$	2.66	77	< .05

NOTE.—The designation of infant-metapelet relationship subgroups is given in the Sample and Design section; subgroups marked by an asterisk are combined in Subsample I and those unmarked in Subsample II (see the text).
[a] One tailed.

congruent instances is shown in Table 3, with the total of 54 child pairs divided into those living in the communal kibbutzim (27 pairs) and those observed in the first (27 pairs) and in the second (25 of the latter 27 pairs) session of the family-based kibbutzim assessments; these three subsamples can be viewed as providing replication as well as reflecting an ecological context.

The relative prevalence of congruent over incongruent relationships was higher in both family-based subsamples (70% and 68%). In the communal group, however, their relative prevalence was about the same (48%).

AQS security scores.—The correlation between the security scores of the two children sorted by the same metapelet were $r = -.31$ (N.S.) in the communal subsample and $r = .53$ and $.38$ ($p = .01$ for both) in the two family-based subsamples.

Thus, results obtained with both measures converge to indicate that the hypothesis of congruence tends to hold in the family-based setting but not in the communal, pointing to the importance of context in determining its prevalence.

Concordance in Attachment Relationships That a Child Establishes with Two Different Metaplot

As we noted in describing the research design, the structure of the communal kibbutzim precluded conducting this facet of the assessments, which were consequently restricted to children housed in the family-based kibbutzim. To establish a degree of replication, the results are presented separately for the subsamples of children we had designated C_1 and C_2 as well as for the combined sample of 50. (Note that the total here is not 52

TABLE 3

Congruence in Strange Situation Classifications of Two Children with the Same Metapelet

	Strange Situation Classification (N)			
Subsamples	Congruent	Incongruent	χ^2	p
Communal	13 (48)	14 (52)	.04	N.S.
Family based (first session)	19 (70)	8 (30)	4.48	.03
Family based (second session) . . .	17 (68)	8 (32)	3.24	.07

Note.—Percentages are given in parentheses.

TABLE 4

CONCORDANCE BETWEEN STRANGE SITUATION CLASSIFICATIONS OF THE SAME CHILD WITH
TWO DIFFERENT METAPLOT

METAPELET 1	METAPELET 2 (N)			STANDARDIZED RESIDUALS			χ^2	p^a
	A	B	C	A	B	C		
Child 1 subsample ($N = 25$):							3.03	N.S.
A	0	1	1	−.2	.1	.0		
	(0)	(4)	(4)					
B	2	7	5	.9	.8	−1.7		
	(8)	(28)	(20)					
C	0	3	6	−.7	−1.0	1.7		
	(0)	(12)	(24)					
Child 2 subsample ($N = 25$):							14.8	.006
A	2	0	3	1.4	−2.2	.8		
	(8)	(0)	(12)					
B	1	11	4	−.9	4.0	−3.0		
	(4)	(44)	(16)					
C	0	0	4	−.5	−1.8	2.2		
	(0)	(0)	(16)					
Total sample ($N = 50$):							12.72	.01
A	2	1	4	1.3	−2.1	.8		
	(4)	(2)	(8)					
B	3	18	9	.0	4.8	−4.8		
	(6)	(36)	(18)					
C	0	3	10	−1.3	−2.7	4.0		
	(0)	(6)	(20)					

NOTE.—Percentages are given in parentheses.
[a] Exact Fisher tests.

[27 M_1 + 25 M_2] because there were two M_2's missing for establishing the correspondence between M_1 and M_2.)

Strange Situation classification.—The joint distribution of classifications of the child with each metapelet is shown in Table 4. Assessed (via chi square) for deviation from chance expectations, the degree of concordance fails to reach statistical significance in the C_1 subsample, but the concordance seen in the C_2 subsample as well as in the combined total group does attain significance ($p < .006$ and .01, respectively); examination of the standardized residuals indicates that similarly secure and resistant-ambivalent classifications are the prime contributors to this concordance.

AQS security scores.—Security scores derived from the sorts of the two caregivers of C_1 children correlated $r = .29$ (N.S.), and those from the sorts of C_2 children correlated $r = .53$ ($p < .001$); for the two subsamples combined, $r = .39$ ($p < .01$). Thus, the pattern of findings—significant concordance in the sample as a whole, with one of the two subsamples showing it to a far stronger degree than the other—was replicated by these data as well.

DISCUSSION

We began this work by assuming—as we have argued before (van IJzendoorn, Sagi, & Lambermon, 1992)—that infants form attachment relationships with their nonfamilial caregivers. In the present case, the rearing conditions of the infants we studied provide strong justification for the validity of that assumption. On the basis of the information that we reported regarding rearing conditions, it is evident that these infants entered into their metaplot's care at an age when their physical survival and psychological comfort depend almost exclusively on the caregiving adult and that for most of them both the metapelet and the infant house remained a major "constant presence" ever since. Moreover, the data show that most metaplot freely chose to care for their charges and that most expressed satisfaction with their role, suggesting that these caregivers had an emotional investment in the children they were rearing. Taken together, these history-related characteristics represent the set of theoretical hallmarks of circumstances in which relationships governed by the attachment system are formed. However, a relevant cautionary note here is that, since we do not know anything about either the relative salience of these defining characteristics or their minima, the argument must remain restricted to this setting.

Some other caveats regarding the nature of infant–nonfamilial caregiver relationships should also be mentioned. Consistent with Sagi et al. (1985), attachments between infants and metaplot were more likely to be insecure compared to what characterized the metasample of U.S. mother-infant relationships (van IJzendoorn, Goldberg, et al., 1992) as well as the sample of Israeli mother-infant dyads (Sagi et al., 1985). It should be noted, however, that, when the distributions of attachments to kibbutz metaplot are compared with those of attachments to professional caregivers in other countries (Goossens & van IJzendoorn, 1990; Howes et al., 1992), the proportions of secure and insecure attachments are quite similar. What factors may underlie this relative overrepresentation of insecure dyads is not clear. One explanation may lie in the nonfamilial caregiving situation itself: the number of infants who need the caregiver's attention simultaneously may affect the latter's ability to respond promptly, which makes it more difficult to form secure attachments. Alternatively, more subtle differences may exist in the organization of attachment behaviors that characterize the mother and the caregiver relationships and hence require that the Strange Situation coding criteria be adjusted accordingly.

We raise this latter possibility because, compared with our findings regarding mothers of kibbutz infants, which showed the presence of very few insecure-avoidant relationships (Sagi et al., 1985; Sagi et al., 1994), some infants were classified as avoidant in each of the six subsamples we examined, albeit the incidence of such was less than that of insecure-ambivalent relationships (an average 11% and 35%, respectively). While avoidant relationships have been repeatedly reported to be seen and consistently interpreted as insecure (Ainsworth et al., 1978; Main & Weston, 1982), it would be problematic if what passes for "avoidance" in a Strange Situation observation conducted with the professional caregiver is in some cases truly "disinterest" in an adult who is not really an attachment figure for the infant. Current assessment systems for security of attachment *presume* an attachment relationship to exist and do not explicitly permit the coder to identify an infant as not attached. In our data, some of the infant-metaplot dyads showed signs of flatness in expression of affect that could be indicative of the absence of a specific bond. This is a topic that clearly requires further study.

The nature and specificity of infant-adult attachment relationships is a major issue in attachment theory and research (e.g., Bretherton, 1985), and it was addressed in the present study by examining the congruence hypothesis. Our Strange Situation data replicated and extended previous findings (Sagi et al., 1985) in showing congruence in the attachment relationships of two different infants with the same metapelet. Not only do these data corroborate findings that have been reported in studies of siblings (Teti & Ablard, 1989) and of twins (Goldberg et al., 1986; Minde et al., 1990), but they also uniquely support the role of interactional histories in determining specific infant-adult attachment relationships—any possible genetic influences were well controlled here since the infants were not biologically related either to the metapelet or to each other.

Note, however, that this congruence in two infants' relationships to their common caregiver was found to characterize only relationships developed in kibbutzim with family-based sleeping arrangements. Although the overall quality of daytime care was similar in both sleeping settings (Sagi et al., 1994), finding that such congruence is far less prevalent in kibbutzim with communal sleeping conditions raises the intriguing and heretofore unexplored possibility that the identity of the person who is there to comfort the infant during the night can have significant effects not only on the quality of the child's relationship with the daytime caretaker but also on the coherence of such relationships across different infants in the same infant house. It appears that the congruence hypothesis is less likely to be sustained in the unusual ecological context of having an unfamiliar individual take on the nighttime role.

Evidence for the congruence hypothesis appears in the AQS data as well. Although one might argue that such congruence could be expected as a result of having the same metapelet provide the AQS profiles for the two children, note that congruence is supported by the Q-sort data only in those settings where congruence in Strange Situation classification is also observed (i.e., family-based sleeping arrangements). We view this result as indicative of convergence across measures and thus as providing multimeasure support to the congruence hypothesis.

It should also be noted that, whereas studies of siblings (Teti & Ablard, 1989; Ward et al., 1988) and twins (Minde et al., 1990; Szajnberg et al., 1989; Vandell et al., 1988) have reported levels of congruence ranging between 30% and 60%, the level obtained in the present study was about 70%. This is a more impressive figure, and, owing to our unique design, any explanation of this high degree of congruence concluded in genetic terms can be ruled out. However, the finding that about 30% of the relationships were incongruent also should not be overlooked. Finding instances of lack of congruence is not surprising given recent meta-analytic data (van IJzendoorn, 1995) showing that, although there is widespread support for the hypothesis of intergenerational transmission of attachment (a hypothesis that depends on the same assumptions concerning the operations of internal working models as does the congruence hypothesis), there is also evidence of instances where such transmission of attachment patterns does not take place.

Concerning the concordance between the attachment relationships that two different nonparental attachment figures construct with the same child, we expected to find these to be unique to each dyad. However, this has proved not to be the case in this study. Some concordance between relationships that the two metaplot developed with the same child was replicated across subsamples as well as measures, particularly in the case of secure and resistant/ambivalent relationships.

We contend that two caregivers who cooperate jointly in raising the same child tend to model caregiving behaviors for each other as well as explicitly co-construct similar representations as the child, hence potentiating the same qualities of attachment relationship in the children in their charge. Recall that most metaplot had been trained in principles of "good" child rearing and that most were personally motivated to do their jobs as best they could; within the homelike context of the kibbutz infant house, these factors may promote the similarity of caregiving behaviors and hence concordance in relationships. In any event, we propose that the likelihood of similarity of attachment representations in both caregivers can be eliminated here—first, the assignment of metaplot to infant houses does not follow the psychological processes that characterize the selection of a spouse, and, second, it can be safely assumed that the attachment representations of the two metaplot were acquired independently of and prior to their assignment to a given infant house. However, the design of the study does not allow the exclusion of the temperament hypothesis proposed by Fox et al. (1991), according to which characteristics of the child elicit similar responses from different caregivers.

The issue of the reciprocal validity that is afforded by convergence between Strange Situation and AQS data can be summarized by addressing two types of findings. First, in testing the central hypotheses of this study—namely, the congruence and the concordance hypotheses—similar results were obtained with each of the two measures: security scores based on the AQS appeared to support or falsify hypotheses derived from attachment theory in a way similar to that in which scores based on Strange Situation classifications do. The Strange Situation procedure indexes the operations of the attachment system under stress and focuses mainly on reunion behavior; the AQS indexes its operations under "normal" conditions and assesses the balance between age-appropriate proximity seeking and exploration (i.e., the secure-base phenomenon). Thus, the convergence of results between these two different indices provides further evidence, in a cross-cultural context, for the validity of the AQS (for additional evidence of such convergence, see Vaughn & Waters, 1990).

The second line of evidence derives from the finding that AQS scores predictably discriminated between subjects classified as secure and insecure in the Strange Situation. This form of reciprocal validation is consistent with findings reported by Bosso, Corter, and Abramovitch (1995) and Teti and McGourty (1994), which were based on mothers' reports, but is inconsistent with Dutch data reported by van Dam and van IJzendoorn (1988), which were based on mothers' sorts of an earlier version of the AQS. In the case of metaplot, a variety of factors that we mentioned before may have promoted their observation and reporting skills. However, this positive view of the sensitivity of the Q-sorts provided by metaplot must be tempered by the recognition that they tended not to discriminate between infants classified as avoidant and those classified as secure on the basis of the Strange Situation. We are hesitant to attach any strong interpretation to this finding because of the small number of cases that it involves; however, should it be replicated in other samples, it will deserve further careful consideration (see also van Dam & van IJzendoorn, 1988). Be that as it may, the degree to which security versus insecurity of attachment is replicated by the AQS and by the Strange Situation data clearly supports claiming reciprocal validity for both instruments.

CONCLUDING REMARKS

The findings of our study converge with the growing body of evidence indicating that infants form attachment relationships with their nonfamilial caretakers; concurrently, however, they also highlight the necessity of thinking carefully both about the conditions under which the relationship has developed and about the assumptions that are built into our current methods of assessment before this evidence is generalized to other samples.

The theoretical gains entailed by studying the relations among attachment relationships are also highlighted in the results that we have reported. The design of the study allowed us to examine the theoretically central assumption that the working model of attachment constructed by the adult on the basis of past and present attachment experiences acts as a template for subsequent caregiving behavior. Expressed in terms of our congruence hypothesis, the data supported this assumption—and finding that it was less likely to operate under the communal sleeping conditions opens up theoretically intriguing questions concerning the effects that differences in ecology may exert on the development of attachment relationships and their interrelations.

Finding that infants tend to form attachment bonds of similar quality with two different nonfamilial caregivers (our concordance hypothesis) contributes a new source of evidence to the body of work on relations among relationships (Hinde & Stevenson-Hinde, 1988), and it also permits some restriction of hypotheses concerning the mechanism that may underlie the phenomenon. In all, moving from the study of particular attachment relationships to a focus on the network of such relationships within which infants develop and construct their working models emerges as essential in both examining currently held assumptions and permitting further extensions of attachment theory.

PART 3:
CONCURRENT MATERNAL SUPPORT
FOR SECURE-BASE BEHAVIOR

INTRODUCTION TO PART 3

Mary Ainsworth's observational studies in Uganda and in Baltimore were designed so as to permit assessments of the mother-infant interaction antecedents to the organization of attachment. In both studies, but most clearly in the Baltimore study, the role of maternal sensitivity to infant signals was highlighted as a key support for the co-construction of a secure attachment relationship between infant and mother. This key finding has influenced many subsequent studies (e.g., Belsky & Isabella, 1988; Belsky, Rovine, & Taylor, 1984; Egeland & Farber, 1984; Grossmann, Grossmann, Spangler, Suess, & Unzner, 1985) and is reproduced in this volume by Pederson and Moran, who used home assessments of secure-base behavior to characterize the security of infant attachment. But demonstrating the association between maternal and infant behavior patterns leaves open questions regarding the origins of maternal behaviors, both in ontogenetic and in phylogenetic perspectives. Furthermore, the focus on the mother's behavior leaves open questions of the infant's contributions to sensitivity; is it easier to be sensitive to some babies' signals than to the signals of others?

The three other reports in this section address these questions. Kondo-Ikemura and Waters provide compelling data indicating that the phylogenetic roots of the secure-base phenomenon and maternal actions in support of infant secure-base behavior are deep in our primate history. Their findings also suggest that the assembly of secure-base behavior is viewed as critically important by macaque mothers and that researchers might profitably explore relations between the social ecology of the group and the organization of secure-base behavior for infants whose parents differ in social position. Posada, Waters, Crowell, and Lay address questions of the origin of maternal supports for secure-base behavior in the mother's own history and current perspective on attachment. Their findings extend to the organization of home behavior the implications for infants of their mothers' representations of attachment reported by Main and Goldwyn (in press-b) and others.

Closing this section, Seifer and Schiller lay out arguments for the integration of relationship and temperament constructs. Their thoughtful essay finds many points of congruence between these two domains, which have frequently been portrayed as competing explanations for individual differences in the organization of secure-base behavior. Seifer and Schiller point out that the two perspectives can be easily and conveniently coordinated in a co-constructivist explanation of secure-base behavior and that arguments to the contrary from either camp impede progress in understanding the phenomena more completely.

MATERNAL BEHAVIOR AND INFANT SECURITY IN OLD WORLD MONKEYS: CONCEPTUAL ISSUES AND A METHODOLOGICAL BRIDGE BETWEEN HUMAN AND NONHUMAN PRIMATE RESEARCH

Kiyomi Kondo-Ikemura and Everett Waters

Research on nonhuman primates played an important role in Bowlby's (1969/1982) interpretation of human infant attachment as an adaptive behavioral control system. The psychological interpretation of this model in terms of the secure-base phenomenon (Ainsworth, 1967, 1973) was similarly influenced by field and laboratory observations of nonhuman primates. Throughout the late 1960s and early 1970s, interactions between experts in human infant attachment and nonhuman primate behavior were frequent and mutually beneficial. Unfortunately, and to the disadvantage of both areas, such interactions are now rare.

The discovery of qualitatively different patterns of attachment among human infants was an important source of this divergence; for much of the 1970s and 1980s, attachment research focused almost exclusively on individual differences, psychometric issues, and construct validation (e.g., Ainsworth, Blehar, Waters, & Wall, 1978; Sroufe & Waters, 1977; Waters, 1978; Waters & Deane, 1985). Recently, language and cognition have taken significant roles in attachment theory and research (e.g., Oppenheim & Waters, in this volume; Owens et al., in this volume). These trends, constructive in themselves, have diminished the relevance and accessibility of attachment study to field and experimental primatologists.[1]

We wish to thank the New York Zoological Society and the South Texas Primate Observatory for their cooperation and assistance in this work.

[1] An exception to this generalization, Stevenson-Hinde (1983) has presented the case for supplementing traditional behavioral assessments with more molar variables, which she describes as measures of "personality" traits. For an example of "personality"-trait measures applied to nonhuman primates, see Bolig, Price, O'Neill, and Suomi (1992).

Another factor attenuating links between attachment and nonhuman primate research is the differing emphasis placed on separation responses. Attachment theory today places little emphasis on how distressed an infant or child is during separation. Instead, infant assessments either employ extended observations of secure-base behavior (without separation) at home (Waters & Deane, 1985) or focus on avoidance and contact resisting during laboratory reunions (Ainsworth et al., 1978); beyond infancy, separation procedures are less useful (Posada, Waters, Cassidy, & Marvin, n.d.) and give way to secure-base observations and narrative (interview) methods. These are not mere preferences or conveniences; any proposed measure is subjected to empirical validation. In contrast, experimental primatologists have focused on distress elicited by social separation and isolation procedures. This is an operationist approach; separation responses are judged to be attachment related by definition and, in any event, of interest in and of themselves. In order to reestablish links between attachment and nonhuman primate research, we must bridge these differences.

One of the goals of this report is to clarify the behavioral referents of the secure-base concept. To do this, we have adapted a widely used measure of human infant secure-base behavior for use with Old World monkeys. The Attachment Q-Set (AQS; Waters & Deane, 1985) is based on Bowlby and Ainsworth's secure-base concept; the items were developed on the basis of extensive naturalistic observations of human infant attachment behavior; and, most important, Q-sort data can be analyzed at the level of specific behavior or in terms of constructs such as security and dependency. We have also developed a Q-set describing the behavior of female Old World monkeys as they support, ignore, or hinder their infants' secure-base behavior. Such a measure is important because attachment theorists have, at times, emphasized the attachment-activating role of maternal care to the exclusion of its maintenance function. This has led to misapprehensions about attachment theorists' views of early experience; it has also led attachment theorists into traitlike characterizations of phenomena that are clearly dyadic and interactive. This has complicated relations between attachment theory and other disciplines, including primatology.

We focused on attachment behavior in Old World monkeys for two reasons. First, they have been used as a model in human attachment research since Harlow's first studies of surrogate mothering (Harlow, 1958). Second, their development has now been studied in detail in both field and laboratory situations. Interestingly, the case for using macaques as a model of human social attachments has rarely been examined in detail. Given that the central hypothesis in human attachment theory is that early attachments serve as prototypes for adult attachment relationships (see Waters & Deane, 1982), one might question the relevance of focusing on a species that does not form adult pair bonds. Species such as marmosets and gibbons, or other species that provide sustained parental care and also maintain relatively monogamous pair bonds in adulthood, would be theoretically preferable; however, their unavailability has restricted opportunities for research.

The present study was conducted on free-ranging Japanese macaques. Our goal was to evaluate the hypothesis that patterns of secure-base behaviors, postulated to index attachment security in human research, are associated with concurrent patterns of supportive maternal behavior. Although the emphasis in human attachment theory and research has been on the effects of early maternal care on subsequent infant attachment behavior, Waters, Kondo-Ikemura, Posada, and Richters (1990) have suggested that the association may owe more to consistency in maternal behavior than to direct effects of early care on later infant behavior. Moreover, the contemporaneous coordination of infant and maternal behavior in the course of secure-base and exploratory behavior is central to our understanding of the function and evolution of attachment relationships and thus deserves attention in developmental and cross-cultural work with both humans and as wide a range of nonhuman species as possible.

Relations between maternal and infant behavior have been reported in a wide range of research on macaques and related species (e.g., Stevenson-Hinde & Simpson, 1981), but the focus has been on discrete (usually time-sampled or sequential) behaviors (for reviews, see Hinde, 1983; and Mineka & Suomi, 1978) that are difficult to relate to the concept of attachment security. As a consequence, this work has been cited only rarely in the human attachment literature. The present study addresses both the suitability of the Q-sort method for research with Old World monkeys and the relevance of macaques and closely related species as models of human attachment. It also provides information about the sensitivity of Q-sort data in detecting individual differences under naturalistic rather than experimentally induced conditions, an issue that is important because effects in longitudinal and naturalistic research, with which we are most often concerned, are typically much smaller and more difficult to detect than, for example, the effects of major separations or controlled laboratory manipulations.

Q-SORT METHODOLOGY

The Q-sort methodology employed in this research has three components: (1) procedures for developing sets of behaviorally specific items used to describe individuals; (2) procedures for assigning a score to each item in a Q-set by sorting the items into rank order (from most descriptive to least descriptive of an individual); and (3) procedures for data reduction and data analysis.

Constructing an Item Pool

A Q-set is a set of items that serves as a vocabulary for describing individuals. Traditionally, Q-set items have been phrased in terms of psychodynamic or personality-trait language, often with strong motivational connotations (e.g., "Feels a lack of personal meaning," "Has a brittle ego-defense system," "Has repressive or dissociative tendencies"). In the present research, the Q-sort method is adapted for use with items that are behaviorally specific and refer specifically to the contexts in which the behaviors occur. In developing this Q-set, we were careful to avoid unnecessary jargon, to state each item in the affirmative (so that low placement does not introduce double negatives), and to define explicitly what low placement means for each item. Waters and Deane (1985) describe in detail the rationale underlying the human AQS. These item characteristics have been incorporated into a revised 90-item version of the infant AQS (Waters, 1987). Steps in adapting the AQS for use with Old World monkeys and for developing a parallel Q-set to describe maternal behavior in support of infant secure-base behavior are described below.

Q-Sort Procedure

The goal of the Q-sort procedure is to assign a score to each item in a Q-set. This typically involves sorting the Q-set items into nine piles, with a specified number of items in each pile. Thus, the subject is described in terms of an array of scores on behaviorally specific items, rather than in terms of a single global rating. Sorts from different observers or different occasions can be compared by correlating item placements across subjects or by computing the correlation between pairs of Q-sort descriptions across items. Alpha reliabilities (Cronbach, 1951) can be computed from these data. The reliability of a Q-sort description can be increased by averaging sorts from multiple occasions or multiple observers (Block, 1961/1978).

This sorting procedure has several advantages over simply rating each item individually or assigning a single global score to a particular construct. First, the Q-sort method does not assume that observers have detailed normative information about each item. That is, the question is always whether item A or item B best describes the subject, not whether the subject should be scored high or low relative to other subjects on a particular item. The method also reduces halo and desirability effects by limiting the number of items that can be placed in each Q-sort pile. (For discussion of these and other advantages of this scaling method, see Bem & Funder, 1978; Block, 1961/1978; and Waters & Deane, 1985.)

Data Analysis

Q-sort data lend themselves to a wide range of analytic strategies. The most common are item-level analysis, scale and cluster scoring, and criterion-construct scoring. In item-level analyses, the Q-sort procedure is employed to assign scores to each item, and then the items are treated as individual variables. Waters, Garber, Gornal, and Vaughn (1983) illustrate a strategy in which individual Q-set items are identified as correlates or noncorrelates of a target behavior (e.g., amount of visual regard received from peers), and then these two categories of items are summarized by cluster analysis. When subjects can be divided into several groups, individual *t* tests or one-way ANOVAs can be used to compare the groups in terms of individual items, or, where appropriate, one-way MANOVAs or T^2's can be used to compare groups in terms of sets of related items (e.g., Park & Waters, 1989). Item-level analysis is primarily useful in the early stages of research, when it is useful to survey a broad range of behavioral domains to determine where important effects are to be found. Then follow-up observational studies with traditional observational measures can be conducted to replicate and examine these results in detail.

Cluster and scale-level analyses involve cluster analysis or psychometric item analysis to identify subsets of Q-set items and then summing each subject's scores on these items to obtain a cluster or scale score. This procedure has two primary advantages over item-level analysis. First, it reduces the number of statistical tests performed. Moreover, the psychometric advantages of aggregation (Block, 1977; Epstein, 1979; Rushton, Brainerd, & Pressley, 1983) accrue to scores based on multiple items. That is, aggregating items reduces error variance and thus reduces its attenuating effect on correlations and on statistical power (Nicewander & Price, 1978). This is achieved at the expense of some of the exploratory/descriptive advantages of item-level analysis.

Criterion construct scoring involves having experts sort Q-set items to describe the hypothetical subject scoring highest on a particular construct. Waters and Deane (1985) describe the development of criterion Q-sort definitions for attachment security, dependency, and sociability. Waters, Noyes, Vaughn, and Ricks (1985) illustrate the development of criterion sorts for social competence and self-esteem in children and methods for empirical analysis of these conceptual definitions. The criterion sort defines a construct in terms of an array of scores. An individual subject can be scored on the construct by computing the correlation between this array of scores and the array of scores that describe that particular subject (i.e., a correlation between N items and N items, within an individual subject). Individual subjects are scored on the construct in terms of the similarity between their own Q-set item profiles and those of the hypothetically high-est-scoring subject. This is typically obtained by computing the correlation (across items) between the Q-sort description of the subject and the Q-sort description of the hypothetical highest-scoring subject. One advantage of this approach is that it makes implicit constructs public. This should be of considerable comfort to researchers who are uneasy with the openness of construct-oriented research.

The criterion-sort method has been very successful in capturing con-structs that are difficult to operationalize in terms of one or a few behavioral criteria (e.g., the ability to use the mother as a secure base from which to explore). Note also that the observers who describe an individual subject need not know what constructs their descriptions will be scored for. The ability to keep observers blind to the constructs under study can minimize halo effects that often contaminate conventional trait-rating methods (Coo-per, 1981). The criterion-sort method also allows researchers to evaluate unanticipated or alternative hypotheses by constructing criterion sorts and scoring subjects on new variables long after data collection is completed. Finally, like scale and cluster scores, criterion scores tend to be more reliable than item-level scores, and they reduce the number of statistical tests per-formed on a given set of data.

METHOD

Subjects

Subjects were 24 mother-infant pairs of Japanese macaques (*Macaca fus-cata*) observed at the South Texas Primate Observatory in Dilly, Texas. They were members of troops totaling 311 adults and 69 infants that range freely in a 50-acre compound.[2] The infants ranged in age from 1 to 3 months, a time when infants actively leave their mothers to explore but are not yet totally independent of them. There were equal numbers of high- and low-ranking females, equal numbers of male and female infants within maternal ranks, and equal numbers of infants above and below 8 weeks of age.[3]

Infant Secure-Base and Exploratory Behavior Q-Set

The AQS (Waters & Deane, 1985) assesses the full range of behaviors addressed in Bowlby's control-systems analysis of infant attachment behav-

---

[2] For a detailed description of this facility, its current status, and its prospects, see Lampe (1983).

[3] Information on infants' age and maternal rank were provided by the South Texas Primate Observatory staff.

ior. The items cover eight domains of behavior: (1) Attachment/exploration balance; (2) Response to comforting and differential responsiveness; (3) Affect; (4) Social interaction; (5) Object manipulation; (6) Independence and dependency; (7) Social perception; and (8) Endurance and resiliency. The Q-set was subsequently revised (Waters, 1987), minimizing unnecessary jargon, stating items in the affirmative (so that low placement does not introduce double negatives), and explicitly stating for each item the behaviors associated with low placement. The revised item set is presented in Appendix A (in this volume).

The first step in developing the Attachment Q-Set for Infant Macaques (AQS-M) was to identify items that could be adopted from the human Q-set with minor revisions (e.g., changing "leaves infant with baby-sitter" to "leaves infant with juvenile or adult female monkeys"). The second step involved writing 32 additional items to capture behaviors that do not have clear analogues in human infant behavior or that refer to situations rarely encountered by human infants. These primarily involved aspects of social interaction, object manipulation, and independence and dependency. The final version of the AQS-M consists of 94 items; these are listed in Appendix C (in this volume).

Maternal Attachment Behavior

In order to describe maternal behaviors that might help organize infant attachment behavior by supporting the infant's secure-base and exploratory behaviors, we developed a Q-set by writing items related to each of the 94 items in the AQS-M and then editing and revising to eliminate redundancy. The Maternal Q-Set for Macaques (MQS-M) consists of 93 items covering eight facets of maternal behavior: (1) Offering contact or comfort; (2) Comforting behavior; (3) Protection from danger; (4) Affect; (5) Caretaking strategies; (6) Promoting independence or teaching; (7) Social interaction with infant; and (8) Self-maintenance behaviors. For completeness, the MQS-M also describes behaviors that might compete with maternal behavior or might be antithetical to it (e.g., object exploration and foraging). We also included marker items related to maternal status and social adjustment. The MQS-M items are listed in Appendix C.

Q-Sort Descriptions of Maternal and Infant Behavior

Observation Procedure

Observations were conducted by Kiyomi Kondo-Ikemura and a biopsychology graduate student whom she trained in the meaning of the Q-set items and Q-sort procedures. Agreement of at least 80% on each Q-set item was established through training observations of macaques and langurs in indoor naturalistic habitats at the New York Zoological Park. Additional agreement trials were conducted at the Texas facility prior to formal data collection.

The target animals (adults and infants) were observed in a randomly constructed order. The two observers worked independently and never focused on the same mother or infant, or on a mother and her own infant, at the same time. After observing a target animal for 90 min, the observer generated a Q-sort description before observing another animal. The total set of 48 observations was distributed over a period of 3 weeks. The two sorts of each animal were averaged to obtain a single composite Q-sort description. Like many other types of behavioral data, Q-sort descriptions are considerably improved by averaging across observers and occasions.

Q-Sort Procedure

As outlined above, scores were assigned to Q-set items by sorting them into nine piles according to a predefined distribution. Items in pile 9 are those most characteristic of the subject during the observation interval. Piles closer to the center (pile 5) contain items that are successively less characteristic of the subject; items in piles 4, 3, and 2, for example, are successively less characteristic (i.e., the opposite) of the subject. Items in pile 1 are least characteristic or most unlike the subject. This sorting is accomplished in three steps. First, the items are sorted into three piles, characteristic (pile A), undecided or neutral (pile B), and uncharacteristic (pile C). Then the items in pile A are subdivided into three piles, most characteristic (pile 9), characteristic (pile 8), and somewhat characteristic (pile 7), with pile 9 on the left. At this point, any number of items is allowed in any pile. Next, pile B is sorted to yield pile 6 (more like than unlike the subject), pile 5 (neutral or not applicable), and pile 4 (more unlike than like the subject). Pile C is then sorted to yield pile 3 (somewhat unlike the subject), pile 2 (unlike the subject), and, on the far right, pile 1 (most unlike the subject).

The sorting is completed by adjusting the number of items per pile to fit a predefined distribution (usually rectangular or quasi normal). Beginning with pile 9, the most characteristic items are selected and the remainder moved to pile 8. The required number of "characteristic" items is selected for pile 8 and the remainder moved to pile 7. This continues until piles 9, 8, 7, and 6 are completed. Then, working toward the center from pile 1, the necessary pile sizes are obtained for the items that are most uncharacteristic, uncharacteristic, etc. The advantage of working from the outside piles toward the middle is that decisions are usually easier to make in the more characteristic and uncharacteristic items and that, when working with quasi-normal distributions, it is easiest to let the large center pile be fixed by default. When this sorting is completed, each item is assigned a score equal to the number of the pile in which it was placed. Items in pile 9 receive a score of 9, etc.

Q-Sort Definition of "Attachment Security"

Working from Bowlby's attachment theory, extensive experience with the human AQS, and familiarity with criterion sorts for human attachment security, Everett Waters sorted the AQS-M to describe the hypothetical infant monkey that is most able to use its mother as a secure base from which to explore. The item placements for the AQS-M security criterion sort are presented in Appendix D (in this volume). The five items specified as most characteristic of the hypothetical most secure infant monkey were the following: (1) "Monitors mother's location and activities"; (2) "Proximity/exploration/proximity cycles are evident"; (3) "Departures from mother are spontaneous"; (4) "Initiates playful interaction with mother"; and (5) "Approaches mother to observe." The first and second items are prototypical secure-base behaviors; the third reflects the expectation that a secure infant is willing to explore (presumably predicated in part on confidence in the mother's availability and responsiveness), and the fourth and fifth items reflect the expectation that a secure infant will be comfortable and confident in the mother's presence.

The five items specified as least characteristic of the hypothetical secure infant monkey were the following: (1) "Adopts awkward and uncomfortable posture when held"; (2) "Easily annoyed with mother"; (3) "Expects mother will be unresponsive"; (4) "Becomes distressed when mother moves away"; and (5) "Transition from contact to exploration is executed awkwardly." These are behaviors deemed to be most uncharacteristic of an infant that is confident of the mother's availability and responsiveness and that is able to use her effectively as a secure base. The similarity of an infant macaque's behavior to this criterion was determined by correlating the array of AQS-M item scores with the array of scores that make up the criterion sort. In principle, therefore, scores range from $+1$ to -1; in practice, they range between and $+.7$ and $-.1$. The alternative to secure-base behavior is lack of secure-base behavior, not the opposite of secure-base behavior.

The fact that Bowlby's attachment theory can be mapped onto the behavior of infant Old World monkeys does not guarantee that the security concept affords a particularly powerful perspective on their behavior. This is an empirical question. Whether our initial criterion sort is the best possible formulation of the security concept for research with infant macaques is also an empirical question. The present approach at least has the advantage of making the security concept more explicit than if we had simply rated infant macaques on attachment security. This facilitates communication across disciplines and holds out the prospect of using empirical data to improve on the present security definition.

RESULTS

There were no significant differences between the security scores of male and female infants (.33 and .40, respectively) or between young and old infants (.35 and .38, respectively). However, infants of high-ranking mothers scored significantly higher than those of low-ranking mothers (.43 and .29, respectively; $p < .05$). Twenty-three of the 93 MQS-M items were significantly correlated with infant security scores; they are organized into the three categories shown in Table 1.

The first of these consists of eight items related to active maternal supervision. The more secure the infant, the more characteristic it is of its mother to keep the infant close even after threatening situations have abated (item 2), when moving from place to place (item 3), and when the infant approaches adults carelessly (item 8). The mother's alertness to environmental changes (item 4) and to changes in the infant's behavior (item 7) are also correlated with infant security. In addition, active involvement in caretaking, as reflected in persistence (items 5, 6), and caution in sharing the infant (item 1) were more characteristic of mothers with more secure infants.

The second category consists of eight items related to the mother's sensitivity to infant signals, responsiveness, and availability. These are closer to the behaviors that have been postulated most often as being critical determinants of attachment security in human infants. In human research, however, the emphasis has been on early maternal behavior as a determinant of subsequent infant secure-base behavior; as noted earlier, our own interest is in the organizing and maintaining role that concurrent maternal behavior plays in relation to secure-base behavior throughout infancy and beyond (see Waters et al., 1990).

The third category of secure-base correlates consists of seven items related to maternal rank and adjustment. The results showed that mothers of secure infants are more likely to behave in a relaxed manner when alone (items 19, 20, 21), with her infant (items 18, 22), and in social situations (items 17, 23). It was more characteristic of these mothers to receive than to offer social bids or grooming. In contrast, mothers of less secure infants scored higher on items indicating that they sought safety in the troop through social proximity to, or social interaction with, a specific adult.

TABLE 1

CORRELATIONS BETWEEN AQS-M SECURITY SCORES AND THE MQS-M

Content Areas	Pearson r
Active supervision	
1. Allows other monkeys to hold infant	−.64**
2. Keeps infant closer for some time after unusual event has ceased	.55**
3. Carries infant when moving from place to place (i.e., doesn't just walk off)	.54**
4. Alert to subtle changes in the environment	.50**
5. Does not hesitate to punish infant in appropriate circumstances	.47*
6. Ceases caretaking behavior if infant wiggles or gets annoyed	−.45*
7. Monitors infant's location and activities consistently	.44*
8. Retrieves infant or drives adults away if infant approaches them (esp. adult males or dominant females)	.44*
Sensitive to infant signals/available/supportive	
9. Occupied in caretaking, to the exclusion of other activities	.64**
10. Devotes more time to infant than to older siblings	.53**
11. Quickly becomes bored with caretaking	−.52**
12. Accepts or tolerates infant using mother's tail or body during play	.50*
13. Changes attitude toward infant frequently	−.46*
14. Prevents infant from leaving in unfamiliar settings	−.42*
15. Recognizes infant signals of fear, etc.	.41*
16. Retrieves infant from play with novel objects	−.40*
Maternal adjustment or rank	
17. Seeks proximity with a specific adult	−.66**
18. Keeps infant close when asleep	−.58**
19. Movement and activities are relaxed	.57**
20. Displays tension movements	−.51*
21. Rests regularly	−.50*
22. Comforting is exaggerated	−.43*
23. Frequently initiates (vs. receives) interaction from other adults	−.42*

* $p < .05$.
** $p < .01$.

DISCUSSION

Closely coordinated face-to-face and feeding behaviors, analogous to those typically defining *maternal sensitivity* in research on human infants (e.g., Ainsworth et al., 1978; Belsky, Taylor, & Rovine, 1984), are not a distinctive feature of infant-mother interaction in macaques. Rather, the mother's willingness and ability to organize her behavior around the infant and to serve as a secure base is probably the critical factor organizing and maintaining the infant's secure-base behavior after the onset of locomotion; this appears to be a more critical factor than either early or concurrent microinteractions.

In contrast to most middle-class human infants, infant macaques risk serious accidental and intentional injury from adult and juvenile conspecifics as soon as they venture far from the mother. This risk is probably much greater than the risk of predation. In such unsafe circumstances, the concepts *secure base from which to explore* and *haven of safety* are much more than mere metaphors. Our results indicate that an infant macaque cannot use its mother as a secure base from which to explore unless she is powerful enough to protect it. But high social rank alone is not enough; to serve effectively as a secure base, the mother must be an active caregiver and supervisor throughout the day; she must be accessible and maintain access to the infant as social situations within the troop change. This is a very challenging task. Indeed, explaining such apparently purposeful behavior requires models at least as complex as the control systems that Bowlby invoked to explain infant secure-base behavior.

Unfortunately, the caregiver's role in organizing and maintaining secure-base behavior has received little attention. Attachment theorists have focused instead on the role of species-specific maternal care as an activator of the attachment control system; the continuity of care and the role of concurrent care in longitudinal outcomes have received little attention. Although attachment theorists may too readily look to early experience for explanations of longitudinal outcomes, such a developmental bias is not a central tenet of attachment theory. The importance of early experience is an empirical question. As Richters and Waters (1990), Waters, Hay, and Richters (1985), and Waters et al. (1990) have emphasized, a viable alternative hypothesis is that individual differences in caregiver behavior are significantly stable and that concurrent care plays a significant role in longitudinal effects. This hypothesis can be examined by assessing concurrent caregiver behavior along with longitudinal outcomes. The outcome of such research is not a test of key attachment concepts; rather, it influences how we formulate for future research Bowlby's control-system model, Ainsworth's secure-base concept, and the notion that mental representations (even those constructed years later) of early experience are important in adult relationships. Supervision, monitoring, and support are ongoing processes in parent-child as well as adult-adult attachments; that they are continuous processes is *central* to attachment theory.

The middle-class human infants most often studied in academic research are relatively safe when they venture off to play and explore; they are certainly very safe in comparison to the infant macaques observed in this study. This may account for the lack of emphasis in human attachment research on variables such as maternal status and vigilance. Unfortunately, as statistics on child abuse and homelessness attest, not all human infants and children are as safe as they should be (Daly & Wilson, 1981; Hausman & Hammen, 1993). Only through closer attention to the organization, functioning, and continuity of maternal behavior over time can attachment theory contribute to prevention and intervention in complex situations such as child abuse and homelessness. An important first step toward this goal

would be programmatic research to develop measures of secure-base support by human caregivers. The Q-sort method illustrated in the present
study may be suitable for this work.

Maternal care variables, especially sensitivity to infant signals and cooperation versus interference with ongoing behavior, are the most consistent
correlates of infant attachment security; the correlations, however, are usually in the range of .1–.3 (Ainsworth et al., 1978; Goldsmith & Alansky,
1987; Lamb, Thompson, Gardner, & Charnov, 1985; van IJzendoorn,
Goldberg, Kroonenberg, & Frenkel, 1992). Much stronger relations between maternal and infant behavior were found in the present study (see
also Pederson & Moran, in this volume).

Several distinctive features of the present study may have contributed
to this difference. First, focusing on the initiating rather than the maintaining role of maternal behavior, attachment researchers have often assessed maternal behavior early in infancy and attachment behavior months
later. We focused, instead, on the secure-base-maintaining function of concurrent maternal behavior. In addition, previous research on maternal behavior has adopted a microanalytic perspective, focusing on the details of
sensitivity to infant signals; in the present study, we give comparable weight
to the organization of maternal behavior over longer periods of time. In a
sense, where previous research focused largely on tactics in infant-mother
interaction, the Q-sort method enabled us to give equal weight to both
tactics and strategy.

Ainsworth's Baltimore longitudinal study was unique in that each infant-mother dyad was observed in naturalistic settings for 12–15 hours in
each quarter of the first year of life; subsequent studies have involved less
than 1 hour of observation, often just a few minutes, in laboratory or constrained (e.g., feeding in a high chair) home situations. In the present study,
subjects were observed for a total of 3 hours in a naturalistic setting. Because
brief observations and constrained situations cannot reliably estimate subjects' typical rates of behavior, correlations based on such observations underestimate the correlations that would be obtained with more representa-
tive (reliable) data (see Block, 1977; Epstein, 1979; and Waters, 1978).

Previous research has relied on global rating scales and time-sampling
methods, neither of which is particularly well suited to the task of measuring
infant secure-base behavior or concurrent maternal behavior. The Q-sorts
employed in the present study are behaviorally specific, they enable the
observer to take into account the behavioral context in which behaviors
occur, and they readily take into account the fact that a wide range of
behaviors and behavior sequences are functionally equivalent in terms of
secure-base functioning. In brief, small correlations do not always imply
weak associations; often, for psychometric reasons, they underestimate important relations. Attachment researchers may have accepted too readily

weak or false negative results regarding the effects of maternal behavior on infant secure-base behavior. Both improved measurement and a broader view of what should be measured can help clarify this important issue.

The Q-sort method permits surveying a much wider range of behavior than we can typically accommodate in time-sampling procedures; it can capture behavioral detail and also summarize the functioning of complex behavior patterns. Most important of all, it makes explicit the behavioral referents of attachment constructs such as security and sensitivity. The Q-sort method will not replace conventional observational methods; as with any other broad-band measure, it is most powerful when used to guide and focus more detailed observational work that builds on the outlines it draws. This can expand the reach of human attachment research and help rebuild bridges that once linked work on human and nonhuman primates.

A CATEGORICAL DESCRIPTION OF INFANT-MOTHER RELATIONSHIPS IN THE HOME AND ITS RELATION TO Q-SORT MEASURES OF INFANT-MOTHER INTERACTION

David R. Pederson and Greg Moran

The development of the Strange Situation (Ainsworth, Bell, & Stayton, 1971; Ainsworth, Blehar, Waters, & Wall, 1978) shifted the focus of the study of attachment relationships from the infant's natural environment to the assessment of individual differences in novel laboratory environments. Paradoxically, as Bretherton (1992) suggested, the dramatic success of this assessment method in supporting investigations of the sequelae of individual differences in early social development may have inhibited the study of the origins of distinct attachment relationships in naturalistic contexts. The success of the Strange Situation served to move research out of the naturalistic domain of the home and into the world of structured separations and reunions, where there are few opportunities to study the dynamics of mother-infant interaction. Yet, according to attachment theory, it is these interactions—particularly the sensitivity and responsiveness of the mother—that are the fundamental precursors to variations in patterns of attachment (Ainsworth et al., 1971; Sroufe & Fleeson, 1986). In this report, we describe a system of classifying attachment relationships at home and relate these classifications to descriptions of maternal and infant attachment-relevant behavior.

The research reported here was supported by grants from the Ontario Mental Health Foundation and from the Social Sciences and Humanities Research Council of Canada. We are grateful to the mothers and infants who participated in this research and to Sandi Bento, Gail Buckland, Jane Myles, Andrea Noonan, and Ann Robson for conducting the home observations. Special acknowledgment is given to Sandi Bento for her assistance in the development of the home-based attachment classification system.

111

ATTACHMENT RELATIONSHIPS AT HOME

Very little attention has been devoted to the delineation of attachment relationships on the basis of naturalistic observations in the home since Ainsworth's initial studies (e.g., Ainsworth, 1963; Ainsworth et al., 1971). In this early work, Ainsworth et al. (1971) described five types of relationships; distinctions among the categories were based almost exclusively on the effectiveness of the infant's use of the mother as a secure base for exploration. Thus, for example, infants in group I were described as clearly using the mother as a secure base from which to explore the familiar context of the home environment; in contrast, group IV infants actively sought contact with the mother in a way that disrupted their exploratory behavior, and the contact did not seem satisfying to either mother or infant. A strong correspondence between these relationship classifications and classifications derived from the Strange Situation assessment was also reported; thus, all eight infants in group I were classified as secure, and all four infants assigned to group IV at home were classified as anxiously attached (three as avoidant and one as ambivalent) in the Strange Situation.

Despite these encouraging initial results, Ainsworth et al. (1978, p. 241) expressed dissatisfaction with their system for classifying relationships from home observations and were confident that it could be improved. They suggested that any revisions should capitalize on insights into the nature of infant-mother relationships that were emerging from research using the Strange Situation and that the description should include aspects of infant-mother interactions beyond the attachment/exploration balance.

In elaborating on Ainsworth's descriptions, we used the avoidant, secure, and ambivalent designations for what we considered to be the at-home parallels of the three patterns of relationships that are observed in the Strange Situation, and we developed descriptions of infant and maternal behaviors likely to be observed in the nonstressful context of the home that would be diagnostic of these patterns. In seeking descriptive criteria that go beyond secure-base behavior, we were strongly influenced by Sroufe's thesis (e.g., Sroufe & Fleeson, 1986, 1988) that relationships are multidimensional, coherent wholes in which each partner plays a reciprocal role in maintaining the underlying structure of the relationship. In our view, it follows from this position that qualitatively different relationships would have different structures that reflect distinct principles or implicit rules that organize the interactions.

Of the three major attachment classifications, the organizing principles of secure relationships have been most clearly identified. Ainsworth et al. (1971, pp. 49–50; see also Biringen, 1990) concluded that the underlying feature of secure relationships is that the infant and mother are in harmony with each other. Interactions are marked by effective secure-base behavior on the part of the infant and by sensitive responsiveness on the part of the mother (Ainsworth et al., 1978). The infant is conspicuously proficient in using the mother as a secure base, balancing investigations of the environment with proximity maintenance and affective sharing with her. The mother, in turn, recognizes and responds to her infant's needs in a prompt and effective manner. This coherent relationship, with interactions organized around a dynamic balance of exploration and secure-base behavior, is characteristic of secure relationships and distinguishes them from avoidant and ambivalent relationships.

Attachment security has often been viewed as the organizing principle for all attachment relationships (see Cummings, 1990), and this focus may have diverted researchers from seeking to specify distinct organizing principles for avoidant and ambivalent relationships in similar detail. Following Main's analyses of the role of avoidance in relationships (e.g., Main & Weston, 1982), we suggest that the predominant organizing principle of an avoidant relationship is that of containing negative affect (for a similar analysis, see Cassidy, 1994). An avoidant relationship is manifested in infant-mother interactions that function primarily to maintain emotional distance, particularly in times of mild stress. Thus, mothers in avoidant relationships are relatively insensitive to signals of infant distress (Cassidy & Kobak, 1988), and, when they do respond to such signals, their response might be to orient the infant's attention to external events rather than to engage in affect-laden interactions focused directly on the distress and its relief. Because emotional closeness is often communicated by physical closeness (Main, 1990), mothers in avoidant relationships are expected to be relatively uncomfortable with physical contact (Ainsworth et al., 1978); for example, they have been reported to express their physical affection by kissing the infant on the head, often with a sort of pecking motion (Tracy & Ainsworth, 1981). In turn, infants in avoidant relationships attempt to soothe themselves when upset rather than to approach their mother for comfort because they have been encouraged in a variety of ways to be independent (Braungart & Stifter, 1991).

The structure of ambivalent relationships and their likely expression in naturalistic interactions appear to be least well understood (Ainsworth et al., 1978; Cassidy & Berlin, 1994; Isabella, 1993). Part of the difficulty is that ambivalent relationships occur relatively infrequently; for example, Ainsworth et al. (1971) identified only four such dyads in their study relating home observations and Strange Situation classifications. Moreover, they reported considerable heterogeneity in the characteristics of the four mothers: two were very dysfunctional, one was intrusive, and the remaining one was very unresponsive. Other investigators have characterized mothers in ambivalent relationships as unresponsive (e.g., Belsky, Rovine, & Taylor, 1984; Cassidy & Berlin, 1994; Isabella, Belsky, & von Eye, 1989; Smith &

113

Pederson, 1988) or as rejecting and inconsistent (Isabella, 1993). The emotional volatility of both infants and mothers is another source of difficulty in developing clear and consistent descriptions of ambivalent relationships. As Cassidy (1994) and Crittenden (1992) have suggested, the infant's negative emotional displays may be a response to the mother's unresponsiveness as well as the unpredictability of her behavior. Thus, being demanding and fussy may be the infant's way of eliciting predictable maternal responses, and the mother's negative emotions may be a product of irritation induced by a fussy infant. Whatever the causes, ambivalent relationships are perplexing to an observer who is attempting to understand the implicit rules and structures guiding the dyadic interactions.

We used the above descriptions (which are detailed more extensively in the Appendix to this report) to classify infant-mother relationships on the basis of a home visit conducted when the infants were 12 months of age. The validity of these classifications was evaluated by relating them to assessments of maternal sensitivity at 8 months and to the mother's Attachment Q-Set (AQS) description of her infant at age 12 months.

MATERNAL SENSITIVITY

A second compelling impetus for return to home-based observations is that our understanding of the role of maternal behavior in the emergence of distinctive attachment relationships has not been elaborated substantially beyond Ainsworth's pioneering work. Ainsworth et al. (1971) reported that mothers of infants classified as securely attached in the Strange Situation were rated as having been more sensitive during earlier home observations than mothers of anxiously attached infants. Consistent with the view that maternal behavior is the primary determinant of attachment security, the magnitude of the effect size reported by these authors was considerable: a difference of about 2.5 standard deviation units between ratings recorded for mothers of secure and of anxious infants. Some subsequent studies that used the same rating scales have also reported significant but much smaller differences (e.g., Egeland & Farber, 1984; Grossmann, Grossmann, Spangler, Suess, & Unzner, 1985); however, other studies have failed to replicate such findings (e.g., Goldberg, Perrotta, Minde, & Corter, 1986; Mangelsdorf, Gunnar, Kestenbaum, Lang, & Andreas, 1990). Goldsmith and Alansky (1987) concluded from their meta-analysis of this body of research that the average effect size is about a third of a standard deviation, a magnitude of difference that is typically labeled as small to moderate (Cohen, 1988).

Such inconsistent results across studies could be viewed as undermining the central assumption made by all attachment theorists, namely, that attachment security is a product of the infant's experiences with a sensitive and appropriately responsive caregiver. This conclusion seems unwarranted on logical grounds alone—it is hard to imagine any tenable alternative postulate about the experiential source of individual differences in attachment security—and it is also inconsistent with findings that variations in maternal psychiatric problems provide a better predictor of attachment security than do infants' clinical characteristics (for a review, see van IJzendoorn, Goldberg, Kroonenberg, & Frenkel, 1992).

An alternative explanation for the difficulty that has been encountered providing solid empirical confirmation of the theoretical link between maternal sensitivity and infant attachment security is that the descriptive techniques used in many studies have failed to capture meaningful variation in maternal interactive behavior. To address this possibility, we developed a Q-sort procedure designed to provide a detailed description of maternal behavior as well as to yield a summary assessment of the mother's sensitivity as indexed by the correlation between the sort of her behavior and a sort describing the behavior of a prototypically sensitive mother (see Pederson et al., 1990).

In contrast to all studies that followed, a unique strength of Ainsworth's original home observations was that they involved more than 60 hours of observations of each mother-infant dyad. Given the practical difficulties of replicating such an extensive data base, we rely on two features of the Maternal Behavior Q-Set to capture meaningful variation in interaction. First, patterned after the Waters AQS (except that the 90 items focus on maternal behavior), our Q-set contains items that prompt observers to focus their attention on attachment-relevant aspects of the interactions (for a listing of items, see App. B, in this volume). Second, we deliberately observe mothers in circumstances where their attention is divided between the demands of their infant and tasks posed by the researchers under the assumption that such circumstances are more likely to reveal differences in maternal sensitivity than observations performed in low-demand circumstances. Under such conditions, 2–4 hours of home observations appear sufficient to provide reliable descriptions.

Using this technique, Pederson et al. (1990) reported that maternal sensitivity scores derived from the Maternal Behavior Q-Set were significantly correlated ($r = .52$) with infant security scores derived from the AQS. In a second study, one of mothers with infants at biological risk for developmental delay, Moran, Pederson, Pettit, and Krupka (1992) reported a lower mean maternal sensitivity score, but the substantial relation between maternal sensitivity and attachment security was replicated in this sample ($r = .49$). Moreover, the trained observers' Maternal Behavior Q-Set sorts—based on approximately 2 hours of observation—were consistent with ratings of maternal sensitivity provided by infant therapists who had a longstanding knowledge of the dyads. These initial studies provided evidence of the theoretically expected association between contemporaneous measures of infant attachment security and maternal sensitivity, suggesting that methodological problems may have accounted for the failure of previous attempts to establish an empirical link between these two constructs. In combination, the Maternal Behavior Q-Set and the AQS appear capable of capturing relevant variation in maternal and infant interactive behavior.

The present study included assessments of maternal sensitivity at both 8 and 12 months and an assessment of the infant's security of attachment at age 12 months. This design made it possible to examine the relation between independent assessments of antecedent as well as concurrent maternal sensitivity and the infant's attachment security. Both preterm and full-term infants were included in the sample. We were interested in the development of infant-mother attachment relationships in a preterm sample because preterm birth is associated with more stress (e.g., Pederson, Bento, Chance, Evans, & Fox, 1987) and preterm infants present more caregiving difficulties (e.g., Goldberg & DiVitto, 1983). Thus, albeit all parents experience stress, individual differences within a sample of low-risk infants are more likely lie below a minimum threshold where stress provides a serious challenge to parental responsiveness. We assumed that the stresses associated with preterm birth would tend to exceed this hypothesized threshold and thus that a preterm sample should provide a better opportunity to observe individual differences in maternal responsivity to infant social cues.

ATTACHMENT BEHAVIOR

As Waters and Deane (1985) suggested, the Q-sort method is amenable to a variety of scoring approaches, although the attachment security score has been by far the most frequently used system. The security score is a reflection of the similarity between the interactions of an observed infant and interactions that attachment experts expect of a secure infant. As we examined the content of high- and low-security items (see App. A, in this volume), we noted that the security score reflects a heterogeneous set of behaviors including secure base, affective sharing, and the absence of fussing. Some items, such as those referring to secure-base behaviors, seem central to the concept of attachment security; other items refer to expected behaviors of secure children, but not necessarily to the concept of security. For example, such items as "recognizing when mother is upset" or "attracted to new toys" may well be an outcome of being in a secure relationship rather than a reflection of security per se.

In order to provide a multidimensional portrait of attachment-related interactions and to make more informative distinctions than is possible with a single security score, we grouped items into what we considered to be attachment-relevant domains. Our first step in constructing the domain scales was to examine the items that experts had judged to be important in defining the hypothetical securely attached infant (i.e., those with a mean placement ≥ 7.5 or ≤ 2.5 on the criterion security sort; see App. A); this ensured that only behaviors conceived to be central to the attachment system would enter into the scales. The resulting pool of 39 items contained (as would be expected) a number of behaviors descriptive of secure-base phenomena; we grouped other items into clusters reflecting the infant's affective sharing with the mother, enjoyment of physical contact, cooperation/ compliance with the mother's wishes, and fussy or difficult behavior. Eight items in this pool were judged as isolated examples of their type and thus could not be formed into any scale. The remaining 51 items of the AQS were then examined, and those items that corresponded to one of the five domains were added to the initial scales.

The items selected for each domain are indicated in Appendix D (in this volume). The infant's score is the average placement of the items on each scale (of course with correction for items conveying negative instances of the domain). We expected that all these scales would differentiate infants in secure from those in nonsecure relationships; moreover, infants in avoidant relationships should show the least enjoyment of physical contact, and those in ambivalent relationships should be characterized by a greater tendency to be fussy and difficult.

METHOD

Subjects

Forty-seven mothers of preterm and 42 mothers of full-term infants were recruited shortly after the infants' births in a hospital in London, Ontario. The preterm infants were selected from the neonatal intensive care unit using the criteria birth weight less than 2,000 grams, gestational age less than 37 weeks, and the absence of gross neurological or physical anomalies at birth. Infants with birth anomalies were also excluded from the full-term group. The birth status and demographic background of these two groups are summarized in Table 1. All but two of the mothers in this predominantly middle-class sample were Caucasian.

Procedures and Measures

Observer training.—Just as in the case of other attachment assessments (such as the Strange Situation and the Adult Attachment Interview), we

TABLE 1

Birth Status and Demographic Characteristics of the Preterm and the Full-Term Samples

	PRETERM (N = 47)		FULL TERM (N = 42)			
	M	SD	M	SD	t(87)[a]	p
Gestational age (weeks) ...	28.2	3.7	39.4	1.2	20.31	< .001
Birth weight (grams)	1,129.9	409.1	3,444.6	448.2	27.01	< .001
Days in hospital	71.0	34.1	3.5	1.3	12.96	< .001
Mother's age	28.0	5.2	29.9	4.8	1.81	N.S.
Mother's education (years)	13.4	2.6	14.5	2.6	1.92	N.S.
Father's education (years)	13.3	2.8	14.0	3.3	2.80	< .01

[a] Unequal variance estimates of *t* were used for the analyses of gestational age and days in hospital.

regard training of observers to be essential for sound home assessments of attachment relationships. In the course of training, observers first become familiar with descriptions of attachment behaviors and classifications by reading Ainsworth et al. (1971), Ainsworth et al. (1978, chaps. 1, 7–8, 14–15), and Sroufe and Fleeson (1986); they also familiarize themselves with the items of the AQS and the Maternal Behavior Q-Set. Their initial home visits are training experiences in which the apprentice and an experienced observer collaborate in discussing the visit, reviewing the running records, and completing the Q-sorts, ratings, and postvisit notes. The extent of collaboration decreases over visits, and training is deemed to be completed when the apprentice observer reaches criterion agreement with the experienced observer (i.e., is within .2 on the Q-sort infant security and maternal sensitivity scores, within 2 points on the Ainsworth scales, and in categorical agreement on the avoidant, secure, and ambivalent relationship classification system).

Home visit procedures.—Two observers conducted a home observation of each infant-mother dyad at 8 and at 12 months of age (ages for the preterm infants were corrected for weeks of prematurity); both were present at each visit, each of which lasted approximately 2 hours. One observer participated in all the home visits, and four different people served as the second observer. For 53 cases, the role of the second observer was performed by a different person at the 8- and 12-month visits. The educational background of the observers ranged from completing two years in a community college program in early childhood education to advanced doctoral studies in developmental psychology. All the observers were female and had extensive experience with young children either as parents or as caregivers. At the 8-month home visits, the Bayley Scales of Infant Development (Bayley, 1969) were administered with the baby seated on the mother's lap; the following interview with the mother provided a context in which the visitor's questions and the infant's needs competed for the mother's attention. At the 12-month home visits, the Bayley scales were administered by one observer (with the infant seated in a high chair) while the mother completed the AQS (Waters, 1987) under the guidance of the second observer; this again was followed by an interview with the mother. Both observers took extensive notes during the visits.

Postvisit procedures.—After the visit, each observer independently described her observations of the infant and mother to a researcher who had no prior knowledge of the dyad (in most cases David Pederson). This description was organized as a semistructured interview and began with a description of what the infant and the mother did when the visitors first arrived. Using the notes the observer had taken during the visit as well as her recollections, the entire visit was then reviewed in detail, with a focus on incidents of the infant's affective sharing, proximity-seeking, and comfort-seeking behaviors with the mother as well as of the infant's exploratory behavior. Consideration was also given to the mother's behavior, including descriptions of her responses to positive and negative affective cues from her infant, her accessibility to her infant in the context of a busy visit, and her anticipation of the infant's needs.

Once the visit was described, the interviewer summarized the impressions of the infant-mother interactions that had been given, and the observer corrected or confirmed these impressions. On the basis of this material, the interviewer and the observer jointly arrived at a relationship classification using procedures modeled after those developed by Ainsworth et al. (1971) and detailed in the Appendix to this report. Following the debriefing interview, each observer independently summarized the visit in a brief written narrative description and then completed the Maternal Behavior Q-Set, the AQS, and the Ainsworth ratings of maternal acceptance-rejection, accessibility-ignoring, cooperation-interference, and sensitivity-insensitivity (Ainsworth et al., 1971).

Derived measures.—The Q-sorts were summarized by generating a maternal sensitivity score from the Maternal Behavior Q-Set and a security score from the AQS, through correlations of the individual sort with the relevant criterion sorts. The AQS sorts were also used to score the five domains of the infants' attachment behavior that we had derived (for a list of items for each dimension, see App. D): Secure-Base Behavior (14 items, Cronbach α = .81), Affective Sharing (three items, α = .76), Compliance (six items, α = .69), Enjoyment of Physical Contact (five items, α = .93), and Fussy/Difficult (14 items, α = .85). There was high interobserver agreement on the Q-sort-derived maternal sensitivity scores at both 8 months (r = .94) and 12 months (r = .95) as well as on the 12-month security scores (r = .95); the observers' scores were averaged for use in subsequent analyses. Because ratings on the four Ainsworth scales proved to be highly intercorrelated both across observers and across scales (r's > .84), an aggregate score, Ainsworth Ratings, was constructed by averaging the four scales. (Results of the analyses of the four individual scales did not differ substantially from analyses using the aggregated measure.)

Assessments of maternal sensitivity were reasonably stable between the 8-month and the 12-month visits: r = .71 for the Q-sort sensitivity scores, and r = .73 for the Ainsworth Ratings. The infant security scores derived from the observers' AQS sorts were moderately correlated with those derived from the AQS sorts provided by the mothers (r = .51, p < .001). The attachment domain scale scores derived from observers' and mothers' sorts were also moderately correlated with r's ranging from .46 to .51 (p's < .001) for all but Affective Sharing, where r = .16 (N.S.). A sample of 89 was available for analyses based on observers' scores, one of 88 for analyses involving mothers' Q-sorts (one mother did not complete the AQS).

RESULTS

Classification of Attachment Relationships at 12 Months of Age

Twenty-five dyads were classified as avoidant, 43 as secure, and 21 as ambivalent on the basis of the 12-month home observations. The 8-month mean Ainsworth Ratings and Q-sort maternal sensitivity scores provided by the observers and the attachment security and attachment domain scores derived from the mothers' Q-sorts at 12 months for these groups are shown in Table 2. (The observers' 12-month sensitivity and security data are not analyzed because these data are based on the same observations that were used to classify the relationships and thus are not methodologically independent of the classifications.)

These eight variables were entered as dependent measures in a 2 (birth group) × 3 (attachment relationship) MANOVA. There was a significant main effect for attachment relationship ($F[16, 150]$ = 6.73, p < .001); neither the birth group main effect ($F[8, 75]$ = 1.97, p > .05) nor the attachment relationship × birth group interaction ($F[16, 150]$ = 1.35, p > .1) was significant. Follow-up univariate ANOVAs revealed a significant effect of attachment relationship for both the Q-sort and the Ainsworth Rating measures of maternal sensitivity at 8 months and for infant attachment security scores and Secure-Base Behavior, Enjoyment of Physical Contact, and Fussy/Difficult scale scores derived from the mothers' Q-sorts at 12 months; the univariate tests for Affective Sharing and Compliance were not significant. Further follow-up tests (Duncan's multiple range test, p < .05) revealed that, 4 months prior to the classification of their attachment rela-

TABLE 2

INTERACTIONS OF MOTHERS AT 8 MONTHS AND INFANTS AT 12 MONTHS IN AVOIDANT, SECURE, AND AMBIVALENT RELATIONSHIPS

| | RELATIONSHIP CLASSIFICATION | | | | | | | |
| | Avoidant (N = 25) | | Secure (N = 43) | | Ambivalent (N = 21) | | | |
	M	SD	M	SD	M	SD	$F(2, 86)^a$	p
Age 8 months (observer's data) maternal sensitivity:								
Ainsworth Ratings	4.83	1.49	7.27	1.45	4.10	2.22	31.72	< .001
Q-sort scores	.02	.39	.58	.31	-.14	.47	31.93	< .001
Age 12 months (mother's AQS):								
Attachment security	.34	.17	.44	.15	.28	.13	8.96	< .001
Domain scores:								
Secure-Base Behavior	5.73	.69	6.16	.59	5.56	.49	8.12	< .001
Affective Sharing	6.18	1.04	6.52	1.10	6.53	.98	.94	N.S.
Compliance	5.45	1.30	5.79	1.20	5.44	1.22	.70	N.S.
Enjoyment of Physical Contact	6.00	1.34	6.82	1.14	7.09	1.29	5.16	< .01
Fussy/Difficult	2.97	.75	3.15	1.00	4.15	.97	10.35	< .001

[a] $df = (2, 86)$, except for maternal data, where $df = (2, 85)$.

tionship, mothers in secure relationships were judged to be more sensitive by the observers than mothers in nonsecure relationships; the mothers in the latter two groups did not significantly differ in sensitivity.

This same pattern of results was obtained for the 12-month data derived from mothers' Q-sorts: mothers in secure relationships described their infants as more secure and as engaging in more secure-base behavior than mothers in avoidant or ambivalent relationships; once again, attachment security scores and Secure-Base Behavior scale scores did not differ between the two nonsecure relationships. Follow-up contrasts for Enjoyment of Physical Contact indicated that mothers in avoidant relationships described their infants as enjoying contact less than mothers in secure or ambivalent relationships. The Fussy/Difficult scores for infants in ambivalent relationships were significantly higher than those for infants in secure or avoidant relationships.

Correlates of 12-Month Maternal Sensitivity and Infant Security Scores

Birth and demographic variables.—Gestational age, birth weight, and number of days in the hospital were not significantly correlated with measures of maternal sensitivity or infant attachment security derived from the observers' records from the 8- or the 12-month visits (the absolute values of the r's ranged from .07 to .18). Infant attachment security scores derived from the mothers' AQSs were marginally but significantly correlated with length of hospitalization ($r = -.23, p < .05$) but not with birth weight ($r = .18$) or gestational age ($r = .18$).

Mother's age showed no significant relation to any of the measures of maternal sensitivity or infant attachment security. Mother's years of education were correlated with observers' assessments of sensitivity and security (r's ranged from .30 to .33, p's $< .01$) but not with the mothers' AQS security scores ($r = .09$). Father's education was correlated with observer maternal sensitivity and AQS security scores as well as the mothers' AQS security scores (r's ranged from .22 to .29, p's $< .05$).

Correlates of 12-month infant attachment security scores.—As shown in Table 3, observers' assessments of maternal sensitivity at both the 8- and the 12-month visits correlated significantly with the AQS indices of infant attachment security.

Because observers' maternal sensitivity scores at age 12 months were based on observations of the same interactions as their infant attachment security scores, no parallel correlations between these two sets of data were computed. Note, however, that using one observer's 12-month maternal sensitivity scores and the other observer's infant attachment security scores

TABLE 3

CORRELATIONS OF 12-MONTH INFANT ATTACHMENT SECURITY SCORES DERIVED FROM OBSERVERS' AND FROM MOTHERS' Q-SORTS

OBSERVERS' DATA	INFANT 12-MONTH AQS ATTACHMENT SECURITY			INFANT 12-MONTH AQS ATTACHMENT SECURITY	
	Observers' Scores	Mothers' Scores	OBSERVERS' DATA	Observers' Scores	Mothers' Scores
8-month maternal sensitivity:			12-month maternal sensitivity:		
Ainsworth Ratings........	.62**	.29*	Ainsworth Ratings........		.44**
Q-sort scores	.61**	.30*	Q-sort scores		.49**

NOTE.—Correlations between observer assessments of maternal sensitivity and infant security at 12 months are not given because they are based on the same observations.

* $p < .01$.

** $p < .001$.

yielded an r of .84 ($p < .001$). All the above correlations were very similar within the preterm and the full-term groups and were not substantially altered in magnitude when the effects of either birth weight or parents' education were partialed out. The correlations of the 8-month assessment of maternal sensitivity with the 12-month assessments of sensitivity and security in those cases in which the same person observed at the two time periods did not differ substantially from the correlations where different persons observed, thus ruling out the possibility that impressions from the earlier visit inflated the correlations between the two time periods.

DISCUSSION

Relationship Classifications

The infant-mother attachment relationship is a hypothetical construct that characterizes the implicit set of rules governing the structure of the dyadic interactions. This structure (described by Bowlby, 1969/1982, as an "internal working model") guides the interactions of both the infant and the mother. Although each dyad may operate under some unique rules, Ainsworth et al. (1978) have shown the theoretical power of clustering these structures into secure, avoidant, and ambivalent forms. The relationship structure cannot be directly observed, but it can be inferred from infant-mother interactions. The procedures for inferring these structures have been most explicitly described in the classification system that Ainsworth et al. (1978) developed for Strange Situation observations.

The Strange Situation offers many advantages for the assessment of infant-mother relationships. It is a standardized procedure, which facilitates comparisons across dyads, and the videotape record can be repeatedly viewed by different observers, thus expediting the establishment of interobserver agreement and cross-research group replication. The most important advantage of the method lies in the extensive research literature reporting antecedent (e.g., Ainsworth et al., 1971; Belsky, Rovine, & Taylor, 1984; Fonagy, Steele, & Steele, 1991), concurrent (e.g., Ainsworth et al., 1978; Braungart & Stifter, 1991; Smith & Pederson, 1988), and subsequent (e.g., Matas, Arend, & Sroufe, 1978; Sroufe, 1983) differences in both child and maternal behaviors related to the three main attachment classifications.

Despite these advantages, the Strange Situation methodology entails at least two limitations to a full understanding of the expression of attachment relationships. First, the novelty of the Strange Situation procedures leads to a description of how the relationship functions in response to the stresses of this particular, unusual context, but how the relationship functions in more typical and presumably ecologically valid contexts is not necessarily revealed. Our home-based relationship classification system is an attempt to/ characterize relationships in the context in which they develop. Second, constraints are placed on the mother's behavior in the Strange Situation both explicitly, by the instructions, and implicitly, by the demand characteristics of the laboratory context; thus, the procedure does not allow an unrestrained assessment of the role that the mother plays in the expression of the relationship. Since it appears that variations in maternal characteristics are more strongly associated with different attachment relationships than are variations in infant characteristics in both normal (e.g., Ainsworth et al., 1978; Belsky, Rovine, & Taylor, 1984; Smith & Pederson, 1988) and clinical (van IJzendoorn, Goldberg, et al., 1992) samples, observation of the mother's role in the expression of the relationship is vital to a more complete understanding of relationship structures.

The validity of our system of relationship classifications was substantiated by two sets of findings. First, mothers deemed to be in secure relationships with their 12-month-olds were judged 4 months earlier to be more sensitive during interactions with their infants than mothers in nonsecure relationships. Attachment theorists (e.g., Ainsworth et al., 1971; Bowlby, 1969/1982; Sroufe, 1985) have consistently maintained that maternal sensitivity is the distinguishing characteristic of mothers in secure relationships. Second, the mothers' AQS descriptions of their infants' attachment-relevant behavior discriminated among the three relationship groupings. Just as maternal sensitivity is the principal characteristic of mothers in secure relationships, attachment security and secure-base behavior are defining features of infants in secure relationships. Consistent with this criterial expectation, infant attachment security and Secure-Base Behavior scale scores derived from the mothers' AQSs were higher for infants in secure than for those in nonsecure relationships.

However, our expectations that affective sharing and compliance would also be more characteristic of infants in secure relationships were not confirmed. In addition to the possibility that our expectations were unfounded, our failure to find a relationship effect for the Affective Sharing scale could also be reasonably attributed to reliability problems: this scale includes only three items, and the agreement between observers' and mothers' scores was very low. The Compliance scale has relatively low internal consistency, and, in addition, it may be difficult for mothers, or for items on the AQS, to detect the subtle differences between the cooperative spirit that motivates secure infants and the defensive compliance that may characterize infants in nonsecure relationships. Alternatively, it may be that further detailed descriptions of distinct aspects of naturalistic interactions may reveal unanticipated patterns of infant-mother interactions that may prompt a reformulation of our notions of the distinctive features of secure relationships.

Ainsworth and Bell (1970) and Main (1990), among others, have noted that infants in avoidant relationships are uncomfortable with physical contact with their mothers; in accordance with this observation, the Enjoyment of Physical Contact scale derived from the mothers' AQSs distinguished infants in avoidant relationships from those in secure and in ambivalent relationships. As Cassidy (1994) has pointed out in her conceptual analysis of affect regulation and attachment, infants in ambivalent relationships would be expected to be emotionally overreactive; confirming this expectation, mothers in ambivalent relationships reported their infants to be fussier and more difficult. Thus, the independent descriptions of both maternal and infant behavior that we obtained in this study proved consistent with predictions from attachment theory and research; the finding that descriptions of infant behavior provided by the mothers distinguished all three attachment relationship classifications is particularly noteworthy.

Although we were successful in using AQS-derived scales to identify infant behaviors that distinguished the three attachment relationship groups, further work on the Maternal Behavior Q-Set is needed to develop analogous scales to index different domains of maternal attachment-relevant behavior. The items in the Maternal Behavior Q-Set were explicitly designed to distinguish sensitive from nonsensitive maternal behavior, and the data indicate that this goal appears to have been successfully attained. Recent conceptualizations of maternal behavior that may characterize mothers in avoidant and in ambivalent relationships (Cassidy, 1994; Cassidy & Berlin, 1994) will be particularly useful in developing additional Q-set items and scales aimed at distinguishing maternal behavior in these two forms of nonsecure relationships.

The proportion of secure dyads (51%) in our study is not markedly dissimilar from the 57% reported by Egeland and Farber (1984) and the 55% reported by Vaughn and Waters (1990). These figures are in contrast with the cross-national average of 65% reported by van IJzendoorn and Kroonenberg (1988), who also note considerable sample-to-sample fluctuation in the frequency distributions of attachment classifications and recommend caution in interpreting variations in single samples.

Preterm/Full-Term Contrasts

We expected that the link between maternal sensitivity and infant attachment security would be stronger within the preterm sample, reasoning that success in overcoming the developmental challenges of prematurity would require greater levels of sensitivity on the part of the mother. Contrary to this expectation, the correlations within each birth group proved to be similar in magnitude. This result may be related to the fact that, by 8 months postterm, mothers of this particular sample of generally healthy preterm infants reported few if any differences in emotional stress as compared to mothers in the full-term group (Pederson et al., 1987). It appears that, although preterm birth is stressful, the dynamics of interaction reflected by the relation between maternal sensitivity and infant attachment security do not differ from those observed in a full-term sample. Other investigators have reported similar findings that, although preterm birth is stressful, there are few if any differences with full-term samples in measures of infant-mother interactions or relationships by the end of the first year (e.g., Crnic, Greenberg, Ragozin, Robinson, & Basham, 1983; van IJzendoorn, Goldberg, et al., 1992).

Predictions of Attachment Security

Assessments of maternal sensitivity at 8 months of age were predictive of independent indices of the infant's attachment security at 12 months as derived from both mothers' and observers' judgments. These results are consistent with the fundamental postulate of attachment theory, namely, that the nature and quality of the attachment relationship is determined by interactions between the infant and the caregiver. Ainsworth has proposed a strong developmental model in which variation in maternal sensitivity is hypothesized to be the direct developmental antecedent of the infant's attachment security (see, e.g., Ainsworth et al., 1978, chap. 8); our findings are consistent with such a model.

Despite this consistency, we favor an alternative conceptualization of the link between maternal sensitivity and infant security (Moran & Pederson, 1992), one in which the conceptual framework shifts from a causally linked model to an organized system. A number of authors have argued for the utility of applying a systems perspective to the study of various aspects of human development (e.g., Fogel & Thelen, 1987; Oyama, 1989), and Hinde's (1987) discussion of dialectical relations between levels of social organization also encourages a shift to thinking about social development beyond the constraints of traditional causal explanations.

In Hinde's model, not only do the actions of each interactant reciprocally influence those of the other, but their past history of interaction also shapes those actions, which, in turn, modify their relationship—and so on ad infinitum. Hinde calls this inherently dynamic but stable interplay among conceptual levels "the dialectics of social behavior." In the current context, this model makes explicit the fact that caregiver behavior cannot be seen in any meaningful developmental sense as being a characteristic of the mother in isolation but must rather be conceived as a reflection of the current interaction between her infant and herself as well as of the current structure of their relationship.

Sroufe and Fleeson (1986, 1988) have also maintained that the caregiver-infant relationship must be understood as an organized whole in which the stable element is the relationship itself, not the characteristics of the interactants. In their view, the social dynamics are conceptualized as changes in the interactive behavior of each individual that are associated with complementary changes in the behavior of the partner. The result is a goal-directed system in which the behavior of each interactant is structured to complement the behavior of the social partner within the constraints of the relationship and in which the interactive behaviors function to maintain the organization of the relationship. Rather than a model in which maternal sensitivity—a characteristic of the mother—determines infant attachment security—a characteristic of the infant—a relationship perspective implies that both the mother's sensitivity and the infant's security are reflections of the dyad's interactional dynamics. Maternal sensitivity and infant security are constructs about the same interactions—in the first instance the observer is focused on the mother's behavior, in the second on the infant's. From a systems perspective, it makes no sense to assume that these two constructs could be independent or that maternal sensitivity "causes" attachment security.

In conclusion, the results of the current study provide a reaffirmation of the strength of Ainsworth's (Ainsworth et al., 1971; Ainsworth et al., 1978) conceptualization of distinct attachment relationships. We have used her original concepts that have proved so powerful in the context of the Strange Situation to develop descriptions of infant-mother relationships as manifested in the less structured naturalistic environment. The resultant descriptions were differentially related to antecedent and concurrent descriptions of maternal and infant interactive behavior in the home. Secure, avoidant, and ambivalent relationships were found to be associated with distinctive styles of naturalistic interactions, and these differences are consistent with the basic tenets of attachment theory.

Although the AQS and the Maternal Behavior Q-Set provided the basis for the association between attachment relationships and distinct patterns of home interaction, both instruments are limited by their emphasis on the secure/nonsecure distinction. It is increasingly evident that our ability to explore the organizational principles and developmental antecedents of avoidant and ambivalent relationships will require the development of descriptions that reflect the unique characteristics of these relationships and not simply their dissimilarity with patterns of interaction in secure relationships.

APPENDIX:
CRITERIAL DESCRIPTIONS USED TO CLASSIFY
ATTACHMENT RELATIONSHIPS BETWEEN MOTHERS AND
THEIR 12-MONTH-OLD INFANTS OBSERVED IN THE HOME

Avoidant (A) Relationships

The goal of an avoidant relationship is to contain negative affect in the context of the relationship. The infant has learned skills of affective control, for example, by distracting herself or finding ways to self-soothe such as lying on the floor or approaching the visitor. The mother responds to her infant's overtures for comfort by redirecting the child's attention outward, both emotionally and physically.

A1 Relationships

We distinguish two types of A1 relationships that seem to differ in terms of the mother's involvement with the infant.

A1a (teaching relationship).—The infant is typically very competent, sociable, and friendly with visitors. Mother and infant often function well together in the restricted domain of cognitive tasks, although the infant may turn away if the mother pushes too hard. Although the relationship is focused on the cognitive domain, there is surprisingly little affective sharing initiated by the infant, even around successes on the developmental assessments (thus distinguishing this dyad from a B1 relationship; see below). The mother is very interested in and devoted to her infant's development, treating cognitive development as a "project" that she regiments with her own program. Because of this involvement, the mother will be intrusive (ratings of 3 or less on Ainsworth's cooperation-interference scale), but the intrusiveness is often subtle. Affection is expressed via praise that is clearly contingent on the infant's performance. As Ainsworth pointed out long ago, the little physical affection that is expressed is often in the form of kissing the infant's head—sort of pecks of affection.

A1b (ignoring relationship).—The infant is competent in controlling affect—if hurt, the infant will attempt to contain tears; the infant may cry but will not seek contact unless very upset. The infant is very independent of the mother, with little or no affective sharing, contact, or interaction. The infant may be more animated and affectionate in interactions with a visitor than with the mother (except for babies who are temperamentally shy or cautious). The mother redirects the infant's overtures for contact outward. When the mother responds to the infant's fusses or cries, she distracts the infant from the affect by offering food, toys, or other diversions. It is often difficult to get a sense of the relationship since both mother and infant operate effectively independently. Perhaps more than any non-B relationship, A1b dyads function smoothly. Neither party in the dyad seems dysfunctional (as long as you forget that you are observing an infant-mother and not an adult-adult relationship). The mother will get low scores on the accessibility-ignoring scale (3 or lower). Some mothers appear dysphoric; others are more interested in interacting with a visitor than with the infant.

A2 Relationships

Unlike A1 relationships, A2 relationships are not smooth. The infant tends to be fussy and will sometimes approach the mother for contact (at other times she will try to comfort herself). The approaches are not satisfactory for either the mother or the infant—sometimes the infant tries too hard to get comfort, and the mother is unresponsive; other times the mother is responsive, and the infant is cool and unresponsive. It is often difficult to discern the differences between A2 and ambivalent (C1; see below) relationships. In both types, there is overt discordance, and infants are fussy and frequently seek proximity. In A2 relationships, fussiness does not have a petulant quality that interferes with settling—A2 infants try (unsuccessfully) to settle themselves and attempt to use the mother as a source of comfort. It is as if they are trying to be A1 infants but cannot contain their negative emotions. They differ from C1 infants in that the fussiness appears to be elicited by factors outside the relationship—such as frustration with toys or falling down—rather than by the relationship itself.

Secure (B) Relationships

Although secure relationships come in various forms, coherence is the key marker for all of them. Both the mother and the infant are relatively easy to describe, both individually and as a dyad. Very few of their behaviors seem puzzling or dissonant. The infant obviously obtains a sense of security from the mother, and the mother is clearly interested in and responsive to her infant.

B1 Relationships

The infant engages in independent exploration, with little proximity seeking. Most infants are outgoing both with the mother and with visitors and engage in frequent affective sharing, with vocalizations and smiles directed toward the mother. Unlike A1 infants, B1 infants have a rich affective repertoire with their mothers and clearly show a preference for her over a visitor in times of stress.

B2 Relationships

Descriptions of B2 relationships at home have not been developed because the distinctive patterns that would distinguish these from other secure relationships in the relatively low-stress context of home observations are not definitive.

B3 Relationships

The infant's secure-base behavior is obvious; the infant explores away from the mother and engages in frequent affective sharing both over a distance and in close proximity. If the infant is upset, contact provides comfort—both the mother and the infant are interested in being sure that the contact is effective. The mother takes delight in her infant, knows her infant, and freely discusses both positive and negative aspects of her behavior. The mother monitors the infant but does allow independent exploration.

B4 Relationships

The infant needs lots of contact and is content when in contact. Sometimes the infant will be fussy (observers get the impression that the fussiness occurs because it is physically impossible to get as close to the mother as the infant wants), but the fussiness has a feisty rather than an angry or a passive tone. It may be difficult to determine differences between B3 and B4 infants in the home setting since many B4 infants explore away from the mother—it is often a matter of noting the amount of contact maintenance that is needed. Some B4 babies also seem to be fussier than one would expect with B3 infants. Mothers tend to encourage dependency and enjoy cuddling with their infants.

Ambivalent (C) Relationships

Ambivalent relationships frequently feature interactions that appear maladaptive and incoherent despite periods of harmony; intense affect, often negative in tone, appears to be a predominant behavioral feature. Observers sometimes find home visits confusing because, although interactions often seem angry and hostile, these emotions are not clearly linked to the actual content of the current interaction. In contrast to avoidant relationships, ambivalent relationships are organized around intense affective interchanges whose seemingly paradoxical function is to maintain

131

close contact and a sense of intense connection between the mother and the infant, thus interfering with exploration.

C1 Relationships

The distinction between A2 and C1 relationships at home is a difficult call. C1 infants are more overtly angry and do not attempt to contain their anger; the mother may have periods of anger as well. There are also moments of coming together. The visits are often confusing since there seems to be little coherence in the behavior of the mother or that of the infant. Researchers who find themselves asking, "Why did the mother (or the infant) do that?" should be thinking about a C1 relationship.

C2 Relationships

The striking feature of C2 infants is their passivity. The infant seems to have given up on being instrumental in meeting attachment needs and will sit and fuss with a helpless, pathetic cry. Often this style spills over to other aspects of behavior so that exploration is unorganized and immature. The infant seems to have an overriding sense that life it too negative and overwhelming and that there is nothing that can be done that will make a difference. The mother is inconsistent, sometimes being responsive and other times seemingly oblivious to her infant, for no discernible reason. This inconsistency also extends to her descriptions of the infant. Sometimes the descriptions are positive but unconnected with the reality of the infant's behavior, and at other times they include superficially lighthearted pejoratives that suggest thinly veiled hostility. Mothers are often given a rating of 1 on Ainsworth's acceptance-rejection scale, although for some mothers rejection is so subtle and mixed with strong acceptance that it is difficult to justify a low score. The rejection often has a dispassionate tone.

IS IT EASIER TO USE A SECURE MOTHER AS A SECURE BASE? ATTACHMENT Q-SORT CORRELATES OF THE ADULT ATTACHMENT INTERVIEW

German Posada, Everett Waters, Judith A. Crowell, and Keng-Ling Lay

Attachment theory hypothesizes that the quality of the child-mother attachment relationship is greatly influenced by the caregiving environment. The principal caregiver is considered to play a crucial role in affecting the organization of a child's attachment behavior and ultimately of her attachment system (Bowlby, 1969/1982). Current caregiver-child interactions, the history of previous interactions, and the context in which the attachment relationship develops determine the organization of a child's attachment behavior.

Because the mother is generally the child's principal caregiver, maternal characteristics in mother-child interactions have been studied in relation to child attachment outcomes. For instance, characteristics such as sensitivity-insensitivity, acceptance-rejection, cooperation-interference, and accessibility-ignoring in maternal behavior at home during the infant's first year were found to be associated with the pattern of attachment behavior that a child shows in the Strange Situation (Ainsworth, Blehar, Waters, & Wall, 1978; Grossmann, Grossmann, Spangler, Suess, & Unzner, 1985). Pederson and Moran (in this volume) report strong associations between observers' ratings of maternal behavior on an aggregate score (Ainsworth Ratings) and on Q-sort descriptions of maternal behavior (summarized as maternal sensitivity) when children were 8 months old at home and observers' Q-sort descriptions of secure-base behavior at home when children were 12 months old.

In order to explain individual differences when mothers interact with

This research was partially supported by a grant from the National Institute of Mental Health (R01 MH-44935).

their children, researchers have looked at variables that hypothetically may be associated with such differences. In the last 9 years, attention has started to turn to caregivers' current conceptualizations of their own attachment relationships and to the relation that such conceptualizations may bear to qualities of both mothers' caregiving and children's attachment behavior. This movement has in part been due to the development of the Adult Attachment Interview (AAI), an instrument specifically designed to assess adults' current narratives of their early attachment relationships (George, Kaplan, & Main, 1984; Main & Goldwyn, 1991).

Briefly, the AAI is a semistructured interview that asks for descriptions of early relationships and attachment-related events and for adults' views of how these relationships and events have affected their adult personality (the AAI is described more fully in the Method section below). There are four major adult attachment categories according to which adults are classified: autonomous, dismissing, preoccupied, and unresolved. The latter three are considered insecure representations or conceptualizations of attachment (the category unresolved was added to the classification system later than the other three categories; because of this, early studies report findings concerning only three groups).

The hypothesis implied in most research using this new instrument is that individuals' current conceptualizations of attachment reflect the organization of their underlying working model of attachment. This model is expected to influence the ways in which a caregiver interacts with her or his child and is therefore presumed to affect the quality of the child-caregiver attachment relationship. Further, the argument hypothesizes that caregivers' working models of attachment are transmitted intergenerationally to the child via what the latter experiences in the mother-child relationship. Correspondence is expected, therefore, between the caregiver's conceptualization of attachment and the organization of the child's attachment behavior.

The AAI classifications have been found to relate to children's secure-base behavior in the Strange Situation in retrospective, concurrent, and prospective studies. Concerning retrospective studies, Main, Kaplan, and Cassidy (1985) assigned security scores to children in the different Strange Situation categories and to parents interviewed with the AAI and reported a significant correlation between adults' internal model of attachment and early infant security of attachment for both mothers ($r = .62$, $p < .001$) and fathers ($r = .37$, $p < .05$); the children were observed at 12 and 18 months of age, and parents were interviewed when their children were 6 years old.

Using a classification system for the AAI that differs from that of Main and her colleagues, Grossmann, Fremmer-Bombik, Rudolph, and Grossmann (1988) found concordance for the secure-insecure dimension in two

German samples. In one of these (Bielefeld), maternal classifications contrasting attachment-valuing and attachment-devaluing representations corresponded with children's Strange Situation secure/insecure classifications in 13 of 15 cases (85%); in the other (Regensburg), the same held true for 35 of 45 cases (78%). As in Main et al.'s (1985) study, the children had been seen in the Strange Situation at age 12 months, and their mothers were interviewed when the child was 5 (Regensburg) or 6 (Bielefeld) years old.

In a Dutch study, van IJzendoorn, Kranenburg, Zwart-Woudstra, van Busschbach, and Lambermon (1991) found that 20 of 26 (77%) mothers were classified in the same attachment category (secure/insecure) that had applied to their 12-month-old children in the Strange Situation some 2–3 years earlier. The results obtained for fathers were not significant (62% level of correspondence). Using a three-group classification system (autonomous, dismissing, and preoccupied for adults, secure, avoidant, and resistant for children), there was not a significant correspondence between the AAI and the Strange Situation for either mothers or fathers.

In a study of kibbutz mothers and children, the secure/insecure attachment classifications of the dyads matched in 76% of the cases in families where children slept at home. However, the correspondence was much lower when sleeping arrangements were communal; the match in this latter case was not significant (Sagi et al., 1993; Sagi et al., 1992).

Studies assessing children's attachment behavior and mothers' conceptualizations of attachment concurrently have reported similar results. Ainsworth and Eichberg (1991) assessed children's quality of attachment at 12–18 months and mothers' conceptualizations of attachment 2–6 months later. These authors reported 80% correspondence between the two classification systems when the children were classified in the avoidant (A), secure (B), resistant (C), and disorganized (D) distribution and 90% correspondence when mother-child pairs of children classified as disorganized were omitted from the analysis. In a study in which children's Strange Situation and mothers' AAI assessments were both conducted when the child was 12 months old, Zeanah et al. (1993) found a significant match between the two assessments; the concordance between children being classed as A, B, or C and their mothers as dismissing, secure, or preoccupied was 75% (κ = .62).

With regard to prospective studies, Levine, Tuber, Slade, and Ward (1991) found that attachment conceptualizations of adolescent mothers during pregnancy and their children's attachment behavior at 15 months of age were significantly related; exact agreement was reported for 62% of the sample (26 of 42 pairs), and agreement on the general secure/insecure distinction was 83% (35 of 42 pairs). Fonagy, Steele, and Steele (1991) interviewed 96 mothers and fathers during the last trimester of pregnancy and found that these parents' attachment classifications significantly matched those their children obtained in a Strange Situation assessment at age 12 months. The overall secure/insecure match for mother-child pairs was 75% (κ = .48, p < .001), and the three-way match was 66% (κ = .38, p < .001); for father-child pairs the association was weaker yet significant (Fonagy, Steele, Moran, Steele, & Higgit, 1991). Finally, Radojevic (1992) interviewed fathers prior to the birth of their children and assessed the quality of the child-father attachment relationship in the Strange Situation when the child was 15 months of age. The secure/insecure distinction yielded a 77% match between children and their fathers; using all four classification categories of both systems decreased this value to 56%.

In sum, all the studies we have reviewed indicate significant levels of correspondence between both attachment classification systems for mother-child pairs, especially when the match is restricted to the secure/insecure distinction. The results are not as strong for father-child dyads, and in one case (van IJzendoorn et al., 1991) no significant association was found.

Since the AAI classification system was originally developed on the basis of differences in the quality of transcripts obtained from parents whose children had been assigned to different groups in the Strange Situation assessment, it is important that studies originating in different laboratories and with independent samples have replicated the concordance reported by Main et al. (1985). However, it remains important to demonstrate that an association between the mother's current conceptualizations of attachment relationships and her child's secure-base behavior also exists in other contexts, that is, in nonemergency, ordinary, everyday life circumstances such as at home. After all, it is in the home where the phenomenon is taking place and being shaped. Also, it is important to seek to demonstrate the hypothesized association between constructs with diverse methodologies. With these considerations in mind, we investigated in this study the relations between Attachment Q-Set (AQS; Waters, 1987) descriptions of children's behavior at home and mothers' attachment conceptualizations assessed with the AAI (George et al., 1984).

In addition, we investigated whether the behavior of children whose mothers were classified on the AAI as unresolved was similar to the secure-base behavior of those whose mothers were classified as dismissing and preoccupied. AAI transcripts are first assigned to a primary classification category (secure, dismissing, or preoccupied), then reclassed with respect to the unresolved category; in this latter step, a classification of unresolved overrides any classification that may have been assigned initially. Dismissing, preoccupied, and unresolved are considered to be insecure (anxious) attachment classifications; the unresolved classification has been associated with (i.e., it is hypothesized to correspond to) the disorganized category of the Strange Situation coding system. This disorganized (D) category was added to the system relatively recently by Main and Solomon (1986), and no data linking it to attachment behavior at home exist. The question that we asked concerns whether the secure-base behavior at home of children of mothers classified as unresolved differs from that of children of mothers classified as insecure (dismissing or preoccupied).

METHOD

Subjects

The sample consisted of 51 mother-child pairs. The children's ages ranged from 50 to 59 months (average = 54 months); 27 were girls and 22 boys, and all were white and came from intact families, except for three children whose parents had separated. The mothers' ages ranged from 26 to 49 years (average = 36.5 years), and their level of education ranged from 12 (high school) to 18 (Ph.D. degree) years (average = 14.7 years). The data obtained from two child-mother pairs could not be used in data analysis because of technical problems with audiotapes of their interviews; thus, the sample was reduced to 49 child-mother pairs.

Measures

The Adult Attachment Interview (AAI)

The mother's current conceptualization of her attachment experiences was assessed with the AAI (George et al., 1984). The AAI is a semistructured interview that asks for descriptions of early relationships and attachment-related events as well as for the adult's view of how these relationships and events have affected her or his adult personality. Subjects' verbal accounts are presumed to reflect their current state of mind regarding attachment.

Classification of an interview is obtained using rating scales for both the subject's parent-child relationship experiences and her or his style of discourse, that is, how past experiences are described and the ability to provide an integrated, coherent, and believable account of these experiences and their meaning. There are four major classifications: secure (autonomous), dismissing, preoccupied, and unresolved. The latter three are considered to reflect insecure representations, or conceptualizations, of attachment.

Subjects classified as *secure* describe early relationship experiences that may be either positive or negative; in either case, they maintain a balanced view of such experiences, value attachment relationships, and view attachment-related experiences as influential to their development. In all, these subjects present coherent, thoughtful, and believable accounts of their attachment experiences. Subjects classified as *dismissing* tend to deny the effects of early attachment experiences or to consider such effects as limited; they often have difficulties recalling specific events and tend to idealize experiences. Subjects classified as *preoccupied* tend to express confusion about past experiences and about attachment figures, and their accounts show a lack of coherence and an inability to gain insight into early events; expressions of anger toward parents or passivity of speech may be present. When deemed appropriate, the classification of *unresolved* is given in addition to one of the other three classifications, superseding it. That is, transcripts are assigned to a primary classification category (secure, dismissing, or preoccupied) and then classified with respect to the unresolved category, which takes precedence for the final classification of a transcript. This category includes subjects who have experienced attachment-related trauma, usually involving the loss of, or abuse by, an attachment figure, that has not been resolved or reconciled.

The interviews were classified by three coders who had been trained by Mary Main. Since the unresolved classification is assigned independently of the three major classifications, interrater agreement was calculated separately for the three major classifications and for the unresolved classification. Agreement was calculated on 39 (of the 49) interview transcripts. Results indicated 77% agreement (κ = .69) for the initial three-way classifications and 85% agreement (κ = .60) for the unresolved classification. Any disagreements on the classification of transcripts were discussed, and the most experienced of the three raters (Judith Crowell) decided on the classification category.

The Attachment Q-Set (AQS)

Children's secure-base behavior at home was assessed with the 90-item version of the AQS (see App. A, in this volume). One 2½–3-hour home visit was conducted by two observers for 33 mother-child pairs and by one observer for 16 pairs. The observers watched child-mother interactions and played with the child; after the visit, each observer independently completed a Q-sort description of the child's behavior. Interobserver reliability coefficients for the 33 children described by two observers ranged between .54 and .89 (average = .78); the two sorts were then averaged into a single composite. The sort provided by a single observer was used in the remaining 16 instances. A child's *security score* was obtained by correlating her or his composite Q-sort description with the criterion sort that describes the theoretically secure child (see App. D). Thus, attachment secure-base behavior is assessed on a continuum of security rather than categorically.

In addition to the global security score, children were also scored on four scales that had been derived (by German Posada and Everett Waters) from the AQS with an independent sample of 45 children by averaging the placement of items contained in the given scale. The items selected were those that were conceptually related to the construct *using the mother as a secure base* and that could be observed in home visits. These items included behavior central to the secure-base phenomenon, child behavior when interacting with her or his mother, and behavior with other adults that was mediated by the mother. A principal component analysis was run, and four factors emerged (Posada & Waters, 1995). Items were assigned to the scales on the basis of their loadings on each factor. In addition, items originally not selected were correlated with the four factors and included if they correlated significantly ($p < .01$) with any of the factors. Each scale was named on the basis of the content of the items included in it. These scales, thus, refer to more specific domains of child behavior covered by the AQS.

The scales are as follows:

1. *Smooth interactions with mother.*—This scale contains 17 items (internal consistency = .91). Some items concern the child's emotional tone when interacting with the mother and her or his readiness to interact with her. Others concern issues of compliance. For example, "Child readily shares with mother or lets her hold things if she asks to"; "Child follows mother's suggestions readily."

2. *Proximity to mother.*—This scale contains 13 items (internal consistency = .77). Some items concern going back to the mother, keeping track of her location, and staying near to or far from her, others going back to the mother when upset, bored, and when needing help. For example, "Child keeps track of mother's location when s/he plays around the house"; "When something upsets the child, s/he goes to mother when s/he cries."

3. *Physical contact with mother.*—This scale contains seven items (internal consistency = .80). Some items concern enjoyment of physical contact. Others are about being comforted by contact with the mother. For example, "Child enjoys relaxing in mother's lap"; "If held in mothers' arms, child stops crying and quickly recovers after being frightened or upset."

4. *Interactions with other adults.*—This scale contains 13 items (internal consistency = .81). Some items refer to readiness to interact, to share, and to enjoy interactions with adult visitors. Others involve interactions with other adults with the mother's encouragement and support. For example, "Child readily lets new adults hold or share thing s/he has, if they ask"; "Child is willing to talk to new people, show them toys, or show them what s/he can do, if mother asks her/him to."

A full listing of items contained in each scale can be found in Appendix D.

Procedures

Subjects were recruited from local nursery schools, through announce-ments placed on bulletin boards in toy stores, and from another study that was ongoing at the time of recruitment. Of the 49 mother-child pairs, 19 were participating in that other project. The study was described to all the subjects, and arrangements were made to conduct a home visit and to inter-view the mother.

Each mother-child pair was visited at home on one occasion for 2½–3 hours. Approximately 1 hour of the home visit was devoted to structured activity between the mother and her child, who were asked to bake cupcakes together using a prepackaged mix; in addition, the mother was asked to read to her child from a story book that the observers had brought along. Many of the behavioral items included in the AQS were easily unveiled in these situations. The observers were especially careful not to disrupt child-mother interactions when they were working together. The rest of the visit was unstructured, and the observers watched the child's behavior and interacted freely with both the mother and the child.

The AAI was conducted at the university laboratory before the home visit for 19 subjects; for the remainder it was conducted after the home visit at a place convenient for the mother (either at home or at the university). Both the interviewers and the coders of the interviews had no access to information about children's behavior observed in the home visits, and the observers of child behavior had no access to information about the mothers' AAI. Mothers were paid $25.00 when the assessments were completed.

RESULTS

The number of mothers in each AAI classification group as well as the means and standard deviations of their children's security scores are presented in Table 1. Over the full sample, children's security scores ranged from −.16 to .70 (average = .40). (This mean is comparable to those ob-tained in other studies—e.g., those of Pederson et al., 1990, who reported a mean of .40, and Park & Waters, 1989, who reported means of .38 for girls and .41 for boys.)

The mothers' AAI classifications were first grouped as either secure (22 mothers, 45%) or insecure (dismissing, preoccupied, and unresolved; 27 mothers, 55%), and their children's security scores were compared. The percentages of mothers in the two groups are comparable to those obtained in other studies. (For a review of studies in nonclinical populations, see van IJzendoorn, 1992; the author reports a summary figure of 48% secure and 52% insecure across five studies.) The mean security score of children of

TABLE 1

SECURITY SCORES FOR CHILDREN OF MOTHERS CLASSIFIED
IN THE DIFFERENT AAI GROUPS

MOTHER's AAI CLASSIFICATION	CHILDREN's SECURITY SCORES		
	M	SD	Range
Secure (N = 22)	.48	.12	.07–.63
Dismissing (N = 9)	.34	.22	−.12–.64
Preoccupied (N = 4)	.48	.18	.32–.70
Unresolved (N = 14)	.29	.27	−.16–.60

secure mothers was .48 (SD = .12), that of children of insecure mothers .33 (SD = .24); the difference is statistically significant (t = 2.57, $p < .01$).[1]

To investigate further differences in children's security scores, planned comparisons were conducted between the secure group and each of the insecure groups. These contrasts indicated that security scores of children of secure mothers were significantly higher than those of children of unresolved mothers (F = 8.30, $p < .01$) and marginally higher than those of children of dismissing mothers (F = 3.03, $p < .09$). There was no significant difference between the security scores of children of secure and preoccupied mothers.

Children of secure and insecure mothers were also compared along each of the four scales derived from the AQS; means and standard deviations for these measures are presented in Table 2. The two groups differed significantly on "Smooth interactions with mother" and were marginally different on "Physical contact with mother"; in both cases, children of secure mothers obtained higher scores than children of insecure mothers. No significant differences were obtained on the other two scales.

Subsequent planned comparisons among all four groups on the scale "Smooth interactions with mother" revealed that children of secure mothers had significantly higher scores than those of dismissing (F = 6.91, $p < .01$) and unresolved (F = 7.03, $p < .01$) mothers. Planned comparisons on the scale "Physical contact with mother" revealed that children of secure mothers obtained marginally higher scores than those of unresolved mothers (F = 3.85, $p < .06$). The means, standard deviations, and range of scores for the four groups on each scale are provided in Table 3.

Finally, a planned comparison analysis was conducted to determine whether the security scores of children whose mothers were classed as unre-

---

[1] The same analysis was conducted using the three original AAI categories (i.e., secure, dismissing, and preoccupied). Results comparing secure (M = .46, SD = .16) and insecure (M = .31, SD = .25) groups were virtually identical.

TABLE 2

Comparison of Secure and Insecure Groups on the AQS Scales

	Secure Group		Insecure Group				
Scale	M	SD	M	SD	t	df	p
Smooth interactions with mother ...	6.9	.8	5.8	1.7	2.72	47	< .01
Proximity to mother.............	5.2	.9	5.1	1.1	.45	47	N.S.
Physical contact with mother.......	6.0	1.4	5.4	1.1	1.84	47	.07
Interactions with other adults......	6.4	1.1	6.4	1.3	.004	47	N.S.

solved ($N = 14$) differed significantly from those of children whose mothers had been classified in either one of the other two insecure categories (dismissing or preoccupied, $N = 13$). The mean of the group of children whose mothers were classified as unresolved was .29 (SD = .27); this did not differ significantly from the mean of .38 (SD = .21) obtained for the other two insecure groups ($F = 2.45$, p = N.S.).

TABLE 3

AQS Scale Scores Obtained for Children of Mothers Classified in the Different AAI Groups

	Children's Scale Scores[a]		
AQS Scales	M	SD	Range
"Smooth interactions with mother":[b]			
Secure ($N = 22$)	6.9	.80	5.2–7.9
Dismissing ($N = 9$)	5.5	1.3	3.7–7.2
Preoccupied ($N = 4$)	7.1	.86	6.0–7.8
Unresolved ($N = 14$)	5.7	1.9	2.9–7.6
"Proximity to mother"			
Secure ($N = 22$)	5.2	.86	3.4–6.8
Dismissing ($N = 9$)	5.5	1.3	3.5–7.3
Preoccupied ($N = 4$)	5.4	1.1	4.3–6.8
Unresolved ($N = 14$)	4.7	.99	3.3–6.3
"Physical contact with mother":[c]			
Secure ($N = 22$)	6.0	1.4	3.7–8.6
Dismissing ($N = 9$)	5.6	.87	3.5–6.9
Preoccupied ($N = 4$)	5.4	1.3	4.3–7.0
Unresolved ($N = 14$)	5.2	1.2	3.9–8.1
"Interactions with other adults"			
Secure ($N = 22$)	6.4	1.1	3.6–8.0
Dismissing ($N = 9$)	6.8	1.1	4.5–8.0
Preoccupied ($N = 4$)	6.1	1.3	5.3–8.0
Unresolved ($N = 14$)	6.2	1.4	2.3–8.0

[a] Average of placement of items contained in the scale.

[b] Mean for the secure group was significantly higher than that for the dismissing and unresolved groups.

[c] Mean for the secure group was significantly higher than that for the unresolved group.

DISCUSSION

The AAI classifications of mothers of preschoolers proved to be significantly associated with their children's secure-base behavior at home: except for children of preoccupied mothers, children of mothers whose transcripts were classified as secure scored higher on the AQS-derived security dimension than children whose mothers were classified as insecure (i.e., dismissing and unresolved). Thus, AAI classifications of mothers as secure or insecure were shown to be related to children's secure-base behavior in ordinary, everyday life circumstances.

This finding extends and supports previous results that were reviewed in the introduction and that show significant associations between mothers' AAI classifications and children's attachment behavior under the mildly stressful conditions of the Strange Situation. In addition, along with previous results presented by Main et al. (1985), our data provide evidence for the association between AAI classifications and secure-base behavior in older children: the majority of previous studies had demonstrated this association for children during their first 2 years of life, and this study extends the findings to preschool children.

As seen in the home, and focusing on specific behavioral domains tapped by the AQS scales used here, children of secure mothers interacted with them more smoothly than children of mothers categorized as dismissing and unresolved; they were more likely to share readily, to participate in give and take, to have a positive emotional tone, and to be compliant. Interactions of children of preoccupied mothers were characterized as being as smooth as those of children of secure mothers; however, since the number of children in each of the three insecure groups is low (especially in the preoccupied category), the absence of a statistically significant difference must be viewed with caution.

Children of secure mothers were also generally judged to enjoy physical contact with their mothers and to derive comfort from it more than children of insecure-unresolved mothers. Analyses of the other two AQS behavioral domains used here—"Proximity to mother" and "Interactions with other adults"—indicated that neither the quality of the child's interactions with other adults nor the extent to which the child tracked the mother and/or appeared aware of her proximity differentiated children of secure from those of insecure mothers.

Although the absence of between-group differences on the scale "Proximity to mother" was contrary to our expectations, this negative finding resembles Fonagy, Steele, and Steele's (1991) report of no differences in proximity- and contact-seeking behavior between children of secure and those of insecure mothers in the Strange Situation. It also conforms to results achieved by Vaughn and Waters (1990), who reported that ratings of proximity seeking in the Strange Situation (in episodes 5 and 8) were found not to contribute to the prediction of secure-base behavior at home as assessed with the AQS.

It is relevant to note here that the behavioral content of our "Proximity to mother" scale addresses the core of the secure-base phenomenon: it refers to "touching base" with the mother, checking on her location, and staying near her and to going to her when upset, bored, or needing help. Yet, regardless of their mothers' AAI classification, the children's home behavior did not differ in this regard even though other domains of interactions were seen to be associated with the mothers' classification as secure or insecure. This finding points out that, on average, children from all groups exhibited secure-base behavior, supporting Bowlby's (1969/1982) contention that the secure-base phenomenon can be observed in all children. At the same time, our findings suggest that the effectiveness of such behavior depends on the quality of the mother-child relationship that is reflected in other domains of children's interactive behavior. Thus, despite the fact that no differences were observed among the groups with respect to secure-base behavior, children of secure mothers exhibited smoother interactions than those of dismissing and unresolved mothers and tended to enjoy physical contact with their mothers more than children of insecure-unresolved mothers.

The findings that we obtained on the AQS scales underscore the importance of studying the relation between specific domains of child-mother interactions—especially those that are central to the secure-base phenomenon—and AAI classifications. It is in the study of such behavioral domains in both children and mothers, that is, what they actually do when interacting, that will allow us to understand how mothers' narratives about attachment relationships come to be associated with children's secure-base behavior.

It is also worth noting that a few of the mothers classified as insecure had children whose security scores were as high as or higher than those of some children of secure mothers (see, e.g., Table 1). Methodological issues—such as measurement error and the representativeness of the mother's narrative and of the child's behavior—aside, these cases suggest that mothers' conceptualizations of attachment do not directly translate into a child's attachment behavior and that other intervening factors also need to be taken into account. For example, the spousal relationship (Howes & Markman, 1989; Isabella & Belsky, 1985), family life stressors (Vaughn, Egeland, Sroufe, & Waters, 1979), and the child's attachment relationship with the father, among other things, are likely to influence how mother and child interact with each other and hence affect the ultimate nature of the child-mother attachment relationship.

Finally, our results support grouping children of unresolved mothers with those of dismissing and preoccupied mothers in the category of insecure attachment. Security scores of children of unresolved mothers did not differ significantly from those of children whose mothers were assigned to either of the two other insecure groups; grouped together, mothers assigned to the insecure classification had children with significantly lower security scores than children whose mothers were secure. Thus, the behavior of children of unresolved mothers—like that of children of dismissing and preoccupied mothers—is organized in ways that depart from the theoretical description of optimal secure-base behavior. Note, however, that our data cannot speak to the hypothesized link between mothers' unresolved classification and children's disorganized attachment since no Strange Situation observations were obtained in this study. Furthermore (and as noted before), the small number of subjects available for contrasts among the three insecure groups calls for caution concerning the reliability of the results of such comparisons.

CONCLUDING REMARKS

The evidence of a significant relation between mothers' current secure/insecure conceptualizations of attachment relationships (i.e., dismissing and unresolved) and their preschool children's secure-base behavior at home supports as well as extends findings from other studies. The fact that this expected association emerges both under circumstances in which the child's attachment system is highly activated—as it is in the Strange Situation paradigm—and in the natural setting of the home lends significant support to a central hypothesis of attachment theory and research in the last years. The task ahead is one of disentangling and demonstrating empirically the mechanisms through which these conceptualizations relate to children's secure-base behavior, their feeling of security, and, ultimately, the organization of their attachment system.

THE ROLE OF PARENTING SENSITIVITY, INFANT TEMPERAMENT, AND DYADIC INTERACTION IN ATTACHMENT THEORY AND ASSESSMENT

Ronald Seifer and Masha Schiller

What are we trying to index when we make assessments of attachment patterns in early life? How do these quality-of-attachment constructs relate to other constructs that are theoretically important to the description and development of attachment relationships? How do parents and children contribute to these developmental processes? What measurement issues are important for the field to consider when evaluating attachment and related constructs? In addressing these questions, we will concurrently examine the nature and assessment of constructs of maternal sensitivity and temperament, both of which have been significant in attachment research and theory.

We begin by describing the core constructs of attachment theory, namely, the attachment system and secure-base behavior. We follow by discussing contextual factors that are thought to be crucial in the development of individual differences in attachment, especially maternal sensitivity. We then consider child characteristics, especially temperament, that may contribute to the operation of the attachment system. In this context, we consider both parental supports for secure-base behavior and the ways by which infants "teach" their parents about the specific behaviors that are required to provide a secure base for the individual child. Assessment issues associated with each of these constructs, connections (theoretical and empirical) among them, and some views on directions for future research are each discussed in turn.

Research reported here was supported by a grant from the National Institute of Mental Health. Direct correspondence to Ronald Seifer, Bradley Hospital, 1011 Veterans Memorial Parkway, East Providence, RI 02915.

146

By focusing on such questions, we hope to shed light on several issues. Attachment theory is broad and complex, but it does have a degree of specificity that is often lost in the empirical literature, where categorization resulting from assessment of the attachment system often assumes the central role. The concept of attachment has specific meaning that applies to a limited set of infant and parent behaviors that does not encompass the entire interactive relationship between infant and caregiver. The theoretical antecedents of attachment are also complex phenomena that in some cases have more precise definitions than is apparent in empirical reports. Further, the different antecedents of attachment patterns may be related to one another by theoretical overlap as well as by overlap in assessment techniques. Finally, the bidirectional nature of the development of early relationships has not been emphasized at all times in the attachment literature. Specifically, the effects that infant characteristics may have on caregiving strategies that promote individual differences in attachment outcomes have not been a focus of empirical work.

By exploring these issues and highlighting areas where attachment theory and research would benefit from clarification, we hope to contribute to efforts (both theoretical and empirical) aimed at further refining the details of attachment theory, to evaluate critically assessment strategies used in studies of attachment and related phenomena, and to identify the antecedents and consequences of individual differences in attachment patterns.

CONSTRUCTS

Attachment and Secure-Base Behavior

Giving a concise definition of *attachment* is not easy. None of the major theoretical treatments provide a simple descriptive definition (e.g., Ainsworth, Blehar, Waters, & Wall, 1978; Bowlby, 1969/1982; Bretherton, 1985; Sroufe & Waters, 1977). Rather, the complexity of the construct is typically described as well as the different ways in which the term *attachment* is employed. In these expositions, attachment is discussed in terms of (1) specific behaviors related to increasing infants' proximity and contact with a caregiver (*attachment behavior*), (2) specific behaviors that decrease proximity to the attachment figure but promote infants' interaction with the environment (*exploration*), (3) the theoretical organization and control of proximity and exploration behavior (*attachment system*), (4) the organizational structure of behaviors observed in context from which a strategy for maintaining attachment relationships is inferred (*attachment strategy*), and (5) the inferred internal bonds that form between infants and their caregivers (*attachment*). The discussion of these issues by Hinde (1982) brings much clarity to an often confusing literature.

Ainsworth et al. (1978) clearly state that *attachment* refers to the affectional bonds that infants form with their caregivers and that endure across time and situations. However, the terms *attachment, attachment behavior, attachment strategy,* and *attachment system* are sometimes used interchangeably, blurring what are in fact important distinctions. Furthermore, *attachment* is used to refer both to the set of behaviors that are related to proximity maintenance and to the organization and balance between such behaviors with the proximity-reducing exploratory behaviors, again leading to some conceptual confusion. Further complicating the issue is whether attachment is conceived as a species-typical pattern of behavior or whether it is viewed as an individual difference among people. Here we attempt to use these terms as they have commonly been used in the past while concurrently trying to minimize their confusion as much as possible.

Discerning the specific attachment behaviors—which include signaling (e.g., crying, reaching, smiling) and approaching (e.g., moving toward, following, clinging)—is relatively simple; however, of greater interest to attachment researchers has been the organizational nature of attachment systems (Sroufe & Waters, 1977). Several important components of this organization have been explored in depth elsewhere (Bowlby, 1969/1982; Bretherton, 1985); these include the infant having a set goal that governs the timing and degree of proximity maintenance; the balance of proximity and distance/exploration, which is often called *secure-base* behavior; and the relative activation of the attachment (proximity) system in circumstances of danger, illness, or separation.[1] This theoretical focus has prompted a large body of empirical work aimed at characterizing individual differences in the organization of children's behavior with regard to attachment systems and the identification of normative patterns of attachment organizations. Central to this work has been the attempt to understand the strategy (Cassidy & Mar-

---

[1] A common phrase used by attachment researchers is "activation of the attachment system" in response to stress or danger. We believe that this usage is somewhat misleading. As Hinde (1982) points out, the attachment system is a theoretical organization of the forces controlling attachment and exploratory behavior. This system is always active. The sense of this phrase is that the attachment-behavior side of the secure-base balance is heightened; i.e., the probability of expressing attachment/proximity behavior is increased. (The difficult issue of how avoidant behavior in the Strange Situation relates to the presumed increased probability of attachment behavior when the system is activated is discussed by Main & Weston, 1982.) Perhaps a more accurate phrase would be that the attachment system is "influenced by stress or danger," implying that the operation of the active system is modified by contextual events. However, rather than coin new language here, we will continue to use the phrase "activation of the attachment system" with the understanding that this nuance of meaning should not be forgotten.

vin, 1992) or plan (Ainsworth et al., 1978) used by the infant in negotiating the balance between proximity and exploration (Sroufe & Waters, 1977).

Perhaps the most fundamental postulate of attachment theory is that, during the first year of life, all children (except those reared under the most severe forms of isolation or neglect) will develop some degree of secure-base behavior with one or more attachment figures (Bowlby, 1969/1982). This type of secure-base behavior is found in some form across different human cultures as well as primate and some nonprimate species (Kondo-Ikemura & Waters, in this volume; Posada, Waters, Crowell, & Lay, in this volume), indicating that there are likely evolutionary roots to this species-typical behavior in humans. Unique to humans is that an extended period of development for secure-base behavior is required, that these behaviors organized with respect to a specific person are not seen in their full form until almost a year after birth, and that they provide a basis for subsequent, more complex social-relationship behaviors.

Secure-base behavior is important for many reasons. First and foremost, the secure-base attachment figure provides protection to the infant in times of danger. Although threats from predators (and perhaps conspecifics) have diminished in our Westernized culture, many environmental threats to the safety and well-being of young infants continue to exist. A secure protective base also enhances the infant's opportunities to engage in a variety of adult-supervised learning experiences; exploratory interactions with objects and social partners that lead to eventual mastery of these domains are believed to be optimal under the auspices of the secure-base attachment figure. Finally, secure-base behavior provides a context in which differentiation of self and other can take place. As has been noted in many contexts (e.g., Stern, 1985; Werner & Kaplan, 1963), the earliest months of life are best characterized as global and undifferentiated with respect to parent-child relationships. Development proceeds from this state to one where an emergent, organized sense of self becomes apparent in the infant. Following an extended period of near total dependence on adult caregivers during the first months of life, secure-base behavior progresses from proximity to exploration, and infants gradually establish relative autonomy from their caregivers (Hofer, 1987; Pipp & Harmon, 1987). Many systems are involved in this transformation, including cognitive appreciation of self-other differentiation, motor skill to effect proximity increase and decrease autonomously, and formation of relationship bonds that mediate social interaction across time and space.

Defining ''Secure-Base Behavior''

What exactly do we mean by *secure-base behavior*? At the behavioral level, it may be conceived as reflecting the balance exhibited by infants between the so-called attachment and exploratory behaviors. The term *balance* should not be interpreted in a quantitative sense; rather, balance is best viewed as a level of adaptation between the competing systems of attachment and exploration behaviors at which establishment of successful attachment (proximity) strategies supports the expression of exploratory behaviors. Note, however, that understanding of the exploratory aspect of secure-base behavior is less well developed within attachment theory, as is evidenced by reserving the term *attachment behaviors* only for those that increase proximity and by the emphasis placed on such behaviors in the Ainsworth Strange Situation assessment of attachment security.

As noted earlier, the specific attachment and exploratory behaviors of interest have been well specified—however, attaching appropriate developmental significance to their relative prevalence remains at a general and qualitative level. By 1 year of age, exploration should predominate in nonstressful conditions but continue to be accompanied by consistent attention and periodic communication and/or contact with attachment figures. Under most circumstances, exploration should lead to developmentally appropriate play (with or without the involvement of the attachment figure), and attachment behaviors should be expressed without anxiety or ambivalence. When the context is more stressful (e.g., when there is perceived danger or the infant is ill or distressed), we expect to see a shift in the attachment/ exploration balance toward closer proximity and less exploration (i.e., the attachment system has been activated).

Infant Strategies and Secure-Base Behavior

Attention to the concept of strategies—evidenced by the quantity and quality of attachment and exploratory behaviors shown by the infant—is the core of attachment research. By invoking the notion of strategy, we imply that the infant seeks to achieve certain goals in the attachment relationship, that the organization of behaviors within the relationship is coherent and transcends time and context, and that the nature of the behaviors exhibited by infants provides insight into the meaning that specific relationships have in their lives. Obviously, we can make no assertion that these strategies, goals, or meanings are articulated by infants or known at a conscious level; rather, the concept is more appropriately understood in much the same manner as the late sensorimotor schemes described by Piaget (1952)—that is, as organized patterns of behavior that represent cumulative behavioral adjustments to the experiences of the first months of life. When these strategies become more conscious is not clear. As symbolic representation and language become more established in toddlers, some have speculated that internal working models are at a higher level of awareness as well (Bretherton, 1990). There is, however, little empirical work on which to base such judgments.

Bowlby's (1969/1982) characterization of this organization of attachment behavior in the language of control-systems theory has been instrumental to the development of the notion of working models of attachment (see Waters, Kondo-Ikemura, Posada, & Richters, 1990). The fundamental qualities of such working models are (1) the set goals of the infant, (2) the repertoire of secure-base behaviors and their effect on maintaining the set goals, (3) the contextual factors (including infant-caregiver history) that influence the relative expression of these behaviors, and (4) manifestations of felt security (for a detailed description of such a model, see Bretherton, 1985). Defined as a *working* model, it is under constant refinement and adaptation as a function of the infant's and parent's experiences. Bretherton (1990) has expanded her perspective on working models to emphasize more conscious linguistic representations as children grow older. However, this aspect of her formulation is more speculative and less widely accepted.

The connection between Bowlby's control-systems perspective and Bretherton's (1985) description of an internal working model may not be intuitively obvious. Bowlby's (1969/1982) approach was pioneering in its application of systems theory to human behavioral phenomena, particularly in the context of early social relationships, where he invoked the working-model approach (see also Hinde, 1982). He articulated this model at the level of attachment and exploratory behaviors and their relative expression. The primary emphasis was on species-typical behavior. Bretherton's model, in contrast, emphasized inferred internal states of infants in addition to behavioral control systems. The emphasis here was more on individual differences in attachment behavior. Despite these differences, these models are quite comparable.

Both models in essence bridge the boundary of different levels of systemic organization (Sameroff, 1983). To digress for a moment, hierarchically organized biological, behavioral, and cultural systems may be described and understood relatively independently of one another. However, these different systems are clearly dependent on one another in their function. For example, biological integrity is necessary for an organism to exhibit the variety of behaviors that we observe in everyday life; similarly, the behavior of individuals in social settings underlies the organization of family and cultural systems (Hinde, 1982). It is at the nexus of individual and social systems where attachment theory is most relevant.

Returning to the models described by Bowlby and Bretherton, the former emphasized observed social behavior and made inferences about individual attachments, while the latter emphasized inner states and feelings regarding social partners and the relation of these inner experiences to social behavior. However, both are clearly concerned with the boundaries of individual and social organization in the context of relationship formation. The coherence of attachment theory depends on these models of different levels of systemic organization converging on a similar understanding of attachment phenomena.

The set goals of the attachment working-model system have been articulated in both behavioral and affective terms. On the behavioral side, maintenance of an appropriate balance of proximity and distance exploration is frequently cited as the goal of the infant (Ainsworth et al., 1978). However, it is the often theoretically implicit level of affective arousal that is believed to be the internal process mediating shifts in this balance. Increased distance or duration of separation heightens infant arousal, leading the infant to engage in attachment (proximity) behaviors in an effort to modulate this arousal to more comfortable levels. Regardless of the transient changes in specific attachment behaviors or proximity set points, the quality of attachment is evaluated by the manner in which the attachment-behavior component of the secure-base behavior is expressed. Thus, the bond is judged to be secure if the parent functions as a safe haven for exploration and perturbations to the attachment system are resolved quickly and without apparent anxiety.

Insofar as the attachment system functions to modulate arousal, it will be more readily activated under certain conditions that may be either external (e.g., presence of an unfamiliar adult or total stimulus load) or internal (e.g., hormonal status or central nervous system organization) to the infant. The degree of activation of the attachment system is directly related to shifts in the attachment/exploration balance evident in secure-base behavior.

Before discussing the antecedents of secure-base behavior, we want to emphasize an important distinction between felt security (an unobserved inner state) and secure-base behavior (an observed set of organized behaviors). As with inner states of people in general and nonverbal infants in particular, we have very limited direct access to measuring the specific emotions that would constitute an infant's inner feeling of security with a caregiver in a given context. All we can examine directly is the organization of the infant's secure-base behavior (specifically with respect to proximity and exploration), obvious signs of affect and arousal exhibited at the behavioral level, and any behavioral manifestations of anxiety surrounding these social interactions. From this complex of behavioral observations, we attempt to infer the infant's underlying state of mind with respect to attachment. Our working hypothesis about the infant's state of mind or felt security then becomes the central feature of the assessment of individual differences in attachment quality.

Development of Secure-Base Behavior: Parenting Sensitivity

Closely associated with normative descriptions of secure-base behavior are propositions concerning the development of individual differences in this set of behaviors. Ainsworth et al. (1978) described infants' experiences with attachment figures (typically parents) during the first year that should be precursors of secure, or of insecure, attachment. These authors' summary construct of parenting sensitivity includes alertness to infant signals, appropriate interpretation of response, promptness of response, flexibility of attention and behavior, appropriate level of control, and negotiation of conflicting goals. While intuitively pleasing, these are behaviors and constructs that are only partially operationalized at any level of detail. Typically, macroscopic assessments of parenting sensitivity have been obtained during the middle of the first year (e.g., Ainsworth et al., 1978) by the use of global summary ratings after direct observations. In contrast, some of the microanalytic studies of dyadic interaction have specified these sensitivity behaviors more precisely in the more limited and controlled face-to-face situation (Cohn & Tronick, 1987). Intermediate between these two strategies is the use of techniques (such as Q-sorts) that quantify individual behaviors and then produce summary aggregates (Pederson et al., 1990).

It is important to emphasize here that sensitivity is not equivalent to parental love, warmth, or affection. There is a technical aspect to being sensitive in that parents must be able to read accurately the signals of their infant, some of which may be unique to the particular baby. Also, the construct of sensitivity emphasizes flexible adaptation on the part of caregivers so that responses to signals are well attuned to the current time and place. Again, skillful understanding and action is involved as the timing and pacing of behavior must be well suited to the individual baby at each general developmental stage and specific state of arousal (see Hinde, 1982). Clearly, success in these interactive skills with young infants will be enhanced when the caregiver's affect is positive and behavior is motivated by warmth and affection for the baby. However, loving feelings and good intentions may well be present in the absence of the technical skills required to interact effectively with a baby.

An approach related conceptually to sensitivity, less often seen in research on attachment precursors, is the development of mutual regulation of affect, a perspective most closely associated with Tronick (1989). In this conceptualization, infant-parent interaction between the ages of 3 and 9 months represents a working out by dyads of their joint mechanisms for regulating affect. The infant is characterized as having internal set goals of maintaining homeostasis, establishing security, experiencing positive emotions, and controlling negative emotions. During dyadic interaction, all these control states are likely to be violated, and the repair of these "interactive errors," repeated over the course of continuing interaction, provides the basis for the development of interactive patterns that begin to transcend time and setting, that is, become part of a relationship representation. The more optimal states of infant arousal are viewed as a set goal of the dyad that motivates their interactive behavior. Infants who experience more successful interactive repair (either by self-regulation or regulation by the caregiver) are more likely to engage in behavior that solicits high-quality interactive behavior from their partner (Gianino & Tronick, 1988). Those attachment figures who consistently provide sensitive affect-regulating experiences lead infants to develop representations of their partners as likely to respond to interactive bids (see also Thompson, 1994).

It has been less well explored at the theoretical level how these experiences of parenting sensitivity or insensitivity accumulate over time in the development of working models of attachment (Waters et al., 1990). The most sophisticated statement currently available is that, if interactions are generally characterized as sensitive, infants will come to expect that their parent (or caregiver) will be available to help modulate negative states of arousal (e.g., Bretherton, 1985). Beyond this general statement, however, we have little theoretical or empirical guidance for seeking evidence concerning the specific supports that parents and other caregivers provide for the development of secure-base behavior.

We speculate that some of the important factors in this regard may be caregivers' consistency over extended time periods, effective (i.e., sensitive) negotiation of daily transitions (e.g., bedtime; Sadeh & Anders, 1993), effective negotiation of special events (e.g., illness, fear episodes, doctor visits), or sensitivity when setting limits. Although the specification of attachment systems during times of stress to the parent-child relationship is clearly articulated and has been extensively studied, it is still unclear whether sensitive parenting during these stressful aspects of daily life is most important or whether it is equally important across all circumstances.

Moving one step further from direct behavior experiences, it is also becoming increasingly evident that parents' cognitive construction of their own relationship history is an indirect factor associated with individual differences in attachment strategies. Parents (particularly mothers) whose narrative accounts of their own childhood relationships with their parents are coded as autonomous (i.e., secure) are likely to have children whose attachment to them is also judged to be secure (Posada, Waters, et al., in this volume; van IJzendoorn, 1995). Conversely, parents whose narratives are coded as dismissing or preoccupied (i.e., insecure) are likely to have children judged to be insecurely attached, typically in correspondence with respect to strategies regarding activation versus dampening of attachment behaviors. Despite the accumulating evidence for this cross-generational correspondence, there is little empirical work that has defined a mechanism by which this transmission. occurs. We know little about how parents' cognitive systems might affect their caregiving sensitivity, how they might be involved in shaping the microscopic aspects of dyadic interaction, or whether these mechanisms may be operative at critical points during their infants' development.

The theoretical relations among parents' working models and parenting behavior are still in their early stages, and little empirical work has been done in this area. However, in the area relating parenting behavior to infant attachment security, where theory and research are more abundant, there remain contradictory findings as to the degree to which the theoretical relation between sensitivity and secure attachment has been established. Parenting sensitivity typically explains only small to moderate portions of individual variability in attachment classification; for example, Goldsmith and Alansky concluded that the effect size of parenting sensitivity predicting attachment security was equivalent to a correlation of .20–.30 (a small to medium effect according to Cohen's, 1988, standards). Pederson and Moran (in this volume) assert that the inconsistency across studies and the smaller than expected effect sizes may result from methodological limitations in some studies. Note also that recent evidence suggests that sensitive maternal behavior in nonhuman primates is related to the infant's attachment behavior (Kondo-Ikemura & Waters, in this volume). Still, some recent work with apparent methodological rigor has not supported the sensitivity-attachment association (Rosen & Rothbaum, 1993; Seifer, Schiller, Sameroff, Resnick, & Riordan, in press). We return to this issue in our subsequent discussion of matters related to assessment.

What beyond the caregiver's behavior during the first year of life might influence variation in the individual differences seen in attachment quality? Infant characteristics such as temperament (particularly self-regulatory ability) and mastery motivation have been proposed as important in this regard (Kagan, 1982; Seifer & Vaughn, in press), and in the following section we explore how such child characteristics may contribute to the development of attachment systems.

Child Contribution to Attachment Systems

Characteristics that have been most often discussed when considering the infant's contributions to the attachment system are the set of behaviors that fall under the rubric of temperament. Infant temperament constructs can be relatively circumscribed or quite broad, depending on one's theoretical perspective (Goldsmith et al., 1987; Goldsmith & Harman, 1994); also, there is some debate over whether temperament is best conceived as a set of behavioral dimensions or as an attribute that distinguishes categorically different types of children (Kagan, 1994; Kagan, Reznick, & Gibbons, 1989). In addition to temperament, a less frequently discussed set of behaviors that are important to the formation of attachment relationships is infant signaling behaviors (Fogel & Thelen, 1987), which will be discussed in a later section. In addressing these issues, we want to emphasize that viewing the child's contributions to the attachment relationship as unidirectional vastly oversimplifies the developmental process; such child characteristics should rather be examined in terms of their effect on the dyadic system and the manner in which they contribute to a caregiver-child co-construction of the relationship (Hinde, 1982).

Temperament

One feature shared by all theories of temperament is that the referents for the postulated constructs are behaviors that are somewhat consistent over time and across settings and that appear early in life. Typically, these include behaviors within the domains of affect; activity; approach to novel objects, events, or people; intensity of behavioral expressions; and general interactive difficulty. Also, some would say that they have biological substrates (Bates, 1980; Goldsmith & Harman, 1994; Rothbart, 1981; Seifer, Sameroff, Barrett, & Krafchuk, 1994; Thomas, Chess, Birch, Hertzig, & Korn, 1963). Although a clear distinction may be drawn between those who view temperament as a behavioral style, relatively devoid of specific content (Thomas et al., 1963), and those who view it as a biobehavioral regulatory system (Rothbart & Derryberry, 1982), both perspectives focus on behaviors that overlap with those considered to be central in indexing individual differences in infants' attachment.

For example, behaviors characterized as temperamental attributes of fear (Rothbart, 1981) or of approach (Thomas et al., 1963) should relate to infants' reaction to the introduction of an unfamiliar adult in the Strange Situation assessment. Temperamental soothability and distractibility (Thomas et al., 1963) will be involved in the degree to which infants return to baseline arousal if they become distressed during separations. Activity level (Bates, Freeland, & Lounsbury, 1979; Rothbart, 1981; Thomas et al., 1963) may influence the degree of exploration and returns to the attachment figure that are observed both in the laboratory and in the home. Orientation, threshold to stimulation, distractibility, and persistence (Thomas et al., 1963) should all be related to the quality of interactions with both objects and people during the exploration phases of secure-base behavior. Bridges, Connell, and Belsky (1988) and Connell and Thompson

(1986) provide evidence that emotional reactivity has cross-episode and cross-age stability in Strange Situation assessments of attachment quality.

Viewed as regulatory systems, temperamental "types" also have a substantial surface relevance to the operation of attachment systems. The temperamental type that has been most vigorously supported is that of behaviorally inhibited children (Kagan et al., 1989), who are characterized as being highly physiologically reactive to novelty as well as very fearful, wary, and behaviorally timid in situations where novelty is a salient feature. All these behaviors are clearly relevant to assessments of attachment quality, particularly in the Strange Situation, where novelty and activation of the attachment system (arousal) are critical features of the assessment technique.

Signaling Behaviors

In addition to examining individual differences in children's dispositions as representing direct mediators of the behavioral patterns studied in attachment assessments, it is equally if not more useful to examine more directly the infant's contribution to the interactive sequences that are thought to be important in the development of working models of attachment. In our earlier discussion of mutual regulation models, we touched briefly on the notion that the ability of infants to manifest "interactive repairs" results in eliciting a higher quality of interactive behavior from their caregivers; achieving such interactive repairs involves the regulation of arousal and the expression of clear and readable signals.

The concept of infants influencing their development (Bell & Harper, 1977) may be viewed more broadly in light of major early developmental accomplishments. As infants grow from the first days through the first year of life, the parent-child relationship shifts from being characterized by the caregiver bearing almost total control over available resources to manage dyadic communication to increasingly joint control of interactive behavior with clearer autonomy on the part of the infant (Kaye, 1982; Stern, 1985; Werner & Kaplan, 1963). From the relationship perspective, part of the developmental task is for the caregiver to allow the infant to teach him or her about the child's newly emerging competencies in participating and directing communicative interactions. For example, the infant's ability to maintain directed gaze, engage in social smiling, make signals regarding differentiated needs, and reference objects in the environment all emerge during the first year. Further, as parents respond to these newly emerging behaviors, infants provide feedback such as maintaining or terminating social interaction, modulating arousal, or exhibiting affect displays. The clarity and organization of the infant's expression of these new behavioral competencies, the caregiver's adaptation to these developmental accomplishments, and the infant's interactional feedback may all be important determinants of the successful development of secure relationships (Sameroff & Emde, 1989).

There are many features of infant behavior that affect their social partners' ability to read the baby's signals. These include clarity of facial expression (which involves organizational features and the timing of facial displays), integration of different modes of expression (e.g., facial, vocal, gestural), the intensity of signaling behavior, the timing and pacing of these signals, and the context in which the behavior is expressed. Some of the work on specifying individual differences in quality of signaling behavior in normally developing infants has been reported by Fogel and Thelen (1987) and Kaye (1982) and that on identifying disturbances in signaling behavior in developmentally delayed infants by Jones (1980); there is also evidence of individual differences in infants' ability to self-regulate their state of arousal using both internal resources (Rothbart, 1981) and social supports (Campos & Stenberg, 1981). A focus on such differences in signaling and self-regulatory behavior would surely enhance our understanding of how the attachment system develops as well as of the origins of the individual differences that we observe in attachment behavior.

Of particular interest in this context is to identify the differences in motivations or goals that different investigators have proposed as governing communicative and interactive systems. As noted above, Tronick (1989) proposes that an optimal state of arousal is a basic set goal of young infants that motivates interactive behavior. In contrast, Fogel and Thelen (1987) invoke the notion of a set of frequently changing control parameters—which may be endogenous or exogenous—that spur transitions during early development. That is, the characteristics of the infant self-regulatory and communicative systems change over time, and these changes in themselves may spur developmental shifts.

Within attachment theory, hypotheses about the underlying motivations or set goals that drive the infant to construct a working model of attachment are still vague. In Bretherton's (1985) "simplified" flow chart of a control system for attachment working models (which is probably the most elaborated example presented to date), the primary goal-setting criterion is maintaining appropriate proximity to the caregiver. Left out of this formulation is the functional utility that the proximity set goals have for the infant; it is unclear whether maintenance of proximity serves the system of affect, of arousal, of cognitive equilibration (perhaps regarding perceived danger), of appetitive drives, or of mastery of the physical and social environment—or any combination thereof. One major task that attachment theory faces is to become more specific about the beneficial ontogenetic consequences that the infant gains by engaging in secure-base behavior and maintaining secure attachment relationships.

As we achieve more precision in identifying the functional goals that social relationships serve for infants, we will be able to describe more clearly the control systems that are operative in the development of later attachments. Conversely, as we understand more clearly the role that infant characteristics play in the interactive process, we will be able to identify more precisely the manner in which such characteristics affect the development of relationships. This would include specification of how infant skills and dispositions contribute to the establishment and maintenance of specific caregiving behaviors and of how mutual adaptations between the infant and the caregiver lead them to establish patterns of secure-base behavior that become specific to individual caregiver-child dyads.

MEASUREMENT ISSUES

We move now from considering theoretical issues to discussing assessment of the attachment-related constructs that we have identified. The two are integrally related since the quality of the empirical measurement will inevitably affect success or failure to confirm theoretical expectations.

Assessment of Attachment

The assessment of secure-base behavior and of quality of attachment has taken two major forms. The first of these is the laboratory Strange Situation developed by Ainsworth (Ainsworth et al., 1978), in which a series of brief episodes are staged for a total of about 20 min (including play, the introduction of an unfamiliar adult, and separations from, followed by reunions with, the caregiver). This protocol is used to activate the attachment system and hence provide an opportunity to observe the quality of attachment behaviors. In the other major approach, in-home observations of the child's behavior with attachment figures are made, and the quality of that behavior is quantified using Q-sort methods described by Waters and Deane (1985).

Strange Situation Assessments

The laboratory Strange Situation strategy relies on the researchers' ability systematically to influence the attachment system of young children (the MacArthur preschool attachment protocol—Greenberg, Cicchetti, & Cummings, 1990—and the Cassidy, 1988, system have extended this type of protocol to children between 1 and 6 years of age). The purpose of activating the attachment system is to alter the secure-base balance away from exploration and toward attachment behavior. Crucial to the classification of the quality of a child's attachment as seen in the Strange Situation is the manner in which attachment behaviors are expressed during reunions with the attachment figure; infants who express such behaviors clearly without either ambivalence or avoidance are judged to be secure. Within this coding framework, the exploration side of the secure-base balance is not characterized in any detail but is assessed only generally in terms of whether (1) developmentally appropriate levels of play are observed that are independent of the attachment figure (particularly during preseparation episodes) and (2) reunion with the attachment figure serves to return the secure-base balance more toward levels of exploration that had been evident in the earlier episodes in the protocol. For example, the small amount of work examining exploration during the Strange Situation has focused on the quality of free play rather than the maintenance of proximity or distance (Belsky, Garduque, & Hrncir, 1984).

The assumption that the Strange Situation protocol succeeds in activating the attachment system has received some support, although the empirical evidence is limited and sometimes equivocal. Physiological arousal in response to the introduction of the stranger and to the separation from the parent has been documented, regardless of the apparent behavioral distress of the child (Sroufe, 1977). Also, cortisol levels are typically (but not always significantly) elevated during the Strange Situation episodes, again regardless of ultimate classification (e.g., Gunnar, Mangelsdorf, Larson, & Hertsgaard, 1989). Physiological arousal is thought to be an important mediator in this context because it is related to both positive and negative emotional states and is readily modulated by internal and social systems (Tronick, 1989). Even when an infant does not overtly display negative affect in response to the stress induced by the Strange Situation protocol, his or her arousal may be elevated to a level beyond the set point optimal for that infant. This deviation from the bioregulatory systemic goal is believed to motivate the expression of attachment behaviors in the social contexts that are constructed in the assessment protocol.

Classifications derived from Strange Situation assessments rely heavily on infants' and young children's reunion strategies. Given this emphasis, how broadly does the Strange Situation assess the infant's overall secure-base behavior? One valid answer to this question is that it addresses only a limited aspect of the phenomenon, namely, the attachment-behavior side of the balance when the system is highly activated, leaving out the exploration side as well as attachment behaviors that would be observed under low-activation conditions. Considered from the perspective of protocol design rather than behaviors scored, an equally valid answer is that, by systematically influencing the activation of the attachment system, critical elements indicative of its quality come into sharper focus—it is only by highlighting the behaviors that increase the degree of relatedness between child and attachment figure that the child's strategy regarding the relationship may be revealed (see also Hinde, 1982).

Attachment Q-Sort

The Q-sort strategy for assessing secure-base behavior is quite different. First, its approach does not rely on procedures that systematically activate the attachment system. Second, the observation period is substantially longer, lasting several hours rather than 20 min. Third, the full potential repertoire of secure-base behaviors is examined in this protocol; the observer's task is to develop an understanding of the behaviors characteristic of the particular child and then to sort a set of 90 behavioral descriptors in terms of their similarity to how the child behaved. The observer sorts— which describe a range of specific child characteristics by which both attachment behaviors and exploration may be expressed—are then often summarized by correlation with sorts of prototypical secure children (this procedure is described in detail in Strayer, Verissimo, Vaughn, & Howes, in this volume). The basic postulate of this Q-sort strategy is that the organization of attachment and exploratory behavior, evident in the sort that describes a particular (or prototypical) child's characteristics, reveals important information about security of attachment.

Other strategies also exist for using Q-sort data. For example, these Q-sort data, which define behavior profiles of individual children, are ideal for examining clustering of individuals. The correlations among different children's sorts provide a clear distance metric defining similarities or differences among groups of children. Similarly, Q-sort items that cluster together across sorts of different children may reveal patterns of behavior that are important to take into account when considering attachment phenomena (Strayer et al., in this volume).

One crucial question raised by the procedural differences between these two approaches to assessment is whether manifestations of secure-base behavior might differ at home and in the structured laboratory situation. For example, is reunion behavior seen in contexts of a highly activated attachment system similar to or different from the attachment behaviors that are seen when the system is less activated? To what extent is there clearly demonstrated conceptual overlap in what is assessed in the Strange Situation and in home-based Attachment Q-sort protocols? What other methods might be used to provide a cross-assessment validation of the constructs postulated by attachment theory? Would it be worthwhile to adopt multiple measurement strategies instead of the single measurements typically in use? Some of the data presented by Sagi et al. (in this volume) speak to these issues. Their study of kibbutz children indicates modest overlap of the two strategies, with some conceptual difficulties, such as the inability when using the Q-sort data to discriminate between children classified as secure and those classified as avoidant in the Strange Situation.

Validation of Attachment Measurements

A more fundamental question concerns the degree to which these two assessment strategies have been validated. To address this question properly, the specific constructs that are the target of validation efforts, and the strategies by which validation might be pursued, should be clearly identified.

As to the latter, in their classic treatment Cronbach and Meehl (1955) argued that validation should involve (1) determination of the universe of items to be examined so that tests can sample from that universe to ensure content validity; (2) demonstration of correspondence of results to those of other theoretically correlated tests, either concurrently in time or predictively to future assessment; and (3) grounding of the validated construct in a logically coherent nomological net, often examined in a bootstrapping fashion. By nomological net, Cronbach and Meehl meant a network of theoretical principles and observed properties that form a coherent set of propositions and evidence about a particular construct. Often, in the conceptualization and validation of constructs, there is a cyclic process by which observed properties require modification of proposed constructs, which may in turn lead to collecting a new and modified set of observed properties, leading to modification of constructs, and so on—this bootstrapping results in ever more precisely identified and empirically validated constructs. Campbell and Fiske (1959) added to this formulation the task of identifying not only those characteristics that co-occur according to theoretical principles but also those that should be discriminated from the construct in question.

Our understanding of the universe of behaviors to be examined when validating attachment constructs comes from several sources, including Bowlby's (1969/1982) rich descriptions, Ainsworth's observational work (Ainsworth et al., 1978), the set of items contained in the Attachment Q-Set (AQS; Waters & Deane, 1985), and the discussion of the organization of attachment behavior provided by Sroufe and Waters (1977). Both the Strange Situation and the Q-Sort assessments of attachment have sampled from this universe of behaviors. However, the history of these assessments has been notable for its lack of critical attention to the utility of the specific behavior items sampled in these protocols (the revision of the Q-Sort being one major exception). That is, how has each of the sampled behaviors (or complexes of behaviors) performed in relation to each other as well as other indicators of attachment? A rare example where this agenda was pursued may be found in the components process analysis of Thompson, Connell, and Bridges (1988). With regard to criterion-related validity, there is a body of evidence that attachment has some measure of concurrent and predictive validity when compared with other constructs that are theoretically correlated with attachment, such as later problem-solving ability and social interactive behavior (e.g., Bates, Maslin, & Frankel, 1985; Matas, Arend, & Sroufe, 1978), although the size of these relations is typically modest (Lamb, 1987).

It is more significant that minimal attention has been directed in attachment research to construct validation issues. The criteria for evaluating secure-base behaviors have been established for the Strange Situation, where there are clear guidelines for assessing the quality of attachment behaviors following separation, and for the Attachment Q-Sort procedure conducted in the home, which attends to a wider array of exploration and attachment behaviors but with a lesser degree of specificity. However, little attention has been paid to the exploration side of secure-base behavior in the Strange Situation. Since no commonly accepted criteria against which to validate these assessments has been available, construct validation remains an essential task to be accomplished. Work devoted to demonstrating that attachment is discriminated from other relationship constructs by these assessment methods has also been limited; to date, the best evidence of such discriminant validity has been with respect to the construct of dependency (e.g., Waters & Deane, 1985).

Given that only two assessment strategies have gained widespread acceptance as indicators of secure-base behavior or of attachment quality, it is difficult to claim that these constructs have been well validated; to date, the most compelling evidence comes from the moderate relation between the Strange Situation and Q-Sort assessments themselves (Bosso, Corter, & Abramovitch, 1995; Sagi et al., in this volume; Vaughn & Waters, 1990). Other validation questions not yet addressed include (1) whether the Strange Situation and the Attachment Q-Sort are equally accurate in identifying individual differences in attachment quality, (2) whether measures of secure-base behavior in normative conditions and of the quality of attachment behaviors under conditions of stress address the same construct, (3) whether the Strange Situation classifications and indices derived from the Attachment Q-Sort (or some other yet-to-be-identified measures) are differentially predictive of future developmental accomplishments, and (4) whether classification or continuous measurement will prove to be the best quantification strategy for maximizing concurrent and predictive associations (Cohen, 1990; see also Strayer et al., in this volume).

It is ironic that so much of the field's attention has been devoted to laboratory Strange Situation assessments when the initial development of the secure-base construct originated in the context of home-based assessments that had been motivated by an ethological perspective, which emphasizes the value of observation in natural settings. In further conceptual and empirical attempts to validate constructs in attachment research, we may be served best by always keeping the ethological/observational roots of these constructs in the foreground—whether using natural observation techniques (where secure-base behavior is the focus) or laboratory techniques (where reunion strategies under stress are emphasized), it is useful to remain constantly aware of the theoretical roots of the construct of attachment.

Assessment of Caregiver Sensitivity

We now turn to issues related to the measurement of behaviors believed to affect the development of individual differences in quality of attachment. This is important for two reasons: first, the predictive power of these variables will inevitably depend on their psychometric characteristics; second, the degree to which attachment constructs may overlap at different developmental periods is important to consider in evaluating the relations between indices of attachment and of their predictors.

We first consider the domain of parenting sensitivity. As noted by others (e.g., Pederson & Moran, in this volume), observations in Ainsworth et al.'s (1978) original work were conducted over an extended period and included multiple home visits. Detailed narrative records of specific behaviors observed in the dyads were compiled, and several rating scales were subsequently scored from these narratives, one of which was maternal sensitivity. Later studies have typically used much more economic data-collection strategies, including fewer visits over shorter developmental spans, with the result that the level of detail in the original work has rarely been duplicated (e.g., Crockenberg, 1981; Mangelsdorf, Gunnar, Kestenbaum, Lang, & Andreas, 1990; Rosen & Rothbaum, 1993; for an exception, see Grossmann, Grossmann, Spangler, Suess, & Unzner, 1985). Hence, although the relation between maternal sensitivity and attachment might in fact be modest (Goldsmith & Alansky's, 1987, meta-analysis estimated the effect size to be equivalent to correlations of .20–.30), it may be that characteristics of the measures that have been used introduce too much error to demonstrate consistently the larger effect posited by attachment theory. The importance of extensive as well as multiple observations cannot be overemphasized.

In studies of parent-child interaction, session-to-session correspondence in particular parental behaviors is typically around .40 (e.g., Seifer,

Sameroff, Anagnostopolou, & Elias, 1992)—obviously, this is well below psychometric standards for reliability of measurement. In our own work, we have noted this same level of correspondence across observations in the assessment of maternal sensitivity. However, when multiple sessions are aggregated, reliable variables can be formed, and these aggregated measurements have proved to be stable (*r*'s of about .80) across time (Seifer et al., in press).

A second important issue is whether viewing parenting sensitivity as a unitary construct is in fact appropriate. As we noted earlier, there are numerous components of parenting sensitivity, each of which taps a different type of parenting skill. There has been little empirical work aimed at examining whether these different aspects of parenting consistently co-occur in a manner that would support a single measure of sensitivity (Seifer et al., in press). Should a global construct of maternal sensitivity prove not to be supported, this might explain the modest effect sizes typically obtained in studies that rely on global indices. Alternatively, current scales may overemphasize the loving/warmth/supportiveness aspects of sensitivity in lieu of assessing the skill-related aspects of identifying, appraising, and appropriately responding to infant signals (Mangelsdorf et al., 1990).

We should also be as concerned with what is *not* included in the construct of sensitivity as with what it comprises. Theoretically, *sensitivity* is not identical to *good parenting*. That is, there are aspects of high-quality parenting that are not included in the sensitivity construct (such as affective involvement and providing a safe environment), and sensitivity is possible in the context of parenting that would otherwise be considered poor. In the same way that attachment does not describe everything about the parent-child relationship, sensitivity does not describe everything about caregiving behavior. To date, however, indices of parenting sensitivity have not yet been examined for their discriminant validity from these other aspects of caregiving behavior.

Finally, it is important to consider whether some aspects of the child's behavior may be implicitly included in assessments of parenting sensitivity. One basic indicator of parenting sensitivity is the determination that, through their interventions, parents are successful in maintaining an optimal state in their infants. However, it is not at all clear that the attribution of sensitivity to parents is warranted by this criterion—the success of the interventions may be at least in part a function of infants' self-regulatory abilities (Belsky & Isabella, 1988). Stated in its extreme form, the notion is that infants with a "good" temperament (e.g., able to modulate arousal quickly and independently) can make caregivers who are not adept at reading and responding to their signals appear highly sensitive.

Studies focused on examining the conditions under which infants can, and cannot, modulate their affect—especially with respect to the presence or absence of parents' intervention—are necessary to answer this question adequately. The body of work that comes closest to following such an agenda has been conducted using the face-to-face paradigm (Cohn & Tronick, 1987; Tronick, 1989). There is some evidence that patterns of reciprocity in mother-infant interaction are important in predicting later attachment (e.g., Isabella & Belsky, 1991; Isabella & Gable, 1991). In general, however, the relations among assessments made in this paradigm with sensitivity and attachment assessments are as yet poorly understood. Adopting a dynamic perspective on relationship formation, we might find that *jointly constructed* interactive patterns that evolve from an early interplay of infant characteristics and caregiving style may ultimately prove to be the most important predictors of later attachment quality.

Assessment of Temperament

Like parenting sensitivity, infant temperament is defined by multiple specific behaviors. In fact, it is an inherently multiconstruct phenomenon as currently conceptualized, and a number of systems are available for defining which are the relevant constructs (Goldsmith et al., 1987). For example, the classic Thomas and Chess system identifies activity, approach, adaptability, intensity, mood, rhythmicity, distractibility, threshold to stimulation, and persistence (Thomas et al., 1963). Style of behavior is emphasized in this system. Other systems are offered by Rothbart (1981) and Goldsmith (in Goldsmith et al., 1987), who emphasize biobehavioral reactivity as reflected in scales of fear, distress to limits, smile and laughter, orientation, soothability, and activity, and by Kagan (Kagan, 1994; Kagan et al., 1989; see also Garcia-Coll et al., 1992), who describes a temperamental type related to behavioral inhibition in novel situations. Whatever one's theoretical preferences, there is also evidence that several key constructs (such as activity, negative emotion, or sociability) are measured with some consistency across questionnaire instruments (Goldsmith, Reiser-Danner, & Briggs, 1991).

The truly important constructs derived from temperament research are *not* the specific behaviors; rather, it is the approach represented by such research to studying behavior early in life that is crucial. Temperament researchers make the assumption that some infant behavioral dispositions transcend time and setting and are relatively independent of contextual support (Goldsmith et al., 1987). Empirical support for this proposition has been discovered in both direct observations and parent reports (Hubert, Wachs, Peters-Martin, & Gandour, 1982; Seifer et al., 1994). The importance of the concept of temperament is that, even in the earliest months of life, infants are seen to behave in part according to internal agendas and are not totally driven by external contextual events. As described in some detail above, this is also a fundamental premise of attachment theory; the major difference is the formulation of goal-directed working models for behaving with relationship partners in attachment theory. However, when temperament is viewed from the perspective of biobehavioral regulation and the idea that interactive partners contribute to this regulatory process is added, temperament and attachment approaches appear far more compatible than is typically portrayed (Kagan, 1982; Sroufe, 1985).

As theories of temperament become increasingly integrated into complex theoretical models (as suggested in the discussion above; see also Calkins, 1994; Hinde, 1982), the assessment of temperament becomes more critical since the ability to use successfully any construct in data analyses that are of high complexity is very much dependent on the precision of its measurement. Currently, the most important measurement issue in temperament research is whether to obtain information using parent reports or direct observations (Seifer et al., 1994). The vast majority of studies examining infant temperament have used parent reports, yet there is little evidence of substantial correspondence between such reports and actual child behavior. In our own recent work, observer-parent correspondence was between .20 and .40 (Seifer et al., 1994)—even when the reliability of observations was assured by aggregating eight weekly sessions. Despite this lack of satisfactory correspondence, many cross-sectional and longitudinal studies have found parent-reported temperament to be an important predictor of the child's other developmental accomplishments (e.g., Bates et al., 1985). The most prudent approach may be to treat direct observations and parent reports of infant temperament as separate constructs until the relations among these measures are better understood.

As with assessments of attachment and sensitivity, there are established options for observation of temperament in the home or laboratory (Garcia-Coll et al., 1992; Goldsmith & Rothbart, 1990; Seifer et al., 1994). In-home observations typically extend over longer time periods and are conducted in a more natural setting, which may permit observing behaviors in a form relatively unaffected by the structure of the laboratory. On the other hand, laboratory assessment affords a degree of control and precision that cannot be achieved in the home. As with attachment and sensitivity, it is likely that the best current strategy for assessing temperament is to include multiple assessments obtained in different settings using different informants.

Connections between Attachment and Sensitivity Constructs

We now consider the theoretical and empirical links among the constructs discussed in preceding sections. The strongest of these lie between sensitivity and attachment. Theoretically, infants gradually construct working models of relationships in the context of interactions with significant caregivers. Two types of phenomena are operative in this process. The first is the species-typical secure-base behavior—and note here that, although this is the least-well-explicated aspect of attachment theory, behaviors characteristic of early parent-child contact may serve as sensitive-period elicitors of secure-base behaviors. For instance, social referencing that begins during the second 6 months of life helps promote exploratory behavior that increases distance between infant and parent; conversely, the infant's ability to read parents' distress while exploring serves to increase proximity-increasing attachment behaviors. We emphasize again that this developmental process is bidirectional—as noted above, we believe that refining the sensitivity construct to encompass jointly constructed caregiver-infant interactive patterns is likely to prove most useful in understanding later variation in patterns of attachment.

The second connection is qualitative and relates ultimately to individual differences in attachment quality. When the sensitivity of caregiving is consistently at high levels, infants both use and come to perceive these attachment figures as a source of affection, a safe haven from danger, and a partner capable of repairing and regulating negative states of affect/arousal. As a result, when their attachment system is activated, infants with a history of sensitive interactions will exhibit attachment behaviors that are expressed in a clear and unambiguous way, without evidence of either over- or under-activated defensive strategies. As noted in our earlier discussion (see also Pederson & Moran, in this volume), the empirical base that supports these theoretical positions is currently a matter of some debate.

Attachment and Temperament

Outlining the theoretical relations between temperament and attachment is more difficult. There have been a series of provocative treatments of this issue (e.g., Kagan, 1982; Sroufe, 1985). On one side of the issue, temperament has been offered as a way of explaining away variability in behavior observed in the Strange Situation; on the other, it has been dismissed as having no utility in understanding attachment security or secure-base behavior. Unfortunately, this controversy has served to obscure the meaningful theoretical relations that do exist between the two constructs while ensuring that temperament and attachment researchers will have as little contact with each other as possible. In fact, there are two important ways in which attachment and temperament might be related. The first is that temperamental variability among infants might influence interpretation of attachment assessments, the second that infant temperament during the first year of life may influence the nature of parent-child interactions that are important in shaping the development of attachment patterns.

As concerns interpreting Strange Situation behavior in the context of the infant's temperament, many have rejected the idea that temperament could account for security/insecurity differences in this procedure (Belsky & Rovine, 1987; Sroufe, 1985; Vaughn, Lefever, Seifer, & Barglow, 1989). Most studies find no direct relation of temperament and attachment security (e.g., Mangelsdorf et al., 1990), although Calkins and Fox (1992) did find that Strange Situation classification was related to subsequently measured behavioral inhibition. Some have posited a less direct effect, arguing that there might be a temperamental component to the apparent activation of attachment behaviors during the procedure (Belsky & Rovine, 1987). This is a nontrivial point since, to the extent that differences between the insecure-avoidant and insecure-resistant classification arise from different antecedents or have different consequences, temperament might play an important role in understanding this aspect of variation in attachment patterns. Another interesting finding is that *change* in temperament may be an important predictor; for example, increases in unadaptable or unpredictable behavior between 3 and 9 months of age have been found to be related to insecure attachment classification (Belsky & Isabella, 1988).

In any event, two important caveats limit current evidence concerning possible relations between temperament and attachment. First, these studies have typically used parent reports to assess temperament (see Belsky & Isabella, 1988). Second, there is as yet little work that has investigated relations between indices of temperament and home-based Q-Sort assessments. In the two studies conducted to date (Seifer et al., in press; Vaughn et al., 1992), correlations have been found between difficult temperament and lower Q-sort security scores, particularly as children grow older.

Because of the emphasis that has been placed on whether temperament "explains" patterns of attachment, little theoretical understanding can be derived from current work. We suggest that shifting to a focus on the second of the two possible links that we have noted would generate more useful results. If parent-child interactions during the months prior to the full behavioral expression of the attachment system do influence its development, then understanding the ways in which temperament might play a part in shaping these interactions would be quite valuable. For example, it is reasonable to expect that, as concerns mutual regulation, children who tend toward more negative mood, whose affect expressions are very intense, and who have more difficulty returning to a positive affective state when aroused are less likely to experience instances of successful mutual regulation, which are potentially important to the development of secure attachment. Similarly, activity level may be important in the development of secure-base behaviors in that highly active children might have difficulty coordinating the proximity/distance balance because of the interference of excess motor behavior. Conversely, low-active children may lack experience in doing so because of a tendency to stay in one place most of the time. Although these possibilities are speculative, they nevertheless point to areas where seeking to understand joint effects of temperament and the attachment system may provide important insights.

From a more methodological viewpoint, one must also consider consequences that follow when this approach is employed in assessing temperament. Parent reports probably confound two types of information: some indication of the child's actual behavior and some indication of the parent's cognitive and emotional processing of that behavior. Direct observation will provide a much cleaner view of the child's behavior, but only if a sample of behavior sufficient to provide reliable measurements is obtained (Seifer et al., 1994). Debate about the relation between temperament—taking the term to mean how infants actually behave—and attachment cannot be productive if the measures of infant behavior have yet to be demonstrated as valid. This is precisely the position in which we find ourselves when comparing parent reports of temperament with attachment assessments.

As with parenting sensitivity, the timing of temperament assessments is also an important issue to consider. When should temperament be expected to show its greatest influence on attachment assessment? If the issue concerns how temperament may be driving specific Strange Situation behavior, then concurrent temperament assessment makes the most sense. When the question concerns how temperament contributes to shaping the parent-child transactions that are important in the development of attachment, then some point in time prior to assessment of attachment would be indicated; timing temperament assessments so that they take place during the periods when parenting sensitivity appears to have its greatest influence could prove to be a productive strategy.

Sensitivity and Child Characteristics

It is also useful to consider the relation between the two influences on attachment that we have discussed—child characteristics and parenting sensitivity. We have already both noted that infant temperament may be important in shaping the parent-infant interactions that ultimately affect the development of secure-base behavior patterns and stressed the importance of understanding early dyadic interactions as a reciprocal process. The manner in which characteristics of both the child and the parent contribute to the dyadic interaction process should be the focus of study since there is every reason to expect that the characteristics of one will influence the behavior of the other (Gable & Isabella, 1992; Isabella & Gable, 1991; Mangelsdorf et al., 1990). Our own work suggests that there is indeed a relation between positive infant mood and greater parenting sensitivity at

6 and 9 months of age (Seifer et al., in press), a relation that was similar to those described by Mangelsdorf et al. (1990). Unfortunately, few studies have focused on such questions, and there are very few empirical data to address this issue with authority.

When seeking to examine empirical connections between the two constructs, in what context should temperament be assessed? If temperament is viewed as relatively insensitive to change in situation, one might consider assessing infant behavior either when the infant is alone or when he or she is interacting with a caregiver. However, there are data to indicate that these changes in situation do indeed have important effects on infant behavior (Seifer et al., 1992); hence, for the purpose of relating temperament to parenting sensitivity (and, ultimately, to attachment), it may be crucial to assess the infant's temperament in the context of parent-child interaction. This presents a methodological problem in that the parent's presence is bound to influence the assessment. However, if the relationship is viewed as the basic unit of analysis (a position that is consistent with attachment theory), examining child characteristics in the context of the relevant relationship is crucial.

Finally, a temperament construct that becomes salient when discussing connections between infant behavior and quality of parenting is that of *goodness of fit* (Thomas et al., 1963). Goodness of fit is a relationship construct whose formal properties can be described in terms similar to those used for the construct of attachment. The dyadic partners behave with each other according to set goals for a variety of infant temperament behaviors that are determined in part by prior expectations, in part by cultural background, and in part by immediate context. When the dyadic system operates close to these set goals, there is a high degree of fit; when their interactions consistently violate these goals, the fit is poor. Hinde (1982) has discussed how the match between characteristics of the dyad and the larger social context must be considered in attachment research; he cites examples in primates of how different strategies regarding proximity and exploration may have different survival implications depending on dominance status in the social group.

It is important to note that goodness of fit should not be construed as a static construct, akin to matching the pieces of a precut jigsaw puzzle. Rather, the partners in the relationship must be viewed as dynamic and changing on the basis of their accumulated interactive histories and as capable of influencing one another in fundamental ways. Further, the degree of fit is not established at some point to remain fixed thereafter but may repeatedly change over time as perturbations and repairs of the interaction take place. The concept of goodness of fit typically is used to describe parents adapting to difficulties presented by their infants; however, it can be applied equally well to the resilient child who adapts to less than optimal caregiving circumstances and hence promotes healthier development of the relationship. In sum, goodness of fit characterizes the "personality" of caregiver-infant relationships in ways that may be enduring over time (i.e., traitlike dimensions) as well as ways that are sensitive to the interactive history at a particular point in time (i.e., statelike dimensions).

Dyads that either fit well together naturally in smoothly maintaining set goals and/or that adapt well to perturbations during interactions will presumably work out a system of sensitive parenting, an appropriate proximity/exploration balance, and a secure attachment. Dyads that achieve a high degree of fit for temperaments associated with arousal of affect (e.g., mood, intensity, distress to limits, soothability) may appear as the most sensitively mutually regulated pairs; this achievement is likely to result from some combination of the infant's level of arousability or control of arousal and the responsiveness of the parent's interventions. In contrast, dyads that do not routinely achieve an adequate degree of fit are likely to be characterized by insensitive parenting and a greater likelihood of disturbances in the secure-base balance as well as an insecure quality of attachment.

CONCLUDING REMARKS

We have discussed three distinct conceptual domains of functioning in families of young infants: the attachment system, parenting sensitivity, and infant characteristics. Each of these domains has a well-defined and logically coherent conceptual base; nevertheless, many uncertainties concerning assessments limit our ability to examine and evaluate empirically the proposed theoretical explanations of the relations among these domains. Chief among these uncertainties are the breadth, scope, and comparative utility of different attachment assessments; the determination of relevant constructs to be considered in assessments of parenting sensitivity; and the use of different informants in assessing infant temperament.

The theoretical connections among these domains remain controversial or poorly explored. The least controversial relation lies between parenting sensitivity and attachment, yet the data to support this connection have been equivocal. The others either are poorly researched or represent questions that have not been addressed empirically; thus, for example, a full theoretical exploration of temperament or sensitivity constructs from a dyadic relational point of view has not been attempted. Finally, the entire theoretical basis for proposing any linkages needs to be evaluated in terms of the limits imposed by measurement constraints.

We conclude our essay by presenting five questions whose resolution we believe to be important in promoting progress in understanding the development of attachment relationships:

1. *What components of parenting behavior are essential in promoting secure-base behavior?*—The current construct of parenting sensitivity is broad and multi-dimensional; we do not know which of the many aspects of sensitivity are operative in the development of attachment systems, and the appropriate levels of analysis are not well specified (ranging from global observation schemes to microanalytic coding). Establishing whether the specific characteristics of sensitivity are appropriately represented in the global summary variables that have been employed can determine whether working with one unified construct or many specific (but related) constructs would be more productive in future research.

2. *What aspects of infant behavior serve to teach parents about the infant's security and the parent's sensitivity?*—The dynamic, transactional nature of early interactions has been little explored in the context of attachment theory; its main focus has been on the parent-to-child direction of effect (implicit in the emphasis on parenting sensitivity), even though the majority of developmentalists postulate bidirectional effects in dyadic interaction. We noted several types of infant interactive characteristics that have been proposed as being potentially important in the development of attachment (e.g., clarity of communication and modulation of arousal) and that could be included in studies of the antecedents of attachment. Continuing research on the contributions of infant temperament is useful, but it will be most productive if conducted in the context of confirming or disconfirming propositions derived from attachment theory rather than that of attempting to challenge the validity of attachment assessments.

3. *Which aspects of infant temperament act to affect secure-base behavior and the attachment system?*—Existing studies have not been consistent regarding which dimensions of temperament are considered in this context. As with parenting sensitivity, the multidimensional nature of the concept of temperament suggests that part of the research agenda should focus on isolating those components of infants' behavioral styles or biobehavioral regulation that are operative in the development of attachment. On theoretical grounds, identifying which temperament constructs are relevant to the development of attachment and explicitly testing these hypotheses will be a significant advance over current approaches.

4. *At what point in development are parenting sensitivity and infant temperament most influential in affecting secure-base behavior and the attachment system?*—The timing of the study of these effects is crucial since, if families are studied at the wrong point in development, associations will not be detected. This issue is complex both conceptually and methodologically. Identification of a sensitive period operating across all, or most, dyads has not been achieved—perhaps the timing of influences is in itself an individual difference. The only sure means of investigating the issue are complicated longitudinal designs that directly compare the same variables at differ-

ent points in development. Such complex research would benefit from strong theoretical predictions.

5. *What are the best criterion variables for assessing the predictive value of constructs presumed to affect attachment?*—There are currently only two established assessments available for use in the first years of life—the Attachment Q-Sort and the Strange Situation. Each of these has some characteristics that have proved useful, but neither has been subjected to the full range of validation. To promote such work, theoretically based propositions need to be made regarding the relative utility of assessing secure-base behavior in natural settings as opposed to assessing reunion strategies under stress as regards concurrent or subsequent prediction in different domains of functioning. Testing such specific theoretical assumptions will require clearer identification of the components of the attachment system that are being indexed in each of these assessments. Obvious validation strategies would include examining associations between Q-sort and Strange Situation assessments.

There are other, more theoretically driven, types of validation that might be attempted. For example, one prediction of attachment theory is that secure quality of attachment will promote more successful exploration of the environment; this can be examined empirically by relating successful nonanxious proximity behaviors to more elaborate or developmentally advanced exploratory behaviors (either closely linked in time or more generally across settings). Similarly, as we more precisely identify the set goals of infants that theoretically motivate the attachment control system, examination of whether secure attachment quality is associated with greater maintenance of these set goals across situations would provide validation of the construct and measurement strategies. These and other approaches that closely link theoretically derived components of attachment constructs with observed infant and caregiver behavior will enhance the validation of these constructs.

PART 4:
LINKING SECURE-BASE PHENOMENA
TO ATTACHMENT REPRESENTATION

INTRODUCTION TO PART 4

Both John Bowlby and Mary Ainsworth adopted an epigenetic viewpoint regarding the trajectory of attachment. That is to say, both saw attachments as directed toward a specific kind of outcome, namely, the internal representation or working model of the attachment figure, the self, and the relationship between the two. Bowlby (1980)—and more recently Bretherton (e.g., 1991)—turned to the concepts of cognitive psychology to flesh out his framework for describing such working models. Clearly, this line of thought has generated much new research, as the program of Main and her associates (e.g., Main & Goldwyn, in press-b) demonstrates. But the connection between mental representations of relationships and the cognitive capacity/limitations of children has not been as closely explored.

The reports in this part were intended to stretch the envelope of understanding(s) surrounding relations between mental/cognitive developmental phenomena and the representation of attachment. Lay, Waters, Posada, and Ridgeway stay most closely within the tradition of the earlier parts in that they consider the relations between the organization of secure-base behavior in preschool-aged children and their responses to mood induction. Bowlby considered both secure-base behavior and defensive processes central to attachment theory; this is the first experimental analysis of the hypothesis that these very different domains are related.

Oppenheim and Waters review the use of storytelling methodologies in research on children's attachment working models; they emphasize that an extended history of child-caregiver discourse may be a necessary condition for the co-construction of such models. They also suggest that narrative models are not the only kinds of representations that can arise in the course of child-parent interaction.

The final report, by Owens et al., brings the questions of representation nearly full circle. Although most attachment researchers have speculated privately regarding associations between early attachment relationships, currently held representations of attachment, and adult love relationships, these thoughts have remained speculative and private because data appropriate to the question were unavailable. Fortunately, methodological advances in assessment (George, Kaplan, & Main, 1984) made possible assessments of current representations of attachment that could be connected to (recollected) childhood experiences. Owens et al. took the next step of connecting those representations with representations of current love relationships by studying both in engaged couples. Their findings document the extent of relations between these two intimate relationships and suggest that one's history in attachment relationships—or at least one's currently held model of such relationships—does indeed play a role in the construction of later love relationships.

ATTACHMENT SECURITY, AFFECT REGULATION, AND DEFENSIVE RESPONSES TO MOOD INDUCTION

Keng-Ling Lay, Everett Waters, German Posada, and Doreen Ridgeway

Despite disagreeing with important elements of classical psychoanalytic theory, John Bowlby considered many of Freud's ideas about infant-parent and adult-adult relationships to be genuine insights. Among the most important of these propositions are (1) that infants have a complex social and emotional life, (2) that early experiences can have lifelong implications, (3) that mental representations of early experiences mediate effects on later behavior and development, (4) that defensive processes play a role in affect regulation, and (5) that loss of an attachment figure—at any age—is an emergency and mourning is a process that serves an adaptive affect-regulation function.

Many of Freud's insights about attachment were rooted more in clinical observation than in formal theory. One of Bowlby's most valuable contributions was recognizing that the value of such observations is independent of the theoretical framework in which Freud cast them. Indeed, he recognized that they could be preserved only by recasting them in a more scientifically respectable theoretical framework. Bowlby's (1969/1982) concept of an attachment behavioral system provided an alternative motivational theory/model that could be expressed in terms of control-systems theory and evolutionary theory. In addition, his working-models concept recast important psychoanalytic insights about mental representation in the language of cognitive psychology.

Address correspondence to Keng-Ling Lay, Department of Psychology, National Taiwan University, No. 1, Roosevelt Road, Section 4, Taipei, Taiwan ROC; Everett Waters and Doreen Ridgeway, Department of Psychology, State University of New York at Stony Brook, Stony Brook, NY 11794; or German Posada, Department of Psychology, University of Denver, Denver, CO 80208.

Attachment theory rests on these two cornerstones: the control-system/ secure-base concept and the cognitive/dynamic concepts of attachment representation and defensive processes. On these foundations Bowlby intended to build a comprehensive theory of close relationships and personality development across the life span. A central postulate of Bowlby's theory is that the secure-base phenomenon is the developmental precursor of the cognitive representations and defensive processes emphasized in his discussions of adult attachment and loss (Bowlby, 1973, 1980). Empirically confirming this postulate and framing a detailed theoretical explanation would represent a milestone in attachment theory. Unfortunately, the link between secure-base phenomena and cognitive representations and defensive processes has not yet been established. Until recently, research on secure-base phenomena centered on the earliest years of life, and research on attachment representations focused on the adult years; this has led some to describe current attachment theory as a theory of infancy and of adulthood, with a great deal in between left to the imagination (Waters, Kondo-Ikemura, Posada, & Richters, 1990).

There are several ways in which we could establish links between secure-base phenomena, cognitive representations, and defensive processes. We could look at longitudinal data relating the secure-base behavior of an individual as an infant to his or her own attachment working models in adulthood. Bowlby's hypothesis would be strongly supported if patterns of secure-base behavior were concordant with the types of cognitive and defensive processes scored in the Berkeley Adult Attachment Interview (AAI; Main & Goldwyn, 1991). Unfortunately, the necessary data are not yet available (see Waters, Merrick, Albersheim, & Treboux, 1995). Of course, a negative result would not disprove the hypothesis that secure-base behavior in infancy and cognitive/representational processes in adulthood are related; it would simply mean that such relations are not evident in long-term Strange Situation/AAI concordance.[1]

Another approach to linking secure-base behavior and cognitive/defen-

[1] The fact that infant Strange Situation classifications tend to be concordant with mothers' Adult Attachment Interview classifications (Ainsworth & Eichberg, 1991; Fonagy, Steele, & Steele, 1991; Grossmann, Fremmer-Bombik, Rudolph, & Grossmann, 1988; Levine, Tuber, Slade, & Ward, 1991; Main, Kaplan, & Cassidy, 1985; Sagi, Aviezer, Joels, Koren-Karie, Mayseless, Sharf, & van IJzendoorn, 1992; van IJzendoorn, Kranenburg, Zwart-Woudstra, van Busschbach, & Lambermon, 1991; Zeanah et al., 1993) is often taken as indication that we may be able to link secure-base behavior with phenomena in the cognitive/representational domain. Logically, however, such data only establish a link between secure-base behavior and adult representations if infants of secure mothers grow up to be secure, etc. But data establishing this would be definitive support for the secure-base/adult representation hypothesis. If we had the longitudinal data necessary to support the mother-infant concordance data, we would not need the mother-infant concordance data.

sive processes would be to examine both in the context of adult love relationships. One example of this type of approach is the Current Relationship Interview, developed by Owens et al. (in this volume), which captures, among other things, some aspects of secure-base use in adult love relationships. Owens et al. have found significant relations between representations of adults' relationships to parents (AAI) and functioning in current love relationships. These are promising indications, but a much stronger case could be made by relating direct observations of adult secure-base use to AAI classifications. Again, the necessary data are not yet available.

Bowlby (1960, 1969/1982) defined *infant attachment* as an emotional bond that ties the infant to one or a few figures across time and distance. Anxiety, anger, detachment, and helplessness figured prominently in the clinical phenomena that inspired his early work on children, as did emotion regulation and defensive processes. Bowlby treated emotion as an important source of information in his control-system model of secure-base behavior. Today it plays a role in most methods of assessing secure-base patterns and attachment working models (Ainsworth, Blehar, Waters, & Wall, 1978; Main, Kaplan, & Cassidy, 1985; Oppenheim & Waters, in this volume; Waters & Deane, 1985). For attachment theorists, flags are raised whenever emotion seems unregulated, out of context, disorganized, or absent. The central role of emotion and emotion regulation in theories of secure-base behavior and working models suggests a third approach to relations between secure-base behavior and cognitive/representational processes— examining secure-base behavior and cognitive/defensive processes concurrently in infancy or childhood.

Methods for assessing secure-base behavior at this age are well developed. But because subjective states are difficult to assess, especially in infants and children, hypotheses about emotion and defensive processes have seemed untestable (Campos, Campos, & Barrett, 1989). The role of defensive processes in attachment is particularly difficult to study empirically because both eliciting stimuli and subjects' responses are often covert and because scoring defensiveness often involves highly subjective judgments. What is familiar to every therapist has remained largely inaccessible to the experimentalist.

Bowlby's work and recent developmental research suggest that representational/defensive processes might be assessed by using mood-induction procedures to elicit individual differences in emotion regulation processes, especially in relation to attachment- and non-attachment-related mood-induction stimuli. Mood induction has been used extensively with children (Kenrick, Baumann, & Cialdini, 1979; Lay, Waters, & Park, 1989; Potts, Morse, Felleman, & Masters, 1986; Ridgeway & Waters, 1987; Underwood, Froming, & Moore, 1977) and has proved to be a very flexible methodology and to entail little risk of undesirable reactions. Unfortunately, research on relations between attachment and emotion has progressed slowly. Only infant-mother face-to-face interactions and separation protest have been studied in detail, and much of this work uses emotional expression merely as a means of studying cognitive development. Emotion regulation too has been the subject of many recent studies, often using mood induction to elicit target responses (Dodge, 1989; Masters, Ford, & Arend, 1983; Thompson, 1994). Little of this research, however, has addressed issues in attachment theory. The role of defensive processes in attachment is particularly difficult to study empirically.

From the 1950s to the early 1970s, both emotion and individual differences were out of favor in developmental psychology. That they stayed on the agenda at all was perhaps largely due to psychologists' enduring interest in temperament constructs (e.g., Buss & Plomin, 1975; Thomas, Chess, Birch, Hertzig, & Korn, 1963). Even with emotion and individual differences returning once again to the mainstream of developmental psychology, temperament research remains a major source of data on emotion in infancy and childhood (see Kohnstamm, 1990). A number of recent studies have found significant correlations between attachment security and positive affect (Vaughn et al., 1992). Such data are most often discussed in terms of the attachment measures' discriminant validity (or lack thereof). Equally likely is the possibility that both attachment security and positive affect (Lay et al., 1989) are related to a third factor, namely, harmonious parent-child interaction. There is a great deal of evidence establishing the basic discriminant validity of attachment measures (Sroufe, 1985); nonetheless, individual differences in emotional responsiveness are certain to play an interesting and important role in secure-base behavior.

Taking a more developmental perspective and looking at temperament constructs as possible moderators of the relation between maternal sensitivity and secure-base outcomes opens up new questions. For instance, do infants with different temperament profiles experience insensitive care differently? Can the behavioral structure of insensitive care affect the development of secure-base patterns, or must the infant also experience negative affect? The same questions can be asked in relation to sensitive care and positive affect. As Waters et al. (1990) pointed out, secure-base behavior is learned. A better understanding of the interactions between maternal sensitivity and the parameters of affective response could reveal much about the types of learning involved and about what is learned, and it could also help integrate complex phenomena such as social referencing (Campos & Stenberg, 1981) into attachment theory.

In this study, we employed standardized mood-induction procedures to examine the relation between attachment security and representational/ defensive processes in childhood. In previous work with mood-induction procedures (Lay et al., 1989; Ridgeway & Waters, 1987), we have noticed that children sometimes report positive responses to negative stimuli. The precise and coherent manner in which these children state and explain such paradoxical responses makes it clear that they are not errors. Such paradoxical responses served as our measure of defensive response. In order to evaluate the specificity of responses to attachment-relevant stimuli, half the stimuli that we used portray the mother as the agent, and half do not mention the mother at all.

This is a critically important manipulation—many studies relating attachment status to emotional responses are correlational or naturalistic and do not address alternative interpretations. Without appropriate controls we cannot distinguish effects of attachment on emotion from effects of individual differences in emotional responsiveness on attachment (i.e., a "happy baby" hypothesis—that purported signs of attachment security reflect only a child's low threshold for positive emotion).

Fortunately, attachment and temperament interpretations of emotion expression lead to very different predictions. Attachment theory predicts that emotional responses (and defensive responses in particular) to attachment and nonattachment stimuli will be very different to different stimuli and across different contexts; temperament theories predict traitlike consistency in emotional response across a wide range of stimuli.

METHOD

Subjects

The study was conducted in the homes of 48 intact, middle-class families residing in suburban Long Island, New York. We observed 21 boys and 27 girls (mean age = 4.5 years, range = 4-2 to 4-11) and their mothers. The children were ranked on the basis of Attachment Q-Set (AQS; Waters, 1987) security scores (see below), and the 16 most secure and 16 least secure children (five boys and 11 girls in each group) were selected for the study. The secure and insecure groups were comparable in mean age (secure = 4.4 years, insecure = 4.5 years).

Materials

Mood-Induction Vignettes

In pilot research, we asked mothers of preschool children to list events that had induced feelings of happiness, excitement, pride, anger, sadness, or fear in their 4-year-olds; we asked that they include both mother-involved and other types of events. From these listings we then selected topics for brief (50–100-word) narrative vignettes. The mood-induction stimuli used in the present study consisted of 24 videotaped readings of such vignettes, 12 for positive and 12 for negative moods; each set contained six "mother-involved" and six "mother-not-involved" situations. To avoid prompting a particular affective response, the texts (listed in the Appendix to this report) were free of mood-descriptive terms.

The readings were videotaped in order to standardize their presentation. Each was presented by an adult female actress who began by saying, "I'm going to tell you about something. Maybe it didn't really happen to you. But I want you to think about it and tell me how you would feel if this really happened to you." In order to minimize carryover from vignette to vignette and to maintain the children's interest, we employed six different actresses, each of whom presented one positive and one negative mother-involved vignette and one positive and one negative mother-not-involved vignette. The camera framed the head and shoulders of the actress, who looked directly toward the camera and spoke in a clear, pleasant voice, adding emphasis where appropriate, but allowing neither vocal tone nor facial expression to suggest either a positive or a negative response to the event. All 24 vignettes were transferred to a single half-inch videocassette. The order of positive and negative and of mother-involved and mother-not-involved vignettes was counterbalanced, with different actresses presenting adjacent vignettes.

Procedures

Prior to each home visit, the attachment observation and the mood-induction procedures were explained to the mother over the telephone. Each mother-child pair was visited once for a period of 2–3 hours by three visitors. The mother received a typed copy of the mood-induction vignettes at the beginning of the visit. The format and tone of the visits was informal; mothers were encouraged to go about their activities and to treat the visitors as they would a visiting neighbor, not as guests. At a convenient time during the visit, the mother and child took 15—20 min to bake and frost cupcakes, using ingredients provided by the visitors. Periodically during each visit, the third visitor asked the child to watch videotaped mood-induction vignettes.

Attachment Assessment

The observations of secure-base behavior were conducted according to procedures described by Waters, Posada, and Vaughn (1994). After the home visit, two of the observers provided independent Q-sort descriptions of the child's behavior. Interobserver reliability (using the Spearman-Brown formula) across the 90 Attachment Q-set items was computed for each subject, yielding a mean reliability of .78 (range = .54–.89). The two Q-sorts were then averaged. Security scores were computed by correlating the composite Q-sort with the 90-item Q-sort description of the "hypothetical most secure child" (see App. D), and this correlation served as the child's attachment security score. The scores of the 16 most secure children ranged from .50 to .70 (average = .56), those of the 16 least secure children from −.12 to .36 (average = .19).

Mood Induction

Our goal was to have each child watch and report emotional responses to as many of the 24 vignettes as possible. Promised a choice of colorful paper stickers, most children watched and responded to 6–10 vignettes (a period of 10–15 min) before becoming inattentive or asking to do something else. After 20–30 min, or at some opportune moment, the child was offered another paper sticker and asked to watch a few more vignettes; most agreed to do so at least twice during the visit. The mean number of vignettes viewed was 18 (range = 11–24). There was no significant difference in the number of stories seen by children in the secure group (M = 18.6, range = 13–24) and those in the insecure group (M = 16.4, range = 11–24).

The Attachment Q-sort observers left the room during the mood-induction sessions. The mother was invited to observe the mood-induction procedure from a position behind the child and visitor; few of them watched for more than the first few vignettes.

Mood Assessment

Because the children were young, we used a modified version of Ridgeway and Russell's (1985) nonverbal paired-comparison procedure to assess emotional response to each mood-induction vignette. The procedure employs cartoon faces similar to the familiar "happy face" icon that portray seven expressions: very happy, moderately happy, slightly happy, neutral, slightly sad, moderately sad, and very sad. Although older children and adults can assign numerical ratings to these faces, a forced-choice paired-comparison task is more appropriate for younger children. In the complete paired-comparisons task, the subject indicates for each of the 21 possible pairs which of the faces is most like the emotion that he or she feels at the moment. The positive/negative mood dimension is scored by counting the number of comparisons in which the more positive face is chosen.

To allow for the children's very young age and the difficulty of completing multiple trials, we used only two of the 21 possible pairs of comparisons—*moderately happy versus neutral* and *neutral versus moderately sad*—to determine the valence of the child's emotional response to each vignette, according to the following rules:

> *Purely positive.*—The child preferred the more positive pair in both sets (i.e., moderately positive over neutral and neutral over moderately sad).
>
> *Purely negative.*—The child preferred the less positive face in each pair (i.e., neutral over positive and moderately sad over neutral).
>
> *Neutral.*—The child preferred the neutral face in both pairs.
>
> *Mixed.*—The child preferred moderately positive over neutral and also moderately negative over neutral.

The entire emotion assessment procedure was audiotaped, and the order and position of the faces in these pairs was counterbalanced. The percentages of positive, negative, neutral, and mixed responses were computed for each type of mood-induction vignette. After the paired comparisons, the child was asked to explain his or her response to the vignette. If during this questioning the child reported both positive and negative responses, the vignette was scored as mixed, regardless of the valence indicated by the initial paired comparisons. After these initial pairs, follow-up pairs (e.g., very sad vs. moderately sad) were administered to quantify the intensity of the response. Follow-up pairs were also administered if a child mentioned a mixed response during the follow-up questioning. Analyses of the valence data and the more thorough quantitative assessment of mood intensity yielded the same pattern of results. Consequently, only the results based on the valence assessments are presented here. (The procedures for administering and scoring the follow-up pairs are available from the authors on request.)

RESULTS

Manipulation and Assessment Check

We first examined the effectiveness of the mood-induction procedures and the accuracy of the children's mood reports. As expected, children reported significantly more "purely positive" than "purely negative" responses to positive vignettes ($t[47] = 18.56$, $p < .0000$) and more "purely negative" than "purely positive" responses to negative vignettes ($t[47] = 11.98$, $p < .0000$). The mean proportions of vignettes scored positive, negative, neutral, and mixed are presented in Table 1. The high level of discrimination between positive and negative vignettes and the low frequency of

TABLE 1

AFFECTIVE STATE INDUCED BY POSITIVE AND NEGATIVE VIGNETTES: RESPONSES TO A
POSITIVE VERSUS A NEUTRAL AND A NEUTRAL VERSUS A NEGATIVE PAIRED COMPARISON

RESPONSE TO INITIAL (+ VS. O AND − VS. O) PAIRED COMPARISONS[a]	RESPONSE DESCRIPTION	VIGNETTE TYPE	
		Positive (%)	Negative (%)
Positive; neutral	Purely positive	80 (20–100)	11 (0–33)
Neutral; negative	Purely negative	3 (0–50)	59 (0–100)
Neutral; neutral	Neutral	2 (0–33)	3 (0–75)
Positive; negative	Mixed	16 (0–75)	26 (0–100)

NOTE.—Ranges are given in parentheses.

[a] Subjects' responses to the positive vs. neutral and the negative vs. neutral paired comparisons. The first term indicates the child's response to the positive vs. neutral paired comparison. The second term indicates the child's response to the neutral vs. negative paired comparison. "Positive; neutral" indicates that the child preferred positive to neutral on one trial and neutral to negative on the other. (As indicated in the text, the order of presentation was counterbalanced.)

purely neutral responses indicate that the mood-induction procedures and the mood assessments worked as intended.[2]

Individual Differences of Attachment and Mood Induceability

The relations between attachment security and responses to positive and to negative mood inductions were examined in separate 2 (attachment status) × 2 (mother involved vs. not involved) ANOVAs. The mean proportions of "purely positive" responses to positive vignettes are presented in the top panel of Table 2.

There was no indication that the most secure children were any more responsive to positive mood inductions than the least secure ones. A 2 × 2 (attachment group × maternal involvement) ANOVA on "purely positive" responses to the positive vignette data revealed only a significant main effect of mother involvement ($F[1, 30] = 4.42, p < .05$); both groups more often responded positively to vignettes that did not involve mother. The relative novelty and concreteness of the mother-not-involved vignettes may have contributed to this result. Neither the main effect of attachment group nor the interaction was significant.

The mean proportions of "purely negative" responses to negative vignettes are presented in the bottom panel of Table 2.

[2] The number of negative responses to the positive vignettes is inflated somewhat by the fact that a number of children said that they were frightened by the fish caught in positive, mother-not-involved vignette 4.

TABLE 2

Children's Responses to Mother-Not-Involved (MNI) and
Mother-Involved (MI) Mood-Induction Vignettes
(N = 16 in Each Group)

| | Purely Positive Responses to Positive Vignettes (Mean % of Vignettes) | | | |
| | Mother-Not-Involved | | Mother-Involved | |
	M	SD	M	SD
Attachment status:				
Most secure	79	18	74	23
Least secure	82	24	73	21
	Purely Negative Responses To Negative Vignettes (Mean % of Vignettes)			
Attachment status:				
Most secure	58	38	44	41
Least secure	45	31	63	33

There was no indication that secure children are less affected by, or in any sense resistant to, negative inductions. A 2 × 2 (attachment group × maternal involvement) ANOVA conducted on the purely negative responses to negative vignettes revealed no significant main effects. Thus, the data do not support a "happy baby" alternative to the secure attachment concept.

There was, however, a significant interaction between attachment group and maternal involvement ($F[1, 30] = 6.14, p < .02$). Secure and insecure children respond very differently to negative mother-involved and mother-not-involved vignettes, in a manner that is clarified by examining defensive responses (positive and mixed) to the negative vignettes.

Defensive Responding: Positive and Mixed Responses to Negative Vignettes

As in our pilot data, and as the results of the negative responses to negative vignettes imply, there was a substantial number of positive—and hence paradoxical—responses to negative vignettes. As mentioned above, we believe that these were not errors since they were associated with transformations or elaborations that made it possible for the child to focus on positive aspects of the vignettes. Because they reduce the expression or the experience of negative affect, we have tentatively labeled such responses *defensive*. That these may be related to attachment status was suggested by the finding of an interaction in the preceding analysis between respon-

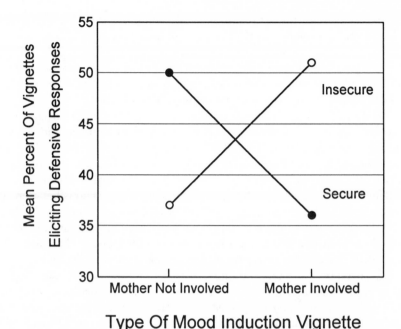

FIG. 1.—Relation between child attachment status (secure vs. insecure) and defensive responses to negative mood-induction vignettes (mother not involved vs. mother involved).

siveness and negative mood inductions, where the dependent variable was limited to "purely positive" responses.

Because both "purely positive" and "mixed" responses to negative vignettes can be construed as defensive, we performed a 2 (attachment status) × 2 (mother involvement) ANOVA including both types of responses in the dependent variable. Neither main effect was significant. The attachment status × mother involvement interaction was significant ($F[1, 30] = 4.95$, $p < .04$). This interaction is illustrated in Figure 1. For secure children, the mean percentage of defensive responses was 50 (SD = 34) for mother-not-involved vignettes and 36 (SD = 37) for mother-involved vignettes. The corresponding mean percentages for insecure children were 37 (SD = 31) for mother-not-involved and 51 (SD = 33) for mother-involved vignettes.

DISCUSSION

Secure-base behavior is central to the Bowlby/Ainsworth perspective on attachment. Individual differences in infant attachment relationships are conceptualized in terms of the infant's ability to use the caregiver as a secure base and the caregiver's ability to respond to infant signals and serve consistently as a secure base over time and situations. Critics of attachment theory have suggested that individual differences such as those assessed in the Strange Situation can be interpreted instead in terms of individual differences in affective response parameters (e.g., Kagan, 1984).

We found no support for such alternative interpretations. Secure subjects were no more responsive to positive mood inductions, and no less responsive to negative mood inductions, than insecure subjects. Although secure infants and toddlers tend to display more positive affect during interaction with their mothers (Vaughn et al., 1992), these differences are best explained as a reflection of the more harmonious interactions between secure children and their mothers. Lay et al. (1989) have demonstrated experimentally that even a minor manipulation favoring harmonious interaction can induce positive affect in preschool-aged children. Surely there are individual differences in affective responsiveness, and to some extent these are traitlike, even heritable (Kohnstamm, 1990). But we should not take temperament explanations for granted. The extent to which stable individual differences in emotion-related responses arise from social experience deserves careful attention. Similar attention should be paid to the role of social relationships in consolidating biases in parameters of affective learning and transforming them into traitlike individual differences.

Our analysis of "defensive" responses revealed a theoretically interesting relation between attachment security and emotion regulation. Although secure and insecure children were equally likely to respond defensively to negative mood inductions, their responses to mother-agent and other-agent vignettes were very different. In the case of the mother-not-involved negative vignettes, the secure child avoids negative affect by cognitively transforming the vignette in a way that reduces its potential for eliciting negative affect. The negative mother-agent vignettes are construed (or appraised) by such a child quite differently. As Freud and Bowlby emphasized, separation or rejection (threatened separation) is construed as an emergency. For the secure child, the level of experienced emotion provides important information that activates a readily available and well-integrated secure-base response system—shutting off the emotion in such instances would be counterproductive.

Faced with a mother-not-involved negative vignette, an insecure child is much less able to transform it and attenuate its impact. This is not a traitlike deficit since, when faced with a negative vignette in which mother is the agent, insecure children show that they can transform the material and redirect attention every bit as well as secure children do in instances of other-agent vignettes. In effect, we propose that, in the case of mother-agent negative vignettes, insecure children are using cognitive mechanisms to prevent the attachment response system from becoming activated. Emotion activates the secure-base system, and secure-base behavior can be ignored or rebuffed. Because the latter is strongly goal oriented, it is understandable that experientially based expectations of maternal unresponsiveness or rejection might engender even stronger negative affect.

Our interpretation has much in common with Lazarus's (1991) cognitive theory of emotion and adaptation. Specifically, our proposition concerning children's use of cognitive processes to transform a potentially aversive vignette into something less aversive parallels what Lazarus calls *short-circuiting of threat:* "Short-circuiting may be thought of as a metaphor . . . for the triggering of defense without anxiety having to play a role. The decision about the danger, and the defense against it, was, in effect, made earlier in the person's life as a result of prior learning and contemporaneously only requires the right cue to elicit it" (pp. 164–165).

Our view of the children's differential responses to the mother-agent and other-agent vignettes suggests something similar to Lazarus's (1991) notion of primary appraisal, which he defines as a person's analysis of whether an event is relevant to his or her well-being. The present results suggest that children who differ in their ability to use mother as a secure base from which to explore also appraise mother-involved (and perhaps mother-not-involved) negative situations differently.

One additional parallel between our interpretation and Lazarus's theory is that both focus on appraisal and coping processes that can occur prior to emotion rather than in response to it. Traditionally, attachment theory has assigned the attachment system a central role in emotion regulation. Here we have cognitive processes controlling arousal and thus whether the attachment system is even engaged. In order to understand the relation between attachment and emotion regulation, attachment theory may have to find its place in a broader theoretical framework such as cognitive self theory. The downfall of many theories begins when they try alone to explain too much.

In an early study of cognitive control over emotion in children, Terwogt, Schene, and Harris (1985) asked 6-year-olds to adopt a detached attitude while listening to a sad story and then interviewed them about their self-control strategies. Although many of their subjects could not describe a specific strategy, denial and maintaining detachment were common, as was imagining themselves somehow involved in the story. Our paradigm was somewhat different in that emotion regulation was spontaneous rather than instructed. The fact that our method had the child imagine experiencing the vignettes may have reduced the likelihood of detachment and hence partially explain the higher rate of seemingly more sophisticated cognitive coping. The subtlety and sophistication of the children's defensive responses to the negative mother-agent and other-agent vignettes deserve further attention from experts in coping skills and in cognitive development.

Although these are the first experimental data to link secure-base behavior to defensive processes, there are already a number of studies relating attachment status to emotionality and emotion regulation. This literature is reviewed in detail by Cassidy (1994). The present study differs from most of this work in several respects that may prove important for future research. First, we found little of interest in merely quantitative dependent variables defined in terms of intensity or threshold of response. Thus, it may be useful in the future to pay greater attention to context and to cognitive processes. Second, we used a simple self-report method to elicit information about each child's emotional experience after each vignette. Most previous studies have assessed only emotion expression, and, although this index can be quite useful, the relation of emotion expression to emotion is complex and not well understood. Clearly, attachment theory is primarily concerned with emotion per se.

Further research is needed before we can say that secure-base behavior and working models can be incorporated into a unified attachment theory. It seems likely that many important issues will turn on research linking appraisal processes, emotion regulation, and behavior. This report illustrates the viability and some of the advantages of an experimental approach to these issues.

APPENDIX: MOOD-INDUCTION VIGNETTES

Each vignette was introduced by an actress saying, "I'm going to tell you about something. Maybe it didn't really happen to you. But I want you to think about it and tell me how you would feel if this really happened to you." The vignettes follow.

Mother-Agent Vignettes

Positive

1. "One day, you were in school, and you drew a picture. And you took it home and showed it to Mommy. And her eyes just popped open. And she said, 'It is beautiful!' And she hugged you, and she wanted to show the picture to everybody. How would that make you feel?"
2. "One day, you and Mommy were home together, and she said she would read you a story. And so you sat up on the bed, Mommy's big bed. And you sat right next to her and snuggled close to her. And she put her

arm around you. And she started to read you the sweetest story. And you sat there together while she read the story. How would that make you feel?"

3. "One day, Mommy's friend was visiting, and you were sitting on Mommy's lap while they talked. And Mommy was telling her friend that you were just the sweetest, best little child any mother could have. And then she smiled at you and said, 'I love you so much!' How would that make you feel?"

4. "One day, Mommy was trying to fix a broken chair, and she just couldn't fix it. And you said, 'It's easy Mommy! All you need is someone to help you!' And so you helped her work on the broken chair. And when one part of the chair was still hard to fix, you saw just how to fix it. And you said, 'Here Mommy, all you have to do is this.' And together you got the job done. And Mommy said, 'Thank you—*my helper.*' How would that make you feel?"

5. "One day, you and Mommy were looking at pictures from when you were a little baby. And Mommy told you that you were really cute. And she told you all kinds of cute little things you used to do. And she really liked talking about these pictures. And she told you all the things about when you were a little baby. How would that make you feel?"

6. "One day, Mommy went into the kitchen to make a cake. And you said, 'Can I help?' And she said, 'Well, you are very grown up now. So *yes,* we can make the cake together.' And she helped you crack some eggs open. And she put her arm on your shoulder while you poured in some milk and cake mix. Then you took turns stirring the cake mix. And Mommy said, 'You are just like me. We are both great cooks!' How would that make you feel?"

Negative

1. "One day, you were at home with your mom. She was working in the living room, and you were playing in your room with your toys. And you didn't hear her, but she had to go out of the house. And she forgot to tell you that she was going. And then you went into the living room to find her, and she wasn't there. And you looked all around the house, and she wasn't anywhere. And you didn't know where she was. You were all alone. How would that make you feel?"

2. "One day, Mommy was cleaning up your room and putting your toys away. And there was one toy you really loved. And after she cleaned up, you couldn't find it. And she couldn't find it either. So Mommy said, 'It doesn't matter if it is gone.' How would that make you feel?"

3. "One day, you were at home playing, and after a while you went into the kitchen to find your mommy. And you walked over to sit on her

lap and hug her. And she said, 'Don't bother me right now. Go play.' How would that make you feel?"

4. "One day, Mommy was watching TV. And you wanted to watch with her. And she just said, 'No, go away; you're in my way. Only grown-ups can watch this.' And she wouldn't let you watch TV with her. How would that make you feel?"

5. "One day, you came home from school, and you wanted to tell Mommy something really important. And Mommy was talking to her friend. And she wouldn't listen. And you said, 'Mommy, Mommy, I've got to tell you. It's important.' And she said, 'No, no, don't interrupt me.' And you said, 'Mommy, I have to tell you.' She became a little bit grouchy and said, 'I am talking to my friend. Don't tell me now. Tell me later.' How would that make you feel?"

6. "One day, you were at home and drawing pictures. And when you finished your picture, you took it to Mommy. And she said, 'I don't think that's a very good job. Go back, and do it again, better.' How would that make you feel?"

Other-Agent Vignettes

Positive

1. "One day, you were in a grocery store, and a lady said to you that you were the winner of a great big bowl of ice cream. You could choose your favorite flavor, and you got to have as much as you wanted. And she brought up a huge bowl with all kinds of little sprinkles, syrup, and everything you wanted. And she gave you a great big spoon, and you got to eat the whole thing up. How would that make you feel?"

2. "One day, after you waited a long time, it was your birthday. And everybody called you the birthday child. And you had a big party, and all your friends came. And they played games and ate birthday cakes, and you got presents. And you opened them, and they were great. How would that make you feel?"

3. "One day, you were at your friend's house. And your friend had a toy that you really enjoyed playing with. It was different from any toy you had ever owned. When your friend saw how much you liked the toy, he/she said, 'You can take it home, and you can keep it.' And his/her mother said, 'It's OK. You can have it.' So you took it home and played with it for a long time every day. How would that make you feel?"

4. "One day, you went to a big park where there was a big lake. And in the lake were lots of fish. And you had a *fishing pole and some string* (net), and you put the *string* (net) in the water, and all of a sudden you caught a *great big* (beautiful) fish. You had always wanted to catch a fish. And now

you had caught the *biggest* (most beautiful) fish ever. How would that make you feel?"[3]

5. "One day you were at your friend's birthday party. And one of the grown-ups said, 'OK, now we are going to have a race. And whoever wins the race will get a great prize!' So all the children lined up, and the grown-up said, '1-2-3-*go!*' And you ran really fast and won the race. And everyone was cheering and shouting your name and telling you how good you were. And they gave you the prize. How would that make you feel?"

6. "Someday you're gonna grow up, and you're gonna be really big and really grown up. And you're gonna get to first grade. And you're gonna have a class of your own. And a teacher of your own. And books. And you're gonna be really grown up. And you get to go to your school everyday. How would that make you feel?"

Negative

1. "One day, some children came to your house to visit, and they played with your most favorite toy. And they liked it so much they wouldn't let you play with it when it was your turn. And they wouldn't let you play with it at all. They just kept it for themselves and played with it. And you didn't get to use it. How would that make you feel?"

2. "You were sleeping one time. And you were having a dream, and in the dream there were some big monsters chasing you, and they wouldn't leave you alone. And they were bothering you. And you were in sleep and didn't know how to get away. How would that make you feel?"

3. "One day, you were walking alone in the woods and on your way to someone's house. Suddenly it got very dark. There were clouds in the sky. And it looked like it was going to rain. And you heard thunder rumbling and lightning cracks. And you saw lightning hit a tree right near you. And the tree fell right down across the path. How would that make you feel?"

4. "One day, you and your class from school went together on a picnic. And everybody brought a snack. And when it was lunchtime, one of your friends had something that looked really good to eat. And you wanted to try it. You friend said it was OK. But the teacher said, 'No, you may not share food with the other children. You must eat your own food. And do not taste the food from another child. And children you must not give food even to your friends.' How would that make you feel?"

5. "One day, you were in the park. And you just bought a big ice cream cone. And you wanted to walk over to a bench and sit down and eat your

[3] The italicized words were the ones used in this research. Replace them with the words in parentheses to avoid a negative response to this vignette.

ice cream. But on the way the ice cream fell right off the cone and landed on the ground. And it was all dirty. And you could not eat it because it was dirty and melting, and you didn't have any money to buy any more. So you got no ice cream at all. And you really wanted it. How would that make you feel?"

6. "One day, you got a telephone call. It was a friend of yours who lives in another town, and your friend said that they had bought you a beautiful present. And they were sending it to you in the mail. So you should wait by the door until the present comes. And you waited and waited and waited, and it didn't come. And the next day you sat by the door of your house, and you waited, and you waited, and you waited. But the present that your friend had promised never came in the mail. How would that make you feel?"

NARRATIVE PROCESSES
AND ATTACHMENT REPRESENTATIONS:
ISSUES OF DEVELOPMENT AND ASSESSMENT

David Oppenheim and Harriet Salatas Waters

John Bowlby was a thorough and imaginative scholar. He was also farsighted in his plans for attachment theory. In evolutionary and control-systems theories, he saw useful alternatives to psychoanalytic motivation models and conceptual foundations that had passed the test of time and could only grow stronger with succeeding generations. Moreover, he perceived how the emerging field of cognitive psychology could play a major role in his efforts to "demystify" psychoanalytic insights about attachment and adjustment. Most important for current directions in attachment theory, he saw in Craik's (1943) concept of internal working models a way of demystifying and thus preserving psychoanalytic insights about the importance of mental representations in development and adjustment.

A great deal of attachment theory and research is based on the control-systems model and the secure-base concept as developed in the first volume of *Attachment and Loss* (Bowlby, 1969) and in Ainsworth's empirical and theoretical papers (e.g., Ainsworth, Blehar, Waters, & Wall, 1979). Here the focus is on infancy, and any attachment representations are necessarily sensorimotor in nature. The later volumes of *Attachment and Loss,* several of Bowlby's later writings (e.g., Bowlby, 1988), and a great deal of recent theory and research have focused on *mental* representations of attachment, which Bowlby referred to as *working models.*

One of the key differences between attachment theory and psychoanalytic theory is Bowlby's consistent emphasis on real rather than intrapsychic events and on ordinary rather than traumatic experiences as determinants of attachment relationships. Both secure-base behavior and attachment working models are said to emerge through everyday child-parent interactions and, although potentially stable, to be open to change in light of new experience. However, despite this emphasis on the importance of real-world experience, attachment theory and research have not as yet detailed how early care leads to secure-base behavior (Waters, Kondo-Ikemura, Posada, & Richters, 1990) or how the transition to mental representations is achieved.

One of Bowlby's most important insights was that what caretakers tell their children about early attachment experiences and related emotions is profoundly important for later adjustment. He found, however, that the cognitive psychology of his day did not provide the tools necessary to translate this insight into a detailed understanding of how attachment working models develop, and it is only more recently that Bretherton (1987, 1990) has taken important steps toward developing his insights in this area.

Bowlby's ideas about the importance of child-parent communication in attachment development are reflected in recent trends in assessment, especially in the use of interviews and children's narratives to assess attachment status. Underlying much of this work is the notion that working models determine key characteristics of children's attachment-related narratives. In the first section of this report, we review recent research based on narrative assessments, noting that, although these studies emphasize working models as determinants of children's narratives, they also rely on (1) the ease and openness in the way children communicate narratives about attachment and other emotionally evocative interpersonal themes and (2) the emotional coherence of these narratives.

We then review Bowlby's thoughts regarding the importance of parent-child verbal communication in the development of attachment security beyond infancy, emphasizing the relevance of recent work on the co-construction of personal narratives through child-parent discourse. The representations that emerge from such co-construction processes bear on the child's experience, interpretation, and representation of concurrent and subsequent attachment-related experience. We highlight both interpersonal narrative/communication processes and intrapersonal aspects of cognitive development as determinants of children's narrative productions, and we suggest that theory and research in both areas have advanced to the point where they can now make important contributions to our understanding of the transition from sensorimotor to mental representations as well as help us make the most out of narrative attachment assessments.

In the final section, we review recent cognitive research that bears on the development and assessment of attachment representations from early to middle childhood. This work suggests a great deal about the likely role of cognitive development in pacing the development of attachment representations and about aspects of narrative and interview data that are most likely to reflect important differences in attachment models. The integration that Bowlby sought between intrapersonal, cognitive processes and interpersonal, communication processes as central determinants in the development of attachment across the life span seems within reach. We propose that progress in this direction is the only way to understand what attachment representations are likely to consist of and how they emerge and evolve during a childhood (or a lifetime) filled with diverse attachment-related experiences.

NARRATIVE ASSESSMENTS OF ATTACHMENT IN CHILDREN

Our focus here is on interview and narrative methods for assessing attachment representations in early and middle childhood. Until recently, most childhood attachment measures derived either from the observational methods that Ainsworth pioneered in Uganda and Baltimore (e.g., the Attachment Q-Set developed by Waters & Deane, 1985) or from her Strange Situation procedure (e.g., Cassidy & Marvin, 1989; Main & Cassidy, 1988). Such measures focus primarily on sensorimotor representations and secure-base behavior, phenomena that may not exhaust everything that Ainsworth and Bowlby had in mind when they spoke of attachment security and working models (Waters et al., 1991). Accordingly, attachment theory and assessment strategies are beginning to rely on children's narrative, language, and cognitive skills in studying internal working models.

Studies Based on Narrative Assessment

In the first study designed to assess internal working models using a narrative approach, Main, Kaplan, and Cassidy (1985) elicited responses from 40 6-year-olds to two types of projective stimuli: an adaptation of the Klagsburn and Bowlby (1976) Separation Anxiety Test (SAT), which consists of six drawings of a mother, father, and school-aged child in situations that could be construed as separation related, and family portrait photographs obtained from the parents. They also recorded conversations between mother and child following a 1-hour separation.

These authors found that the 6-year-old subjects who had been classified as securely attached in infancy gave coherent, elaborated, and open responses to the separation pictures and also tended to volunteer information about their own separation experiences. Subjects classified as avoidant in infancy described the children in these pictures as sad but could not say what the child might do to cope with the situation, whereas those classified as disorganized were usually completely silent or gave irrational or bizarre responses. In response to the family photograph, secure subjects tended to smile, look, and comment on the picture, whereas subjects classified as avoidant in infancy turned away from the photograph, dropped it, or handed it over to the examiner. Disorganized subjects showed depressed affect or became disorganized in response to the picture (Kaplan & Main, 1985).

The conversational discourse patterns of these 6-year-olds also paralleled their Strange Situation classifications in infancy. Dyads in which the child had been classified as secure were fluent, discussing a wide range of topics. Those in which the classification had been avoidant were restricted in discourse, emphasizing impersonal topics, showing little elaboration, and asking rhetorical questions. Dyads including a child who had been judged disorganized were dysfluent and had many false starts.

Thus, it appears that secure children are able to remain organized when confronted with emotionally laden attachment themes and to talk openly about a wide range of emotions, including anger and sadness. Insecure children's narratives are different, indicating that such children may experience difficulties in remaining organized when confronted with descriptions of separation and other attachment-related situations, may provide incoherent responses, or may have difficulties regulating their emotions.

Cassidy (1988) classified 6-year-olds' attachments to their mothers on the basis of observations of a separation-reunion sequence and interviewed these children using a story-stem technique and a puppet procedure that focused on their views of the self in relationships. She rated the children's story completions for security and classified subjects as *secure* when the child in the story was described as being valuable, the relationship with mother as warm, and mother as available when the child was distressed; as *avoidant* when the child was rejected, the need for help or the importance of the relationship denied, and successful resolutions brought about entirely by the child; and as *hostile* when the child was hostile or violent or showed bizarre behavior and the relationship with the mother was disorganized.

Results showed some links between ratings of security derived independently from the interviews and the observations: there was a good match between secure and avoidant categorizations of reunions and the corresponding story completion categories, but there was no correspondence between the latter and reunion-based ambivalent and controlling classifications. Cassidy's analyses of the narratives constructed by secure as opposed to insecure children point to individual differences in the content of the narratives, with secure children tending to provide more positive descriptions of mother-child interaction than insecure children.

Extending attempts to develop narrative assessments of attachment to even younger children, Bretherton, Ridgeway, and Cassidy (1990) developed a story-completion task for assessing the internal working models of preschoolers' attachments. In this procedure, children were presented with story stems enacted dramatically using appropriate dolls and props and asked to complete the stories. In addition, standardized prompts were used to elicit elaborations and to clarify issues in the stories. The stems described situations that were deemed likely to elicit attachment themes (e.g., separation and reunion, a child finding a monster in the bedroom). Separate criteria for security and insecurity were developed by the authors for each of the stories. In general, stories were considered *secure* when parents were presented as available, interactions were warm, and the child could cope with the stress constructively; they were considered *insecure* when children avoided the story issue, gave incoherent responses, or could not bring the story to a resolution.

In addition to interviewing the children, Bretherton et al. observed them during a mother-child separation-reunion sequence. Results showed that children classified as secure on the basis of story completions were more likely to have secure reunions than those classified as insecure. In addition, story security scores were related to 18-month Strange Situation classifications. Thus, this study suggests that narratives of secure and insecure children differ in both the content and the coherence of the stories, and, moreover, the findings point toward the difficulties that insecure children have in remaining behaviorally and emotionally regulated when confronted with attachment themes.

Oppenheim (1990) also studied preschoolers' attachment narratives, comparing them with observations of separations and reunions as well as teacher reports regarding the children's adaptation to preschool. Story stems were designed to describe situations that vary in the stress that they may elicit, and each included a separation or a stressor (e.g., mother and father are going out to the movies; the little boy/girl falls down and hurts himself/herself) and a reunion or a resolution (e.g., mother and father return from the movies; the little boy/girl runs to his/her mommy). After each story segment, the subjects were asked what the child might do and how the child might feel. Their narrative responses were rated for emotional openness, positive emotional tone of the child-mother interaction, and the constructiveness of the resolution of the story. To assess security of attachment to the mother, the children were observed during two separation and reunion sequences conducted on separate occasions in the children's preschool prior to the beginning of the school year.

Findings showed that children whose stories were rated as more emotionally open and who described more positive mother-child interactions appeared more independent: they explored the classroom more before separating from their mothers and did not seek close physical proximity to their mothers following reunion. Furthermore, these children were rated by their teachers as having higher self-esteem and as seeking attention in more appropriate ways. As in previous studies, Oppenheim found that the important differences between secure and insecure children involved both the content of the narratives and the emotional openness of the children in sharing their narratives with others.

Two additional studies have focused solely on the Separation Anxiety Test (SAT), which, although designed as a semiprojective test, also elicits narratives about attachment themes. Slough and Greenberg (1990) developed a revised version of the SAT in which children are presented with six pictures describing a child of the same sex in various situations involving separations from the parents that range from mild (parents tuck the child in bed and leave the room) to more stressful (parents go away for 2 weeks). The pictures were presented with a brief explanation, and the children were asked what the protagonist might feel and why and what he or she might do. In addition, they were asked what *they* might do in similar situations. Slough and Greenberg hypothesized that, whereas secure children would be able to express confidence during easy separations but would also be able to express any concerns or feelings of sadness in the more stressful situations, insecure children might claim self-reliance in all instances, respond illogically, or avoid the topic.

Children's responses to the three "severe separation" pictures were rated on an attachment scale, and their responses to the three "mild" pictures were rated on a self-reliance scale. All responses were coded for avoidance and emotional openness, and the ratings were given twice, once when the child referred to himself/herself, and once when the reference was to the hypothetical child. A separation-reunion observation conducted concurrently to assess the security of the children's attachments to their mothers was rated for security and for avoidance.

Results showed that children rated as more secure and less avoidant during the separation-reunion sequence had SAT responses that were rated higher on attachment and self-reliance and lower on avoidance, particularly when the child was referring to himself or herself. A similar but weaker pattern was found when subjects were referring to the hypothetical child. Slough and Greenberg also found that children who obtained the same self-reliance scores when referring to self and to the hypothetical child had the highest security ratings, followed by children whose scores for self were higher than their scores for the other, and then by those whose scores for the other were higher than their scores for the self. Finally, children who had the same avoidance SAT scores when referring to self and other were rated more secure and less avoidant than children whose scores for self and other differed.

In the second study to employ the SAT, Shouldice and Stevenson-Hinde (1992) hypothesized that the same organization of attachment seen on reunions of 4½-year-olds and their mothers can be revealed in children's responses to separation pictures. On the basis of verbatim transcripts of children's responses, the authors coded measures of emotional openness (e.g., appropriate expression, avoidance, denial, overreaction, anxiety) as well as interruption, somatic responses, passive solutions, and incoherence. Children's attachment classifications were based on reunion responses from Cassidy and Marvin's (1989) separation-reunion procedure. The authors' hypothesis was confirmed in general. Secure children gave the highest percentage of appropriate negative responses and a lower percentage of inappropriate responses and exhibited fewer persistent denials, overpositive feelings, interruptions, and passive responses. Fewer secure than insecure children showed incoherence. Additionally, more avoidant children gave an avoidant response than any other type of response, ambivalent children displayed most anger, and more controlling/disorganized children showed incoherence.

Taken together, these studies point to important associations between children's narratives about attachment, elicited using a range of procedures, and both concurrent and earlier observational assessments of attachment. In general, investigators have interpreted these results as supporting the notion that young children construct internal working models with respect to attachment (Shouldice & Stevenson-Hinde, 1992) and as suggesting that children's attachment narratives are valid reflections of these models (Slough & Greenberg, 1990). As such, narrative measures provide a new window on attachment relationships and the relation of secure-base behavior to such relationships. However, it is also important to note that narrative assessments of attachment are as much a measure of how children construct narratives about affective themes and communicate those to others as they are assessments of internal representations.

Thus, we suggest that it may be useful to think of narrative assessments of attachment as measuring children's abilities to construct narratives about emotionally laden, personal topics and to share these narratives with others. The shift in perspective that we propose does not imply that internal working models are not also reflected in children's narratives; rather, our goal is to add an additional perspective that should enrich our understanding of the interpersonal and intrapersonal contributions to narrative assessments of security. Specifically, a shift to the narrative and communication viewpoint introduces consideration of two important influences on children's narratives: their history of emotional communication and narrative co-construction and the cognitive bases underlying children's narrative construction. These influences, which we deem to be significant, may be overlooked when children's narratives are viewed solely as direct reflections of the working models that they have constructed internally from their experiences. Before we continue with these ideas, however, let us first examine the evidence for our claim that narrative assessments of attachment rely as much on *how* children communicate and talk about attachment themes as on *what* they say.

*Are Narrative Assessments of Attachment Security Based on
What Children Say or on How They Communicate?*

As mentioned earlier, the renewed emphasis on the concept of working models provided the impetus for recent work on narrative assessments of attachment (Bretherton, 1985; Main et al., 1985). In general, the assumption guiding studies on the representation of attachment has been that the characteristic mode of interaction between a child and his or her parents is represented in an internal working model of that relationship. These models can be accessed through a variety of techniques that elicit attachment themes but contain ambiguity so that the child can reveal his or her own expectations, beliefs, and perceptions. Furthermore, following Bowlby's view that children form representations that are based on perceptions of their actual interpersonal environments and are *not* usually influenced by internal fantasies or distortions, it could be expected that, whereas secure children would construct narratives describing mostly positive interactions between parent and child, insecure children would provide responses describing mostly negative interactions, perhaps corresponding to those assumed to be related to the specific type of insecurity (i.e., avoidant, resistant, or disorganized) that characterizes their actual relationships.

In other words, one might expect that the *content* of children's responses would reveal the *content* of the internal working model. Little has been specified, however, about the degree of elaboration and detail of the narrative responses or about their overall organization or coherence. Nonetheless, to the degree that working models are represented in memory and are subject to developmental changes that involve both social and cognitive input, structural as well as content differences should emerge from the narrative assessment literature.

A careful inspection of how researchers have analyzed children's attachment narratives reveals just such an interesting and complex picture. With regard to secure children, the assessment of attachment narratives has often been based on the content of the narratives. Secure children, in general, describe positive interactions in which parental figures are supportive, benign, and helpful and children cooperative. The classification of insecure children, however, has been based to a large extent on their difficulties in communicating about attachment (and other emotional) themes and not only on the content of the responses.

For example, Cassidy (1988), Main et al. (1985), and Oppenheim (1990) all report that insecure children are less emotionally open, with *emotional openness* defined by *how* the child discusses emotions (i.e., by the ability to balance self-containment with self-disclosure or to provide coherent reasons for emotional states) and less by *what* the child says (i.e., whether positive or negative events or characters are described). In a similar vein, Slough and Greenberg (1990) discriminated between secure and insecure children on the basis of avoidance, a strategy by which children show their difficulties in communication by distancing themselves from the topic. In this case, it is the *absence* of certain themes and the active distancing of the child from the emotional material that provide the basis for the judgment, not the specific content of the response. Oppenheim (1990) used a similar criterion in judging the emotional tone of story completions describing parent-child interactions as being avoidant on the basis of the child's failure to include the mother figure in the story even after she was introduced in it by the interviewer.

Another approach that researchers have used to assess insecurity in children's narratives is to focus on the incoherent or bizarre responses that insecure children provide (Bretherton et al., 1990; Oppenheim, 1990; Main et al., 1985; Shouldice & Stevenson-Hinde, 1992). Incoherence and bizarre qualities have often been judged by how well the child's responses relate to the story stems or pictures, or by how the elements of the responses connect to each other, and less by their content. The reliance on difficulties in communication rather than on the content of responses is clearest when no verbal content is provided by the child. Thus, for example, Main et al. (1985) rated children as insecure on the basis of behavioral responses to the stimuli such as remaining silent, becoming disorganized, throwing the props, or becoming frozen.

It may appear, therefore, that, while judgments of insecurity rely on organizational features of children's responses or on their difficulties communicating about attachment themes, judgments of security are more directly based on the content of responses. However, a closer look reveals that the judgment of security is also complex. For example, Main et al. (1985) reported that emotionally open children describe both positive and negative aspects of their relationships with relative ease and without excessive anxiety or disruption of the communicative process. Along similar lines, Cassidy (1988) pointed out that secure children describe themselves realistically, including both negative and positive aspects in their descriptions. In fact, children who insist on describing themselves only in positive terms tended to be classified insecure/avoidant on the basis of their reunion observations. In this case, reliance on the positive content alone would have resulted in misclassifications.

In general, therefore, it appears that some of the most powerful discriminations between secure and insecure children come from judging individual differences in ease, openness, and coherence of emotional communication and from examining how children construct narratives about attachment themes and communicate them to others. The content of the narratives is important as well, but that content gains its meaning from the interpersonal, communicative context in which it is placed.

Defensive Exclusion as an Explanation of the Difficulties of Insecure Children: Is It Incompatible with a Communication Approach?

How can we explain the differences between the narratives of secure and insecure children? Several investigators (e.g., Slough & Greenberg, 1990) have noticed that the scoring of insecurity in narrative assessments is based (or at least "based in part") on difficulties in communication and have invoked the concept of defensive exclusion to explain these findings. According to this idea (advanced in Bowlby, 1980), information that is too painful for the child is excluded from awareness and processing and is represented in an additional internal working model that lies outside of awareness. Thus, children who rely on defensive exclusion will have difficulties constructing emotionally coherent responses to attachment stimuli because such stimuli force them to respond to the class of information that they are trying to exclude.

Taking an alternative view, we suggest that incoherent responses result from children's difficulties in emotional communication and narrative construction. We further suggest, following Bowlby (1988) and Bretherton (1991), that the source of these difficulties lies in disturbances of parent-child communication and co-construction processes that leave children without the emotional and narrative skills required to provide a coherent response to attachment themes presented in story or picture form. Thus, while Slough and Greenberg view incoherent responses as resulting from the operation of an intrapsychic mechanism, we highlight the role of interpersonal influences.

A rapprochement between these two views seems possible if we remember that Bowlby hypothesized that the origins of defensive exclusion lie, in fact, in difficulties in parent-child communication. Defensive exclusion can be seen as the intrapersonal outcome of interpersonal difficulties in communication about emotions. It can further be proposed that the link between the interpersonal and the intrapersonal may occur in one of two ways. As we will elaborate in detail in the next section, Bowlby suggested that, under certain circumstances, parents may actively try to distort their children's veridical perceptions and pressure them to exclude or distort information. Alternatively, and perhaps more commonly, parents may not directly pressure children to distort their perception of events but rather fail to provide them with the appropriate emotional support or scaffolding that is needed to process and integrate a complex, negative situation. The child may be left overwhelmed, confused, or frightened and, in order to cope with these difficult feelings, may resort to defensive exclusion.

PARENT-CHILD COMMUNICATION AND ATTACHMENT

Our discussion of narrative assessments and defensive exclusion high-lights the interpersonal influences on cognitive and communication pro-cesses and on the development of security throughout the life span. The notion that ineffectual parent-child communication patterns have a strong influence on children's security and emotional development is not new to attachment theory, and it had been suggested by Bowlby in some of his later writings (e.g., Bowlby, 1988). On the basis of a review of attachment studies recent at that time, Bowlby wrote that "the striking differences in which [parent-child] communication is either free or restricted [are] of great relevance for understanding why one child develops healthily and another becomes disturbed" and that the "degree of freedom of communication in the pairs destined to develop a secure pattern of attachment is far greater than it is in those who do not" (Bowlby, 1988, p. 131).

Moving beyond normative attachment studies to his own clinical experi-ence and related research, Bowlby also speculated about the types of dis-torted parent-child communication patterns that may lead to insecurity. In general, his belief was that particularly harmful are childhood situations in which the child's accurate perceptions of painful events related to the self or others are negated or distorted by adults who tell the child what it is that he or she feels or should feel. In the essay "On Knowing What You Are Not Supposed to Know and Feeling What You Are Not Supposed to Feel" (in Bowlby, 1988), Bowlby gives the example of children who had witnessed the suicide of one of their parents and had subsequently been pressured by the surviving parent to believe that they were mistaken in what they had seen or heard and that the death had not been a suicide but had rather been the result of illness or accident. The parent discredited the child's perceptions in such instances by ridiculing them or by insisting that the child was confused by what he or she had seen on television or by some bad dream.

Parents may also press children to shut away information related to internal states or feelings. This occurs most commonly in situations of loss, when children are told to be brave and commended for not showing their pain or anger. More subtle instances involve parent-child relationships char-acterized by role reversal (e.g., Main & Cassidy, 1988). Although in such situations it may appear that children are being overindulged, in fact many demands are made on them, particularly to prefer the parent's needs over their own. One result of such pressures is that the child conforms to the parent's version of the situation and constructs a one-sided view of the parent as generous and loving and of the child as good and caring, while shutting away information about seeing the parent being ungrateful, de-manding, and selfish as well as their own natural feelings of anger.

Sexual abuse may also create situations in which there is a wide gap between what happens to the child and how it is talked about, or co-constructed, within the family. There will often be sharp divergences between the abusive parent's behavior toward the child in public or during daytime and in private or at night, when abuse most commonly occurs. Moreover, failure to acknowledge the abuse frequently continues years after the behavior may have stopped. This leaves the victim split between two very different realities—one of the good daytime parent and one of the abusive nighttime parent—and left with great uncertainty as to what is real and what is not, both in the objective external world and in the subjective internal world.

Beyond being generally harmful to children's healthy development, the importance of such experiences is that all involve *distorted parent-child communication patterns,* particularly when communication about *negative, conflictual emotions* is concerned. Not only do children exposed to such situations lack the emotional scaffolding needed to cope with and integrate painful situations, but they also find themselves in circumstances that undermine their own efforts to make sense of their experience. As a result, they are left with great difficulties communicating about emotional and conflictual situations, be it with the parent or with partners in other relationships. Furthermore, because central and important aspects of the self system emerge and develop in the context of close relationships (Cassidy, 1988; Emde, Biringen, Clyman, & Oppenheim, 1991; Lock, 1986; Sroufe & Fleeson, 1986), problems in communication with others render the child vulnerable to difficulties maintaining communication between parts of the self as well (Bretherton, 1987, 1990).

Bowlby's examples focus on instances of deviations from healthy development, and recent research on parent-child co-construction of narratives complements his clinical focus with evidence from studies of normative developmental trends and variation. This work has shown that from an early age—almost as soon as they become capable of talking—children engage in conversations about emotions with their parents (Bretherton, Fritz, Zahn-Waxler, & Ridgeway, 1986; Fivush, 1991a, 1991b). Thus, children's ability to talk about emotional and personal issues emerges in the context of conversations with their parents and represents the joint contributions of both child and parent (Oppenheim, Emde, Wamboldt, & Winfrey, 1995). At the early stages, the contribution made by the latter may be large: the parent needs to provide much of the structure for the child's narrations, filling in the gaps and tailoring the input to the child's level of skill. Children can gradually assume more conversational responsibility, and parents can modify their own input accordingly. However, because conversations about emotional, conflictual, or personal issues can provide important opportunities to introduce values and preferences regarding emotional experience and expression, it seems likely that many parents would want to continue engaging in such co-constructions until their children are well into adolescence or even early adulthood.

Recent empirical work supports the proposition that children acquire important narrative skills in the context of parent-child conversations. For example, McCabe and Peterson (1991) found that children of parents characterized by "topic-extending," elaborative discourse styles produced longer and more detailed narratives 1 year later than did children of "topic-switching" parents. Similarly, Fivush (1991a, 1991b) noted that children whose mothers used many orienting and evaluative devices often used these devices themselves in their independent narratives 1 year later. Adding to this line of research, Hudson (1990) found that children of "high elaborative" mothers were more engaged with an experimenter and responded to proportionally more of the latter's information requests than children of less elaborative mothers.

Focusing more on emotional issues, and thus more relevant to attachment research, a recent study of parent-child co-construction of affect and conflict narratives showed associations between the level of intersubjectivity and shared affect in children's dyadic co-constructions and the coherence and number of prosocial themes in their independent narratives (Oppenheim et al., 1995). Moreover, this study showed separate contributions arising from children's interactions with their mothers and fathers. In all, the line of research exemplified by these studies provides conceptual guidelines that can be applied to research on attachment. Specifically, some of the links between attachment in infancy and narrative assessments of internal working models conducted in later years may be mediated by co-construction processes such as those studied by Oppenheim et al. (1995) and Reese and Fivush (1993).

Cognitive Development and Narrative Assessments

One important determinant of the quality of children's narratives involves cognitive mechanisms that provide the basic building blocks required to construct a story. Recent advances in research on script representations, narrative production skills, and the child's emerging "theory of mind" have important implications for studies that rely on narratives for assessing attachment, both at a more abstract, conceptual level as well as for scoring and interpreting children's narrative productions.

Event Representation

Bowlby argued that the young child uses experiences with the caregiver to construct a mental model of the caregiver and of the self in relation to the caregiver. This requires the ability to form, manipulate, and integrate representations of such experiences, and Bowlby used the term *internal working model* to characterize the coordination and integration of these representations. Recent studies of very young children suggest that, by the middle of the second year, children routinely abstract from recurring everyday life events representations of their temporal sequences and expectations about typical outcomes (see Fivush & Hudson; 1990; Nelson & Hudson, 1988). Referring subsequent experiences to these representations and expectations makes the experiences much more accessible to memory, even over periods of weeks and months (e.g., Nelson, 1986). Bauer and her colleagues (Bauer & Shore, 1987; Bauer & Thal, 1990) reported a parallel effect in children as young as 20 months of age by demonstrating that, whereas the presence of causal relationships made it easier for children to copy simple behavioral sequences demonstrated by the experimenter, similar sequences without causal links proved difficult to reconstruct.

This work has several implications for the types of working models that we may attribute to preschool children as well as for narrative assessment methods. First, it suggests that the earliest attachment-related representations may arise even while the child's secure-base behavior is in full bloom. Thus, there is likely to be a period during which both secure-base behavior and cognitive/narrative assessments can be used concurrently and hence afford an excellent opportunity to study the mechanisms that underlie the transition from sensorimotor to cognitive attachment representations. Second, it also suggests that early attachment representations include not only outcomes but also temporal-causal elements. If so, then representations of attachment-related experiences may begin to introduce biases in recall and render some experiences more memorable than others, even before the child's communication skills can fully support standard narrative assessment procedures. Perhaps, following on Bauer et al.'s elegant methods, children's recall of causally (vs. randomly) sequenced attachment- (vs. nonattachment-) related events could be used to assess both the development of and individual differences in very early attachment representations.

Development of Narrative Production Skills

In order to use narrative assessment to the greatest advantage, it is important to have a detailed picture of the child's ability to organize knowledge for verbal presentation. Children's first narratives are based on simple production rules that provide little more than an "and then . . . , and then . . . ," framework for their stories (Waters & Hou, 1987). Despite the evidence, mentioned above, that sensitivity to temporal-causal relations emerges as early as 20 months of age, children's narratives are not consistently organized by explicit causal links until well into the elementary school years (Waters & Hou, 1987). Unfortunately, this long transition from early awareness of temporal-causal relations to consistent temporal-causal organization in narrative productions will often make it difficult to distinguish between developmental level and the structure of underlying representations. Reference to psychological motives and the ability explicitly to organize narratives around one of the character's goals are not characteristic of children's narratives until after the third grade (around age 11–12). It is only then that we see clear episode structure in their productions.

We might, of course, find earlier evidence of organized narrative productions by providing organizational cues (e.g., story stems) and working with highly familiar materials (e.g., materials that draw on typical mother-child interaction). In addition to their potential value in normative assessment, such procedures could be used to test the hypothesis that secure children are advanced relative to others in the development of narrative skills, a hypothesis that we think follows from the recent research on differences in mother's communication styles (more as opposed to less elaborative) and the developmental patterns documented in the narrative production work. If this proved to be the case, we would then want to look more closely for the experiential basis for such early narrative coherence in mother-child interaction and ask whether maternal sensitivity and secure-base support are uniquely important, or merely a subset of the experiences that lead to narrative skills. We would also want to ask whether narrative skills and coherence are general or domain specific. In research on adults, Crowell et al. (1992) have demonstrated that the coherence of attachment- and that of non-attachment-related narratives are unrelated.

One of the most interesting connections between research on narrative production and attachment assessment lies in the relations among narrative organization, content elaboration, and recall. As Crowell, Treboux, O'Connor, and Waters (1995) indicate, the *coherence* and *completeness* of an Adult Attachment Interview transcript, along with the subject's *ability to remember events* and *provide examples* of critical events, are central to the distinction between secure and anxious classifications. Although these characteristics are not easily explained by classic attachment theory, cognitive psychologists immediately recognize that they are closely related to each other.

Any narrative production is likely to be longer, more detailed, and more accessible to subsequent recall tests if it has clear temporal-causal organization. This is equally true of children's and of adults' productions (Waters & Hou, 1987). In addition, repeated production of similar story lines is likely to lead to increased content elaboration as individuals take advantage of earlier representations to fill in details and expand the story line. Waters, Hou, and Lee (1993), for example, asked third-grade children to produce a narrative from a prompt-word outline and then to produce a second story from the same outline a week later. The children were free to employ either the same or a different story line on the second occasion, and the results showed that children who employed the same story line both times produced second narratives that were better organized and more richly elaborated. On the basis of their findings, the authors proposed that semantic relatedness is a key factor in content elaboration.

Similar trends of content elaboration have been reported by Nelson and Gruendel (1986) for repeated script assessments. This suggests that individual differences in children's experience of consistency in caregiver interaction might influence the evolution, coherence, and elaboration of personal narratives. If so, it becomes critically important to discover what enables the child to abstract such consistency from these interactions.

Theory of Mind

A third domain of research in cognitive development that seems relevant to attachment representations is "theory-of-mind" research (Astington, Harris, & Olson, 1988; Butterworth, Harris, Leslie, & Wellman, 1991; Wellman, 1990). A number of psychologists and philosophers have argued that, before co-constructing social meanings of other people's behavior, a child must discover or infer that others experience the world in a manner similar to the way in which he or she experiences it (Frye & Moore, 1991). Although precursors to this fundamental social awareness emerge during the first 2 years of life (e.g., Bretherton, 1991; Leslie, 1987; Premack, 1991), it is not until the advent of language and concomitant developments in conceptual representation that young children can refer to nonobserved, mental states (i.e., a theory of [other people's] mind) in explaining and predicting social behavior.

Flavell, Miller, and Miller (1993) suggest that a theory of mind entails at least the following beliefs or inferences about the mind: (1) that it exists; (2) that it has connections to the physical world; (3) that it is separate from, and differs from, the physical world; (4) that it can represent objects and events inaccurately as well as accurately; and (5) that it actively mediates interpretations of reality and experiences of emotion. Although researchers disagree about the order in which these postulates are acquired (Astington & Gopnik, 1991; Chandler, 1988; Hobson, 1991), by 5 years of age children understand relatively completely that other people have mental experiences and that they construct their own representations of reality. It might be expected that children would draw these important conclusions sooner about a primary caregiver than about people in general. This is certainly a testable hypothesis, as is the hypothesis that theory-of-mind postulates are

212

acquired sooner if a child experiences consistent patterns of care and coherent explanations of caregiver's behavior and emotions. These are important issues because the concept of a working model (Bowlby, 1988) would seem to entail having a working theory of mind.

One important conclusion that emerges from this body of cognitive research is that the child's theory of mind continues to develop throughout middle childhood. Important later developments include (1) increasing sensitivity to the psychological characteristics of individuals (Livesley & Bromley, 1973), (2) increasing differentiation of psychological causes of behavior (Miller & Aloise, 1989; Skinner, 1991; Whiteman, 1967), and (3) the recognition that it is useful to understand a person's unique characteristics (personality) and experiences when trying to understand what they say or do (Gnepp & Gould, 1985; Rholes, Newman, & Ruble, 1990; Yuill, in press). These findings have two important implications. The first is that, in terms of content and structure, early attachment representations may be qualitatively different from later ones. In addition, assessment strategies and speculations about the effects of experience on attachment representations should take into account the child's age-related ability to understand and make attributions about caregiver behavior.

CONCLUSION

The narrative co-construction perspective can propel attachment research to address important questions. Many of the studies that we have reviewed were designed to link early or concurrent observational assessments of attachment to narrative assessments of internal working models, and their successes have provided the necessary first step for furthering research in this domain. We are now ready to address additional questions, and this is where the work on parent-child communication can be helpful. We need to know more about the mechanisms linking early attachment to later narrative assessments, and parent-child communication and co-construction processes may prove to be one such important developmental mechanism. Clinical experience as well as a few studies (e.g., Egeland, Jacobvitz, & Sroufe, 1988; Werner & Smith, 1982) suggest that supportive relationships later in life can help provide a benign perspective on early insecure attachments and dampen some of their negative effects. One aspect of such supportive relationships may be that they provide a co-construction context in which new ways to view the past are explored and articulated. As long as we focus on narrative assessments solely as a means of tapping internal models generated by the individual, we may miss recognizing the contributions made by the interpersonal world to such narratives and to their underlying representations. Recognition of the inherently social nature of narratives leads us to pay more attention to the interpersonal co-construction processes that may contribute to them.

Focus on narrative/communication processes also raises important methodological issues. When children's completions of story stems or responses to pictures are viewed as reflections of a relatively stable internal working model, less attention may be given to the process by which narratives are elicited, including the exact nature of the probes and questions used by the examiner. However, focus on narrative characteristics alerts us to the fact that such forms of assessment of internal working models are also co-constructions (albeit of a more standardized nature) and that the examiner's probes and questions may play an important, if less understood, role in shaping children's responses.

At a more general level, taking a narrative/communication perspective reminds us of the transactional nature of attachment processes. In the case of infants, we may be less inclined to forget the dyadic, transactional nature of attachment relationships, the mutual influences between caregiver and child, and the relationship specificity of the attachment construct (e.g., Sroufe & Fleeson, 1986). However, as we move to studying older children and adults, we may inadvertently slip back to viewing attachment as an internal, traitlike, stable entity that resides "inside" the head of the person rather than as a complex, transactionally determined, and contextually sensitive construct. It is the latter view that will lead us to explore multiple influences and outcomes of attachment bonds as well as their dynamic changes throughout the life span, thus keeping attachment research open to conceptual and empirical advances in related areas. Attachment research also needs to remain open to new interpretations of key constructs in light of empirical and theoretical advances.

We have also suggested that cognitively oriented research on scripts, narrative skills, and theory of mind have important implications for studies employing narrative assessments of children's internal working models of attachment. The contributions of these research domains are both conceptual and methodological, deepening our understanding of findings from previous studies and pointing to new directions for research. As we advance in our understanding of the cognitive "building blocks" required to produce a coherent narrative, we will be able to be more accurate in interpreting the difficulties that children may have in constructing narratives about emotional themes. This point is particularly important in studying young children (e.g., Bretherton, Ridgeway, and Cassidy, 1990), childhood being a period in which marked individual differences in the rate of cognitive development are common.

Cognitive theory and research can also play important roles in the design of attachment assessments. They can help identify and distinguish among features of narrative productions that might be useful to quantify, and they also help us see that current attachment assessments are quite heterogeneous with regard to the cognitive skills that they require. Results based on a particular measure may depend very much on whether it engages narrative production skills, event representation, or the child's theory of mind. Each of these factors is interesting and important, but it is also essential to keep the distinctions among them in mind. Perhaps most important, cognitive research challenges attachment research to be more specific about the concept of working models. To make the best use of cognitive development theory and research, attachment theorists need to become more exacting in their definitions of cognitive constructs and in the way they frame empirical questions. This is very much what Bowlby had in mind when he included cognitive psychology among the foundations of attachment theory.

THE PROTOTYPE HYPOTHESIS AND THE ORIGINS OF ATTACHMENT WORKING MODELS: ADULT RELATIONSHIPS WITH PARENTS AND ROMANTIC PARTNERS

Gretchen Owens, Judith A. Crowell, Helen Pan, Dominique Treboux, Elizabeth O'Connor, and Everett Waters

Freud (1940) viewed the infant-mother relationship as a prototype that influenced the formation and course of later love relationships. Attachment theory shares with psychoanalytic theory the assumption that attachment experience in infancy is a major influence on later love relationships (Bowlby, 1973; Waters, Johnson, & Kondo-Ikemura, 1995). Bowlby (1973, 1980, 1988) preserved Freud's insight regarding the importance of early experiences and took some of the mystery out of the link between early experience and later affect, cognitions, and behavior by proposing that internal "working models" of self and other are constructed out of interactions with the primary attachment figure. He also described these representations as dynamic, in the sense that they are always "under construction" and can change, not only in the course of psychotherapy, but also in light of experiences within later attachment relationships.

Across the life span, individuals may develop attachment-like relationships with several different partners, including mothers, fathers, siblings, and other relatives, nonfamilial caregivers, peers, and—during adolescence and adulthood—romantic partners and spouses. While these relationships differ in a variety of ways, any of them can serve as a context for important

This research was funded by National Institute of Mental Health grant R01-MH-4493501, awarded to Everett Waters and Judith Crowell. The scoring system for the Current Relationship Interview was developed as part of Gretchen Owens's Ph.D. thesis. Direct correspondence concerning measures to Judith Crowell, Department of Child Psychiatry, Putnam Hall, State University of New York at Stony Brook, Stony Brook, NY 11794. Direct other correspondence to the authors at the Department of Psychology, State University of New York at Stony Brook, Stony Brook, NY 11794.

attachment experiences (i.e., receiving care, using another as a base for exploration, or using another as a safe haven when aroused or threatened). Attachment researchers have considered parents (or other primary caregivers) as the most influential in terms of the construction of internal working models of attachment and models of the self, but the fact that most people participate in relationships with multiple partners presents current attachment theory with an array of difficult questions. Does early experience leave us with a generalized attachment representation that contributes to the development and course of all later love relationships? Are there also (or instead) representations associated with specific relationships? How are representations of early (child-parent) and later (adult-adult) relationships related? Are there patterns of concordance consistent with the notion that early representations significantly influence the nature of later representations? How do adults' representations of early experience and of current relationships influence the development and quality of romantic relationships? The answers to these questions will shape our understanding of how relationship experience is represented and how past experience influences subsequent relationships.

Empirical research on these questions depends on the design of relevant assessment tools. Although the Strange Situation paradigm (Ainsworth, Blehar, Waters, & Wall, 1978) has long been employed for assessing toddlers' attachments, the first tool to emerge for use with adults was the Adult Attachment Interview (AAI; George, Kaplan, & Main, 1984; Main & Goldwyn, in press-a; Main, Kaplan, & Cassidy, 1985). Rather than focusing on the relationship with a particular person, the AAI addresses the individual's overall "state of mind" with regard to attachment (i.e., his or her general way of thinking about attachment relationships). The AAI has opened up a wide range of possibilities for research on adults' and adolescents' attachment-related working models (see van IJzendoorn & Bakermans-Kranenburg, in press) and relations between current working models of attachment and other variables (Crowell & Treboux, in press).

In order to examine how closely adults' models of their current love relationships correspond to the generalized attachment models believed to be accessed by the AAI, we developed a parallel instrument, the Current Relationship Interview (CRI), and employed both measures in the first stage of a longitudinal study of engaged couples. In this report, we present data on concordance between AAI and CRI classifications and the relation of a given individual's AAI classification to behavior in a love relationship as described by the partner.

The present data address three principal issues. First, how similar are representations of attachment to parents and representations of attachment to an adult partner in a love relationship (AAI-CRI concordance)? Is the correspondence between AAI and CRI classifications within the individual great enough to suggest that representations of child-parent and current adult love relationships are integrated within a single overall model of attachment? Positive results would lend support to Freud's prototype hypothesis, whereas finding substantial differences in the two representations would suggest that separate models are maintained for different relationships or different types of relationships.

Second, we were interested in testing the degree of similarity between the two partners' descriptions of their current romantic relationship (CRI-CRI concordance) as well as between their descriptions of their respective child-parent relationships (AAI-AAI concordance). Finally, these data address the important issue of learning across relationships (Waters, Kondo-Ikemura, Posada, & Richters, 1990). If, as Sroufe and Fleeson (1986) argue, the child internalizes the roles of both the attached and the caregiving partners and carries this relational history into subsequent relationships, we can predict that someone who has experienced sensitive and responsive care during childhood (i.e., has been securely attached) will be able to provide similar care to an adult partner in future relationships. By evaluating the correspondence between an individual's AAI security classification and his or her partner's description of their current relationship, we test the hypothesis that past experiences in attachment relationships help forecast both a person's behavior and the security of his or her partner in future love relationships. Our data permit evaluation of this hypothesis at the level of overall classifications (concordance between subject's AAI and partner's CRI) and at the level of individual dimensions relevant to attachment security (e.g., love and rejection).

METHOD

Subjects

Subjects were 45 engaged couples, part of a larger sample who volunteered to participate in the Stony Brook Relationship Project, a longitudinal study of relationship formation in young adults. Their ages ranged from 20 to 26 for the women ($M = 23.40$, SD = 1.59) and from 20 to 31 for the men ($M = 25.02$, SD = 2.31). The sample was 92% white, 2% black, and 5% Hispanic. Most were from middle-class, intact homes (72% had parents who were still married, while the parents of 27% of the participants were divorced or separated and of 1% widowed). At the time of the interview, the couples had been dating for a mean of 4.3 years (SD = 2.15), with a range of 1–11 years, including an engagement period that averaged 14 months (range = 1 month–3 years).

Measures

Adult Attachment Interview

The AAI (George et al., 1984) is a semistructured interview designed to elicit a subject's recollections about relationships with parents and other significant attachment figures during childhood. The interviewer asks about childhood experiences with parents, significant separations and losses during childhood, and the current status of the child-parent relationship.

The scoring system was developed by Mary Main and Ruth Goldwyn in conjunction with the development of the interview. Scoring of the interview is based on (*a*) descriptions of childhood experiences in parent-child relationships, (*b*) the language used to describe past experiences, and (*c*) the ability to give an integrated, believable account of experiences and their meaning (Main & Goldwyn, 1991). The interview is scored from a transcript using scale points that, in the coder's opinion, characterize the degree to which each parent was loving, rejecting, neglecting, involving, and pressuring. A second set of scales is used to assess the subject's state of mind and discourse style: overall coherence of transcript and of thought, idealization, insistence on lack of recall, active anger, derogation, fear of loss, metacognitive monitoring, and passivity of speech. The scale scores are used to assign the adult to one of three major attachment classifications: secure, insecure/dismissing, and insecure/preoccupied. These parallel the secure, avoidant, and resistant/ambivalent classifications of the Ainsworth Strange Situation scoring system (Ainsworth et al., 1978).

Individuals are classified as secure if they can readily and spontaneously describe a wide range of childhood experiences, understand and attach plausible explanations to (good or bad) experiences with their parents, value attachment relationships, and view attachment-related experiences as influential in their development. They are classified as insecure if their reports and explanations lack "coherence," that is, if their responses seem inconsistent or implausible. From this we infer a deficiency in the underlying "working model" that ordinarily links memories of past experience with the meaning and interpretations of past experience. As in the Strange Situation, there are two major subgroups within the insecure group. Individuals classified as insecure/dismissing tend to deny or devalue the effect of early attachment relationships, have difficulty recalling specific events, often idealize experiences, and usually describe an early history of rejection. Those classified as insecure/preoccupied tend to display confusion about their past experiences and are unable to gain insight into early events, and their current relationships with parents tend to be marked by active anger or by passivity and attempts to please parents.

Individuals may be classified as unresolved in addition to one of the three major classifications. These adults have experienced attachment-related traumas such as a loss or abuse. Their discussions of the traumatic experience are characterized by lapses in monitoring of reasoning (e.g., indications of disbelief that the event occurred), lapses in monitoring of discourse (e.g., eulogistic speech in discussing a death), or extreme behavioral responses (e.g., displaced reactions). The scoring system gives the unresolved classification precedence over the major classification in categorizing the individual, and the relationship is considered insecure.

Several recent studies (e.g., Bakermans-Kranenburg & van IJzendoorn, 1993; Crowell et al., 1992) have established the discriminant validity of the security classifications based on ratings of AAI transcripts, demonstrating the validity of the AAI vis-à-vis social desirability, cognitive complexity, narrative style, IQ, or general social adjustment. Researchers have shown that AAI security classifications are stable over a period of 18 months (Benoit & Parker, 1994; Waters & Crowell, 1994). Classifications are also associated with reports of marital conflict (Cohn, Silver, Cowan, Cowan, & Pearson, 1992; O'Connor, Pan, Waters, & Posada, 1995; O'Connor et al., 1993).

Current Relationship Interview

The CRI was devised by Crowell (1990) in order to investigate how adults mentally represent their attachment to a dating or marriage partner, as reflected in how they speak about their relationships. The intent was to design an interview that paralleled the structure and content of the AAI as closely as possible but targeting the current love relationship of the subject. The interview covers the person's dating history, the nature of the present relationship and characteristics of the partner, and routine behaviors within the relationship, especially those related to seeking and providing support. To get an overview of how subjects view their relationship, questions are also included about the effects of the relationship on them, what they have learned from being in the relationship, and their hopes and fears for the future of the relationship.

The scoring system (Owens & Crowell, 1993) also parallels the format of the AAI. The 23 dimensions fall into five general categories, each scored on a nine-point rating scale. Three of the scales assess the person's observations of and experience in adult-adult relationships: how warm the parents' marriage was, the degree of conflict in the parents' marriage, and the intensity of the subject's previous dating relationships. Three scales assess how the person depicts his or her partner along the dimensions of being loving, rejecting of attachment, and open in communication. Six scales describe the rater's impression of the subject: how open he or she is in communicating with the partner, how skilled he or she is at taking another person's perspective, how satisfied he or she is with the partner, how dependent he or she is on the partner or on others, to what extent he or she seems to value intimacy, and how much he or she values autonomy. Four scales measure the subject's and the partner's abilities to assume a caregiving role and a nurturance-seeking (attachment) role. Finally, the subject's discourse style is rated on the same seven dimensions used in the AAI: anger, derogation of partner and of attachment in general, idealization of the partner (or the relationship), passive speech, fear of losing the partner, and overall coherence of the transcript.

These scale scores are used to assign the subject to one of three attachment classifications that parallel the AAI classification system: secure, insecure/dismissing, and insecure/preoccupied. The secure classification is given to subjects who coherently and believably describe the relationship with a partner; in most cases the partner provides security and comfort and is someone in whose availability subjects are confident. Insecure subjects are less coherent in discussing their relationships, less likely to express a valuing of intimacy and/or autonomy, and less able to function as a secure base for the partner. The dismissing classification is assigned when subjects avoid attachment concerns either by denying or minimizing the limitations of a rather unloving partner or by focusing on other facets of life instead of the relationship. Preoccupied subjects appear confused or angry about the relationship or the partner's behavior and may be anxious about the partner's ability to fulfill their needs for support and closeness.

To provide an analogue to the AAI Unresolved Loss and Unresolved Trauma scales, one final scale, Effects of Loss on Present Relationship, was added. On the CRI, the Loss scale is limited to losses of peers (either romantic partners or close friends), but not just through death: distance or dissension may also lead to unresolved feelings that interfere with the present relationship. High scores on this scale lead to a major classification of unresolved; a secondary classification of secure, dismissing, or preoccupied is also assigned.

Self-Report Measures

The Dyadic Adjustment Scale (DAS; Spanier, 1976) includes a list of 14 common sources of conflict within relationships (e.g., finances, household tasks, religion); three additional topics pertinent to the engagement period and an open-ended space for "other" were added. For each item, the subject was asked to indicate how often he or she and the partner have disagreed or quarreled about that topic during the previous 6 months. The DAS also includes a scale for reporting satisfaction with the relationship, rated from "extremely unhappy" to "perfectly happy."

Procedure

Each couple came to the Department of Psychology twice within the 3 months before their wedding date. A battery of tests and questionnaires, two interviews (AAI and CRI), and a videotaped interaction were completed by the end of the two 2-hour sessions. Each subject was individually interviewed with the CRI in the first session and with the AAI in the second session.

The CRIs were scored blind from typed transcripts, without knowledge of the subject's identity or any other information about the subject. Half the transcripts were scored independently by a second coder; disagreements in major classification were resolved in conference with a third coder (JAC). The scorers gave the same classification as secure, dismissing, or preoccupied 85% of the time and agreed on whether the person was secure or insecure 87% of the time (κ = .79 and .75, respectively, p < .0001 for both).

Each AAI transcript was scored by one of three researchers who had received AAI training with Mary Main; 25% were also scored by a second rater. Disagreements were resolved in conference. Overall, these scorers achieved 77% agreement for secure/dismissing/preoccupied classifications and 80% agreement for security/insecurity (κ = .56 and .60 respectively, p < .001 for both).

RESULTS

Like the Strange Situation, the AAI and the CRI can be scored in terms of (*a*) a secure-insecure dichotomy, (*b*) one secure and either two or three discrete insecure groups, or (*c*) numerous secure and insecure subgroups. The level of analysis chosen for a particular study depends on theoretical and practical considerations. In our primary analyses, we focus on the secure-insecure dichotomy since this approach affords the greatest statistical power as we address concordance questions. Nonetheless, breakdowns for specific insecure groups (i.e., dismissing, preoccupied, and unresolved) are included wherever they are of descriptive or hypothesis-generating value. Cohen's kappa and Fisher's exact probability test were used to evaluate the significance of the secure/insecure cross-tabulated data, while chi-square was employed for three- and four-group analyses.

*Difference between the Percentage of Subjects Scored as Secure
on the AAI and on the CRI*

For descriptive purposes, we first compared rates of secure attachment attained on the AAI and the CRI. Fifty-six percent of the subjects in the present sample were classified as secure on the AAI; this is comparable to the rates for middle-class nonclinical samples (55%–60%) summarized in van IJzendoorn and Bakermans-Kranenburg's (in press) meta-analysis. Among the insecure subjects, 77% were dismissing; in the van IJzendoorn and Bakermans-Kranenburg samples, insecure subjects were more evenly split between dismissing and preoccupied. A number of factors could contribute to this difference: sampling error, the fact that ours is a community rather than a university sample, or regional differences in child rearing and family behavior.

Attachment theory does not afford a specific prediction about relative rates of security to be expected from AAI and CRI interviews. With the opportunity to construct and revise over many years a working model of the child-parent relationship, one might expect higher rates of security on the AAI than on the CRI. On the other hand, romantic partners (unlike parents) are chosen freely; both courtship and the process of leaving unsatisfying relationships might have been expected to inflate the rate of secure attachment in our CRI data. In actuality, the rates of secure attachment scored from the two interviews were similar: 50 of 90 subjects (56%) for the AAI and 42 of 90 (47%) for the CRI. The difference between these rates was not significant ($p = .42$).

Because the CRI is a new measure, it is also important to consider issues of discriminant validity that have already been addressed for the AAI. In the present case, the most important of these concern the relations of CRI classifications to measures of marital discord and satisfaction. Clearly, on the basis of content alone there should be some association between the CRI and such marital variables; the issue is whether the classifications carry additional unique information. To evaluate this, we calculated point-biserial correlations between CRI secure/insecure assignments and scores from two sections of the DAS: the global satisfaction rating and the total score on the conflict items. Security on the CRI was significantly associated with marital variables ($r = .36$ for satisfaction and $r = -.45$ for conflict, $p < .001$ for both). As expected, the correlations are significant, but they are not nearly so large as to raise concerns that the CRI is little more than a measure of marital satisfaction.

Similarities between Individuals' Perspectives on Their Relationships
with Parents (AAI) and a Romantic Partner (CRI)

If attachment working models formed in childhood serve as important prototypes for subsequent conceptualizations of romantic relationships, one would expect significant associations between individuals' AAI and CRI status. Our results support this prediction; overall, 64% of the subjects received

TABLE 1

CONCORDANCE OF CURRENT RELATIONSHIP INTERVIEW (CRI) AND ADULT ATTACHMENT
INTERVIEW (AAI) CLASSIFICATIONS

AAI CLASSIFICATIONS	CRI CLASSIFICATIONS			
	Secure	Dismissing	Preoccupied	Unresolved
Secure..............	30	14	6	0
	(33)	(16)	(7)	(0)
Dismissing..........	6	16	2	0
	(7)	(18)	(2)	(0)
Preoccupied........	0	1	2	0
	(0)	(1)	(2)	(0)
Unresolved.........	6[a]	3[b]	2[c]	2[d]
	(7)	(3)	(2)	(2)

NOTE.—Secondary classifications for subjects classified unresolved on the AAI were as follows: [a] four secure, two dismissing; [b] one secure, two preoccupied; [c] one preoccupied, one dismissing/preoccupied; and [d] one dismissing, one dismissing/preoccupied. Percentages are given in parentheses.

the same AAI and CRI ratings as secure or insecure (expected = 49%; κ = .29, $p < .002$). Of the 50 subjects classified as secure on the AAI, 30 were also secure on the CRI; of the 40 classified as insecure on the AAI, 28 were also insecure on the CRI.[1] Table 1 presents the cross-tabulation of subjects' AAI classifications with their own CRI classifications. For descriptive purposes, the complete four-group classifications are presented. As noted earlier, the CRI scoring system includes a set of rating scales that parallel the scales used to score the AAI. To examine similarities between child-parent and romantic partner relationships further, we computed Pearson correlations between corresponding AAI and CRI scales. The results of these analyses are presented in Table 2.

Overall, only three of these 11 correlations were significant for the full sample. However, when data from males and females were analyzed separately, a clear sex difference emerged in the pattern of results. In the male subsample, all correlations were positive, and seven of the 11 values reached the conventional level of significance (mean r for significant correla-

[1] In order to determine whether concordance is a function of how the AAI and CRI classifications are grouped, we also examined AAI-CRI concordance using three groups (secure, dismissing, preoccupied) and four groups (secure, dismissing, preoccupied, unresolved). For the three-group analysis, unresolved subjects were assigned to their secondary (secure, dismissing, or preoccupied) classification. Concordance was significant in both analyses; using three groups concordance was 61% (expected = 41%; κ = .34, $p < .0001$), and using four groups it was 56% (expected = 37%; κ = .30, $p < .0001$). For all three analyses, concordance was also significant when males and females were analyzed separately.

TABLE 2

PEARSON CORRELATIONS BETWEEN ANALOGOUS ADULT ATTACHMENT INTERVIEW (AAI)
AND CURRENT RELATIONSHIP INTERVIEW (CRI) SCALES

AAI/CRI SCALE	PAST EXPERIENCE SCALES		
	Full Sample	Males	Females
Mother loving/Partner loving	.15	.35**	−.03
Mother rejecting/Partner rejecting	.13	.36**	−.05
Father loving/Partner loving	.09	.20	.01
Father rejecting/Partner rejecting.............	.15	.36**	−.01
	CURRENT STATE OF MIND/DISCOURSE STYLE		
Anger at mother/Anger at partner.............	.14	.28*	.08
Idealization of mother/Idealization of partner ...	.14	.16	.09
Derogation of mother/Derogation of partner....	.05	.25*	−.15
Anger at father/Anger at partner..............	.45***	.45***	.47***
Idealization of father/Idealization of partner	.19*	.11	.26*
Derogation of father/Derogation of partner.....	.11	.01	.22
Coherence on AAI/Coherence on CRI	.43***	.54***	.33*

NOTE.—Because positive correlations are expected between comparable AAI and CRI scales, all significance levels
are for one-tailed tests.
* $p < .05$.
** $p < .01$.
*** $p < .001$.

tions = .37); in the female subsample, only three of 11 correlations were significant. The pattern of results reveals significant effects from both mother and father for males. For females, on the other hand, past experiences with neither mother nor father correlated with partner scales, while the state-of-mind variables evidenced a stronger paternal influence. Because attachment theory does not specifically predict such differences, these results need to be replicated and extended before engaging in extensive speculation concerning their implications.

The issue of possible sex differences is an important one in attachment research. As Posada, Liu, and Waters (1994) point out, the absence of mean differences between the sexes in Strange Situation data does not preclude sex differences in how infant attachment data relate to other variables. Posada et al. illustrate this point by showing strong sex differences in the correlations of attachment security with socialization outcomes in preschool-aged children. Sex-related patterns would seem even more likely in adult attachment data. In light of the present results, correlations involving AAI or CRI scales should be computed separately for males and females, and the sexes should be combined only if the results are comparable in both groups.

Correspondence between AAI Security Classifications of the Two Partners in the Romantic Relationship

In some formulations of the prototype hypothesis, it is proposed that individuals seek out partners with whom they can have relationships similar to those they had with their parents. In the present data, this would be reflected in a tendency for secure individuals to seek secure partners—or perhaps to avoid anxious ones—and for anxious people to enter into relationships with others who are similarly anxious (i.e., preoccupied or dismissing about attachment). This interpretation was not supported by the AAI concordance data; analysis of the correspondence between partners' security on the AAI revealed a 56% concordance rate (25 of 45 pairs; $\kappa = .10$, N.S.; Fisher's exact probability $= .35$). Using a three-group typology, 53% (24 pairs) received the same classification as secure, dismissing, or preoccupied; this dropped to 47% (21 pairs) for the four-group system (which includes a separate unresolved classification).

In their meta-analysis, van IJzendoorn and Bakermans-Kranenburg (in press) found similar levels of concordance when they pooled data from five studies investigating correspondence between spouses' AAI classifications. In their sample, 51% received the same three-group classification as the spouse, comparable to the 53% who matched the partner in ours. Although none of the studies listed by van IJzendoorn and Bakermans-Kranenburg reported significant correspondence, the added statistical power of pooled samples led to significant results in the meta-analysis. The issue, however, is not whether the association is greater than zero but whether it is great enough to suggest that attachment-related prototypes are important in establishing and maintaining romantic relationships. The present results, as well as those of van IJzendoorn and Bakermans-Kranenburg, suggest that prototype effects on partner selection are either weak or operate only in some relationships.

Correspondence between CRI Security of Male and Female Partners

CRI security was concordant (i.e., both partners were classified as secure or as insecure) in 35 of the 45 couples (78%; $\kappa = .56$, $p < .0001$). This strikingly high concordance rate is consistent with two interpretations: one, that people seek out (or stay with) romantic partners whose working models of adult love relationships are similar to their own and, the other, that, over the course of time, the two partners' working models of their shared relationship converge. The validity of these interpretations is an empirical issue; either or both processes could prove to be significant in mate selection. Longitudinal data from dating, rather than engaged, couples could help us evaluate the first hypothesis: if attachment styles act as one of the many filters involved in mate selection (so that people are more likely to find and/ or stay with those who share their perspective on romantic relationships), then mismatched couples would be expected to break up with greater frequency than those whose approaches to attachment coincide. Data on the stability of CRI classifications (i.e., tendency toward change leading to similar classifications) during the same interval could address the second hypothesis, that of convergence over time.

Correspondence between One Partner's AAI and the Other's CRI

As Bretherton (1990) and Sroufe and Fleeson (1986) have noted, both Ainsworth and Bowlby recognized the importance of bidirectional influences in relationship formation, an issue that is developed further in Oppenheim and Waters's (in this volume) discussion of the "co-construction processes" through which working models are formed. An important aspect of the co-construction concept is that the ability to formulate a coherent model (perhaps especially early in relationships) is greatly influenced by the coherence of the partner's behavior and discourse. In the present data, such processes would be reflected in relations between one partner's CRI classification and the other partner's AAI classification. We predicted that a person would be more able to form a coherent model of the current relationship (as reflected in a secure CRI) if the partner presented the coherent behavior and discourse associated with a secure AAI classification.

To avoid dependencies in the data, and because the previous analyses alerted us to the possibility of differential patterns in males and females, we examined subject CRI–partner AAI concordance (secure-insecure dichotomy only) separately in male and female subjects. For females, CRI security ratings matched their partners' AAI security in 69% of the cases (31 of 45; $\kappa = .37, p = .006$). For males, CRI security matched the partner's AAI security in 64% of the couples (29 of 45; $\kappa = .30, p = .02$). These results suggest that, for both sexes, working models of current relationships are constructed in light of the partner's behavior and discourse to a significant degree; they are not merely representations of early experience. Identifying the specific behaviors and discourse processes associated with secure and insecure AAI status deserves high priority in future research.

A person's own AAI status, of course, may also contribute to the process of evolving a working model of a current relationship. Although the present sample is too small to support a formal analysis of such effects, directions for future research become evident when the data are presented separately for AAI-classified secure and insecure subjects, as in Table 3. Among *secure* (AAI) subjects with a secure (AAI) partner, 12 of 15 females (80%) and 11

TABLE 3

CONCORDANCE BETWEEN SUBJECTS' SECURITY CLASSIFICATIONS ON THE CURRENT
RELATIONSHIP INTERVIEW (CRI) AND THE PARTNER'S SECURITY ON THE ADULT
ATTACHMENT INTERVIEW (AAI) AS A FUNCTION OF SUBJECT'S AAI SECURITY

| | PARTNER'S AAI STATUS | | | |
| | Females | | Males | |
STATUS	Secure	Insecure	Secure	Insecure
Subjects with secure AAI classification:				
Secure on CRI....................	12	3	11	4
Insecure on CRI	3	6	4	7
Subjects with insecure AAI classification:				
Secure on CRI....................	6	3	2	1
Insecure on CRI	5	7	7	9

of 15 males (73%) were classified as secure on the CRI. In contrast, among
insecure (AAI) subjects with a secure (AAI) partner, only six of 11 females
(54%) and two of nine males (22%) were classified as secure on the CRI.
This suggests that secure (AAI) subjects are better able to benefit from
whatever behavioral and discourse-related assets a secure (AAI) partner
brings to a relationship (or that insecure subjects are less able to do so).

This complexity is made all the more interesting by indications that
there may be sex differences in the relation between AAI and CRI classifications. Among insecure (AAI) subjects with a secure partner, six of 11
females (55%) but only two of nine males (22%) obtained secure CRI classifications. This could represent a greater vulnerability to the partner's characteristics on the part of females. Alternatively, it could reflect a tendency
for males to construct working models later in the relationship or to do so
over a longer period of time, in which case their models might be better
characterized as "under construction" than as insecure. Larger samples and
assessment at different points in relationships are necessary to resolve these
issues.

DISCUSSION

Freud's (1940) prototype hypothesis remains a central, if untested,
tenet of attachment theory. There are four major challenges to research on
the prototype hypothesis. The first is a problem of definition. As Waters
and Deane (1982) point out, there are "stronger" and "weaker" versions of
the prototype hypothesis. The ability to decide among alternative formula-

tions on the basis of theory alone would be impressive evidence of the power of attachment theory. For the present, however, we cannot deduce much about the nature of attachment representations or their likely effects from theory alone; we are still dependent on an interplay between theory, description, and experimentation.

Measurement and validity issues present a second type of problem. It must be remembered that neither the AAI nor the CRI directly measures the content of a working model. Instead, they provide narratives that are judged to be more or less coherent, and the relation between level of coherence and any underlying working model is inferred, not measured. Research is hampered also by the fact that the AAI and the CRI are expensive to administer and score. Unfortunately, the prospects for more economical measurement are unclear. Self-report measures developed by Hazan and Shaver (1987) and by some others seem to have attachment-related correlates but show little correspondence with AAI classifications (Crowell, Holtzworth-Munroe, Treboux, Waters, & Stuart, 1993). The relation between AAI classifications and projective measures is also inconsistent at best (Sroufe, personal communication). It is difficult to measure something until you know what it is; accordingly, it may be better to turn to cognitive psychology rather than psychometrics for solutions. In the meantime, it is important to keep in mind the distance between attachment measures and the constructs with which they are theoretically linked; Meehl (1973) has argued persuasively that work under such conditions is nevertheless philosophically defensible—as well as having been standard procedure throughout the history of science.

A third difficulty arises from the fact that most formulations of the prototype hypothesis presume some degree of continuity or coherence in individual development across 20 or more years. There are few empirical data to confirm such assumptions (Waters, Merrick, Albersheim, & Treboux, 1995), and we have to employ alternative designs that incorporate replication and convergence of diverse strategies. It will be particularly useful to have longitudinal data that can help establish whether the AAI reflects working models that were already present in childhood, as opposed to current models of childhood experiences (as argued by Main). Even then, issues that cannot be resolved by cross-sectional or short-term longitudinal designs will remain to be considered.

A final difficulty in conducting research on the prototype hypothesis has been the problem of age- and construct-appropriate assessment. Clearly, the Strange Situation serves as a reliable anchor for early behavioral assessment, but, until the development of the AAI, there was no way to assess internal working models of attachment. The CRI is particularly important in adding to what can be done in this regard because it permits us to determine whether a single attachment working model characterizes adulthood or whether there exist multiple models that are associated with different relationships. The data presented in this report provide useful information on several aspects of the prototype issue and point to important directions for research on several others, as elaborated in the following sections.

One Model or Many?

Several of the analyses that we have presented converge on the conclusion that individuals have multiple, yet related, working models of close relationships, not just a single model developed in the child-parent relationship or completely independent models related to the particulars of specific relationships. First is the fact that, although AAI and CRI concordance for secure/insecure classifications is statistically significant, it is far from perfect (64%); correlations between the individuals' current state of mind toward the two relationships are also moderate at best. (The task of understanding discordant classifications—whether the explanation lies in past experience, previous relationships, or the current relationship—deserves high priority in attachment research. It would be of special interest to know whether unusual or traumatic experiences play a significant role.)

As further evidence that the models being accessed by the AAI and CRI are not identical, AAI and CRI classifications showed different results when we examined the concordance between the two partners as secure or insecure: between-partner concordance for secure/insecure status was only 56% (N.S.) on the AAI yet 78% ($p < .0001$) on the CRI. The much higher value obtained with the CRI suggests that models of current relationships are co-constructed along the lines described by Oppenheim and Waters (in this volume). Interestingly, infant attachment data show the same pattern: low concordance between infant Strange Situation classifications with mother and with father separately (Fox, Kimmerly, & Schafer, 1991) yet clear consistency between maternal AAI and infant Strange Situation classifications, which assess both dyad members' models of their shared relationship (Main et al., 1985).

These results do not support the notion that formulations of the prototype hypothesis should include predictions of assortative mating based on individuals' generalized state of mind regarding attachment. It is possible, of course, that a person with a particular AAI working model might prefer partners with certain *behavioral* characteristics. However, this would not necessarily entail similarity in attachment working models; the partner's behavior could be just as attractive if it reflected cultural or temperamental characteristics and were unrelated to the partner's attachment working models.

Behavioral Correlates of Attachment Working Models

A second prototype-related issue addressed in this report is whether AAI classifications have behavioral correlates that affect relationship formation. The Bowlby-Ainsworth perspective places considerable emphasis on the child's behavioral manifestations of attachment, particularly the secure-base phenomenon, as well as on the associations between parents' caregiving behaviors and their children's attachment behaviors. Additionally, numerous AAI studies have documented the link between adults' internal attachment representations and their parenting of their children. Thus, insofar as attachment working models influence ordinary behavior in relationships, they are important not only to the individuals who construct them but also to their partners in close relationships.

Perhaps the most intriguing finding from the present research was that the set of expectations, attitudes, and behaviors that individuals presumably learned in the context of early attachment relationships influenced not just their own but also their *partner's* security in the later romantic relationship. We tested the hypothesis that a person would find it difficult to formulate a coherent model of a romantic relationship (i.e., be classified as secure on the CRI) if the partner brought to the relationship an insecure working model (as determined using the AAI). This prediction was based on the expectation that a person with an insecure AAI classification would act in an incoherent and/or inconsistent fashion in the relationship and would be a poor partner in the process of co-constructing an understanding of the relationship. Our results supported this prediction; for both males and females, participants with secure (AAI) partners were more likely (and those with insecure partners less likely) to form secure (CRI) models of the relationship. Consequently, people who had a secure overall perspective on attachment (AAI), but who were paired for whatever reason with an insecure partner, were often able to help the partner attain a secure CRI classification but were themselves twice as likely to be scored insecure rather than secure in the partner relationship.

Thus, it appears that what is internalized during early interactions with the parents is not simply a prototype for the type of partner one will seek out for later relationships, as asserted by Freud, but instead a set of behaviors that allow the individual to recreate aspects of earlier relationships with subsequent partners (as suggested by Sroufe & Fleeson, 1986). In future research, we need to take a closer look at interactions between couples in order to detail the distinguishing behaviors exhibited by individuals from each of the AAI classification groups and to identify the relational patterns that emerge from the two partners' separate approaches to attachment.

Research on the behavioral correlates of the AAI presents an interesting opportunity to examine another of the central tenets of attachment theory, namely, the notion that infant-adult attachments and adult-adult love relationships are the same kind of relationship. For Bowlby and Ainsworth, this implies that both draw on the species-specific attachment control system to regulate secure-base behavior.[2] From this, it follows that some of the same (or analogous) types of interactions and caregiver/partner behavior would be prepotent or even necessary to initiate and maintain such relationships. We might hypothesize, therefore, that experience using the partner as a secure base (see Waters & Deane, 1985) and experience receiving secure-base support from the partner (see Kondo-Ikemura & Waters, in this volume) would be stronger correlates of relationship formation or representation than behaviors such as negative affect per se or the generic communication skills commonly assessed in marital therapy research (e.g., Heyman & Vivian, 1994; Weiss & Heyman, 1990). Sharing developmental antecedents would be an important indication that infant-adult and adult-adult attachments are similar in kind.

CONCLUDING COMMENTS

Our results are consistent with the notion that early experience influences later relationships. However, we found little support for the "strong" form of the prototype hypothesis, that is, the idea that a working model formed in a child's interactions with his or her primary caregiver subsequently serves as the framework for understanding all later love relationships. Representations of early attachment experience had only a modest effect on conceptualizations of current relationships. However constrained or biased by early experiences, an adult's mental model of his or her romantic relationship is clearly open to ongoing experiences within that relationship. In fact, our CRI concordance results suggest that romantic partners co-construct their conceptualizations of their shared relationship (see also Oppenheim & Waters, in this volume).

Representations of the child-parent relationship seem most likely to influence the development and course of adult relationships through effects on behavior. Insecure adults can form secure working models (especially if the partner is secure), but they may behave in ways that engender conflict and also make it difficult for a partner to understand or predict relationship transactions. This conclusion raises a number of important questions. What mechanisms link representations of early attachment experience to behavior in romantic relationships? How does one partner's behavior influence the

---

[2] Although one can construct multiple attachment working models, the nervous system provides only a single attachment control system.

other's understanding of a romantic relationship? How do representations of an ongoing relationship influence behavior? Research on these questions would benefit from collaboration with cognitive psychologists interested in belief systems and conceptual change and with social psychologists interested in stereotyping, prejudice, persuasion, and attitude change. The relations of attachment working models to interpersonal attraction and relationship formation are also areas in which attachment theorists could profitably collaborate with experts in traditional areas of social psychology (e.g., Shaver & Hazan, 1994; Simpson & Harris, 1994).

APPENDIX A

THE ATTACHMENT Q-SET (VERSION 3.0)

Developed by Everett Waters

Version 3 of the Attachment Q-Set (AQS) consists of 90 individual statements that are descriptive of the behavior of infants and young children observed during periods of interaction with primary caregivers. These items were selected with the intention that they would provide a comprehensive characterization of the secure-base behavior of the child with respect to the caregiver, as observed over a period of from 2 to 6 hours. In ideal circumstances, multiple observers would describe the behavior of the child over multiple settings and occasions. Such circumstances constitute conditions for the most reliable and valid assessments of individual differences along the continuum of optimal to maladapted secure-base behavior. While multiple observers, multiple settings, and multiple occasions constitute the ideal, in practice researchers have reported reliable and valid assessments under less than ideal circumstances (e.g., single observers on single occasions). As originally conceived, the AQS was meant to be completed by observers trained in the meanings of the items with respect to the Bowlby/Ainsworth theory of attachment. In practice, researchers have achieved satisfactory results using less well-trained observers, even when these observers are parents who describe the behavior of their own child.

Content areas and individual items were suggested by developmental researchers with expertise in the area of infant-parent attachment. The initial item pool was refined by Waters and Deane (1985) and reduced to 100 items. The current version of the AQS contains 90 items. These items represent a subset and an extension of the 100-item pool described by Waters and Deane (1985). The 90-item Q-set retains the general content of items from the original 100 items while eliminating much of the psychological jargon present in the original items. Efforts were made also to simplify the sentence constructions, to eliminate double negatives, and to make the items more accessible to less well-trained observers such as parents. Also eliminated from the Q-set were items that were rarely or never observed during home observations (e.g., behavior of the subject in unfamiliar environments) and items that may have been observed routinely but that yielded very limited variability over a range of ages. Finally, most of the items in the current Q-set have explicit definitions of the meanings implied by low placement. The 90-item AQS is now considered the standard and should replace the original 100-item Q-set in most research applications. *Researchers should note that several dated versions of the 90-item Q-set have been circulated. Although the content in these different dated versions is the same, there are some discrepancies in the formatting of the items across versions. For future reference, the "official" date for Version 3.0 of the 90-item Q-set should be "Waters (1987)."*

Like most Q-sets, the AQS is completed by assigning items to categories using a fixed distribution. That is, the observer is instructed to sort the items into nine categories in terms of their salience or relevance to the child being described. Items that are more characteristic or like the child are given high placements (i.e., categories 7–9), and items that are less characteristic or unlike the child are placed in the low categories (i.e., categories 1–3). Items that are neither characteristic nor uncharacteristic and/or items that were not observed are sorted to the center of the item distribution (i.e., categories 4–6).

The particular distribution of items to categories can be tailored to the needs and logistics of specific projects; there is no specific "required" distribution. However, in our own work we have found that less well-trained observers, especially parents, find a rectangular or even distribution of items to categories easier to learn and use than distributions with different shapes (e.g., quasi normal). Our instructions to all observers, after sufficient time to make the relevant observations on the child, are to divide the items into three broad categories (descriptive of the child, not descriptive of the child, and neither/cannot judge) with approximately equal numbers of items in each category. Following this initial division, the observer further subdivides each of the three categories into three. After checking and adjusting the numbers of items in each category, the final distribution should be 10 items in each of the nine categories (i.e., for a rectangular distribution). The resulting "Q-sort description" of the child provides a broad picture of the child's secure-base behavior and personality attributes as ascertained in the context of caregiver-child interaction.

The Q-sort data can be scored in several ways. At the most molecular level, individual items can be evaluated and related to external criteria. Between-group comparisons at the item level can provide important descriptive information about how two (or more) reference groups (e.g., males vs. females) organize their secure-base behavior and other aspects of attachment behavior toward primary caregivers.

A second level of analysis is provided by summary scales made up of items with related content (e.g., Pederson & Moran, in this volume; Posada, Gao, et al., in this volume; Strayer, Verissimo, Vaughn, & Howes, in this volume). Usually, the researcher will be concerned to establish the internal consistency of such scales using an index such as Cronbach's alpha. Because the aggregated scales accumulate "true" scale variance, they tend to have desirable statistical properties. However, as shown in Appendix D, equally thoughtful and experienced investigators can construct rational scales from the item set that do not show much resemblance at the level of underlying constructs. That is, a given item may appear on very different scales in two different research projects, and, conversely, different items may appear on a scale with the same name across projects.

The final and most global level of scoring is provided by the "criterion" sort method. In constructing a criterion sort, experts are asked to sort the items as they would describe a hypothetical individual extreme with respect to some dimension of interest (e.g., attachment security). After establishing appreciable congruence among experts (e.g., Posada, Gao, et al., in this volume), the several expert sorts are averaged to produce the composite criterion definition of the construct (in the language of the Q-set). Q-sort descriptions of individual subjects can be compared with the criterion sort (usually in the form of a Pearson correlation coefficient) and receive a score reflecting the degree of congruence between the individual and the criterion. Waters (1987) provides criterion sorts for the constructs "Security" and "Dependency" with the 90-item version of the AQS. The full text of the 90 items is provided in the following list, which is sorted with respect to the Security criterion.

AQS ITEMS[1]

21.   Child keeps track of mother's location when he plays   8.8
around the house. Calls to her now and then; notices her
go from room to room. Notices if she changes activities.
    Middle: Child isn't allowed or doesn't have room to
play away from mom.
    Low: Doesn't keep track.

---

[1] Items are sorted in descending order with respect to the AQS Security criterion. Figures in the right-hand column indicate an item's placement in the Security criterion.

36.   Child clearly shows a pattern of using mother as a base   8.8
from which to explore. Moves out to play; returns or
plays near her; moves out to play again, etc.
Low: Always away unless retrieved, or always stays
near.

71.   If held in mother's arms, child stops crying and quickly   8.8
recovers after being frightened or upset.
Low: Not easily comforted.

18.   Child follows mother's suggestions readily, even when   8.5
they are clearly suggestions rather than orders.
Low: Ignores or refuses unless ordered.

41.   When mother says to follow her, child does so. (Do not   8.5
count refusals or delays that are playful or part of a
game unless they clearly become disobedient.)

53.   Child puts his arms around mother or puts his hand on   8.5
her shoulder when she picks him up.
Low: Accepts being picked up, but doesn't especially
help or hold on.

60.   If mother reassures him by saying, "It's OK," or, "It   8.5
won't hurt you," child will approach or play with things
that initially made him cautious or afraid.
Middle: Never cautious or afraid.

80.   Child uses mother's facial expressions as a good source of   8.5
information when something looks risky or threatening.
Low: Makes up his own mind without checking
mother's expressions first.

90.   If mother moves very far, child follows along and   8.3
continues play in the area she has moved to.
Middle: Child isn't allowed or doesn't have room to
play away from mom.

42.   Child recognizes when mother is upset. Becomes quiet or   8.2
upset himself. Tries to comfort her; asks what is wrong,
etc.
Low: Doesn't recognize; continues play; behaves
toward her as if she were OK.

1. Child readily shares with mother or lets her hold things   8.0
   if she asks to.
   Low: Refuses.

70. Child quickly greets his mother with a big smile when she   8.0
    enters the room. (Shows her a toy, gestures, or says, "Hi,
    Mommy.")
    Low: Doesn't greet mother unless she greets him
    first.

14. When child finds something new to play with, he carries   7.8
    it to mother or shows it to her from across the room.
    Low: Plays with the new object quietly, or goes where
    he won't be interrupted.

15. Child is willing to talk to new people, show them toys, or   7.7
    show them what he can do if mother asks him to.

19. When mother tells child to bring or give her something,   7.7
    he obeys. (Do not count refusals that are playful or part
    of a game unless they clearly become disobedient.)
    Low: Mother has to take the object or raise her voice
    to get it away from him.

44. Child asks for mother to and enjoys having her hold,   7.7
    hug, and cuddle him.
    Low: Not especially eager for this. Tolerates it, but
    doesn't seek it; or wiggles to be put down.

77. When mother asks child to do something, he readily   7.7
    understands what she wants. (May or may not obey.)
    Middle: Child is too young to understand.
    Low: Sometimes puzzled or slow to understand what
    mother wants.

11. Child often hugs or cuddles against mother without her   7.5
    asking or inviting him to do so.
    Low: Child doesn't hug or cuddle much, unless
    mother hugs him first or asks him to give her a hug.

28. Child enjoys relaxing in mother's lap.   7.5
    Middle: Child never sits still.
    Low: Prefers to relax on the floor or on furniture.

85. Child is strongly attracted to new activities and new toys. 7.5
   Low: New things do not attract him away from
familiar toys or activities.

32. When mother says "no" or punishes him, child stops 7.2
misbehaving (at least at that time). Doesn't have to be
told twice.

47. Child will accept and enjoy loud sounds or being 7.2
bounced around in play if mother smiles and shows that
it is supposed to be fun.
   Low: Child gets upset, even if mother indicates the
sound or activity is safe or fun.

55. Child copies a number of behaviors or ways of doing 7.0
things from watching mother's behavior.
   Low: Doesn't noticeably copy mother's behavior.

64. Child enjoys climbing all over mother when they play. 7.0
   Low: Doesn't especially want a lot of close contact
when they play.

66. Child easily grows fond of adults who visit his home and 7.0
are friendly to him.
   Low: Doesn't grow fond of new people very easily.

9. Child is lighthearted and playful most of the time. 6.5
   Low: Child tends to be serious, sad, or annoyed a
good deal of the time.

22. Child acts like an affectionate parent toward dolls, pets, 6.5
or infants.
   Middle: Child doesn't play with or have dolls, pets, or
infants around.
   Low: Plays with them in other ways.

40. Child examines new objects or toys in great detail. Tries 6.5
to use them in different ways or to take them apart.
   Low: First look at new objects or toys is usually brief.
(May return to them later, however.)

83. When child is bored, he goes to mother looking for 6.5
something to do.

Low: Wanders around, or just does nothing for a while, until something comes up.

86. Child tries to get mother to imitate him or quickly notices and enjoys it when mom imitates him on her own.   6.5

89. Child's facial expressions are strong and clear when he is playing with something.   6.5

5. Child is more interested in people than in things.   6.3
Low: More interested in things than people.

27. Child laughs when mother teases him.   6.3
Middle: Mother never teases child during play or conversations.
Low: Annoyed when mother teases him.

49. Runs to mother with a shy smile when new people visit the home.   6.3
Middle: Child doesn't run to mother at all when visitors arrive.
Low: Even if he eventually warms up to visitors, child initially runs to mother with a fret or a cry.

4. Child is careful and gentle with toys and pets.   6.2

12. Child quickly gets used to people or things that initially made him shy or frightened him.   6.0
Middle: Never shy or afraid.

48. Child readily lets new adults hold or share things he has, if they ask to.   6.0

87. If mother laughs at or approves of something the child has done, he repeats it again and again.   5.8
Low: Child is not particularly influenced this way.

46. Child walks and runs around without bumping, dropping, or stumbling.   5.7
Low: Bumps, drops, or stumbles happen throughout the day (even if no injuries result).

62.   When child is in a happy mood, he is likely to stay that   5.5
way all day.
>*Low:* Happy moods are very changeable.

16.   Child prefers toys that are modeled after living things   5.2
(e.g., dolls, stuffed animals).
>*Low:* Prefers balls, blocks, pots and pans, etc.

45.   Child enjoys dancing or singing along with music.   5.2
>*Low:* Neither likes nor dislikes music.

73.   Child has a cuddly toy or security blanket that he carries   5.2
around, takes to bed, or holds when upset. (Do not
include bottle or pacifier if child is under 2 years old.)
>*Low:* Can take such things or leave them, or has
none at all.

68.   On the average, child is a more active type person than   5.0
mother.
>*Low:* On the average, child is a less active type
person than mother.

84.   Child makes at least some effort to be clean and tidy   5.0
around the house.
>*Low:* Spills and smears things on himself and on
floors all the time.

3.   When he is upset or injured, child will accept comforting   4.8
from adults other than mother.
>*Low:* Mother is the only one he allows to comfort
him.

37.   Child is very active. Always moving around. Prefers   4.8
active games to quiet ones.

39.   Child is often serious and businesslike when playing away   4.7
from mother or alone with his toys.
>*Low:* Often silly or laughing when playing away from
mother or alone with his toys.

43.   Child stays closer to mother or returns to her more often   4.7
than the simple task of keeping track of her requires.

> *Low:* Doesn't keep close track of mother's location or activities.

51.   Child enjoys climbing all over visitors when he plays with   4.7
      them.
      Middle: He won't play with visitors.
      Low: Doesn't seek close contact with visitors when he
      plays with them.

24.   When mother speaks firmly or raises her voice at him,   4.5
      child becomes upset, sorry, or ashamed about displeasing
      her. (Do not score high if child is simply upset by the
      raised voice or afraid of getting punished.)

72.   If visitors laugh at or approve of something the child   4.5
      does, he repeats it again and again.
      Low: Visitors' reactions don't influence child this way.

78.   Child enjoys being hugged or held by people other than   4.5
      his parents and/or grandparents.

7.   Child laughs and smiles easily with a lot of different   4.3
      people.
      Low: Mother can get him to smile or laugh more
      easily than anyone else.

29.   At times, child attends so deeply to something that he   4.3
      doesn't seem to hear when people speak to him.
      Low: Even when deeply involved in play, child
      notices when people speak to him.

35.   Child is independent with mother. Prefers to play on his   4.3
      own; leaves mother easily when he wants to play.
      Middle: Not allowed or not enough room to play
      away from mother.
      Low: Prefers playing with or near mother.

20.   Child ignores most bumps, falls, or startles.   4.2
      Low: Cries after minor bumps, falls, or startles.

57.   Child is fearless.   4.0
      Low: Child is cautious or fearful.

67.   When the family has visitors, child wants them to pay a   4.0
      lot of attention to him.

82.   Child spends most of his playtime with just a few favorite   4.0
      toys or activities.

52.   Child has trouble handling small objects or putting small   3.8
      things together.
      Low: Very skillful with small objects, pencils, etc.

59.   When child finishes with an activity or toy, he generally   3.8
      finds something else to do without returning to mother
      between activities.
      Low: When finished with an activity or toy, he
      returns to mother for play, affection, or help finding
      more to do.

17.   Child quickly loses interest in new adults if they do   3.5
      anything that annoys him.

50.   Child's initial reaction when people visit the home is to   3.5
      ignore or avoid them, even if he eventually warms up to
      them.

8.   When child cries, he cries hard.   3.3
      Low: Weeps, sobs, doesn't cry hard, or hard crying
      never lasts very long.

26.   Child cries when mother leaves him at home with   3.3
      baby-sitter, father, or grandparent.
      Low: Doesn't cry with any of these.

58.   Child largely ignores adults who visit the home. Finds his   3.2
      own activities more interesting.
      Low: Finds visitors quite interesting, even if he is a
      bit shy at first.

76.   When given a choice, child would rather play with toys   3.2
      than with adults.
      Low: Would rather play with adults than toys.

13.   When the child is upset by mother's leaving, he continues   2.7
       to cry or even gets angry after she is gone.
       Middle: Not upset by mom leaving.
       Low: Crying stops right after mom leaves.

23.   When mother sits with other family members or is   2.7
       affectionate with them, child tries to get mom's affection
       for himself.
       Low: Lets her be affectionate with others. May join
       in, but not in a jealous way.

56.   Child becomes shy or loses interest when an activity looks   2.7
       like it might be difficult.
       Low: Thinks he can do difficult tasks.

31.   Child wants to be the center of mother's attention. If   2.5
       mom is busy or talking to someone, he interrupts.
       Low: Doesn't notice or doesn't mind not being the
       center of mother's attention.

10.   Child often cries or resists when mother takes him to bed   2.3
       for naps or at night.

30.   Child easily becomes angry with toys.   2.3

69.   Rarely asks mother for help.   2.3
       Middle: Child is too young to ask.
       Low: Often asks mother for help.

 6.   When child is near mother and sees something he wants   2.2
       to play with, he fusses or tries to drag mother over to it.
       Low: Goes to what he wants without fussing or
       dragging mother along.

25.   Child is easy for mother to lose track of when he is   2.0
       playing out of her sight.
       Middle: Never plays out of sight.
       Low: Talks and calls when out of sight. Easy to find;
       easy to keep track of what he is playing with.

63.   Even before trying things himself, child tries to get   2.0
       someone to help him.

2.   When child returns to mother after playing, he is   1.8
        sometimes fussy for no clear reason.
        Low: Child is happy or affectionate when he returns
        to mother between or after playtimes.

61.   Plays roughly with mother. Bumps, scratches, or bites   1.8
        during active play.(Does not necessarily mean to hurt
        mom.)
        Middle: Play is never very active.
        Low: Plays active games without injuring mother.

65.   Child is easily upset when mother makes him change   1.8
        from one activity to another. (Even if the new activity is
        something the child often enjoys.)

81.   Child cries as a way of getting mother to do what he   1.8
        wants.
        Low: Mainly cries because of genuine discomfort
        (tired, sad, afraid, etc.).

54.   Child acts like he expects mother to interfere with his 1.5
        activities when she is simply trying to help him with
        something.
        Low: Accepts mother's help readily, unless she is in
        fact interfering.

74.   When mother doesn't do what child wants right away, he 1.5
        behaves as if mom were not going to do it at all. (Fusses,
        gets angry, walks off to other activities, etc.)
        Low: Waits a reasonable time, as if he expects mother
        will shortly do what he asked.

33.   Child sometimes signals mother (or gives the impression) 1.3
        that he wants to be put down and then fusses or wants to
        be picked right back up.
        Low: Always ready to go play by the time he signals
        mother to put him down.

34.   When child is upset about mother leaving him, he sits   1.2
        right where he is and cries. Doesn't go after her.
        Middle: Never upset by her leaving.
        Low: Actively goes after her if he is upset or crying.

38.   Child is demanding and impatient with mother. Fusses   1.2
        and persists unless she does what he wants right away.

75.   At home, child gets upset or cries when mother walks out   1.2
        of the room. (May or may not follow her.)
            Low: Notices her leaving; may follow, but doesn't get
        upset.

88.   When something upsets the child, he stays where he is   1.2
        and cries.
            Low: Goes to mother when he cries. Doesn't wait for
        mom to come to him.

79.   Child easily becomes angry at mother.   1.0
            Low: Doesn't become angry at mother unless she is
        very intrusive or he is very tired.

APPENDIX B

MATERNAL BEHAVIOR Q-SET

Developed by David R. Pederson and Greg Moran

Details of the development of the Maternal Behavior Q-Set are presented in Pederson et al. (1990). The original pool of items was constructed on the basis of previous theoretical and empirical descriptions of maternal behavior indicative of Ainsworth's construct of maternal sensitivity (Ainsworth, Bell, & Stayton, 1971; Ainsworth et al., 1978). These items describe a wide range of maternal behavior including her interactive style, her sensitivity to her infant's state, feeding interactions, and the extent to which the home reflects the infant's needs. An attempt was made to provide a broad spectrum of descriptors of maternal behavior, although all items are to some degree related to maternal sensitivity. Items that are most directly relevant to the concept of maternal sensitivity focus on the mother's ability to recognize and detect communicative signals from her infant that call for a response or provide an opportunity for interaction with her infant, to respond in a timely fashion to these signals, and to respond in an appropriate manner. These content areas were used as an aid in generating potential items rather than descriptions of theoretically distinct domains of maternal behavior. The original items were refined by a process of repeated sorting by a group of university faculty and senior graduate students in infant development. Items that could not be reliably interpreted were discarded until a set of 90 items was established.

Ten judges (faculty and graduate students at the University of Western Ontario) who were knowledgeable about attachment theory and research and experienced with observing infant-mother interactions were asked to use the Q-set to describe their conceptualization of the prototypically sensitive mother interacting at home with her 12-month-old infant. Interrater reliability for this "criterion sort" was acceptable (r's > .82). The criterion score was generated from these descriptions by averaging the placement for each item across judges. A mother's sensitivity score is the correlation between an observer's sort describing the mother's behavior and these criterion scores.

Observer training and the context of the home observations are described in Pederson and Moran (in this volume). From our experience, there are three features of the procedures that are fundamental in producing valid descriptions of maternal behavior relevant to attachment constructs. First, the observers must be familiar with attachment relationship constructs both as described by Ainsworth et al. (1971) in the home and by Ainsworth et al. (1978) in the Strange Situation. Second, for at least part of the time during home observations, the mother's attention should be diverted from an exclusive focus on her infant by giving her a questionnaire, an interview, or some other task. It is more difficult to discern individual differences in sensitivity when all the mother's attention is focused on her infant. Third, the observers should take extensive notes during and immediately after the visit. These notes should focus on the baby's secure-base behavior (proximity seeking and comfort in contact), affective sharing, fussiness, and resistance and on the mother's availability to the infant, her responses to her infant's positive and negative signals, and her monitoring of her infant while occupied with tasks we have given her.

The observer is instructed to complete a Q-sort on the basis of her best judgment of the characteristics of the relationship that she has observed. The items are forced into a rectangular distribution with 10 items in each of nine piles. Items in pile 1 are those considered to be least characteristic of the mother's behavior and so on up to items in pile 9, which are judged to be most characteristic. The sort should not simply reflect the relative frequency of each behavior; rather, we encourage the observers to use their social-cognitive abilities to assess the extent that each item is characteristic of the relationship. Thus, the observer may discount a particular interaction because she sees it as being contextually idiosyncratic or base a rating on a brief incident that she views as particularly revealing. The explicitly behaviorally referenced items (e.g., item 89 referring to a diaper change) must go into middle piles if they are not directly observed. Similarly, if baby did not whimper or cry, the items referring to the mother's responsiveness to distress must also go in the middle, although in this case information from the interview or maternal behavior in response to other baby signals may give the sorter confidence to move the items out of the three middle piles after the initial sort. It would be very unlikely that these items would end up in piles 8 or 9 or 1 or 2 even in these circumstances.

MATERNAL BEHAVIOR Q-SET ITEMS[1]

12.   Interprets cues correctly as evidenced by baby's response.   9.00

54.   Interactions revolve around baby's tempo and current state.   9.00

9.   Responds consistently to baby's signals.   8.92
         Low: Responses are unpredictable or arbitrary.

29.   Slows pace down; waits for baby's response in face-to-face interactions.   8.83

63.   Monitors and responds to baby even when engaged in some other activity such as cooking or having a conversation with visitor.   8.83

60.   When baby is distressed, is able to quickly and accurately identify the source.   8.75

53.   Well-resolved interaction with baby—interaction ends when baby is satisfied.   8.58
         (Also consider termination of ongoing interactions that baby is enjoying.)

6.   Interactions appropriately vigorous and exciting as judged from baby's responses.   8.50

66.   Arranges her location so that she can perceive baby's signals.   8.25

46.   Cues baby, and waits for response in feeding.   8.17

64.   Responds immediately to cries/whimpers.   8.17

58.   Aware of baby's moods and fluctuations in state.   8.08

[1] Figures in the right-hand column refer to the sensitivity criterion weights that we developed for mothers interacting with their 12-month-old infants. Note that items are presented in the order of their ranking with respect to the sensitivity criterion.

61.	Seems to be aware of baby even when not in the same room.	8.08
1.	Notices when her baby smiles and vocalizes.	8.00
5.	Notices when baby is distressed, cries, fusses, or whimpers.	7.92
23.	Respects baby as individual, that is, able to accept baby's behavior even if it is not consistent with her ideal.	7.67
47.	Balances task and baby's activities in feeding.	7.67
67.	When in the same room as baby, provides baby with unrestricted access to her.	7.67
15.	Aware of how her moods affect baby.	7.58
45.	Encourages baby's initiatives in feeding.	7.58
44.	Balances task and baby's activities when changing diapers.	7.42
10.	Greets baby when reentering room.	7.25
18.	Structures environment considering baby's *and* own needs. (Consider the balance in this item.)	7.17
24.	Knows a lot about her baby; good informant.	7.17
34.	Seeks face-to-face interactions.	7.00
42.	Is animated in social interactions with baby.	6.92
22.	Resolves negative feelings about baby; that is, has some negative feelings about baby but can set these aside in interacting with baby.	6.83
36.	Predominantly positive mood about baby.	6.75
40.	Praise directed toward baby.	6.75
38.	Displays affection by touching.	6.50

37.	Comments are generally positive when speaking about baby.	6.25
86.	Encourages interaction of baby with visitor; for example, invites visitor to hold baby; ensures that baby is "introduced" to visitor (e.g., "Look who's here!").	6.25
35.	Points to and identifies interesting things in baby's environment.	6.17
49.	Environment is safe, "baby proofed."	6.17
90.	Often brings toy or other object within baby's reach and attempts to interest her in it.	6.08
33.	Creates interesting environment.	6.00
39.	When holding, cuddles baby as a typical mode of interaction; molds baby to self.	6.00
32.	Provides age-appropriate toys.	5.83
21.	Is delighted over baby.	5.75
89.	Very alert to "dirty diaper"; seems to change diapers as soon as indication of need.	5.75
30.	Plays games with baby such as peek-a-boo, patty cake.	5.67
31.	Makes an effort to take baby on "outings" such as shopping, visiting friends.	5.58
79.	Frequently repeats words carefully and slowly to the baby as if teaching meaning or labeling an activity or object.	5.58
82.	Feels at ease leaving the child with a baby-sitter in the evening.	5.50
48.	Provides nutritional snacks.	5.08
85.	Is very reluctant to leave the baby with anyone other than husband or close relative. (Determine from interview.)	5.08

27. Seems "long suffering" in her attitude about her maternal duties.   4.67

56. Very concerned that baby is well dressed and attractive at all times.   4.33

72. At first glance, home shows little evidence of presence of infant.   4.33

25. Idealizes baby—does not acknowledge negative aspects.   4.25

43. Kisses baby on head as major mode of expressing affection.   4.25

81. Makes frequent use of playpen in order to permit carrying out normal household chores.   4.25

14. Scolds baby.   4.08

17. Worried about spoiling; has lots of "shoulds" about baby's care.   3.92

69. Seems overwhelmed, depressed.   3.92

75. Attempts to involve baby in games or activities that are obviously beyond the child's current capability.   3.83

50. Sometimes will interfere with appropriate activity if it is likely to get baby messy or soiled.   3.75

41. Flat affect when interacting with baby.   3.67

51. Disturbed by baby becoming messy during feeding; these concerns sometimes interfere with feeding.   3.58

26. Critical in her descriptions of baby.   3.50

76. Sometimes will break off from the child in mid-interaction to speak to visitor or attend to some other activity that suddenly comes to mind.   3.50

83. Leaves the room without any sort of "signal" or 3.50
    "explanation" to the baby (e.g. "I'll be back in just a
    minute").

77. Often "parks" the baby in front of the television in an 3.42
    attempt to keep her entertained.

70. Responds accurately and promptly to signals of distress, 3.33
    but often ignores (is unresponsive to) signals of positive
    affect.

87. Seems awkward and ill at ease when interacting directly 3.08
    with the baby face to face.

13. Is irritated by demands of baby. 2.75
        (Note information from interview including
    comments on caregiving demands.)

80. Seldom speaks to the baby directly. 2.67

84. Sometimes seems to treat baby as an inanimate object 2.67
    when moving her around or adjusting her posture.

19. Perceives baby's negative behavior as rejection of her; 2.58
    takes misbehavior "personally."

65. Not skillful in dividing her attention between baby and 2.58
    competing demands; thus misses baby's cues.

20. Seems to resent baby's signals of distress or bids for 2.50
    attention.

55. Repeated series of interventions in search for best 2.42
    method to satisfy baby; often resorts to trial and error.

78. Nap times are determined by mother's convenience 2.42
    rather than the immediate needs of the baby.
        (Determine from interview.)

88. Often seems to forget baby is present in the room during 2.33
    interaction with visitor.

11. Sometimes is aware of baby's signals of distress, but 2.25
    ignores or does not respond immediately to these signals.

62.	Preoccupied with interview—seems to ignore baby.	2.17
71.	When baby is in a bad mood or cranky, often will place baby in another room so that she will not be disturbed.	2.08
16.	Will often interfere with baby's ongoing appropriate behavior. *Low:* Stands back, and lets baby carry on with activity without interruption.	2.00
3.	Often interprets baby's signals according to own wishes and moods.	1.92
59.	Rough or intrusive in interactions with baby.	1.75
28.	Teases baby beyond point where baby seems to enjoy it.	1.67
52.	Fails to interrupt activity by her baby that is likely to be dangerous.	1.67
74.	Often misses "slow down" or "back off" signals from baby during face-to-face play.	1.58
73.	Content and pace of interactions with the baby seem to be set by mother rather than according to baby's responses.	1.50
68.	Often appears to "tune out" and not notice distress or bids for attention.	1.42
4.	Response so delayed that baby cannot connect mother's response with the action that initiated it.	1.33
8.	Responses to baby's communications are inconsistent and unpredictable.	1.33
7.	Responds only to frequent, prolonged, or intense signals.	1.25
57.	Subjects baby to constant and unphased barrage of stimulation; baby overwhelmed.	1.25
2.	Unaware of or insensitive to baby's signs of distress.	1.00

APPENDIX C

BACKGROUND AND SORTING INSTRUCTIONS FOR THE ATTACHMENT Q-SET FOR INFANT MACAQUES AND THE MATERNAL Q-SET FOR MACAQUES

Developed by Kiyomi Kondo-Ikemura and Everett Waters

The Attachment Q-Set for Infant Macaques (AQS-M) and the Maternal Q-Set for Macaques (MQS-M) were developed to assess the role of concurrent maternal support in the maintenance of infant secure-base behavior. The AQS-M was designed to parallel the same secure base phenomena assessed by the Attachment Q-Set (AQS; Waters & Deane, 1985). The MQS-M was designed to assess maternal behaviors that are relevant to the infant's success across time and situations in using her as a secure base from which to explore and as a haven of safety. Several sources of information contributed to the construction of these Q-sets. These included conceptual analysis of the secure-base phenomenon, the content of the AQS used with humans, Kondo-Ikemura's years of observational experience as a primatologist, and observations of captive macaques, langurs, and other Old World monkeys during the development of the Q-sets.

The items of the human infant AQS cover eight domains of behavior: (1) attachment/exploration balance; (2) response to comforting and differential responsiveness; (3) affect; (4) social interaction; (5) object manipulation; (6) independence and dependency; (7) social perception; and (8) endurance and resiliency. The first step in developing the AQS-M was to identify items that could be adopted from the human AQS with minor revisions (e.g., changing "leaves infant with baby-sitter" to "leaves infant with juvenile or adult female monkeys"). The second step involved writing 32 additional items to capture behaviors that do not have clear analogues in human infant behavior or that refer to situations rarely encountered by human infants. These primarily involved aspects of social interaction, object manipulation, and independence and dependency.

In order to describe maternal behaviors that might help organize infant attachment behavior by supporting the infant's secure-base and exploratory behaviors, we developed a Q-set by writing items related to each item in the infant behavior Q-set and then editing and revising to eliminate redundancy. The MQS-M consists of 93 items covering eight facets of maternal behavior: (1) offering contact or comfort; (2) comforting behavior; (3) protection from danger; (4) affect; (5) caretaking strategies; (6) promoting independence or teaching; (7) social interaction with infant; and (8) self-maintenance behaviors. For completeness, this Q-set also describes behaviors that might compete with maternal behavior or might be antithetical to it (e.g., object exploration and foraging). We also included marker items related to maternal status and social adjustment.

Both the MQS-M and the AQS-M are sorted in the same manner as the AQS, using nine categories. Thirteen (14 for the AQS-M) items are placed in the center category (i.e., category 5), ten items in each of the remaining eight categories. A useful observational strategy is first to watch the subject(s) for up to 1 hour and afterward perform a sort and then perform additional sorts after further observation or on separate occasions. Averaging each item across several sorts increases the reliability and representativeness of the data. It can also be useful to average across multiple observers from the same time interval. A criterion for scoring the infant's ability to use the mother as a secure base, based on a single conceptual sort by E. Waters, is provided in Appendix D. Also provided in Appendix D is a criterion for dependency, based on a similar sort by E. Waters.

Both Q-sets seem appropriate for use with a wide range of Old World monkeys. Among New World monkeys, informal observations suggest that these Q-sets are less well suited for work with *Callitrichidae* (marmosets and tamarins). We have not observed *Cebidae* (howlers, spider monkeys, etc.). It is difficult to assess the usefulness of these Q-sets for the great apes because their housing in captivity does not often give free rein to secure-base patterns. Researchers interested in secure-base behavior in nonhuman primates are encouraged to revise these item sets to suit the behavior of the species they study.

Following are the items in the AQS-M and MQS-M. The items in the AQS-M are sorted according to their placement in the criterion sort for secure-base behavior.

ATTACHMENT BEHAVIOR Q-SET FOR INFANT MACAQUES[1]

18.   Infant returns to mother and actively solicits comfort   9.00
      from mother when wary, fearful, or otherwise upset.
      Low: Sits, freezes, or screams until mother retrieves.

24.   Infant clearly shows a pattern of using mother as a base   9.00
      from which to explore. Moves out to play, returns, or
      plays near her and moves out to play again, etc.
      Low: Always away from mother or near mother
      when playing around.

43.   Returns from exploration and play are spontaneous in   9.00
      nonthreatening situation; mother does not have to
      retrieve infant.
      Low: Does not return to mother unless he is called or
      retrieved by mother or unless something upsets him.

83.   Infant returns to mother between bouts of social play.   9.00
      Low: Sits alone between bouts of social play.

87.   Departures from mother are spontaneous; infant departs   9.00
      from mother on his own.
      Low: Does not depart from mother unless mother
      prompts him or other monkeys invite him to play.

4.   When infant screams, screaming stops as soon as mother   8.00
      holds him for comfort.
      Low: Screaming continues even after mother holds
      him for comfort.

7.   Infant keeps track of mother's location when he plays   8.00
      away from her; when mother moves or changes activities,
      infant follows visually.
      Middle: Does not move away very much from
      mother.

30.   Infant is playful most of the time.   8.00
      Low: Infant tends to be quiet and withdrawn.

---

[1] Values in the right-hand column indicate placement in the Security criterion sort
for AQS-M items.

35.   When infant is distressed or injured, mother is the only   8.00
       one he allows to comfort him.
            Low: Would accept comforting from monkeys other
       than mother if offered.

45.   Infant clings on mother in a comfortable posture and   8.00
       position when in contact with mother.
            Low: Does not cling on mother, or clings in an
       awkward posture or position when in contact with
       mother.

67.   Even if the object makes infant afraid or cautious, he will 8.00
       approach it if mother approaches or examines it first.
            Middle: Never cautious or afraid.
            Low: Does not approach; remains wary or afraid. (If
       infant is held by mother, remains clinging or avoiding.)

76.   Infant plays at distance beyond mother's reach (> 0.3 m).   8.00
            Low: Plays within mother's reach.

81.   Infant explores widely and plays throughout space   8.00
       available.
            Low: Only explores or plays in a small portion of
       available space.

15.   When infant makes contact with mother, he seeks   7.00
       mother's ventral surface.
            Low: Content even if he cannot make contact with
       her ventrum.

26.   Infant approaches mother to observe what she is doing;   7.00
       shows much interest in mother's behaviors.
            Low: May or may not be attentive mother's
       behaviors, but rarely approaches her to observe what she
       is doing.

31.   When something looks dangerous or threatening, infant   7.00
       looks at mother as a good source of information.
            Low: Decides what to do without using mother's
       behaviors as a cue.

34.   If allowed, infant moves along with mother as she goes   7.00
        from place to place; does not have to be called or
        carried; does not become distressed.
            Middle: Decision to move along with mother is not
        left with infant (e.g., mother retrieves infant before
        moving).
            Low: Would be left behind unless mother actively
        calls or carries him; does not move play when mother
        moves.

40.   When infant plays with objects, he allows mother to   7.00
        examine them.
            Middle: Mother ignores what he has or steals rather
        than sniffing, touching, or looking at it.
            Low: Carries away objects, or protests when mother
        tries to examine them.

51.   When something in environment frightens infant, his   7.00
        fear is reduced if he moves closer to mother or is held by
        her.
            Low: Remains fearful, even if he approaches and is
        held by mother.

69.   Infant spends more time away from mother than he does   7.00
        in proximity, contact, or interaction with her.
            Low: Spends more time in proximity, contact, or
        interaction with mother than in exploration or play away
        from mother (excluding sleeping time).

70.   Infant is interested in what mother eats; watches closely,   7.00
        and wants the same kinds of food.
            Low: Little interest in mother's food or her choice.

77.   Infant prefers ventro-ventral position when in contact   7.00
        with mother.
            Middle: No clear preference in position.
            Low: Content even when he can't make
        ventro-ventral position, or avoids ventro-ventral position
        when in contact with mother.

78.   Infant retreats exclusively to mother when frightened.   7.00
            Low: Retreats to any of several monkeys when
        frightened.

88.   Infant approaches mother and stays closer than usual   7.00
when unusual happenings occur (e.g., social trouble
including group members, sudden environment changes,
etc.). (He does not necessarily approach quickly or
vocalize about the event.)
    Low: Does not approach mother when unusual
happenings occur.

90.   Infant is curious; when monkeys other than mother   7.00
manipulate small objects, infant approaches or/and
observes carefully.
    Low: Little interest in monkeys other than mother
manipulating objects.

1.   Infant is attracted to unusual or novel noises, objects, or   6.00
movements in environment (even if he returns to
mother).
    Low: Ignores or avoids unusual or novel noises,
objects, or movements in environment.

3.   Infant tries to wrestle with mother or directs playful   6.00
mouth-open or play-solicit posture to mother if no other
monkeys are available.
    Low: Even if there are no playmates, infant does not
direct playful behaviors toward mother.

11.   Infant approaches adult monkeys other than mother to   6.00
play, explore, or otherwise interact, without hesitation.
    Low: Avoids other adult monkeys, and does not
approach them.

22.   Infant accepts mother's leaving without following or   6.00
screaming if left in the company of juveniles or adult
females other than mother.
    Middle: Never becomes distressed by mother's leaving
in any situations.
    Low: Follows mother's leaving with distress or
screams, even if with juveniles or adult females.

25.   If infant notices play group, he actively joins in. (May or   6.00
may not play with peers actively, but tries to play in the
same manner as peers are doing.)
    Low: Avoids or ignores play group.

28.   In coordination with mother's activity cycles; when   6.00
        mother sleeps, infant also sleeps; when mother is awake,
        infant is also awake, etc.
        Low: Infant's activity cycles are not synchronized.

32.   Infant initiates social play with peers or juveniles.   6.00
        Middle: Too young for social play.
        Low: May respond to play invitations, but does not
        initiate social play on his own.

33.   When infant is in mother's ventrum, he sucks (mouths)   6.00
        on nipple.
        Low: Indifferent to nipple contact even when he is in
        mother's ventrum.

59.   Infant is strongly attracted to the objects that other   6.00
        monkeys are handling or that are brought into play.
        Low: Peer's playthings do not attract him.

60.   When infant is attacked by other monkeys, he calls   6.00
        mother for help and waits for her rescue.
        Low: Escapes or counterattacks on his own without
        mother's help.

64.   Infant uses a part of mother's body as a play object or   6.00
        jumping platform.
        Middle: Mother does not allow.

72.   When mother takes infant to an unfamiliar area which is   6.00
        new to them or not usually used, infant is closer to
        mother than usual.
        Low: Unfamiliar area does not change infant's
        closeness to mother.

80.   Infant will go greater distance or longer time from   6.00
        mother than he will allow mother to go from him.
        Low: Tolerates both mother-initiated and
        self-initiated separation and distance equally.

91.   Infant grooms mother or shows similar behavioral   6.00
        pattern to mother's coat.
        Middle: Never touches mother's coat.

Low: Not interested in mother's coat care, or only interested in her coat as a plaything.

9.   When infant returns from exploration or play, he clings   5.00
     on mother and/or sucks on her nipple.
         Low: Makes casual contact or proximity with mother.

13. When social play gets rough and active, infant continues   5.00
     to play confidently.
         Low: Not confident in rough play; victimized,
     freezes, flees, or screams.

14. Infant repeats or persists in activities that have proved to 5.00
     be difficult for him.
         Low: When something has proved to be difficult for
     him, infant does not try again.

19. Infant examines objects (either animate or inanimate) in   5.00
     detail; manipulates or carries them for a long time.
         Low: Examines objects briefly, and leaves them.
     (Infant may examine them later.)

23. Infant tries to interrupt mother when she cares for   5.00
     siblings or other infants.
         Middle: There are no siblings, or mother is not
     concerned about other infants.

27. Infant accepts being held or carried by monkeys other   5.00
     than mother.
         Middle: No effort to hold or carry from others.
         Low: Refuses or protests.

29. When mother leaves infant, he becomes distressed and   5.00
     follows with calling or screaming and tries to cling on
     her.
         Middle: Stays or follows without distress.
         Low: Sits right where he is and screams.

36. When mother approaches infant, he notices immediately   5.00
     and looks at or approaches her in a hurry.
         Low: Does not respond to mother's approaching him
     until she is close to him or picks him up.

38.   Infant is interested in social environment; watches social   5.00
      interactions between adults closely.
            Low: Does not watch social interactions between
      adults very closely.

46.   Infant walks, runs, and climbs without bumping,   5.00
      stumbling, or falling.
            Low: Bumps, stumbles, or falls occur during play.

49.   Infant is very active, always moving around when he is   5.00
      awake. Prefers active play to quiet play.
            Low: Prefers low-intensity play.

50.   Infant ignores most bumps, falls, or startles.   5.00
            Low: Runs to mother, screams, or stops play/sits
      alone etc.

58.   Infant accepts necessary restraint and limits set by   5.00
      mother.
            Low: Resists necessary restraint and control.

86.   Infant quickly gets used to observer or observation   5.00
      situation that initially made him wary.
            Middle: Not initially wary of observer or observation
      situation.
            Low: Remains wary of observer and observation
      situation.

89.   Infant seeks mother's help when exploration or play   5.00
      becomes difficult or is blocked.
            Low: Deals with a difficulty on his own, or moves to
      different activity; does not seek mother's help.

92.   Infant periodically interrupts active social play to   5.00
      approach and make contact with mother. (May or may
      not return and continue social play.)
            Low: Does not interrupt active social play to seek
      mother; may return to her after the bout of play.

 2.   Infant seeks to be held or carried or protected by adult   4.00
      monkeys other than mother when she is occupied with
      other activities.

> *Low:* Does not ask for caretaking from adults other than his own mother.

6.   When mother interacts with adult monkeys, infant tries to intervene; climbs on or between them.   4.00
Low: Tolerates or joins in mother's social interactions.

10.   When adult monkeys other than mother approach or sit nearby, infant stops play, freezes, or returns to mother.   4.00
Low: Play or exploration is not disrupted when adults approach.

17.   Infant will solicit care or interaction from one or two adult males.   4.00
Low: Ignores or avoids any adult males.

21.   Infant ignores, avoids, or rejects play invitations.   4.00
Middle: Infant is too young for social play.

44.   Infant solicits and cooperates with grooming from juveniles or adults other than mother.   4.00
Middle: Monkeys other than mother never groom infant.
Low: Avoids or does not cooperate with grooming from juveniles or adults other than mother.

61.   When mother is nearby, infant is bolder or more confident to play or explore.   4.00
Low: Infant's boldness/tentativeness is the same regardless of mother's location.

65.   Infant shows great interest in nonsocial exploration or play.   4.00
Low: Only interested in social play.

66.   When infant spontaneously returns to mother in nonthreatening situation, proximity or contact with mother is brief.   4.00
Low: Proximity or contact with mother lasts more than 1 min (without infant's sleeping).

73. When exploration or solitary play is interrupted, infant   4.00
gives up easily.
> *Low:* Resumes the activity after the interruption.

79. Infant will engage in quiet social play with peers, but   4.00
avoids active chasing- and wrestling-type play.
> *Middle:* Does not play at all.
> *Low:* Prefers vigorous social play.

85. Infant prefers climbing and running to exploring or   4.00
manipulating small things.
> *Low:* Prefers manipulatory play to gross motor play.

93. When mother is feeding, sleeping, or manipulating   4.00
objects, infant tries to interrupt if he is unoccupied; calls
or climbs on her.
> *Low:* Tolerates or joins in mother's nonsocial
activities; does not demand to be the center of her
attention.

94. Infant is fearless with new objects or animals when he   4.00
first encounters them.
> *Middle:* There are no new objects or animals other
than monkeys.
> *Low:* Afraid of new objects or animals when he first
encounters them.

5. Infant approaches one or two adult males within 1 m.   3.00
> *Low:* Does not approach any adult males on his own.

12. In addition to or instead of keeping track of mother   3.00
visually, infant returns to her repeatedly even in calm
situation.
> *Low:* During play or exploration, infant monitors
mother's location and activity without having to
approach.

20. When infant becomes frightened and returns to mother,   3.00
he clings on her for long time even after the frightening
event is over.
> *Low:* Ready to resume play once frightening event is
over.

39. When mother punishes infant's behaviors, he returns to 3.00
the same behaviors without wariness of further
punishment.
Low: Does not repeat punished behaviors, or does so
with care or cautiously.

42. Infant ignores peers' activities; finds his own activities 3.00
more interesting.
Low: Stays with peers rather than playing on his
own.

48. Infant hesitates to approach or retreats quickly from play 3.00
objects or peers.
Low: Is confident during exploration and play; takes
initiative with peers and playthings.

53. Infant solicits or cooperates with grooming from mother. 3.00
Middle: Mother never grooms infant.
Low: Avoids or does not cooperate with mother.

62. Infant screams or throws tantrums as a way of getting 3.00
objects from mother, resisting her control, or intruding
on her behaviors.
Low: Makes demands to mother without screams or
tantrums unless injured or frightened.

71. When infant finishes with an activity or discards an 3.00
object, he finds something to do first without returning
to mother between activities.
Low: Returns to mother for rest, affection, or
interaction before finding a new plaything or activity.

74. Infant wants to be carried when moving long distance. 3.00
Middle: Too young to walk long distance.
Low: Walks by himself.

75. When infant screams, he screams hard and for a long 3.00
time.
Middle: Never screams.

84. Infant plays roughly and in cruel way with peers. (Peers 3.00
scream or withdraw from play.)
Middle: Play is never very active.
Low: Plays active games without hurting peers.

8.   Infant adopts awkward posture when carried by mother.   2.00
        Low: Adjusts his posture to mother's movement.

16.   Infant screams or throws tantrums when mother   2.00
        physically rejects his bid for contact. (May or may not
        persist in trying to establish contact.)
        Middle: Mother never physically rejects infant.

41.   Infant is sometimes unaware of mother's location and has   2.00
        to search for her when returning.
        Low: Even if social situation becomes chaotic, infant
    knows where mother is and returns to her without
    mistakes.

47.   Infant engages in self-directed behaviors other than coat   2.00
        care (e.g., manipulates or licks fingers, thumbs, chest,
        genitals, etc.).
        Low: Infant's self-directed behaviors consist of coat
    care.

52.   When infant returns to mother after play or exploration,   2.00
        he seeks signs of tolerance or acceptance from mother
        before he clings on; pauses, signals, or waits for mother
        to complete contact.
        Middle: Infant approaches mother but never makes
    physical contact on his own.
        Low: Tries to cling on mother directly, without
    pausing to seek signs of tolerance or acceptance from
    her. (Mother may show her acceptance and sit still or
    reach for infant.)

55.   Infant vocalizes or moves closer showing distress when   2.00
        mother moves more than 10 m away or out of sight.
        Middle: Mother never moves more than 10 m away
    or out of sight.
        Low: Notices mother's moving away without
    screaming or approaching.

56.   Infant displays distress-related motor patterns (e.g.,   2.00
        auto-orality, stereotypies, etc.) in low-stress situations or
        long after stressful experiences pass.
        Low: Does not display such patterns, or displays
    them after stressful experiences pass.

82. Infant scratches body persistently when alone and   2.00
     unoccupied (no evident wound, mange, etc.).
          Low: Rests, plays, or grooms without persistent
     scratch.

37. Infant is demanding; fusses and interrupts mother's   1.00
     behaviors if she does not do what he wants immediately.
          Low: Patient; sits and watches if mother does not
     respond immediately. (He may or may not repeat
     demand.)

54. When mother does not respond to infant's bids for care   1.00
     or attention, he immediately throws tantrums or gives up
     and walks off to other activities.
          Low: Waits for a response or repeats bids rather than
     throwing tantrums or giving up immediately; acts as if
     mother will shortly do what he asked.

57. Infant jerks or throws tantrums in response to competent   1.00
     maternal caretaking (e.g., grooming, retrieving under
     threat, feeding, etc.).
          Low: Accepts mother's caretaking without jerks or
     annoyance unless it is necessarily uncomfortable.

63. When mother moves away from infant in calm situation,   1.00
     infant produces distressed vocalization, clings strongly, or
     throws tantrum.
          Low: Notices and/or follows without distressed
     vocalization, strong clinging, or throwing tantrum.

68. Infant gets off mother's ventrum but stops near mother   1.00
     or wants to be held again.
          Low: Once he gets off mother's ventrum, infant goes
     directly to play.

MATERNAL Q-SET FOR MACAQUES

1. Mother moves around when infant is playing at a distance. (Infant's
    keeping track of mother may be difficult.)
         Low: Sits in conspicuous place, or does not move repeatedly
    from place to place.

2. Mother makes eye contact with infant when holding him in her arms.

   Middle: Lack of eye contact is due to infant.

   Low: Avoids or is indifferent to eye contact with infant even if infant tries make eye contact.

3. When mother observes social conflicts between monkeys or unusual happenings, she retrieves, restrains, or stays in proximity with infant.

   Low: Does not keep infant closer even when she observes social conflicts or unusual happenings.

4. Mother punishes infant for slight provocation or misbehaviors. (Punishment should consist of biting, grasping, open mouth, etc.; does not imply simple rejection.)

   Middle: Infant never bothers mother much.

   Low: Doesn't punish infant at all or only after serious or persistent misbehaviors.

5. Mother prevents infant from approaching or interacting with most adult females.

   Low: Allows infant to approach or initiate social interactions with any adult females.

6. Mother is quick to retrieve infant in response to slight strange noises or happenings.

   Low: Does not retrieve infant unless happenings may cause infant danger.

7. Mother is often made uncomfortable by infant's behaviors in ventrum; moves infant's position, jerks, or shows other annoyed behaviors regularly.

   Low: Comfortable with infant in ventrum (regardless of frequency of holding infant).

8. Mother allows other monkeys to hold, carry, groom, or otherwise take care of infant. (Caretaking should consist of physical contact.)

   Middle: No effort at caretaking from others.

   Low: Actively refuses or retrieves infant if other monkey attempts caretaking.

9. When infant emits distressed vocalization during exploration or

play, mother is quick to respond; calls, approaches, or retrieves infant.

Low: No response to infant's distressed vocalization.

10. Mother displays bizarre movements or stereotypies that are obviously out of context in the situation.
    Low: Does not display any abnormal behavior.

11. When infant moves away from mother, she goes after him without preventing him from continuing his activities.
    Middle: Mother accepts infant's moving away from her, even over long distances, without taking any action.
    Low: Mother retrieves or restrains infant to keep him close to her when he moves away.

12. When infant returns to mother in nonthreatening situations, she looks at him and embraces him affectionately.
    Low: Whenever infant returns to mother, she simply accepts him without looking at him.

13. Mother attacks, chases, or bites other monkeys hard in slight social trouble; she is aggressive and bad tempered.
    Low: Escapes quickly, screams, or shows fear grimace in slight social trouble; she is timid and weak.

14. Mother is bold with novel objects and approaches them to explore when first exposed to them.
    Low: Mother is wary of novel objects even after other monkeys examine them.

15. Mother grooms other monkeys or solicits being groomed when they are nearby (not referring to her own infant).
    Low: Does not groom other monkeys when they solicit it, or avoids being groomed.

16. When infant approaches novel animals, mother retrieves him; when he manipulates novel objects, mother takes them away.
    Low: Allows infant to approach novel animals or manipulate novel objects.

17. Mother has much interest in infants other than her own: inspects parts of their bodies, tries to hold them, etc.

Low: Even when other infants are nearby, mother does not show any interest in them.

18. If infant is away from mother, she calls, approaches, or retrieves him unless he is occupied with play or exploration.
    Middle: Infant is always active during exploration or play.
    Low: Does not notice or ignores when infant sits at a distance without playing or exploring.

19. In general situations, mother looks at infant to check his location and activities when she is at a distance from him; when infant moves, mother follows him visually, etc.
    Middle: Infant is never away.
    Low: Rarely checks infant's location and activities.

20. Mother's responses to infant's signals are often delayed (signal = infant produces distressed call, approaches to be picked up or carried, etc.).
    Low: Mother's responses to infant signals are prompt. (Mother's responses may or may not be positive.)

21. Mother plays many roles in order to regulate distance between her and her infant: follows, calls, retrieves, or restrains infant.
    Low: Does not play any role in regulating distance between her and her infant.

22. Mother refuses to carry infant in most situations; makes infant walk on his own.
    Low: Carries infant according to situation or infant's request (e.g., when moving a long way or escaping attack or owing to infant's illness or fatigue).

23. Treatment of infant is rough and careless; drags infant, stamps on him, pushes him hard, etc.
    Low: Treatment of infant is careful and tender.

24. In nonthreatening situation, mother will interact with, care for, or supervise infant in favor of interaction with other adults.
    Low: When other adults seek interaction, mother responds to them in favor of interaction with, caring for, or supervising infant.

25. Mother keeps infant close to her, even after unusual events are over.

Low: Leaves or releases infant right after unusual events are over.

26. Mother accepts or is tolerant of infant using her body or tail for or during play.
    Middle: Infant never uses mother's body as a play object.
    Low: Withdraws or punishes infant playing on her body.

27. Once infant goes off mother's ventrum, she rejects his bid for contact and/or turns her back for a while.
    Low: Holds infant right away even after he goes off and wants to be held again.

28. When infant approaches or pauses near mother, she looks at him or retrieves him if necessary.
    Low: Ignores infant's approaching.

29. Mother accepts infant's moving beyond 1 m.
    Low: Prevents infant from moving beyond 1 m.

30. When mother sits and infant is in mother's ventrum, she embraces him with one or both arms.
    Low: Does not embrace infant in her ventrum when sitting.

31. When infant is not distressed, she ignores or rejects infant's approach, bid for contact, or signals if she is engaged in social activities.
    Low: Accepts or tolerates infant's approach, bid for contact, or signals in favor of social interactions with others.

32. Mother prevents infant from approaching or interacting with most adult males.
    Low: Allows infant to approach or initiate social interaction with any adult male.

33. Mother encourages infant to leave by pushing him away gently, gradually departing from him, etc.
    Low: Does nothing to make infant leave her; waits for his departure.

34. Mother shares food with infant; allows him to eat the same food or to take food from her.

Low: Does not allow infant to eat along with her; pushes infant from food or moves away; will not share food.

35. When infant initiates physical contact with mother in nondistress context, mother rejects or avoids his bid.
    Low: Accepts physical contact on any occasion.

36. When infant gets involved in social conflicts, mother is bold to retrieve him or counterattack his adversary even at the risk of conflict with other adults.
    Low: Mother is timid to retrieve infant and/or does not help infant.

37. Mother is inconsistent in responding to infant's bid for contact or interaction; sometimes she is responsive, other times unresponsive.
    Low: The level of mother's responsiveness is consistent.

38. Mother inspects infant's body routinely even without obvious need. (Inspection does not necessarily equal grooming; inspection means manipulating infant's body to find or look at dirt or injury; groom means parting fur and picking up a small object in stereotyped way.)
    Low: Only inspects infant's body in response to seeing some obvious problem, or rarely inspects him.

39. If mother is moving and infant approaches to make contact, she walks more slowly or pauses to let him approach.
    Low: Walks at her own pace.

40. When infant initiates social play with peers or juveniles, mother retrieves or restrains infant most times.
    Low: Allows infant to initiate social play with any peers or juveniles.

41. When other adult monkeys (or older juveniles) are nearby or taking care of infant, mother is not uneasy about letting him move farther away and for a longer time.
    Low: Other monkeys' supervision of infant does not change mother's supervision of infant.

42. Mother notices infant's response to caretaking in nonthreatening situations; mother adjusts her behaviors when infant shows annoyance during grooming or carrying.

Low: Persists despite infant's annoyed behaviors; infant shows further annoyance.

43. When mother goes out of infant's sight, she keeps in touch with him by occasional vocalization in nonthreatening situations.
    Low: Does not vocalize to keep in touch with infant when she goes out of his sight unless something happens.

44. Mother allows infant to sit close to her or follow closely when she forages food (i.e., she is not concerned about his stealing the food she finds).
    Middle: Infant is always carried (i.e., cannot approach and steal).
    Low: Keeps infant at a distance when she is looking for food.

45. Even when infant has been punished and has stopped misbehaviors, mother repeats or continues punishment.
    Middle: Never punishes.
    Low: When infant stops misbehaviors, she stops punishment.

46. When infant is distressed and returns to mother for contact, she holds him in ventrum right away.
    Low: Ignores, delays, or rejects infant's request for contact; does not hold him.

47. Mother bites, pushes to a degree that causes infant to scream long or hard or to flee or avoid mother for a short time.
    Low: Mother's punishment stops without injury or making him avoid her.

48. Mother refuses to divide attention between infant and other young monkeys when infant is in ventrum; pushes them away or moves away from them.
    Low: Responds to other young monkeys even when she is caring for infant in ventrum.

49. Mother imposes or persists in grooming or coat care despite infant's protest or effort to explore.
    Low: Only grooms or cares for infant's coat when infant accepts.

50. Mother grooms infant whenever he solicits grooming or rests in ventrum.
    Low: Rarely grooms infant even when he solicits.

51. Mother stays alone rather than with other adult monkeys.
    Low: Stays with other adult monkeys most of the time.

52. Mother allows infant to examine or groom her coat without moving, pushing him away, or shaking her body.
    Middle: Infant never manipulates her coat.
    Low: Prevents infant from manipulating her coat.

53. Mother tries to hold or carry infants other than her own if they obviously need immediate care.
    Low: Does not take care of other infants in any situation.

54. In changing or alarming situation, mother has to look for infant before she retrieves him; she does not know where he is.
    Low: Even when the situation is chaotic, mother retrieves infant without mistakes.

55. When mother initially ignores infant's call or contact seeking, she gives in if infant persists.
    Middle: Mother never refuses.
    Low: Refuses even if infant persists.

56. Mother pushes infant away or withdraws nipples when he tries to suck on them.
    Low: Accepts nipple contact whenever he is in ventrum.

57. When social play gets rough and/or infant screams or is victimized, mother retrieves him.
    Low: Lets infant continue rough play regardless of his behaviors.

58. If mother and infant walk together, she pauses or adjusts to his pace.
    Low: Walks at her own pace (infant has to keep up).

59. Mother is occupied in feeding when food is available.
    Low: Mother's feeding duration is short.

60. Mother stays close to other monkeys who have the same age infants as her own.
    Middle: Stays away from any monkeys.
    Low: Stays close to monkeys who do not necessarily have the same age infants as her own.

61. When infant is attacked or threatened or otherwise emits distress call, mother retrieves him right away.
    Low: Retrieval of infant is delayed or does not occur; infant often returns to mother on his own.

62. Mother prefers specific adult female companions.
    Low: No preference among adult female companions.

63. Comforting infant is active or exaggerated; mother not only retrieves infant but also embraces, rocks, or sometimes lip smacks to infant when she comfort him.
    Middle: Mother never comforts infant.
    Low: Comforting of infant is casual; just looks at and holds him.

64. Mother signals intention to change her location by looking at, gesturing toward, or vocalizing to infant.
    Low: Changes her location without signaling infant.

65. Bouts of caretaking are brief; mother ceases infant's care without clear interrupting events or strong signals from infant.
    Low: Bouts of caretaking are long once it starts.

66. When infant tries to play with mother (e.g., playfully pulls her body, approaches with open mouth, etc.), she rejects and/or punishes him.
    Low: Tolerates or responds to infant's playful interactions.

67. Mother scratches body persistently when alone and unoccupied. (No evident wound, mange, etc.)
    Low: Rests, grooms, or interacts socially without persistent scratch.

68. Mother maintains proximity to a specific adult male most of the time.
    Low: Avoids any adult males.

69. Mother retrieves, restrains, or moves closer to infant if his activity might lead to fall or other injury.
    Low: Does not retrieve, restrain, or move closer to infant in situations that might lead fall or injury.

70. Mother is interested in infant's exploration or play; approaches him to observe his activities.

Low: May or may not be attentive to infant's activities, but rarely approaches him to observe his activities.

71. Mother retrieves, restrains, or maintains proximity with infant when she becomes distressed (wary, fearful, sick, troubled in social interaction, etc.).
    Low: Becomes less attentive to infant, or even avoids him.

72. Mother prevents infant from being involved in social conflict; when infant approaches certain monkeys who are dominant or may cause infant trouble, mother retrieves or restrains infant.
    Low: Only responds to infant after he is involved in social conflict.

73. Mother relies solely on physical acts to control infant (e.g., restrains or retrieves by grasping a foot, punishes by biting, instead of lip smacking, grooming, facial expression, or gesture).
    Low: Does not rely solely on physical control; uses gesture or vocalization as well to control infant's behaviors.

74. Mother interferes with infant play in nonthreatening situations, when she observes infant playing with peers.
    Low: Doesn't interfere with infant's social play; calls or retrieves infant after social play bout except in threatening situations.

75. Mother will sleep even when infant is playing at a distance.
    Middle: Infant never goes away.
    Low: Only sleeps if infant is retrieved first or plays nearby.

76. Mother holds or carries infant even if he wants to explore or walk by himself.
    Low: Allows infant to leave ventrum or walk by himself.

77. When infant is not distressed, mother ignores or rejects his approach, bid for contact, or signals if she is engaged in nonsocial activities (e.g., resting, feeding, self-grooming, etc.).
    Low: Accepts or tolerates infant's approach, bid for contact, or signals.

78. When infant is exploring objects, mother takes the objects away from him to examine them by herself.
    Low: Does not intrude on infant's exploration unless the objects are novel or dangerous.

79. When mother is holding infant, she allows other monkeys to touch, manipulate, or otherwise approach infant.
     Low: Turns away or threatens other monkeys showing interest in infant while she is holding him.

80. Mother continues to hold infant when he seeks comfort from her, but then she removes or leaves infant before he departs for exploration on his own.
     Low: Allows infant to stay in her ventrum until he begins to explore.

81. When mother takes infant to an unfamiliar area that is new to them or not usually used, mother retrieves or restrains infant more often than usual.
     Low: An unfamiliar area does not change mother's supervision of infant.

82. When infant goes farther from mother, she looks at infant more closely.
     Low: Supervision does not increase in proportion to the distance that the infant gets from his mother.

83. Mother uses wide space available for activities.
     Low: Stays in the same place.

84. When infant gets involved in social trouble, mother is quick to come to his aid by attacking his adversaries.
     Low: Tries to remove infant from social conflicts; they escape together.

85. Mother retrieves infant even before he finishes exploration or play; she doesn't give infant enough time to explore or play on his own.
     Low: Allows infant to explore as long as he wants.

86. Once infant makes contact with mother, mother allows infant to sit in ventrum or to ride on her as like as he wants to.
     Low: Limits duration of being in ventrum or riding; periodically removes infant.

87. Mother is active, always moving around.
     Low: Stays still; spends long periods sitting or resting (unless interrupted by other monkeys).

88. Mother adjusts infant's position or posture when he clings on her in awkward position or posture.

    Low: Does not show concern about infant's position or posture.

89. Mother leaves infant even if infant screams, follows in a hurry, or otherwise becomes upset.

    Low: Returns to infant, carries him along, or leaves him only when he tolerates it.

90. Mother devotes more time to grooming, coat care, or other caretaking of infant than to that of siblings or peers.

    Low: Devotes equal or less time and effort to care of infant than to that of siblings or peers.

91. Mother screams hard and for long time over social trouble.

    Low: Does not show any excitement unless social trouble is serious enough to cause harm to her or her infant.

92. Mother adapts to infant's activity cycles, sleeping when he sleeps, waking when he wakes.

    Low: Mother's activity cycles aren't synchronized with infant's.

93. Mother carries or holds infant in an odd or unskillful way.

    Low: Carries or holds infant skillfully and in standard posture for his age.

SCORING KEY FOR Q-SORT CRITERIA AND DERIVED SCALES IN THE ATTACHMENT Q-SET AND THE ATTACHMENT Q-SET FOR INFANT MACAQUES ITEM SETS

The Attachment Q-Set (AQS) contains 90 items, the Attachment Q-Set for Infant Macaques (AQS-M) 94. For the Pederson and Moran scales, comp. = compliance, SB = secure base, F/D = fussy/difficult, EPC = enjoys physical contact, and AS = affective sharing. For the Posada, Gao, et al. scales, SIM = smooth interactions with mother, PCM = physical contact with mother, IOA = interactions with other adults, and PM = proximity to mother.

TABLE D1

Scoring Key

Item No.	Placement in AQS Security Criterion	Placement in AQS Dependency Criterion	Pederson-Moran AQS Scales	Posada, Gao, et al. AQS Scales	Placement in Macaque Security Criterion	Placement in Macaque Dependency Criterion
1	8	5.2	Comp.	SIM	6.0	4.0
2	1.8	5.8	F/D	SIM	4.0	4.0
3	4.8	2	SB	PCM	6.0	6.0
4	6.2	4.8			8.0	7.0
5	6.3	5.8			3.0	2.0
6	2.2	7.2		SIM	4.0	6.0
7	4.3	2.4		IOA	8.0	8.0
8	3.3	4.6	F/D		2.0	4.0
9	6.5	3	F/D	SIM	5.0	9.0
10	2.3	6	F/D		4.0	6.0
11	7.5	7.4	EPC	PM	6.0	2.0
12	6	2.8		IOA	3.0	9.0
13	2.7	7.4	F/D		5.0	3.0
14	7.8	6.2	AS	PM	5.0	4.0
15	7.7	4	SB	IOA	7.0	8.0
16	5.2	5			2.0	6.0
17	3.5	4.4		IOA	4.0	2.0

Item No.	Placement in AQS Security Criterion	Placement in AQS Dependency Criterion	Pederson-Moran AQS Scales	Posada, Gao, et al. AQS Scales	Placement in Macaque Security Criterion	Placement in Macaque Dependency Criterion
18	8.5	5.6	Comp.	SIM	9.0	7.0
19	7.7	5.4	Comp.	SIM	5.0	4.0
20	4.2	3	F/D		3.0	7.0
21	8.8	8	SB	PM	4.0	6.0
22	6.5	4.8			6.0	1.0
23	2.7	7			5.0	8.0
24	4.5	5.4		SIM	9.0	6.0
25	2	2.8	SB	PM	6.0	3.0
26	3.3	7.6	F/D		7.0	8.0
27	6.3	4			5.0	2.0
28	7.5	6.4	EPC	PCM	6.0	5.0
29	4.3	4			5.0	5.0
30	2.3	5	F/D		8.0	5.0
31	2.5	8.4			7.0	5.0
32	7.2	4.6	Comp.	SIM	6.0	3.0
33	1.3	5.2	SB	PCM	6.0	8.0
34	1.2	5	SB	PM	7.0	7.0
35	4.3	1		PM	8.0	7.0
36	8.8	3.6	SB	PM	5.0	7.0
37	4.8	4.4			1.0	6.0
38	1.2	7.2	F/D	SIM	5.0	3.0
39	4.7	5			3.0	3.0
40	6.5	4			7.0	6.0
41	8.5	6.8	Comp.	SIM	2.0	1.0
42	8.2	5			3.0	5.0
43	4.7	8.6		PM	9.0	8.0
44	7.7	7.4	EPC	PCM	4.0	4.0
45	5.2	5			8.0	7.0
46	5.7	4.6			5.0	5.0
47	7.2	5	SB		2.0	5.0
48	6	4		IOA	3.0	5.0
49	6.3	5.2			5.0	3.0
50	3.5	5.4		IOA	5.0	2.0
51	4.7	2.6		IOA	7.0	5.0
52	3.8	5			2.0	2.0
53	8.5	6	EPC	PCM	3.0	8.0
54	1.5	4		SIM	1.0	7.0
55	7	5.4			2.0	6.0
56	2.7	5.6			2.0	4.0
57	4	2.4			1.0	3.0
58	3.2	3.8		IOA	5.0	5.0
59	3.8	1.2		PM	6.0	3.0
60	8.5	3	SB	IOA	6.0	3.0
61	1.8	4.6	F/D		4.0	5.0
62	5.5	4	F/D	SIM	3.0	5.0
63	2	7.8			1.0	5.0
64	7	6	EPC	PCM	6.0	7.0
65	1.8	5	Comp.	SIM	4.0	4.0
66	7	3.6		IOA	4.0	2.0
67	4	4.4		IOA	8.0	5.0

Item No.	Placement in AQS Security Criterion	Placement in AQS Dependency Criterion	Pederson-Moran AQS Scales	Posada, Gao, et al. AQS Scales	Placement in Macaque Security Criterion	Placement in Macaque Dependency Criterion
68	5	5			1.0	7.0
69	2.3	1.2		PM	7.0	1.0
70	8	5.6	AS	SIM	7.0	7.0
71	8.8	3.4	SB	PCM	3.0	3.0
72	4.5	5.4			6.0	5.0
73	5.2	5.6			4.0	3.0
74	1.5	6.2	F/D	SIM	3.0	6.0
75	1.2	8	SB		3.0	4.0
76	3.2	2.8		IOA	8.0	1.0
77	7.7	5.2			7.0	9.0
78	4.5	2.4		IOA	7.0	9.0
79	1	5.2	F/D	SIM	4.0	5.0
80	8.5	4.6	SB		6.0	6.0
81	1.8	7.4	F/D	SIM	8.0	2.0
82	4	4.8			2.0	4.0
83	6.5	7			9.0	8.0
84	5	4.6			3.0	4.0
85	7.5	3.4			4.0	4.0
86	6.5	6.2	AS		5.0	4.0
87	5.8	6.6			9.0	1.0
88	1.2	4.4	SB		7.0	6.0
89	6.5	4.8			5.0	6.0
90	8.3	7.2	SB		7.0	3.0
91					6.0	7.0
92					5.0	9.0
93					4.0	6.0
94					4.0	4.0

REFERENCES

Ainsworth, M. D. S. (1963). The development of infant-mother interaction among the Ganda. In B. M. Foss (Ed.), *Determinants of infant behavior* (Vol. 2). London: Methuen.

Ainsworth, M. D. S. (1967). *Infancy in Uganda: Infant care and the growth of love.* Baltimore: Johns Hopkins University Press.

Ainsworth, M. D. S. (1973). The development of infant-mother attachment. In B. M. Caldwell & H. Ricciuti (Eds.), *Review of child development research* (Vol. 3). Chicago: University of Chicago Press.

Ainsworth, M. D. S., & Bell, S. M. (1970). Attachment, exploration, and separation: Illustrated by the behavior of one-year-olds in a strange situation. *Child Development, 41,* 49–67.

Ainsworth, M. D. S., Bell, S. M., & Stayton, D. J. (1971). Individual differences in Strange Situation behavior of one-year-olds. In H. R. Schaffer (Ed.), *The origins of human social relations.* London: Academic.

Ainsworth, M. D. S., Blehar, M. C., Waters, E., & Wall, S. (1978). *Patterns of attachment: A psychological study of the Strange Situation.* Hillsdale, NJ: Erlbaum.

Ainsworth, M. D. S., & Eichberg, C. G. (1991). Effects on infant-mother attachment of mother's unresolved loss of an attachment figure or other traumatic experience. In C. M. Parkes, J. Stevenson-Hinde, & P. Marris (Eds.), *Attachment across the life cycle.* New York and London: Tavistock/Routledge.

Ainsworth, M. D. S., & Wittig, B. A. (1969). Attachment and the exploratory behavior of one-year-olds in a strange situation. In B. M. Foss (Ed.), *Determinants of infant behavior* (Vol. 4). London: Methuen.

Anderson, C. W., Nagle, R. J., Roberts, W. A., & Smith, J. W. (1981). Attachment in substitute caregivers as a function of center quality and caregiver involvement. *Child Development, 52,* 53–61.

Arend, R., Gove, F. L., & Sroufe, L. A. (1979). Continuity of individual adaptation from infancy to kindergarten: A predictive study of ego-resiliency and curiosity in pre-schoolers. *Child Development, 50,* 950–959.

Astington, J. W., & Gopnick, A. (1991). Theoretical explanations of children's understanding of the mind. *British Journal of Developmental Psychology, 9,* 7–32.

Astington, J. W., Harris, P. L., & Olson, D. R. (Eds.). (1988). *Developing theories of mind.* Cambridge: Cambridge University Press.

Aviezer, O., van IJzendoorn, M. H., Sagi, A., & Schuengel, C. (1994). "Children of the dream" revisited: 70 years of collective early child-care in Israeli kibbutzim. *Psychological Bulletin, 116,* 99–116.

Bakermans-Kranenburg, M. J., & van IJzendoorn, M. H. (1993). A psychometric study of the Adult Attachment Interview: Reliability and discriminant validity. *Developmental Psychology*, **29**, 870–879.

Baldwin, J. M. (1895). *Mental development in the child and the race*. New York: Macmillan.

Bates, J. E. (1980). The concept of difficult temperament. *Merrill-Palmer Quarterly*, **26**, 299–319.

Bates, J. E., Freeland, C. A., & Lounsbury, M. L. (1979). Measure of infant difficultness. *Child Development*, **50**, 794–803.

Bates, J. E., Maslin, C. A., & Frankel, K. A. (1985). Attachment security, mother-child interaction, and temperament as predictors of behavior-problem ratings at age three years. In I. Bretherton & E. Waters (Eds.), *Growing points of attachment theory and research. Monographs of the Society for Research in Child Development*, **50**(1–2, Serial No. 209).

Bauer, P. J., & Shore, C. M. (1987). Making a memorable event: Effects of familiarity and organization on young children's recall of action sequences. *Cognitive Development*, **2**, 327–338.

Bauer, P. J., & Thal, D. J. (1990). Scripts or scraps: Reconsidering the development of sequential understanding. *Journal of Experimental Child Psychology*, **50**, 287–304.

Bayley, N. (1969). *The Bayley Scales of Infant Development*. New York: Psychological Corp.

Beit-Hallahmi, B., & Rabin, A. I. (1977). The kibbutz as a social experiment and as a child-rearing laboratory. *American Psychologist*, **32**, 532–541.

Bell, R. Q., & Harper, L. V. (1977). *Child effects on adults*. Hillsdale, NJ: Erlbaum.

Belsky, J., Garduque, L., & Hrncir, E. (1984). Assessing performance, competence, and executive capacity in infant play: Relations to home environment and security of attachment. *Developmental Psychology*, **20**, 406–417.

Belsky, J., & Isabella, R. (1988). Maternal, infant, and social contextual determinants of attachment security. In J. Belsky & T. Nezworski (Eds.), *Clinical implications of attachment*. Hillsdale, NJ: Erlbaum.

Belsky, J., & Rovine, M. (1987). Temperament and attachment security in the Strange Situation: An empirical rapprochement. *Child Development*, **58**, 787–795.

Belsky, J., Rovine, M., & Taylor, D. G. (1984). The Pennsylvania Infant and Family Development Project: 3. The origins of individual differences in infant-mother attachment: Maternal and infant contributions. *Child Development*, **55**, 718–728.

Belsky, J., Taylor, D. G., & Rovine, M. (1984). The Pennsylvania Infant and Family Development Project: 2. The development of reciprocal interaction in the infant-mother dyad. *Child Development*, **55**, 706–717.

Bem, D., & Funder, D. (1978). Predicting more of the people more of the time. *Psychological Review*, **85**, 485–501.

Benoit, D., & Parker, K. C. H. (1994). Stability and transmission of attachment across three generations. *Child Development*, **65**, 1444–1456.

Biringen, Z. (1990). Direct observation of maternal sensitivity and dyadic interactions in the home: Relations to maternal thinking. *Developmental Psychology*, **26**, 278–284.

Block, J. (1971). *Lives through time*. Berkeley, CA: Bancroft.

Block, J. (1977). Advancing the psychology of personality: Paradigmatic shift or improving the quality of research. In D. Magnusson & N. Endler (Eds.), *Personality at the crossroads*. Hillsdale, NJ: Erlbaum.

Block, J. (1978). *The Q-sort method in personality assessment and psychiatry research* (Reprint). Palo Alto, CA: Consulting Psychologists. (Original work published 1961)

Block, J. H. (1983). Differential premises arising from differential socialization of the sexes: Some conjectures. *Child Development*, **54**, 1335–1354.

Block, J. H., & Block, J. (1980). The role of ego-control and ego-resiliency in the organization of behavior. In W. A. Collins (Ed.), *Development of cognition, affect, and social relations* (Minnesota Symposia on Child Psychology, Vol. **13**). Hillsdale, NJ: Erlbaum.

Bolig, R., Price, C., O'Neill, P., & Suomi, S. (1992). Subjective assessment of reactivity level and personality traits of rhesus monkeys. *International Journal of Primatology*, **13**, 287–306.

Bosso, O. R., Corter, C. M., & Abramovitch, R. (1995). *Attachment security in three-year-old first born children: Relations to Strange Situation classifications and to behavior toward a younger sibling.* Unpublished manuscript, University of Toronto, Department of Psychology.

Bowlby, J. (1958). The nature of the child's tie to his mother. *International Journal of Psycho-Analysis*, **39**, 350–373.

Bowlby, J. (1960). Grief and mourning in infancy and early childhood. *Psychoanalytic Study of the Child*, **15**, 9–52.

Bowlby, J. (1973). *Attachment and loss: Vol. 2. Separation.* New York: Basic.

Bowlby, J. (1980). *Attachment and loss: Vol. 3. Loss, sadness, and depression.* New York: Basic.

Bowlby, J. (1982). *Attachment and loss: Vol. 1. Attachment* (2d ed.). New York: Basic. (Original work published 1969)

Bowlby, J. (1988). *A secure base: Clinical applications of attachment theory.* London: Tavistock.

Braungart, J. M., & Stifter, C. A. (1991). Regulation of negative reactivity during the Strange Situation: Temperament and attachment in 12-month-old infants. *Infant Behavior and Development*, **14**, 349–364.

Bretherton, I. (1985). Attachment theory: Retrospect and prospect. In I. Bretherton & E. Waters (Eds.), *Growing points of attachment theory and research. Monographs of the Society for Research in Child Development*, **50**(1–2, Serial No. 209).

Bretherton, I. (1987). New perspectives on attachment relations: Security, communication, and internal working models. In J. Osofsky (Ed.), *Handbook of infant development* (2d ed.). New York: Wiley.

Bretherton, I. (1990). Open communication and internal working models: Their role in attachment relationships. In R. Thompson (Ed.), *Socio-emotional development* (Nebraska Symposium on Motivation, Vol. **36**). Lincoln: University of Nebraska Press.

Bretherton, I. (1991). New wine in old bottles. In M. Gunnar & L. A. Sroufe (Eds.), *Concepts of self* (Minnesota Symposia on Child Psychology, Vol. **23**). Hillsdale, NJ: Erlbaum.

Bretherton, I. (1992). The origins of attachment theory: John Bowlby and Mary Ainsworth. *Developmental Psychology*, **28**, 759–775.

Bretherton, I., Oppenheim, D., Prentiss, C., & the MacArthur Narrative Group. (1990). *MacArthur story-stem battery.* Unpublished manual, University of Wisconsin, Madison.

Bretherton, I., Ridgeway, D., & Cassidy, J. (1990). Assessing internal working models of the attachment relationship: An attachment story completion task for 3-year-olds. In M. T. Greenberg, D. Cicchetti, & E. M. Cummings (Eds.), *Attachment in the preschool years: Theory, research, and intervention.* Chicago: University of Chicago Press.

Bretherton, I., et al. (1986). Learning to talk about emotion: A functionalist perspective. *Child Development*, **56**, 530–548.

Bridges, L. J., Connell, J. P., & Belsky, J. (1988). Similarities and differences in infant-mother and infant-father interaction in the Strange Situation: A component process analysis. *Developmental Psychology*, **24**, 92–100.

Brislin, R. W. (1980). Translation and content analysis of oral and written material. In H. C. Triandis & R. W. Brislin (Eds.), *Handbook of cross-cultural psychology/social psychology.* Boston: Allyn & Bacon.

Buss, A., & Plomin, R. (1975). *A temperament theory of personality.* New York: Wiley.

Butterworth, G. E., Harris, P. L., Leslie, A. M., & Wellman, H. M. (Eds.). (1991). Perspectives on the child's theory of mind (Special Issue). *British Journal of Developmental Psychology*, **9**(1–2).

Calkins, S. D. (1994). Origins and outcomes of individual differences in emotion regulation. In N. A. Fox (Ed.), *The development of emotion regulation: Biological and behavioral considerations. Monographs of the Society for Research in Child Development*, **59**(2–3, Serial No. 240).

Calkins, S. D., & Fox, N. A. (1992). The relations among infant temperament, security of attachment, and behavioral inhibition at twenty-four months. *Child Development*, **63**, 1456–1472.

Campbell, D. T., & Fiske, D. W. (1959). Convergent and discriminant validation by the multitrait-multimethod matrix. *Psychological Bulletin*, **56**, 81–105.

Campos, J., Campos, R., & Barrett, K. (1989). Emergent themes in the study of emotional development and emotion regulation. *Developmental Psychology*, **25**, 394–402.

Campos, J. J., & Stenberg, C. (1981). Perception, appraisal, and emotion: The onset of social referencing. In M. E. Lamb & L. Sherrod (Eds.), *Infant social cognition*. Hillsdale, NJ: Erlbaum.

Cassidy, J. (1988). Child-mother attachment and the self in six-year-olds. *Child Development*, **59**, 121–134.

Cassidy, J. (1994). Emotion regulation: Influences of attachment relationships. In N. A. Fox (Ed.), *The development of emotion regulation: Biological and behavioral considerations. Monographs of the Society for Research in Child Development*, **59**(2–3, Serial No. 240).

Cassidy, J., & Berlin, L. J. (1993). The insecure/ambivalent pattern of attachment: Theory and research. *Child Development*, **65**, 971–991.

Cassidy, J., & Kobak, R. R. (1988). Avoidance and its relation to other defensive processes. In J. Belsky & T. Nezworski (Eds.), *Clinical implications of attachment*. Hillsdale, NJ: Erlbaum.

Cassidy, J., & Marvin, R. (1987). *Attachment organization in three- and four-year-olds: A classification system*. Poster presented at the International Conference on Infant Studies, Washington, DC.

Cassidy, J., & Marvin, R. (1989). *Attachment organization in three- and four-year-olds*. Unpublished coding manual, University of Virginia and Pennsylvania State University.

Cassidy, J. A., & Marvin, R. S., with the MacArthur Working Group on Attachment. (1992). *Attachment organization in three- and four-year-olds: Procedures and coding manual*. Unpublished coding manual, Pennsylvania State University.

Cattell, R. B. (1944). Psychological measurement: Normative, ipsative, interactive. *Psychological Review*, **51**, 292–303.

Chandler, M. (1988). Doubt and developing theories of mind. In J. W. Astington, P. L. Harris, & D. R. Olson (Eds.), *Developing theories of mind*. Cambridge: Cambridge University Press.

Cohen, J. (1988). *Statistical power analysis for the social sciences* (2d ed.). Hillsdale, NJ: Erlbaum.

Cohen, J. (1990). Things I have learned (so far). *American Psychologist*, **45**, 1304–1312.

Cohn, D. A., Silver, D. H., Cowan, C. P., Cowan, P. A., & Pearson, J. (1992). Working models of childhood attachment and couple relationships. *Journal of Family Issues*, **13**, 432–449.

Cohn, J. F., & Tronick, E. Z. (1987). Mother infant face-to-face interaction: The sequence of dyadic states at 3, 6, and 9 months. *Developmental Psychology*, **23**, 68–77.

Connell, J. P., & Thompson, R. (1986). Emotion and social interaction in the Strange Situation: Consistencies and asymmetric influences in the second year. *Child Development*, **54**, 733–745.

Cooper, W. H. (1981). Ubiquitous halo. *Psychological Bulletin,* **90,** 218–244.

Craik, K. (1943). *The nature of explanation.* Cambridge: Cambridge University Press.

Crittenden, P. (1992). Quality of attachment in the preschool years. *Development and Psychopathology,* **4,** 209–241.

Crnic, K. A., Greenberg, M. T., Ragozin, A. S., Robinson, N. M., & Basham, R. B. (1983). Effects of stress and social support on mothers and premature and full-term infants. *Child Development,* **54,** 209–217.

Crockenberg, S. B. (1981). Infant irritability, mother responsiveness, and social support influences on the security of infant-mother attachment. *Child Development,* **52,** 857–865.

Cronbach, L. (1951). Coefficient alpha and the internal structure of tests. *Psychometrika,* **16,** 297–334.

Cronbach, L. J., & Meehl, P. E. (1955). Construct validity in psychological tests. *Psychological Bulletin,* **56,** 281–302.

Crowell, J. A. (1990). *Current Relationship Interview.* Unpublished manuscript, State University of New York at Stony Brook.

Crowell, J. A., Holtzworth-Munroe, A., Treboux, D., Waters, E., Stuart, G. L., & Hutchinson, G. (1993). *Are working models of attachment available to conscious awareness? The Adult Attachment Interview versus self-reports of attachment relationships.* Manuscript submitted for publication.

Crowell, J., & Treboux, D. (in press). A review of adult attachment measures: Implications for theory and research. *Social Development.*

Crowell, J., Treboux, D., O'Connor, E., & Waters, E. (1995). *Stability of attachment representations and experiences of life events in newly married couples.* Paper presented at the meeting of the Society for Research in Child Development, Indianapolis.

Crowell, J., Waters, E., Treboux, D., Feider, O., O'Connor, E., Posada, G., & Golby, B. (1992). *Discriminant validity of the Adult Attachment Interview.* Manuscript submitted for publication.

Crowell, J. A., Waters, E., Treboux, D., Feider, O., O'Connor, E., Posada, G., & Golby, B. (1994). *Discriminant validity of the Adult Attachment Interview.* Manuscript submitted for publication.

Cummings, E. M. (1990). Classification of attachment on a continuum of felt security: Illustrations from the study of children of depressed parents. In M. T. Greenberg, D. Cicchetti, & E. M. Cummings (Eds.), *Attachment in the preschool years: Theory, research, and intervention.* Chicago: University of Chicago Press.

Daly, M., & Wilson, M. (1981). Child maltreatment from a sociobiological perspective. In R. Rizley & D. Cicchetti (Eds.), *Developmental perspectives on child maltreatment* (New Directions for Child Development, Vol. 11). San Francisco: Jossey-Bass.

Dodge, K. (1989). Coordinating responses to aversive stimuli: Introduction to a special section on the development of emotion regulation. *Developmental Psychology,* **25,** 339–342.

Edelman, G. M. (1987). *Neural Darwinism: The theory of neuronal group selection.* New York: Basic.

Edwards, A. L. (1990). Construct validity and social desirability. *American Psychologist,* **45,** 287–289.

Egeland, B., & Farber, A. E. (1984). Infant-mother attachment: Factors related to its development and changes over time. *Child Development,* **55,** 753–771.

Egeland, B., Jacobvitz, D., & Sroufe, L. A. (1988). Breaking the cycle of abuse. *Child Development,* **59,** 1080–1088.

Emde, R. N., Biringen, Z., Clyman, R. B., & Oppenheim, D. (1991). The moral self of infancy: Affective core and procedural knowledge. *Developmental Review,* **11,** 251–270.

Epstein, S. (1979). The stability of behavior: 1. On predicting most of the people much of the time. *Journal of Personality and Social Psychology, 37,* 1097–1126.

Fivush, R. (1991a). Gender and emotion in mother-child conversations about the past. *Journal of Narrative and Life History,* 1, 325–341.

Fivush, R. (1991b). The social construction of personal narratives. *Merrill-Palmer Quarterly,* 37, 59–82.

Fivush, R., & Hudson, J. A. (Eds.). (1990). *Knowing and remembering in young children.* Cambridge: Cambridge University Press.

Flavell, J. H., Miller, P. H., & Miller, S. A. (1993). *Cognitive development.* Englewood Cliffs, NJ: Prentice-Hall.

Fogel, A., & Thelen, E. (1987). Development of early expressive and communicative action: Reinterpreting the evidence from a dynamic systems perspective. *Developmental Psychology,* 23, 747–761.

Fonagy, P., Steele, M., Moran, G., Steele, H., & Higgit, A. (1991). Measuring the ghost in the nursery: A summary of the main findings of the Anna Freud Centre–University College London Parent-Child Study. *Bulletin of the Anna Freud Centre,* 14(pt. 2), 115–132.

Fonagy, P., Steele, H., & Steele, M. (1991). Maternal representations of attachment during pregnancy predict the organization of infant-mother attachment at one year of age. *Child Development,* 62, 891–905.

Fox, N. A. (1977). Attachment of kibbutz infants to mother and metapelet. *Child Development,* 48, 1228–1239.

Fox, N. A., Kimmerly, N. L., & Schafer, W. D. (1991). Attachment to mother/attachment to father: A meta-analysis. *Child Development,* 62, 210–225.

Freud, S. (1940). An outline of psychoanalysis. In J. Strachey (Ed. and Trans.), *The standard edition of the complete psychological works of Sigmund Freud* (Vol. 23). London: Hogarth.

Frye, D., & Moore, C. (Eds.). (1991). *Children's theories of mind: Mental states and social understanding.* Hillsdale, NJ: Erlbaum.

Gable, S., & Isabella, R. A. (1992). Maternal contributions to infant regulation of arousal. *Infant Behavior and Development,* 15, 95–107.

Gao, Y., Posada, G., & Waters, E. (1995). *Cultural expectations and maternal descriptions of children's secure base behavior.* Manuscript submitted for publication.

Garcia-Coll, C. T., Halpern, L. F., Vohr, B. R., Seifer, R., & Oh, W. (1992). Stability and correlates of change of early temperament in preterm and full-term infants. *Infant Behavior and Development,* 15, 137–154.

George, C., Kaplan, N., & Main, M. (1984). *Attachment interview for adults.* Unpublished manuscript, University of California, Berkeley.

George, C., Kaplan, N., & Main, M. (1985). *The Berkeley Adult Attachment Interview.* Unpublished protocol, Department of Psychology, University of California, Berkeley.

Gianino, A., & Tronick, E. Z. (1988). The mutual regulation model: The infant's self and interactive regulation coping and defense. In T. Field, P. McCabe, & N. Schneiderman (Eds.), *Stress and coping.* Hillsdale, NJ: Erlbaum.

Gnepp, J., & Gould, M. E. (1985). The development of personalized inferences: Understanding other people's emotional reactions in light of their prior experiences. *Child Development,* 56, 1455–1464.

Goldberg, S., & DiVitto, B. A. (1983). *Born too soon.* San Francisco: Freeman.

Goldberg, S., Perrotta, M., Minde, K., & Corter, C. (1986). Maternal behavior and attachment in low-birth-weight twins and singletons. *Child Development,* 57, 34–36.

Goldsmith, H. H., & Alansky, J. (1987). Maternal and infant temperamental predictors of attachment: A meta-analytic review. *Journal of Consulting and Clinical Psychology,* 55, 805–816.

Goldsmith, H. H., Buss, A. H., Plomin, R., Rothbart, M. K., Thomas, A., Chess, S., Hinde, R. A., & McCall, R. B. (1987). Roundtable: What is temperament? Four approaches. *Child Development,* **58,** 505–529.

Goldsmith, H. H., & Harman, C. (1994). Temperament and attachment: Individual and relationships. *Current Directions in Psychological Science,* **3,** 53–57.

Goldsmith, H. H., Rieser-Danner, L. A., & Briggs, S. (1991). Evaluating convergent and discriminant validity of temperament questionnaires for preschoolers, toddlers, and infants. *Developmental Psychology,* **27,** 566–579.

Goldsmith, H. H., & Rothbart, M. (1990). *The Laboratory Temperament Assessment Battery* (Version 1.3; Locomotor Version). University of Oregon.

Goossens, F. A., & van IJzendoorn, M. H. (1990). Quality of infants' attachment to professional caregivers: Relations to infant-parent attachment and day-care characteristics. *Child Development,* **61,** 832–837.

Gottlieb, G. (1991). Experiential canalization of behavioral development: Theory. *Developmental Psychology,* **27,** 4–17.

Greenberg, M. T. (1984). *Working paper on the measurement of attachment during the preschool years.* Unpublished manuscript, University of Washington.

Greenberg, M. T., Cicchetti, D., & Cummings, E. M. (Eds.). (1990). *Attachment in the preschool years: Theory, research, and intervention.* Chicago: University of Chicago Press.

Grossmann, K., Fremmer-Bombik, E., Rudolph, J., & Grossmann, K. (1988). Maternal attachment representations as related to patterns of infant-mother attachment and maternal care during the first year. In R. A. Hinde & J. Stevenson-Hinde (Eds.), *Relationships within families: Mutual influences.* Oxford: Clarendon.

Grossmann, K., Grossmann, K. E., Spangler, G., Suess, G., & Unzner, L. (1985). Maternal sensitivity and newborns' orientation responses as related to quality of attachment in northern Germany. In I. Bretherton & E. Waters (Eds.), *Growing points of attachment theory and research. Monographs of the Society for Research in Child Development,* **50**(1–2, Serial No. 209).

Gunnar, M. R., Mangelsdorf, S., Larson, M. L., & Hertsgaard, L. (1989). Attachment, temperament, and adrenocortical activity in infancy: A study of psychoendocrine regulation. *Developmental Psychology,* **25,** 355–363.

Harlow, H. R. (1958). The nature of love. *American Psychologist,* **13,** 673–685.

Hausman, B., & Hammen, C. (1993). Parenting in homeless families: The double crisis. *American Journal of Orthopsychiatry,* **63,** 358–369.

Hazan, C., & Shaver, P. (1987). Romantic love conceptualized as an attachment process. *Journal of Personality and Social Psychology,* **52,** 511–524.

Heyman, R., & Vivian, D. (1994). *Rapid Marital Interaction Coding System* (Version 1.5). Unpublished document. (Available from the authors at Marital Therapy Clinic, Department of Psychology, State University of New York at Stony Brook, Stony Brook, NY 11794)

Hinde, R. A. (1982). Attachment: Some conceptual and biological issues. In C. M. Parkes & J. Stevenson-Hinde (Eds.), *The place of attachment in human behavior.* New York: Basic.

Hinde, R. A. (Ed.). (1983). *Primate social relationships: An integrated approach.* Oxford: Blackwell.

Hinde, R. A. (1987). *Individuals, relationships, and culture.* Cambridge: Cambridge University Press.

Hinde, R. A., & Stevenson-Hinde, J. (Eds.). (1988). *Relationships within families: Mutual influences.* Oxford: Clarendon.

Hobson, R. P. (1991). Against the theory of "theory of mind." *British Journal of Developmental Psychology,* **9,** 33–51.

Hofer, M. A. (1987). Early social relationships: A psychobiologist's view. *Child Development*, **58,** 633–647.

Holt, E. B. (1931). *Animal drive and the learning process* (Vol. 1). New York: Holt.

Howes, C., & Hamilton, C. E. (1992a). Children's relationships with caregivers: Mothers and child care teachers. *Child Development*, **63,** 859–866.

Howes, C., & Hamilton, C. E. (1992b). Children's relationships with child care teachers: Stability and concordance with parental attachments. *Child Development*, **63,** 867–878.

Howes, C., Hamilton, C., & Allhusen, V. (1995). *Using the Attachment Q-Set to describe non-familial attachments: Child-caregiver attachments.* Manuscript submitted for publication.

Howes, C., Phillips, D. A., & Whitebook, M. (1992). Thresholds of quality: Implications for the social development of children in center-based child care. *Child Development*, **63,** 449–460.

Howes, P., & Markman, H. J. (1989). Marital quality and child functioning: A longitudinal investigation. *Child Development*, **60,** 1044–1051.

Hubert, N. C., Wachs, T. D., Peters-Martin, P., & Gandour, M. J. (1982). The study of early temperament: Measurement and conceptual issues. *Child Development*, **53,** 571–600.

Hudson, J. A. (1990). Constructive processes in children's autobiographic memory. *Developmental Psychology*, **26,** 180–187.

Isabella, R. A. (1993). Origins of attachment: Maternal interactive behavior across the first year. *Child Development*, **64,** 605–621.

Isabella, R. A., & Belsky, J. (1985). Marital change during the transition to parenthood and security of infant-parent attachment. *Journal of Family Issues*, **6,** 505–522.

Isabella, R. A., & Belsky, J. (1991). Interactional synchrony and the origins of infant-mother attachment: A replication study. *Child Development*, **62,** 373–384.

Isabella, R. A., Belsky, J., & von Eye, A. (1989). Origins of infant-mother attachment: An examination of interactional synchrony during the infant's first year. *Developmental Psychology*, **25,** 12–21.

Isabella, R. A., & Gable, S. (1991). *Infant behavior and the origins of infant-mother attachment.* Paper presented at the meeting of the Society for Research in Child Development, Seattle.

Jones, O. (1980). Prelinguistic skills in Down's syndrome and normal infants. In T. Field, S. Goldberg, D. Stern, & A. M. Sostek (Eds.), *High risk infants and children: Adult and peer interactions.* New York: Academic.

Kagan, J. (1982). *Psychological research on the human infant: An evaluative summary.* New York: W. T. Grant Foundation.

Kagan, J. (1984). *The nature of the child.* New York: Basic.

Kagan, J. (1994). On the nature of emotion. In N. A. Fox (Ed.), *The development of emotion regulation: Biological and behavioral considerations. Monographs of the Society for Research in Child Development*, **59**(2–3, Serial No. 240).

Kagan, J., Reznick, J. S., & Gibbons, J. (1989). Inhibited and uninhibited types of children. *Child Development*, **60,** 838–845.

Kaplan, N., & Main, M. (1985, April). Internal representations of attachment at six years as indicated by family drawings and verbal responses to imagined separations. In M. Main (Chair), *Attachment: A move to the level of representation.* Symposium conducted at the meeting of Society for Research in Child Development, Toronto.

Kaye, K. (1982). *The mental and social life of babies.* Chicago: University of Chicago Press.

Kenrick, D., Baumann, D., & Cialdini, R. (1979). A step in the socialization of altruism and hedonism: Effects of negative mood on children's generosity under public and private conditions. *Journal of Personality and Social Psychology*, **37,** 747–755.

Klagsburn, M., & Bowlby, J. (1976). Responses to separation from parents: A clinical test for young children. *British Journal of Projective Psychology and Personality Study,* **21,** 7–27.

Kohnstamm, G. (Ed.). (1990). *Handbook of temperament in childhood.* New York: Wiley.

Kraemer, G. W. (1992). A psychobiological theory of attachment. *Behavioral and Brain Sciences,* **15,** 1–28.

Krentz, M. (1983, April). *Qualitative differences between mother-child and caregiver-child attachments of infants in family day care.* Paper presented at the meeting of the Society for Research in Child Development, Detroit.

Lamb, M. E. (1987). Predictive implications of individual differences in attachment. *Journal of Consulting and Clinical Psychology,* **55,** 817–824.

Lamb, M., Thompson, R., Gardner, W., & Charnov, E. (1985). *Infant-mother attachment: The origins and developmental significance of individual differences in Strange Situation behavior.* Hillsdale, NJ: Erlbaum.

Lampe, D. (1983, July). Give me a home where the snow monkeys roam. *Discover,* **9**(7), 36–43.

Lavi, Z. (1990). *Kibbutz members study kibbutz children.* New York: Greenwood.

Lay, K. L., Waters, E., & Park, K. A. (1989). Maternal responsiveness and child compliance: The role of mood as a mediator. *Child Development,* **60,** 1405–1411.

Lazarus, R. (1991). *Emotion and adaptation.* New York: Oxford University Press.

LeBlanc, M., Cote, G., & Loeber, R. (1991). Temporal paths in delinquency: Stability, regression and progression analyzed with panel data from an adolescent and a delinquent male sample. *Canadian Journal of Criminology,* **33,** 23–44.

Legendre, L., & Legendre, P. (1984). *Écologie numérique: La structure des donées écologiques.* Paris: Masson.

Leslie, A. M. (1987). Pretense and representation: The origins of "theory of mind." *Psychological Review,* **94,** 412–426.

Levine, L. V., Tuber, S. B., Slade, H., & Ward, M. J. (1991). Mothers' mental representations and their relationship to mother-infant attachment. *Bulletin of the Menninger Clinic,* **55,** 454–469.

Livesley, W. J., & Bromley, D. B. (1973). *Person perception in childhood and adolescence.* London: Wiley.

Lock, A. J. (1986). The role of relationships in development: An introduction to a series of occasional articles. *Journal of Social and Personal Relationships,* **3,** 86–89.

Loeber, R. (1982). The stability of antisocial and delinquent behavior: A review. *Child Development,* **53,** 1431–1446.

Maccoby, E., & Feldman, S. (1972). Mother attachment and stranger reactions in the third year of life. *Monographs of the Society for Research in Child Development,* **37**(1, Serial No. 146).

Main, M. (1990). Parental aversion to infant-initiated contact is correlated with the parent's own rejection during childhood: The effects of experience on signals of security with respect to attachment. In K. E. Barnard & T. B. Brazelton (Eds.), *Touch: The foundation of experience.* Madison, CT: International Universities Press.

Main, M., & Cassidy, J. (1988). Categories of response to reunion with the parent at age six: Predictable from infant attachment classifications and stable over a one-month period. *Developmental Psychology,* **24,** 415–426.

Main, M., & Goldwyn, R. (1991). *Adult attachment classification system.* Unpublished manuscript, University of California, Berkeley, Department of Psychology.

Main, M., & Goldwyn, R. (1994). *Adult attachment rating and classification systems.* Unpublished manuscript, University of California, Berkeley, Department of Psychology.

Main, M., & Goldwyn, R. (in press-a). Adult attachment classification system. In M. Main

(Ed.), *Behavior and the development of representational models of attachment.* Cambridge: Cambridge University Press.

Main, M., & Goldwyn, R. (in press-b). Interview based adult attachment classifications: Related to infant-mother and infant-father attachment. *Developmental Psychology.*

Main, M., Kaplan, N., & Cassidy, J. (1985). Security in infancy, childhood, and adulthood: A move to the level of representation. In I. Bretherton & E. Waters (Eds.), *Growing points of attachment theory and research. Monographs of the Society for Research in Child Development,* **50**(1–2, Serial No. 209).

Main, M., & Solomon, J. (1986). Discovery of a new, insecure-disorganized/disoriented attachment pattern. In M. Yogman & T. B. Brazelton (Eds.), *Affective development in infancy.* Norwood, NJ: Ablex.

Main, M., & Weston, D. R. (1982). Avoidance of the attachment figure in infancy: Descriptions and interpretations. In C. M. Parkes & J. Stevenson-Hinde (Eds.), *The place of attachment in human behavior.* New York: Basic.

Mangelsdorf, S., Gunnar, M., Kestenbaum, R., Lang, S., & Andreas, D. (1990). Infant proneness-to-distress temperament, maternal personality, and mother-infant attachment: Associations and goodness of fit. *Child Development,* **61,** 820–831.

Masters, J. C., Ford, M., & Arend, R. (1983). Children's strategies for controlling affective responses to aversive social experience. *Motivation and Emotion,* **7,** 103–116.

Matas, L., Arend, R. A., & Sroufe, L. A. (1978). Continuity of adaptation in the second year: The relationship between quality of attachment and later competence. *Child Development,* **49,** 547–556.

McCabe, A., & Peterson, C. (1991). Getting the story: A longitudinal study of parental styles in eliciting narratives and developing narrative skill. In A. McCabe & C. Peterson (Eds.), *Developing narrative structure.* Hillsdale, NJ: Erlbaum.

McKeown, B., & Thomas, D. (1988). *Q-methodology.* Pasadena, CA: Sage.

Meehl, P. (1973). *Psychodiagnosis: Selected papers.* Minneapolis: University of Minnesota Press.

Miller, P. H., & Aloise, P. A. (1989). Young children's understanding of social causes of behavior: A review. *Child Development,* **48,** 257–285.

Minde, K., Corter, C., Goldberg, S., & Jeffers, D. (1990). Maternal preference between premature twins up to age four. *Journal of the American Academy of Child and Adolescent Psychiatry,* **29,** 367–374.

Mineka, S., & Suomi, S. J. (1978). Social separation in monkeys. *Psychological Bulletin,* **85,** 1376–1400.

Miyake, K., Chen, S., & Campos, J. J. (1985). Infant temperament, mother's mode of interaction, and attachment in Japan: An interim report. In I. Bretherton & E. Waters (Eds.), *Growing points of attachment theory and research. Monographs of the Society for Research in Child Development,* **50**(1–2, Serial No. 209).

Moran, G., & Pederson, D. R. (1992, March). *The role of attachment theory in the analysis of early mother-infant interaction: Targeted description and meaningful interpretations.* Paper presented at the Symposium on Childhood and the Family, Quebec.

Moran, G., Pederson, D. R., Pettit, P., & Krupka, A. (1992). Maternal sensitivity and infant-mother attachment in a developmentally delayed sample. *Infant Behavior and Development,* **15,** 427–442.

Nelson, K. (Ed.). (1986). *Event knowledge: Structure and function in development.* Hillsdale, NJ: Erlbaum.

Nelson, K., & Gruendel, J. (1986). Children's scripts. In K. Nelson (Ed.), *Event knowledge: Structure and function in development.* Hillsdale, NJ: Erlbaum.

Nelson, K., & Hudson, J. (1988). Scripts and memory: Functional relationships in development. In F. E. Weinert & M. Perlmutter (Eds.), *Memory development: Universal changes and individual differences.* Hillsdale, NJ: Erlbaum.

Nicewander, W. A., & Price, J. M. (1978). Dependent variable reliability and the power of significance tests. *Psychological Bulletin,* **85,** 405–409.

Norusis, M. J. (1992). *SPSS: Base system user's guide.* Chicago: SPSS.

O'Connor, E., Pan, H., Waters, E., & Posada, G. (1995). *Attachment classification, romantic jealousy, and aggression in couples.* Paper presented at the meeting of the Society for Research in Child Development, Indianapolis.

O'Connor, E., Pan, H., Posada, G., Crowell, J., Waters, E., & Teti, D. (1993, March). *The Adult Attachment Interview and women's reports of marital discord and spouses' conflict behavior.* Paper presented at the meeting of the Society for Research in Child Development, New Orleans.

Oppenheim, D. (1990). *Assessing the validity of a doll-play interview for measuring attachment in preschoolers.* Unpublished doctoral dissertation, University of Utah.

Oppenheim, D., Emde, R. N., Wamboldt, F. S., & Winfrey, N. (1995). *Associations between mother- and father-child co-constructions and children's narratives about affective themes: The role of emotion regulation.* Manuscript submitted for publication.

Oppenheim, D., Sagi, A., & Lamb, M. E. (1988). Infant-adult attachments and their relation to socioemotional development four years later. *Developmental Psychology,* **24,** 427–433.

Owens, G., & Crowell, J. (1993). *Current Relationship Interview scoring system.* Unpublished manuscript, State University of New York at Stony Brook.

Oyama, S. (1989). Ontogeny and the central dogma: Do we need the concept of genetic programming in order to have an evolutionary perspective? In M. R. Gunnar & E. Thelen (Eds.), *Systems and development* (Minnesota Symposia on Child Psychology, Vol. **22**). Hillsdale, NJ: Erlbaum.

Park, K. A., & Waters, E. (1989). Security of attachment and preschool friendships. *Child Development,* **60,** 1076–1081.

Paulhus, D. L. (1984). Two-component models of socially desirable responding. *Journal of Personality and Social Psychology,* **46,** 598–609.

Pederson, D. R., Bento, S., Chance, G. W., Evans, B., & Fox, A. M. (1987). Maternal emotional responses to preterm birth. *American Journal of Orthopsychiatry,* **57,** 15–21.

Pederson, D. R., Moran, G., Sitko, C., Campbell, K., Ghesquire, K., & Acton, H. (1990). Maternal sensitivity and the security of infant-mother attachment: A Q-sort study. *Child Development,* **61,** 1974–1983.

Piaget, J. (1952). *The origins of intelligence in children.* New York: International Universities Press.

Pipp, S., & Harmon, R. J. (1987). Attachment as regulation: A commentary. *Child Development,* **58,** 648–652.

Posada, G., & Waters, E. (1995). *Spousal conflict and aggression: Relations to attachment security.* Manuscript in preparation.

Posada, G., Waters, E., Cassidy, J., & Marvin, R. S. (n.d.). [Q-sort observations of secure-base behavior at home are not strongly related to security classifications based on separation and reunion behavior in the laboratory at age 3 years]. Unpublished raw data, University of Denver.

Potts, R., Morse, M., Felleman, E., & Masters, J. (1986). Children's emotions and memories for affective narrative content. *Motivation and Emotion,* **10,** 39–57.

Premack, D. (1991). The infant's theory of self-propelled objects. In D. Frye & C. Moore (Eds.), *Children's theories of mind.* Hillsdale, NJ: Erlbaum.

Radojevic, M. (1992, July). Predicting quality of infant attachment to father at 15 mo·

from pre-natal paternal representations of attachment: An Australian contribution. In M. H. van IJzendoorn (Chair), *Intergenerational transmission of attachment.* Symposium conducted at the meeting of the International Congress of Psychology, Brussels.

Reese, E., & Fivush, R. (1993). Parental styles of talking about the past. *Developmental Psychology,* **27,** 596–606.

Rholes, W. S., Newman, L. S., & Ruble, D. N. (1990). Understanding self and others: Developmental and motivational aspects of perceiving persons in terms of invariant dispositions. In E. Higgins & R. Sorrentino (Eds.), *Handbook of motivation and cognition: Foundations of social behavior* (Vol. **2**). New York: Guilford.

Richters, J., & Waters, E. (1990). Attachment and socialization: The positive side of social influence. In M. Lewis & S. Feinman (Eds.), *Social influences and socialization in infancy.* New York: Plenum.

Richters, J. E., Waters, E., & Vaughn, B. (1988). An empirical classification system for the Strange Situation. *Child Development,* **59,** 512–522.

Ridgeway, D., & Russell, J. A. (1985). *A nonverbal scale for emotion.* Unpublished manuscript, Colorado State University, Fort Collins.

Ridgeway, D., & Waters, E. (1987). Behavioral and physiological correlates of mood induction procedures with children. *Journal of Personality and Social Psychology,* **52,** 620–625.

Rosen, K. S., & Rothbaum, F. (1993). Quality of parental caregiving and security of attachment. *Developmental Psychology,* **29,** 358–367.

Rosenblum, L., & Pauley, G. (1984). The effects of varying environmental demands on maternal and infant behavior. *Child Development,* **55,** 305–315.

Rothbart, M. K. (1981). Measurement of temperament in infancy. *Child Development,* **52,** 569–587.

Rothbart, M. K., & Derryberry, D. (1982). Theoretical issues in temperament. In M. Lewis & L. T. Taft (Eds.), *Developmental disabilities: Theory, assessment, and intervention.* New York: Spectrum.

Rushton, J. P., Brainerd, C. J., & Pressley, M. (1983). Behavioral development and construct validity: The principle of aggregation. *Psychological Bulletin,* **94,** 18–38.

Sadeh, A., & Anders, T. F. (1993). Infant sleep problems: Origins, assessment, interventions. *Infant Mental Health Journal,* **14,** 17–34.

Sagi, A., Aviezer, O., Joels, T., Koren-Karie, N., Mayseless, O., & Sharf, M. (1993, March). The correspondence of mother's adult attachment representation with infant-mother attachment relationship in stable and unstable contexts. In K. E. Grossmann (Chair), *Attachment development: The meaning of attachment representation in longitudinal, ecological and cross-cultural perspective.* Symposium conducted at the meeting of the Society for Research in Child Development, New Orleans.

Sagi, A., Aviezer, O., Joels, T., Koren-Karie, N., Mayseless, O., Sharf, M., & van IJzendoorn, M. H. (1992, July). Infant-mother attachment relationship in traditional and non-traditional kibbutzim. In M. H. van IJzendoorn (Chair), *Intergenerational transmission of attachment.* Symposium conducted at the meeting of the International Congress of Psychology, Brussels.

Sagi, A., & Koren-Karie, N. (1993). Day-care centers in Israel: An overview. In M. Cochran (Ed.), *International handbook of day-care policies and programs.* New York: Greenwood.

Sagi, A., Lamb, M. E., Lewkowicz, K. S., Shoham, R., Dvir, R., & Estes, D. (1985). Security of infant-mother, -father, and -metapelet attachments among kibbutz-reared Israeli children. In I. Bretherton & E. Waters (Eds.), *Growing points of attachment theory and research. Monographs of the Society for Research in Child Development,* **50**(1–2, Serial No. 209).

Sagi, A., van IJzendoorn, M. H., Aviezer, O., Donnell, F., & Mayseless O. (1994). Sleeping away from home in a kibbutz communal arrangement: It makes a difference for infant-mother attachment. *Child Development, 65,* 988–1000.

Sameroff, A. J. (1983). Developmental systems: Contexts and evolution. In W. Kessen (Ed.), P. H. Mussen (Series Ed.), *Handbook of child psychology: Vol. 4. History, theory, and methods.* New York: Wiley.

Sameroff, A. J., & Emde, R. N. (1989). *Relationship disturbances in early childhood: A developmental approach.* New York: Basic.

Schneider-Rosen, K. (1990). The developmental reorganization of attachment relationships: Guidelines for classification beyond infancy. In M. T. Greenberg, D. Cicchetti, & E. M. Cummings (Eds.), *Attachment in the preschool years: Theory, research, and intervention.* Chicago: University of Chicago Press.

Seifer, R., Sameroff, A. J., Anagnostopolou, R., & Elias, P. K. (1992). Mother-infant interaction during the first year: Effects of situation, maternal mental illness and demographic factors. *Infant Behavior and Development, 15,* 415–426.

Seifer, R., Sameroff, A. J., Barrett, L. C., & Krafchuk, E. (1994). Infant temperament measured by multiple observations and mother report. *Child Development, 65,* 1478–1490.

Seifer, R., Schiller, M., Sameroff, A. J., Resnick, S., & Riordan, K. (in press). Attachment, maternal sensitivity, and temperament during the first year of life. *Developmental Psychology.*

Seifer, R., & Vaughn, B. (in press). Relationships among mastery motivation and attachment within a general theory of competence. In R. H. MacTurk, E. J. Hrncir, & G. A. Morgan (Eds.), *Mastery motivation: Conceptual origins and applications.* Norwood, NJ: Ablex.

Shaver, P., & Hazan, C. (1994). Attachment. In A. Weber & J. Harvey (Eds.), *Perspectives on close relationships.* Boston: Allyn & Bacon.

Shouldice, A., & Stevenson-Hinde, J. (1992). Coping with security distress: The separation anxiety test and attachment classification at 4.5 years. *Journal of Child Psychology and Psychiatry, 33,* 331–348.

Simpson, J., & Harris, B. (1994). Interpersonal attraction. In A. Weber & J. Harvey (Eds.), *Perspectives on close relationships.* Boston: Allyn & Bacon.

Skinner, E. A. (1991). Development and perceived control: A dynamic model of action in context. In M. R. Gunnar & L. A. Sroufe (Eds.), *Self processes and development* (Minnesota Symposia on Child Psychology, Vol. 23). Hillsdale, NJ: Erlbaum.

Slough, N. M., & Greenberg, M. T. (1990). Five-year-olds' representations of separation from parents: Responses from the perspective of self and other. In I. Bretherton & M. W. Watson (Eds.), *Children's perspectives on the family* (New Directions for Child Development, Vol. 48). San Francisco: Jossey-Bass.

Smith, P. B., & Pederson, D. R. (1988). Maternal sensitivity and patterns of infant-mother attachment. *Child Development, 59,* 1097–1101.

Sneath, P. H. A., & Sokal, R. R. (1973). *Numerical taxonomy.* San Francisco: Freeman.

Spanier, G. (1976). Measuring dyadic adjustment: New scales for assessing the quality of marriage and similar dyads. *Journal of Marriage and the Family, 38,* 15–28.

Sroufe, L. A. (1977). Wariness of strangers and the study of infant development. *Child Development, 48,* 731–746.

Sroufe, L. A. (1983). Infant-caregiver attachment and patterns of adaptation in preschool: The roots of maladaptation and competence. In M. Perlmutter (Ed.), *Development and policy concerning children with special needs* (Minnesota Symposia on Child Psychology, Vol. 16). Hillsdale, NJ: Erlbaum.

Sroufe, L. A. (1985). Attachment classification from the perspective of infant-caregiver relationships and infant temperament. *Child Development, 56,* 1–14.

Sroufe, L. A., & Fleeson, J. (1986). Attachment and the construction of relationships. In W. Hartup & Z. Rubin (Eds.), *Relationships and development*. Hillsdale, NJ: Erlbaum.

Sroufe, L. A., & Fleeson, J. (1988). The coherence of relationships. In R. A. Hinde & J. Stevenson-Hinde (Eds.), *Relationships within families: Mutual influences*. Oxford: Clarendon.

Sroufe, L. A., & Waters, E. (1977). Attachment as an organizational construct. *Child Development*, **48**, 1184–1199.

Stephenson, W. (1953). *The study of behavior: Q-technique and its methodology*. Chicago: University of Chicago Press.

Stern, D. (1985). *The interpersonal world of the infant*. New York: Basic.

Stevenson-Hinde, J. (1983). Individual characteristics: A statement of the problem. In R. A. Hinde (Ed.), *Primate social relationships: An integrated approach*. Oxford: Blackwell.

Stevenson-Hinde, J. (1985). *Q-sort attachment data and temperament*. Paper presented at the meeting of the Society for Research in Child Development, Toronto.

Stevenson-Hinde, J., & Simpson, M. J. A. (1981). Mother's characteristics, interactions, and infants' characteristics. *Child Development*, **52**, 1246–1254.

Strayer, F. F. (1989). Co-adaptation within the peer group: A psychobiological study of early competence. In B. Schneider, G. Atilia, J. Nadel, & R. Weisman (Eds.), *Social competence in developmental perspective*. Dordrecht: Kluwer Academic.

Szajnberg, N. M., Skrinjaric, J., & Moore, A. (1989). Affect attunement, attachment, temperament, and zygosity: A twin study. *Journal of the American Academy of Child and Adolescent Psychiatry*, **28**, 249–253.

Takahashi, K. (1990). Are the key assumptions of the "Strange Situation" procedure universal? A view from Japanese research. *Human Development*, **33**, 23–30.

Terwogt, M., Schene, J., & Harris, P. (1985). Self-control of emotional reaction in young children. *Journal of Child Psychology and Psychiatry*, **27**, 357–366.

Teti, D. M., & Ablard, K. E. (1989). Security of attachment and infant-sibling relationships: A laboratory study. *Child Development*, **60**, 1519–1528.

Teti, D. M., & McGourty, S. (1994, June). *Using mothers vs. observers in AQS assessments: Theoretical and practical issues*. Paper presented at the International Conference on Infant Studies, Paris.

Teti, D. M., & McGourty, S. (in press). Characteristics of Q-sort descriptions by mothers and observers. *Child Development*.

Thelen, E., & Ulrich, B. D. (1991). Hidden skills: A dynamic systems analysis of treadmill stepping during the first year. *Monographs of the Society for Research in Child Development*, **56**(1, Serial No. 223).

Thomas, A., Chess, S., Birch, H. G., Hertzig, M. E., & Korn, S. (1963). *Behavioral individuality in early childhood*. New York: New York University Press.

Thompson, R. A. (1994). Emotion regulation: A theme in search of definition. In N. A. Fox (Ed.), *The development of emotion regulation: Biological and behavioral considerations. Monographs of the Society for Research in Child Development*, **59**(2–3, Serial No. 240).

Thompson, R. A., Connell, J. P., & Bridges, L. J. (1988). Temperament, emotion, and social interactive behavior in the Strange Situation: A component process analysis of attachment system functioning. *Child Development*, **59**, 1102–1110.

Tiger, L., & Shepher, J. (1975). *Women in the kibbutz*. New York: Harcourt Brace Jovanovich.

Tracy, R. L., & Ainsworth, M. D. S. (1981). Maternal affectionate behavior and infant-mother attachment patterns. *Child Development*, **52**, 1341–1343.

Tronick, E. Z. (1989). Emotions and emotional communication in infants. *American Psychologist*, **44**, 112–119.

Underwood, B., Froming, W., & Moore, B. (1977). Mood, attention, and altruism: A search for mediating variables. *Developmental Psychology,* **13,** 541–542.

Valenzuela, M., & Lara, V. (1987). Nutrition and attachment in an impoverished Chilean population: The use of the Attachment Q-Set in support of Strange Situation assessments. In B. E. Vaughn (Chair), *The Q-sort method in attachment research.* Symposium conducted at the meeting of the Society for Research in Child Development, Baltimore.

van Dam, M., & van IJzendoorn, M. H. (1988). Measuring attachment security: Concurrent and predictive validity of the parental attachment Q-set. *Journal of Genetic Psychology,* **149,** 447–457.

Vandell, D. L., Owen, M. T., Wilson, K. S., & Henderson, V. K. (1988). Social development in infant twins: Peer and mother-child relationships. *Child Development,* **59,** 168–177.

van IJzendoorn, M. H. (1992). Intergenerational transmission of parenting: A review of studies in nonclinical populations. *Developmental Review,* **12,** 76–99.

van IJzendoorn, M. H. (1995). Associations between adult attachment representations and parent-child attachment, parental responsiveness, and clinical status: A meta-analysis on the predictive validity of the Adult Attachment Interview. *Psychological Bulletin,* **117,** 387–403.

van IJzendoorn, M. H., & Bakermans-Kranenburg, M. J. (in press). Attachment representations in mothers, fathers, adolescents, and clinical groups: A meta-analytic search for normative data. *Journal of Consulting and Clinical Psychology.*

van IJzendoorn, M. H., Goldberg, S., Kroonenberg, P. M., & Frenkel, O. J. (1992). The relative effects of maternal and child problems on the quality of attachment: A meta-analysis of attachment in clinical samples. *Child Development,* **63,** 840–858.

van Ijzendoorn, M. H., Kranenburg, M. J., Zwart-Woudstra, H. A., van Busschbach, A. M., & Lambermon, M. W. (1991). Parental attachment and children's socio-emotional development: Some findings on the validity of the Adult Attachment Interview in the Netherlands. *International Journal of Behavioral Development,* **14,** 375–394.

van IJzendoorn, M. H., & Kroonenberg, P. M. (1988). Cross-cultural patterns of attachment: A meta-analysis of the Strange Situation. *Child Development,* **59,** 147–156.

van IJzendoorn, M. H., Sagi, A., & Lambermon, M. W. (1992). The multiple caretaker paradox: Some data from Holland and Israel. In R. C. Pianta (Ed.), *Beyond the parent: The role of other adults in children's lives* (New Directions for Child Development, Vol. 57). San Francisco: Jossey-Bass.

Vaughn, B. E., Egeland, B., Sroufe, A., & Waters, E. (1979). Individual differences in infant-mother attachment at twelve and eighteen months: Stability and change in families under stress. *Child Development,* **50,** 971–975.

Vaughn, B. E., Lefever, G. B., Seifer, R., & Barglow, P. (1989). Attachment behavior, attachment security, and temperament during infancy. *Child Development,* **60,** 728–737.

Vaughn, B. E., Stevenson-Hinde, J., Waters, E., Kotsaftis, A., Lefever, G. B., Shouldice, A., Trudel, M., & Belsky, J. (1992). Attachment security and temperament in infancy and early childhood: Some conceptual clarifications. *Developmental Psychology,* **28,** 463–473.

Vaughn, B. E., Strayer, F. F., Jacques, M., Trudel, M., & Seifer, R. (1991). Maternal descriptions of two- and three-year-old children: A comparison of attachment Q-sorts in two socio-cultural communities. *International Journal of Behavioural Development,* **14,** 279–291.

Vaughn, B. E., & Waters, E. (1990). Attachment behavior at home and in the laboratory:

Q-sort observations and Strange Situation classifications of one-year-olds. *Child Development,* **61,** 1865–1973.

Waddington, C. H. (1942). Canalization of development and the inheritance of acquired characters. *Nature,* **150,** 563–564.

Wallon, H. (1934). *Les origines du caractère chez l'enfant.* Paris: Boivin.

Ward, M. J., Vaughn, B. E., & Robb, M. D. (1988). Socio-emotional adaptation and infant-mother attachment in siblings: Role of the mother in cross-sibling consistency. *Child Development,* **59,** 643–651.

Waters, E. (1978). The reliability and stability of individual differences in infant-mother attachment. *Child Development,* **49,** 483–494.

Waters, E. (1987). *Attachment Behavior Q-Set* (Revision 3.0). Unpublished instrument, State University of New York at Stony Brook, Department of Psychology.

Waters, E., & Deane, K. E. (1982). Infant-mother attachment: Theories, models, recent data, and some tasks for comparative developmental analysis. In L. Hoffman, R. Gandelman, & H. Schiffman (Eds.), *Parenting: Its causes and consequences.* Hillsdale, NJ: Erlbaum.

Waters, E., & Deane, K. E. (1985). Defining and assessing individual differences in attachment relationships: Q-methodology and the organization of behavior in infancy and early childhood. In I. Bretherton & E. Waters (Eds.), *Growing points of attachment theory and research. Monographs of the Society for Research in Child Development,* **50**(1–2, Serial No. 209).

Waters, E., Garber, J., Gornal, M., & Vaughn, B. (1983). Q-sort correlates of visual regard among preschool peers: Validation of a behavioral index of social competence. *Developmental Psychology,* **19,** 550–560.

Waters, E., Hay, D. F., & Richters, J. (1985). Infant-parent attachment and the origins of prosocial and antisocial behavior. In D. Olweus, J. Block, & M. Radke-Yarrow (Eds.), *The origins of prosocial and antisocial behavior.* New York: Academic.

Waters, E., Johnson, S., & Kondo-Ikemura, K. (1995). *Do preschool children love their peers?* Manuscript submitted for publication.

Waters, E., Kondo-Ikemura, K., Posada, G., & Richters, J. E. (1990). Learning to love: Mechanisms and milestones. In M. R. Gunnar & L. A. Sroufe (Eds.), *Self processes and development* (Minnesota Symposia on Child Psychology, Vol. **23**). Hillsdale, NJ: Erlbaum.

Waters, E., Merrick, S. K., Albersheim, L. J., & Treboux, D. (1995, March). Attachment security from infancy to early adulthood: A 20-year longitudinal study. In J. A. Crowell & E. Waters (Chairs), *Is the parent-child relationship a prototype of later love relationships? Studies of attachment and working models of attachment.* Symposium presented at the meeting of the Society for Research in Child Development, Indianapolis.

Waters, E., Noyes, D. M., Vaughn, B. E., & Ricks, M. (1985). Q-sort definition of social competence and self-esteem: Discriminant validity of related constructs in theory and data. *Developmental Psychology,* **21,** 508–552.

Waters, E., Posada, G., & Vaughn, B. E. (1994). *The Attachment Q-Set: Hyper-text advisor.* Unpublished computer software, State University of New York at Stony Brook, Department of Psychology.

Waters, H. S., & Hou, F. (1987). Children's production and recall of narrative passages. *Journal of Experimental Child Psychology,* **44,** 348–363.

Waters, H. S., Hou, F., & Lee, Y. (1993). Organization and elaboration in children's repeated production of prose. *Journal of Experimental Child Psychology,* **55,** 31–55.

Weiss, R. L., & Heyman, R. (1990). Observation of marital interaction. In F. Fincham & T. Bradbury (Eds.), *The psychology of marriage.* New York: Plenum.

Wellman, H. M. (1990). *The child's theory of mind.* Cambridge, MA: MIT Press.

Werner, H., & Smith, R. S. (1982). *Vulnerable but invincible: A longitudinal study of resilient children and youth.* New York: McGraw-Hill.

Werner, H., & Kaplan, B. (1963). *Symbol formation: An organismic-developmental approach to language and the expression of thought.* New York: Wiley.

Whiteman, M. (1967). Children's conceptions of psychological causality. *Child Development,* **38,** 143–156.

Yuill, N. (in press). Children's conception of personality traits: A critical review and analysis. *Human Development.*

Zeanah, C. H., Benoit, D., Barton, M., Regan, C., Hirshberg, L. M., & Lipsitt, L. (1993). Representations of attachment in mothers and their one year old infants. *Journal of the American Academy of Child and Adolescent Psychiatry,* **32,** 278–286.

EXPANDING THE STUDY OF THE FORMATION OF
THE CHILD'S RELATIONSHIPS

Christoph M. Heinicke

As a set, the reports included in this *Monograph* seek to expand the conceptualization and study of attachment. The editors and authors have indeed done an excellent job of presenting the "new growing points" within this field. My comments will focus on three of the issues that they raise: (1) How do we continue the study and conceptualization of secure-base behavior? (2) How do we take into account the multiple-relationship context of attachment? (3) How do we expand our conceptualization of attachment to include variations in individual adaptations and the development of relationships?

Two statements that John Bowlby made during our many exciting conversations serve as an introduction to these comments. When I expressed discomfort with the reduction of attachment to five behavioral responses, he answered that the scientific study of essential phenomena requires some simplification; later conceptualization and further research involve revision and a better fit. He also often joked with me: "Jimmy Robertson, you, Miss Freud, and I can pretty much agree on how children respond to being separated from their mothers. It is when we come to interpret these responses that we get into difficulty."

Theorizing about Secure-Base Behavior

How then do we observe and theorize about secure-base behavior? Is the focus to be on species-specific behavioral responses or on an organization of behavior involving individual differences in internal representations and defensive adaptations? I begin by making a few historical comments to show how the various reports in this *Monograph* reflect the continuing development of thought about this issue.

Although considerable consensus concerning the behavior that is seen when children are separated from their parents prevailed in the 1950s (Freud & Burlingham, 1944; Heinicke, 1956; Robertson & Bowlby, 1952), the theoretical interpretation of the nature of these responses differed greatly. Impressed by the profound reaction that follows the breaking of the mother-child tie, Bowlby (1958) reasoned that its intensity could not be explained by a process whereby the child forms such attachment solely through being gratified by a primary caretaker.

Turning to ethology, he postulated instead that the attachment of the 12-month-old infant is made up of a number of component instincts that bind him or her to the mother: "To have a deep attachment for a person is to have taken them as the terminating object of our instinctual responses" (Bowlby, 1959, p. 13). The profound responses to separation were seen as "built into the organism" and adaptive from an evolutionary point of view; concepts such as internal working models and defense against affect were not included in this formulation at that time.

With Bowlby's active encouragement, and with the help of Gill (Rapaport & Gill, 1959), I attempted my own integration of the behavioral observations, global ratings, and experiential processes set off by the trauma of separating parents from their 2-year-old child (Heinicke & Westheimer, 1965). Following Freud (1926/1959), in our interpretation of the results of the study that we undertook, separation anxiety was understood in the context of the "intensification of need." It was hypothesized that anxiety is aroused when parents are no longer there to satisfy either immediate or anticipated needs. Children whose relationship history was associated with the expectation of being cared for would tolerate more "tension due to need," but all 2-year-olds would typically show some anxiety.

The next question became, What are those needs and "tensions due to need?" The need to be physically cared for and to experience a satisfying feeding experience was stressed, but equally important was the child's need to be loved, particularly so in relation to an emerging sense of self (Heinicke & Westheimer, 1965, p. 328). As a function of the separation, the main source of approval was removed; indeed, we observed that, although resisting any intimate contact in the first 3 days, the children in our study soon desperately sought approval from the nursery staff.

As the separation continued and the longing and associated anger increased, defensive adaptations came into play both to maintain the previous relationship and to prevent these intense feelings from overwhelming contact with, and approval from, the visiting parents. The children's longing and anger could be seen in the way they devoured the candy that the parent brought them while suppressing any direct expression of feelings toward that parent.

In her article on the origins of attachment theory, Bretherton (1992) has indicated how Bowlby revised his original conception of attachment to include mental representations. The reports in this *Monograph* both reflect that growth in theory and continue to struggle with it.

In approaching the question of the universality of secure-base behavior, Posada, Gao, et al. suggest that the hypothesis that it reflects a species-specific behavior could be tested by whether appears in a variety of cultures. While mothers using the Attachment Q-Set did indeed report a predominance of secure-base behavior in seven different cultures, this generality can be interpreted in different ways. One can stress (1) that the generality is driven by a species-specific response; (2) that, as the authors suggest, "what has been selected for in the course of human evolution can be better understood in terms of a propensity to organize an attachment behavioral system within the context of child-caregiver interactions" (p. 28), and (3) that the proved universality of some form of family caretaking system is associated with both the generality of secure-base behavior and the extensive individual differences in the development of that behavior.

As already indicated, the authors' findings support the generality of secure-base behavior in that infants in all cultures were characterized as behaving more like (than unlike) the hypothetical American child whose Q-sort profile indexes optimal secure-base behavior. However, despite this evidence of cross-cultural consistency, the absolute levels of similarity both within and across cultures were in fact rather low. That is, extensive individual variation in the organization of attachment behavior was the rule. Although the authors show that the mother's observations were not simply a function of their ideal conceptualization of secure-base behavior, issues of universality, cultural differences, and the extent of individual variations would have been greatly illuminated by Q-sorts based on observations in the naturalistic setting made by research observers. The nature of the sources of the generality of secure-base behavior thus remains an ongoing question.

Attachment in the Context of Relationships

Expansion of the conceptualization and study of the relationship context in which attachment develops has also occurred in the last decades and is furthered by the reports in this *Monograph*. Bretherton (1992) has documented the significant addition that inclusion of a focus on the caretaker's responsiveness made to the study of attachment. In their classic observational study, Bell and Ainsworth (1972) reported that maternal sensitivity in the first quarter of the first year was associated with a more harmonious mother-child relationship and less crying in the fourth quarter. Ainsworth, Blehar, Waters, and Wall (1978) interpreted these findings as indicating the development of the infant's expectation of being cared for, based on the child's prior satisfying versus rejecting experiences with the mother. I will return to the concept of the child's expectation of care later; what is important to stress here is the historic placement of attachment responses within an expanding conceptualization and study of relationships. Mary Ainsworth and I have enjoyed over the years being part of an exciting adventure; just as she encouraged a generation of brilliant students, so she also gave continuing support to her colleagues. I regard her emphasis on maternal sensitivity that emerged from her naturalistic mother-infant observations as among her greatest contributions (see also Bretherton, 1992).

Several reports in this *Monograph* present innovative ways of continuing the study of the transactions between caretaker and infant attachment. Thus, Sagi et al. (in this volume) stress the formative input of nonparental relationships by showing that two infants cared for by the same metapelet tend to have the same attachment experience and develop similar bonds to that caretaker. Interestingly, this prevailed only among infants who returned to their families at night and who also had the same metapelet beyond the first year. The authors suggest that the children's nighttime experience in the communal sleeping condition may be important in accounting for this difference. I would add that the more extensive family and caretaker relationship experiences of one group could lead the child to a more developed capacity for relationships and, in turn, lead to a more sensitive and consistent response to what the metapelet brought to the interaction. In any case, what this research highlights is that relationship experiences and the development of attachment in one setting are likely to influence these developments in other relationship settings.

The transactional, mother-infant context of the study of attachment is further highlighted by the study of the maternal behavior and infant security in Old World monkeys (Kondo-Ikemura & Waters). This study is first of all an example of the method that is stressed throughout the *Monograph*, namely, the collection of observations of longer duration, made in a naturalistic setting, and organized by the Q-sort methodology. A further generic point in the study of attachment is stressed by this study, namely, the importance of the mother's ongoing active supervision and sensitivity in *maintaining* infant secure-base behavior. In our own path-analysis model of the parent's responsiveness to the child's need interacting with the security of the child as observed in the home, we found that this transaction was maintained throughout the first 4 years of life and was in turn associated with the maintenance of a positive relationship between the parents (husband-wife) during that time (Heinicke & Guthrie, 1992; Heinicke & Lampl, 1988).

This ongoing association of maternal sensitivity and Q-sort assessment of infant security is further substantiated by Pederson and Moran. Both the stability and the transactional nature of the mother-infant relationship is stressed by their findings. As powerful as the Strange Situation has proved to be in distinguishing attachment patterns (Ainsworth et al., 1978), it focuses on the child's responses, especially to reunion, and it does not include either categorization of maternal behavior or the larger context of the transaction as it occurs in various settings. Expansion of methods to include such factors is clearly needed for the "new growing points" of the study of attachment.

Individual Variation in Adaptation

Several of the reports also focus on conceptualizing the nature of the child's attachment in ways that complement and expand the well-known trilogy of avoidant, anxious, and secure. Using both a Chicago and a Montréal sample of children between 24 and 36 months of age, Strayer, Verissimo, Vaughn, and Howes describe the analytic steps involved in moving from the 100 Waters AQS items to assigning these to seven descriptive domains that, in turn, are then grouped (reduced) to three clusters. In addition to the traditional correlations of Q-sort profiles with criterion profiles that yield indexes of security and dependency, the authors provide us with additional reliable scales of Proximity/Exploration Balance, Differential Responsiveness to Caregiver, Positive Affect, Sociability, Independence, Social Perceptiveness, and Endurance. This empirical derivation of these scales provides a most valuable additional analytic tool for the use of the AQS. Comparison of diverse cultural samples—such as is made in this study—becomes possible, and the use of individual dimensions of the primary social relationship opens up possibilities for a variety of analyses. For example, for theoretical reasons we would expect that the antecedents and correlates of proximity/exploration, independence, and endurance (task persistence) are likely to be different.

Similarly, Lay, Waters, and Posada expand our concept of attachment and its regulation by empirically demonstrating the activation of defensive processes in relation to mood induction stimuli. Thus, secure—as opposed to insecure—children reacted with less defensiveness to negative vignettes involving the mother. In insecure children, who have developed experientially based expectations of maternal unresponsiveness or rejection, mother-agent negative vignettes engender stronger negative affect, and so cognitive (defensive) mechanisms prevent the attachment response system from becoming activated. The key concept derived from this and other research is that, when the child does not expect positive care, the maternal stimulus activates the negative affects of anxiety, anger, and intense longing. These affects, which are potentially overwhelming, may lead to anxious expression or may be suppressed and regulated by distancing from the stimulus. As Lay et al. point out, this conception of defense is similar to Lazarus's (1991) concept of "short-circuit" as part of emotion regulation.

The role of defense in the organization of the child's relationship development is indeed further informed by current research focusing on emotion regulation as a means "of maintaining the relationship with the attachment figure" (Cassidy, 1994, p. 230). The nature of the child's emotion expression (regulation) is linked to the parent's sensitivity to the child's needs. If the infant believes that her emotion signals will be responded to sensitively, she is most likely to signal her wishes directly and freely and to share her emotions (positive and negative) with the parent (Cassidy, 1994). By contrast, the insecure/avoidant child copes with a history of caretaker rejection by minimizing emotion expression. For the infant overtly to express her anger about the rejection is dangerous because she risks further alienating the attachment figure; moreover, if she increases her demands, she also risks further rejection. The extreme distress and difficulty of being calmed on reunion seen in the ambivalent/insecure child is also understood as a way of maintaining the relationship: for the infant to relax and allow herself to be soothed is to run the risk of losing contact with the inconsistently available parent (Cassidy, 1994).

This functional view of emotion regulation—namely, that it is adaptive in maintaining the relationship to the caretaker—is well documented. As a complementary elaboration, concepts of defense and anxiety can be used to focus on the child's efforts to reach a greater equilibrium by either suppressing or expressing her intense emotions; thus, they represent ways of gaining emotional control without necessarily being motivated by the need to maintain the relationship to the caretaker.

Related to the above, Seifer and Schiller comment on the function of defense by ruling that, when the sensitivity of caregiving is consistently at high levels, infants both use and come to perceive the attachment figure as a source of affection, a safe haven from danger, and a partner capable of repairing and regulating negative states of affect/arousal. As a result, when their attachment system is activated, infants with a history of sensitive interactions will exhibit attachment behaviors that are expressed in a clear and unambiguous way, without evidence of either over- or underactivated defensive strategies.

My discussion has been confined to those *Monograph* reports and the related literature relevant to three aspects of the study of attachment that continue to be "new" growing points. How, first of all, do we define *secure-base behavior* and distinguish it from felt security? Do we focus on demonstrating the universality of secure-base behavior or study the antecedents and correlates of felt security? I found the following formulation particularly helpful in this regard.

As with inner states of people in general and nonverbal infants in particular, we have very limited direct access to assessing the specific emotions that would constitute an infant's inner feeling of security with a caregiver in a given context. All we can examine directly is the organization of the infant's secure-base behavior (specifically with respect to proximity and exploration), obvious signs of affect and arousal exhibited at the behavioral level, and any behavioral manifestations of anxiety surrounding these social interactions. From this complex of behavioral observations, we attempt to infer the infant's underlying state of mind with respect to attachment. Our working hypothesis about the infant's state of mind or felt security then becomes the central feature of the assessment of individual differences in attachment quality (Seifer and Schiller).

I have also commented—both elsewhere as well as in discussing individual reports in this *Monograph*—on the need to place the development of attachment in a multiple-relationship context. The importance of the *configuration* of relationship influences as well as the *continuity* of those relationship influences is documented by the work reported here. Finally, I have noted the continuing need for the reconceptualization of the organization of the attachment responses that is evidenced in this *Monograph;* for example, felt security, affect arousal, and defense are all studied and used as constructs in these innovative reports.

In sum, this *Monograph* and the related research on emotion regulation suggest to me further expansion in a number of areas. First, in a rapidly changing primary caretaker environment, what profile of transactions with what caretakers comes to be associated with the experience of security? For example, what type of relationship to her family, partner, and community resources, combined with a positive alternate care opportunity for her child, promotes the mother's sensitivity to her child?

While this emphasis on relationship is crucial, the reports in this *Monograph* as well as other emerging research suggest that the study of attachment needs to involve conceptualization and research on adaptive and regulatory mechanisms. As in the studies reported here, such conceptualization can focus on regulation in the service of maintaining the relationship. Thus, Crittenden and Claussen (1994) state that, "with preoperational maturation, the defended Type A (avoidant) strategy, including the *inhibited, compulsive caregiving*, and *compulsive compliant* subgroups, becomes a regulatory strategy of seeking sufficient proximity to attachment figures for protection, yet sufficient distance to avoid intrusion, rejection, and punishment" (p. 2). Complementing the above, our own research on child and caregiver responses to separation from 6 months to 4 years asks what adaptive mechanisms—such as defensive suppression or expression of affect—help restore the child's own functioning and prevent debilitating levels of anxious or depressed states (Heinicke, Recchia, Berlin, & James, 1993). This emphasis on infant adaptive capacities provides a link to the assessment of other stable infant characteristics such as soothability, activity level, and cognitive abilities.

From the above, I conclude further that the study of attachment needs to be expanded not only to include multiple relationships but also by incorporating conceptions and assessments of the child's and caretaker's mode of individual adaptation (i.e., regulating mechanisms, defenses, etc.). Adaptations may focus on maintaining the relationship and/or on maintaining the sense of personal equilibrium. This expansion is of interest not only because it provides a more differentiated picture of the networks of factors that influence relationship development but also because such a network of variables must be included if we hope to assess the effect of a relationship-focused early intervention.

Turning to potential intervention, this *Monograph* has emphasized again the key role of caretaker sensitivity in affecting the development of a secure attachment in the child. If we consider this transaction as an outcome variable—meaning that we wish to influence its development—what network of variables must be addressed? Here, a considerable body of research can be summarized as follows: the mother's prebirth and ongoing adaptive competence and capacity to sustain positive relationships (especially those with her partner) anticipate her responsiveness to the needs of her infant and the development of security in her child in the period from 1 month to 4 years of age (Heinicke, in press).

This suggests that early family intervention efforts, such as home visiting, need to focus not only on the child and parent-child behavior but also on the individual functioning of the caretakers and the context of their experienced support. The intervenor (home visitor) becomes part of that ongoing comprehensive support and working effort (Olds & Kitzman, 1993). Review of controlled follow-up intervention studies that have assessed and attempted to intervene in different family domains suggests the following hypotheses: (1) Pervasive and sustained gains in parent-child and child social-emotional development are corollaries of changes in the multirisk mother's adaptation-competence and partnership quality. (2) Efforts to change this network of functioning are most likely to be successful if the mother (and partner) can develop a sustained and working relationship with the intervenor (Heinicke, 1991).

To reflect accurately intervention effects (which experience suggests are not likely to be overwhelming), multiple and repeated assessments of individual adaptation (parent's, child's) and relationship variables are necessary. For example, the new mode of dimensional analysis of the Attachment Q-Set (Strayer et al.), defining Proximity/Exploration Balance, Differential Responsiveness to Caregiver, Positive Affect, etc., is very likely to reflect intervention effects that could not be detected by summed criterion scores of security and dependency.

Thus, further conceptualization and new assessments develop in parallel and are necessary for a successful strategy of research on what aspects of the family system are subject to change and how to bring about that change. I believe that we can indeed define the intervention conditions that will lead to change in attachment (Lieberman, Weston, & Pawl, 1991). The results of such intervention research will in turn stimulate yet new growing points in attachment theory and research.

References

Ainsworth, M. D. S., Blehar, M. S., Waters, E., & Wall, S. (1978). *Patterns of attachment: A psychological study of the strange situation.* Hillsdale, NJ: Erlbaum.

Bell, S. M., & Ainsworth, M. D. S. (1972). Infant crying and maternal responsiveness. *Child Development, 43,* 1171–1190.

Bowlby, J. (1958). The nature of the child's tie to his mother. *International Journal of Psycho-Analysis, 39,* 1–23.

Bowlby, J. (1959). Separation anxiety. *International Journal of Psycho-Analysis, 41,* 1–25

Bretherton, I. (1992). The origins of attachment theory: John Bowlby and Mary Ainsworth. *Developmental Psychology, 28,* 759–775.

Cassidy, J. (1994). Emotion regulation: Influences of attachment relationships. In N. Fox (Ed.), *The development of emotion regulation: Biological and behavioral considerations. Monographs of the Society for Research in Child Development, 59*(2–3, Serial No. 240).

Crittenden, P. M., & Claussen, A. H. (1994). *Validation of two procedures for assessing quality of attachment in the preschool years* [Abstracts]. International Conference on Infant Studies, Paris.

Freud, A., & Burlingham, D. (1944). *Infants without Families.* New York: International Universities Press.

Freud, S. (1959). Inhibitions, symptoms and anxiety. In J. Strachey (Ed. and Trans.), *The standard edition of the complete psychological works of Sigmund Freud* (Vol. 20). London: Hogarth. (Original work published 1926)

Heinicke, C. M. (1956). Some effects of separating two-year-olds from their parents: A comparative study. *Human Relations, 9,* 105–176.

Heinicke, C. M. (1991). Early family intervention: Focusing on the mother's adaptation-competence and quality of partnership. In D. G. Unger & D. R. Power (Eds.), *Families as nurturing systems: Support across the life span.* New York: Haworth.

Heinicke, C. M. (in press). Determinants of the transition to parenting. In M. H. Bornstein (Ed.), *Handbook of parenting.* Hillsdale, NJ: Erlbaum.

Heinicke, C. M., & Guthrie, D. (1992). Stability and change in husband-wife adaptation, and the development of the positive parent-child relationship. *Infant Behavior and Development, 15,* 109–127.

Heinicke, C. M., & Lampl, E. (1988). Pre- and post-birth antecedents of 3- and 4-year-old attention, I.Q., verbal expressiveness, task orientation and capacity for relationships. *Infant Behavior and Development,* **11,** 381–410.

Heinicke, C. M., Recchia, S., Berlin, P., & James, C. (1993). *Manual for coding global child and parent-child ratings.* Unpublished manuscript, Department of Psychiatry, University of California, Los Angeles.

Heinicke, C. M., & Westheimer, I. (1965). *Brief separations.* New York: International Universities Press.

Lazarus, R. S. (1991). *Emotion and adaptation.* New York: Oxford University Press.

Lieberman, A. F., Weston, D. R., & Pawl, J. H. (1991). Preventive intervention with anxiously attached dyads. *Child Development,* **63,** 199–209.

Olds, D., & Kitzman, H. (1993). Review of research on home visiting for pregnant women and parents of young children. *The Future of Children,* **3,** 54–92.

Rapaport, D., & Gill, M. M. (1959). The points of view and assumptions of metapsychology. *International Journal of Psycho-Analysis,* **40,** 1–10.

Robertson, J., & Bowlby, J. (1952). Responses of young children to separation from their mothers. *Courrier of the International Children's Centre* (Paris), **2,** 131–140.

COMMENTARY

A COMMUNICATION PERSPECTIVE ON ATTACHMENT RELATIONSHIPS
AND INTERNAL WORKING MODELS

Inge Bretherton

To retain its vitality, a theory must be translated into assessments. The publication of several new instruments for assessing patterns of attachment in *Growing Points of Attachment Theory and Research* (Bretherton & Waters, 1985) was therefore an important milestone. In that *Monograph,* Waters and Deane (1985) presented the first version of their Attachment Q-Set (AQS) to facilitate observational studies of secure-base behavior in the home environment, especially beyond the first year of life. At the same time, several other assessments, including the Adult Attachment Interview (AAI; Main, Kaplan, & Cassidy, 1985), were introduced that moved the study of attachment quality to the level of representation. The current *Monograph* successfully builds on the earlier one, but it also expands our repertoire of theory-relevant assessments, with a special emphasis on Ainsworth's concept of the *secure base.* In what follows, I focus on a number of issues raised by this new and exciting collection that strike me as particularly promising for theory development.

Assessing Attachment Relationships, Secure-Base Behavior,
and Maternal Sensitivity

The notion of a secure base from which an individual can move out to master the environment stems from Ainsworth's graduate work at the University of Toronto under her mentor, William Blatz (Salter, 1940). Ten years later, after becoming a member of John Bowlby's research team in

London, Ainsworth realized that this concept meshed well with ideas that Bowlby was independently developing from ethological studies of imprinting. Subsequently, the concept of the secure base came to play a major role in the formulation of attachment theory, particularly through Ainsworth's delineation of qualitative differences in attachment relationships based on her innovative observational studies.

Ainsworth and her colleagues discovered that sensitive maternal responding to infant signals during home observations of feeding, crying, holding, and face-to-face episodes in the first 3 months of life predicted more harmonious patterns of infant-mother interaction and secure-base behavior during the last quarter of the first year. Furthermore, maternal sensitivity also predicted patterns of infant behavior in a 20-min laboratory separation-reunion procedure when the infants were 1 year of age. This procedure, known as the Ainsworth Strange Situation, hence became a valuable and productive shortcut method for examining the quality of mother-infant attachment (Ainsworth & Bell, 1969, 1970; Ainsworth, Bell, Blehar, & Main, 1971; Ainsworth, Bell, & Stayton, 1971, 1974; Ainsworth, Blehar, Waters, & Wall, 1978; Bell & Ainsworth, 1972; Blehar, Lieberman, & Ainsworth, 1977; Stayton & Ainsworth, 1973; Tracy & Ainsworth, 1981; Tracy, Lamb, & Ainsworth, 1976).

An adverse side effect of the Strange Situation's subsequent success has been that patterns of infant-mother attachment became defined almost solely in terms of patterns of attachment behavior observed during this procedure. Yet, as Strayer, Verissimo, Vaughn, and Howes note, although infants' secure-base and security-seeking behaviors in the Strange Situation and at home are conceptually related, they are not isomorphic. For example, infants who cry little and show optimal secure-base behavior in the familiar home environment protest the mother's departure in the unfamiliar laboratory setting where the Strange Situation is usually conducted. By contrast, a subgroup of infants who respond without crying to the mother's departure and avoid her on reunion in the Strange Situation are quite likely to cry more at home. To gain a clearer picture of naturally occurring variations of secure-base behavior in a familiar environment, one cannot therefore directly extrapolate from infants' Strange Situation behavior.

Pederson and Moran deserve tremendous credit for developing criteria that will allow other researchers to identify secure, avoidant, and ambivalent attachment relationships in the context of mother-infant interactions at home rather than having to rely on the Strange Situation. Their use of a dialogue process to clarify and extend observer notes is an especially interesting technique. Having to respond to queries from an attachment expert who did not participate in the home visit presumably forced the observers to state their descriptions, intuitive judgments, and inferences more clearly and explicitly. I suggest that these dialogically created descriptions would be even more valuable for future research if the authors used them to supplement their manual of home-based attachment patterns with a greater variety of concrete examples.

That Pederson and Moran found it difficult to distinguish between home-based attachment classifications for subgroups A2 (avoidant) and C1 (ambivalent) was particularly intriguing. In many previous studies, researchers had lumped infants who were identified as ambivalently or avoidantly attached on the basis Strange Situation behavior together into a single insecure group, in part because they were unable to discriminate between them in other contexts. Pederson and Moran's work may serve as encouragement to take a closer look. In their study, both A2 and C1 relationships were described as not smooth. The primary distinction between the A2 and the C1 groups related to the causes of infant fussiness and the degree of overt anger in the relationship. In A2 relationships, infant fussiness was associated with identifiable nonrelationship factors (frustration with a toy, falling over), and mothers responded to infant cries by distracting the infant. In C2 relationships, on the other hand, the cause of infant fussiness could not be clearly identified, and both infant and mother were more overtly angry (although there were also moments of coming together). If replicable, these are subtle but conceptually important distinctions.

Inspired by Waters and Deane's (1985) example, Pederson and Moran also devised and validated a Maternal Behavior Q-Set (MBQS) to assess maternal sensitivity and thus complement the revised AQS (Waters, 1987). That the home-based attachment classifications successfully predicted mother-rated AQS security scores and observer-rated MBQS sensitivity scores adds to the potential of both Q-sets for meaningful evaluation of individual differences in infant and maternal interactive behavior at home in a less time- and labor-intensive manner than the narrative procedures originally developed by Ainsworth. On the other hand, while the discovery that ambivalent infants are the fussiest group and that avoidant children are less prone to seek physical contact with the mother (as shown by the AQS subscales) is in accord with previous findings, it does not fully capture the richness of the classificatory descriptions provided by Pederson and Moran. Perhaps the Pederson and Moran observer field notes could suggest additional AQS and MBQS items that would allow us to use these Q-sets together in order to assess patterns, and not just dimensions, of attachment relationships.

An advantage of the AQS is that it can be used to tap mothers' and other caregivers' perceptions with reasonable confidence in their validity, given that mother- and observer-sorted scores for the same infants tend to be correlated. Nevertheless, the Pederson and Moran data show that trained observers seem to make sharper discriminations in their placement of Q-set items, as demonstrated by the much greater mean differences between observers' and mothers' security ratings of infants who fit the avoidant and ambivalent home-based attachment classifications.

Not surprisingly, mother-observer AQS/MBQS correlations within and between sessions tend to be lower than interobserver correlations. The latter are extraordinarily high, especially when one observer's AQS and the other observer's MBQS for the same session are compared. Although secure-base behavior defines secure infants and sensitivity defines security-providing mothers, Pederson and Moran argue strongly that what we are really assessing here is a harmonious collaboration between mother and infant. They therefore conclude that the mother-infant relationship must be understood as one system: maternal (and presumably also paternal) sensitivity always occurs in relation to a particular infant, just as an infant's secure-base behavior occurs in relation to a particular mother.

Whereas it is difficult to argue with the claim that bidirectional co-regulatory (Fogel, 1993) influences operate in the mother-infant dyad, maternal influences have so far been easier to document than infant effects, not only in Ainsworth's original studies, but in subsequent research as well. For example, Fonagy, Steele, and Steele (1991) reported that Strange Situation classifications at 1 year of age can be predicted with an impressively high degree of accuracy from *prenatal* assessments of mothers' reflections on their own childhood attachments. This suggests that a parent's responses to infant signals are likely to be filtered through already extant conceptions of attachment relationships and cultural prescriptions.

In support of this view, van IJzendoorn, Goldberg, Kroonenberg, and Frenkel (1992) found that better predictions of Strange Situation classifications can be made on the basis of maternal mental health measures than from assessments of child characteristics. Along the same lines, Washington, Minde, and Goldberg (1986) have shown that sensitive maternal behavior in response to initially difficult infants is associated with positive change, whereas insensitive maternal behavior in response to initially easy infants leads to greater difficulty in the relationship later on. Similarly, in the Pederson and Moran study, no difference in the size of sensitivity-security correlations was obtained for dyads with premature infants, who must have been considerably more challenging in the early months.

Despite these findings concerning the importance of maternal behavior, I agree with Seifer and Schiller that we need to study individual differences in *bi*-directional responsiveness at all points in the relationship. Imperfect correlations between early maternal sensitivity and later harmonious interaction may be due to infants who are better able than others actively to recruit their mothers' capacity for sensitive responsiveness, just as some mothers may be more adept than others at tuning in to difficult infants. As Seifer and Schiller argue, goodness of fit is not predetermined or likely to remain unchanged over time without the continued reciprocal adjustment of both partners in the attachment relationship. Using the AQS in conjunction with the MBQS during the negotiation of infant milestones or during other transitions may help us better understand perturbations and reequilibrations in attachment relationships that occur when infants acquire new skills and abilities and they or their parents are exposed to new external challenges. To use the AQS and MBQS for this purpose, however, might require the addition of some developmentally sensitive items. I was somewhat surprised to see that age differences in secure-base behavior were rarely mentioned in the reports contained in this *Monograph*, even though the age of the children participating in the various studies ranged from 8 months to 5 years.

Is Attachment Universal?

Although Ainsworth's initial ideas regarding links between maternal sensitivity and individual differences in attachment security originated in her Uganda study (Ainsworth, 1967), further cross-cultural research of attachment issues was slow to emerge. The frequent use of the Strange Situation in cross-cultural studies during the 1980s (see Bretherton & Waters, 1985) has been especially controversial, given that the meaning of this procedure for infants and parents may differ by culture. For this reason, Ainsworth herself has urged that cross-national attachment research should preferably focus on home observations of attachment interactions and infants' negotiation of the attachment/exploration balance.

Using the AQS in inventive new ways, Posada, Gao, et al. demonstrated that mothers' perceptions of secure-base behavior vary more within than between cultures. Most intriguing to me, however, were their findings regarding mothers' and experts' Q-set descriptions of the ideal infant/child. These suggest that mothers and experts in a variety of cultures across several continents tend to prefer an infant who engages in positive social interaction and exploration but seeks maternal support when under stress.

Had culturally based differences in secure-base behavior been detected, however, their interpretation in cultural terms would have been difficult. Variations that are based on findings from single samples do not necessarily reflect stable cross-national differences (see the cross-cultural meta-analysis of Strange Situation studies by van IJzendoorn & Kroonenberg, 1988). Without a number of replication studies, it is therefore not clear what to make of the cross-national differences that emerged on the AQS *subscales* developed by Posada, Gao, et al. Nevertheless, I cannot help but comment on their finding that German mothers valued physical contact more than mothers of other nationalities. It stands in stark contrast to the earlier report by Grossmann, Grossmann, Spangler, Suess, and Unzner (1985), in which avoidant Strange Situation classifications were overrepresented with respect to U.S. samples, a finding that was ascribed to the (untested) assumption that German mothers train their infants to become independent by *discouraging* close bodily contact.

The AQS-based studies by Posada, Gao, et al. and Strayer et al. suggest that, in line with Bowlby's (1982/1969) ethological perspective, the pursuit of an etic (universal) approach to the study of secure-base behavior has merit. An etic perspective is also justified by a number of cross-national studies reporting correlations between Strange Situation classifications and later social behavior that are consonant with attachment theory (e.g., Grossmann, Fremmer-Bombik, Rudolph, & Grossmann, 1988; Sagi, van IJzendoorn, Aviezer, Donnell, & Mayseless, 1994).

The successful study of the etic aspects of attachment does not mean, however, that an emic (culture-specific) approach should be abandoned. On the contrary, we need to know much more about how specific cultures integrate infant-parent attachment into their overall framework of social relationships and cultural beliefs (for a discussion, see Bretherton, 1992). One example is provided by the work by Tronick, Winn, and Morelli (1985) among the Efe, a seminomadic people subsisting on foraging, horticulture, and hunting in the African rain forest. Young Efe infants receive more care (including nursing) from other adult women than from their own mothers, except at night. Despite this multiple mothering system, 6-month-old infants begin to insist on more focalized relationships with their own mothers, although other female caregivers continue to play a significant role. Tronick et al. explain this practice in terms of the Efe's closely spaced huts that offer little privacy and make cooperation and sharing highly valued behaviors.

These findings suggest that cultural prescriptions play an important role in adult responses to infant attachment behavior even in a society that much more closely resembles the conditions of human evolution than our own. To better explore such cultural variations in attachment organization, attachment researchers need to develop ecologically valid, theory-driven observational and interview measures that are tailored to specific cultures and based on a deeper knowledge of parents' and children's culture-specific folk theories about family relationships and attachment. The AQS and MBQS used conjointly might become useful for the investigation of cultural differences in mother-infant attachment interactions, especially if each Q-set were supplemented by culturally sensitive items.

Internal Working Models, Affect Communication, and Child Narratives

Not only have the last 10 years seen an increase in research based on and inspired by the availability of the AQS, but there has also been a surge of studies using and extending the representational attachment measures introduced by Main et al. (1985). All these measures were conceptually derived from and validated against Ainsworth's Strange Situation classification system for infants.

Taken together, these studies document interesting connections between sensitive and emotionally open communication by attachment partners *within* parent-child attachment relationships and each partner's separate capacity to talk *about* attachment issues openly and coherently with a nonjudgmental interviewer (Bretherton, 1991). As I see it, the crucial theory-based links are between a child's experience of sensitive open communication with parents, feelings of security, well-modulated affect, and coherently organized internal working models of self and attachment figures.

Oppenheim and Waters invite us to take a new look at studies of children's attachment narratives by underscoring the role played by affect regulation, co-constructive processes, and cognitive development. Their arguments, especially those regarding affect regulation, reminded me of related ideas propounded by Bowlby in 1951 before the formulation of attachment theory and further elaborated in his later writings:

> Nothing helps a child more, I believe, than being able to express hostile and jealous feelings candidly, directly, and spontaneously, and there is no parental task more valuable, I believe, than being able to accept with equanimity such expressions of filial piety as "I hate you, mummy" or "Daddy, you're a beast." By putting up with these outbursts we show our children that we are not afraid of hatred and that we are confident it can be controlled; moreover, we provide for the child the tolerant atmosphere in which self-control can grow. ... As in politics, so with children. In the long run tolerance of opposition pays handsome dividends. (1979, p. 12)

Given a tolerant attitude on the part of parents, Bowlby (1951) maintains, the emotions of anxiety and guilt (which experienced in excess characterize mental ill health) will develop in a moderate and organized way. However, such tolerance is likely to be difficult for parents whose feelings toward their children are distorted by unconscious conflicts stemming from attachment experiences in their families of origin.

In later writings, Bowlby advanced the view that parents' ability openly to acknowledge and respond to their children's emotional communications leads to the establishment of internal working models of self and attachment figures that remain open to change:

> Thus the family experience of those who grow up anxious and fearful is found to be characterized not only by uncertainty about parental

support but often also by covert yet strongly distorting parental pressures: pressure on the child, for example, to act as caregiver for a
parent; *or to adopt, and thereby to confirm, a parent's false models—of self, of
child and of the relationship.* Similarly the family experience of those who
grow up to become relatively stable and self-reliant is characterized not
only by unfailing parental support when called upon but also by a
steady yet timely encouragement toward increasing autonomy, and *by
the frank communication by parents of working models—themselves, of child
and of others—that are not only tolerably valid but are open to be questioned
and revised.* . . . The inheritance of mental health and mental ill health
through the medium of family microculture ... may well be far more
important, than is their inheritance through the medium of genes.
(Bowlby, 1973, pp. 322-323; italics mine)

These statements suggest that Bowlby saw the parental role of secure base
as pertaining to children's exploration of their inner, and not just their
outer, world.

Parents are unlikely to be able to fulfill the role of psychological secure
base adequately, however, if they consistently misconstrue, disavow, or ignore infant signals (in support of this claim, see Beeghly & Cicchetti, 1994;
Escher-Graeub & Grossmann, 1983). Misleading, inappropriate, or absent
feedback from a parent or other attachment figure not only is likely to be
distressing or confusing but may also undermine an infant's ability to construct adequate, well-organized internal working models of self and the
attachment figure by bringing defensive processes into play (Bretherton,
1990, 1993; for similar ideas, see also Stern, 1985). Sensitive, emotionally
responsive parental behavior toward children, on the other hand, is likely
to lead to more positive affective experiences for both parties (Bowlby, 1982/
1969) and at the same time help the child construct internal working models
of self and parent that are not pervasively fraught with defensive distortions
and dissociations. Interestingly, Pederson and Moran provide further support for this notion by noting that the spontaneous interactive behaviors of
mothers and infants in insecure relationships are quite confusing and much
harder to follow than mother-infant interchanges in relationships classified
as secure.

The communication perspective on attachment rests on the assumption
that parents transmit their own patterns of relating to children, initially
through behavioral-affective interaction patterns, but later also through verbal dialogue about past, future, and hypothetical experiences. This does not,
of course, imply that the child passively takes in interpretations furnished
by parents and other attachment figures. Rather, children filter parental
communications through their own developing system of understandings.
In this view, misattributions on the part of the children may sometimes
be due to cognitive difficulties rather than deliberate parental falsification,

although in a secure relationship, characterized by open communication between parents and children, such misunderstandings are much more likely to be corrected.

Thus, when Oppenheim and Waters suggest that children's responses in the various narrative assessments are "as much a measure of how children construct narratives about affective themes and communicate those to others as they are assessments of internal representations" (p. 203), I would respond that, in the context of a communication approach to attachment theory, these issues are two different aspects of the same phenomenon. Difficulties dealing with negatively charged story situations presented by friendly examiners may, at least in part, be reflections of past attachment communication problems with parents in which defensive processes interfered (and still interfere) with the construction of well-functioning internal working models. Whereas I agree with Oppenheim and Waters's plea for a greater emphasis on interpersonal rather than intrapsychic processes (see their discussion of Slough & Greenberg, 1990), I contend that defensive processes originate and are maintained by interpersonal interactions and should not therefore be regarded as purely intrapsychic. In fact, as Muir (1994) aptly noted, most defensive strategies require the collaboration of others in order to work and are hence best viewed as transpersonal.

This having been said, I welcome Oppenheim and Waters's emphasis on the importance of emotional communication in interpreting children's attachment narratives during story completions and similar procedures. Researchers investigating preschoolers' attachment representations (including me) have not always sufficiently clarified underlying assumptions about the theoretical connections between emotionally open communication and adequate, adaptable internal working models. Furthermore, a focus on emotional communication helps us make sense of the sometimes unrealistic content of even secure children's attachment narratives. Well-organized internal working models may enable coherent and constructive resolutions of story problems with which children are presented in these assessments, but the content of their solutions need not necessarily reflect actual behavior by parents or children (e.g., we do not assume that fathers shoot monsters in the bedroom or even pretend to do so, but narratives that consistently portray the father in this fashion may nevertheless imply expectations of protective responses by a parent in response to a child's fear).

I feel compelled in this connection to clarify Bowlby's attitude toward fantasy. Oppenheim and Waters, as well as other authors represented in this volume, repeatedly claim that Bowlby was more interested in actual events than in intrapsychic processes and that he was interested in ordinary life events as contrasted to trauma. Stated this way, their remarks could be misleading.

Bowlby's writings do not, in fact, show that he was uninterested in intrapsychic phenomena. However, unlike some of his psychoanalytically oriented colleagues (particularly Melanie Klein), Bowlby insisted that such material needed to be interpreted within an individual's framework of meanings and actual experience: "The more details one comes to know about the events in a child's life, and about what he has been told, what he has overheard and what he has observed but is not supposed to know, the more clearly can his ideas about the world and what may happen in the future be seen as perfectly reasonable constructions" (Bowlby, 1979, p. 23). In another relevant statement, taken from a paper on mourning, Bowlby and Parkes (1970) recommend that *magical thinking* and *fantasy* are terms to be used with extreme caution. They strongly urged that terms such as *denial of reality* and *fantasy* should be avoided and should be replaced instead by phrases such as "disbelief that X has occurred," "belief that Y may still be possible," or "making plans to achieve Z," in order to see the world more from the patient's perspective.

In short, Bowlby suggests that fantasies and other phenomena traditionally interpreted in terms of psychoanalytic defense mechanisms (e.g., projection, isolation) can alternatively be viewed as comprehensible misattributions due to a patient's attempts to make sense of the world as he or she has experienced it or has been told to experience it. For example, Bowlby (1961) cites a case study describing an aloof and apathetic man who had lost his mother at 5 years of age but had been unable to grieve over her death. Although this patient had no recollections of any events prior to his mother's death, he reported memories of leaving his bedroom door open at night during several years of his later childhood "in the hope that a large dog would come to him, be very kind to him, and fulfill all his wishes" (Bowlby, 1961, p. 485).

Similarly, Bowlby (1988) described a 6-year-old girl who had developed a terror that creatures looking like chairs and other pieces of furniture—she called them "daleks"—would fly across the room to strike her. The child kept cowering and ducking as if expecting to be attacked, leading her therapist to believe that she was hallucinating. However, it turned out that the child's father had an extremely violent temper, and it was verifiably established that he had repeatedly broken furniture and thrown it at the child as well beaten and thrown her across the room when she was a toddler. Again, the fear of unreal "daleks" had its roots in an actual experience. As Bowlby (1988) remarked, what is so glibly dubbed a fantasy is often a reflection of grim reality.

The clinician's goal, then, should be to use "fantasy" material to ferret out the reality that lies beneath the camouflage rather than treating the fantasy as having been caused by purely internal mechanisms such as libidinal and aggressive drives. This includes the recognition of the substitution of metaphors for repressed traumatic experiences. When faced with unrealistic (and sometimes strikingly metaphoric) material produced by preschool children during attachment story completion tasks, we cannot know what events underlie these productions without clinical probing. Nevertheless, those who use these assessments from an attachment-theoretic perspective assume a connection between the child's story completions and his or her actual attachment experiences, even though this connection may not be straightforward and may be indexed only in very general terms by the child's style of responding.

Finally, Oppenheim and Waters's emphasis on co-constructive processes in the development of internal working models highlights the lack of attachment theory–based studies of how parents communicate with their children about affective experiences. Bowlby (1980) has discussed this issue primarily in terms of parental pressure to adopt a distorted version of reality (i.e., telling the child that an event that he or she witnessed did not really happen or happened very differently). Oppenheim and Waters add that parents' failures to respond may have equally confusing effects on a young child.

I suggest, however, that the positive side of the picture also deserves careful examination. Young children frequently encounter events and experiences that are difficult to comprehend (such as medical procedures; see Steward, 1993). In such circumstances, parental input can help them make sense of their experiences and cope with them rather than leaving them emotionally overwhelmed or afraid. Unfortunately, we have little idea of how parents succeed in providing such clarifying input.

Some hints regarding these issues can be gleaned from investigators who study the development of self within a different research tradition. For example, Miller and her colleagues (Miller, Hoogstra, Mintz, Fung, & Williams, 1993), who were interested in the development of a relational self as mediated by narratives, present a detailed case study of the dialogues between a 23-month-old boy and his mother that ensued after she read him Beatrix Potter's story *Peter Rabbit*. The child requested many additional readings of the story, using retellings (co-constructed with his mother) to work through the various upsetting story issues (facing danger alone, getting lost) that did not accord with his own experience of rabbits and people in gardens. Interestingly, once the boy had worked out his personal worries and concerns about the story, the need for retellings vanished. It is particularly notable that the child's mother accepted and supported his attempts to cope with the story's affective challenges. A quite different outcome might have ensued had his mother insisted instead that he stick to the "facts" of the story. (Related studies in the same vein are reviewed by Nelson, 1989, 1993.)

In my view, attachment researchers have much to learn about the role of parents as psychological secure bases from studies of co-constructive processes in children's developing understanding of the affective and interpersonal world. I therefore join Oppenheim and Waters's call to researchers interested in the study of children's attachment narratives to become conversant with the literature on children's narrative development (especially studies of joint storytelling and remembering). Young children's incoherent responding may index insecure attachment, but—in some instances—it could also be the result of frustration elicited by overly complex tasks or even insensitive testers. In other words, a child's responses must always be interpreted in terms of his or her socioemotional and cognitive level as well as the extent and kind of co-constructive support offered by the people who administer these assessments. Conversely, however, I am also convinced that researchers with an interest in studying children's narrative development or memory development from a social constructivist perspective have much to gain from the techniques and ideas of researchers studying children's attachment representations through story completion and related techniques. I have tried to address some of these issues in two previous papers (Bretherton, 1993; Bretherton, Prentiss, & Ridgeway, 1990), but much more needs to be done.

Internal Working Models and Attachment Patterns: Personal or Relational?

By 1985, a few studies had reported that infants' Strange Situation attachment classifications with father and mother were frequently discordant. That is, some infants could be secure with one parent and insecure with the other, underscoring the view that attachment is a relational, not an individual, quality. These findings still hold, even though meta-analyses have since shown that the incidence of concordant attachments to mother and father is greater than chance (Fox, Kimmerly, & Schafer, 1991).

The nonconcordance findings suggest that a child often develops a different conception or working model of self for every attachment relationship (akin to William James's, 1890, proposal that an individual has as many social selves as relationships). The question hence arises as to whether and how these separate selves are integrated in the course of development (Bretherton, 1985) or whether the internal working model of self developed in the primary attachment relationship becomes the dominant influence (as suggested by Main et al.'s, 1985, findings). An alternative conception is that children integrate working models constructed in various attachment relationships into a metamodel. If so, we could think of it as a unitary (averaged) structure or, alternatively, as one based on the insight that experiences of self differ by relationship.

Sagi et al. address some of these questions with respect to nonfamilial caregivers (metaplot in kibbutzim). Would two different infants be classified similarly when observed with the same metapelet in the Strange Situation (caregiver effect), and, conversely, would infants observed in the Strange Situation with two different metaplot obtain congruent attachment classifications with both (infant effect)?

The Sagi et al. study revealed neither a clear infant nor a clear caregiver effect but, instead, weak bidirectional effects. From a communication perspective—wherein sensitive or insensitive patterns of caregiving teach infants particular forms of relating—it would reasonable to expect a greater caregiver than infant effect because the mother comes to the relationship with more highly developed personal and culture-specific expectations and interpersonal skills. The findings, however, are also consonant with the hypothesis that individual infants call forth somewhat similar responses from different caregivers. In other words, the study suggests that sensitive caregiving is only partially a quality of the caregiver and that it also depends on the quality of feedback provided by a particular infant in a particular relationship (supporting Pederson and Moran's ideas).

An advantage of the kibbutz study is that genetic factors that might be operative in relationships with biological parents can be ruled out and that, unlike parents who might resemble each other because of assortative mating, the metaplot did not choose to work with each other but were assigned to their positions by the kibbutz. Genetic factors and assortative mating have been adduced to explain the statistically significant but by no means perfect concordances between attachment to mother and father in previous studies by those rejecting an infant temperament explanation (see the meta-analyses in Fox et al., 1991). That the assortative mating hypothesis is partially justified emerges from van IJzendoorn and Bakermans-Kranenburg's (in press) study showing that secure men and women (assessed via the AAI) marry each other more often than expected by chance, thereby also inflating expected concordances of infants' attachment to mother and father. It is not clear how to reconcile the Sagi et al. study with other findings indicating that at least initially the adult caregiver is more influential in setting the tone of the relationship.

The question whether attachment quality and internal working models are relationship specific was also addressed by Owens et al., but these authors tackled the issue at the representational level, using the AAI (Main et al., 1985) in conjunction with a recently developed parallel Current Relationship Interview (CRI) for dating couples. Owens et al.'s objectives were to administer both interviews in order to investigate weak and strong forms of what they call the "prototype hypothesis" in attachment relationships.

Under the strong form of this hypothesis, childhood attachment patterns determine adult styles of relating. I contend, however, that Owens et al. were precluded from examining this strong version in their study because AAI classifications do not rest on descriptions of the content of an individual's experiences with parents in the family of origin but are primarily indexed by the degree of coherence and emotional openness with which adults can discuss their early attachment experiences (be they supportive or adverse). It is the parent's current "state of mind with respect to attachment" that tends to be concordant with the infant's Strange Situation classification and with child assessments at 6 years of age, not descriptions of how the parent was treated by his or her own parents as a child.

Nevertheless, given the current status of attachment theory, the Owens et al. study makes extremely important contributions and raises very important new questions. From a communication perspective on attachment representations, AAI classifications index an individual's ability to consider and discuss attachment issues with emotional openness and coherence. Hence, concordance between individuals' style of responding to the AAI and to the CRI would be expected. Clearly, such an expectation is only weakly supported here. Owens et al. found that, of 50 individuals whose AAIs were classified as secure-autonomous, 20 responded insecurely when interviewed about their romantic relationships using the CRI; 14 of these individuals adopted a dismissing and the remaining six a preoccupied strategy. Even more surprisingly, several individuals who were classified as secure-autonomous on the AAI and who had secure-autonomous AAI partners responded insecurely to the CRI, and, conversely, a few who were insecure on the AAI and had insecure AAI partners nevertheless responded securely to the CRI.

Irrespective of the fact that concordances in the AAI/CRI cross-classification matrix are statistically significant overall, these findings do not suggest that the AAI and CRI classifications assess a traitlike ability to talk about attachment relationships in a particular manner. Instead, they suggest that openness or defensiveness in communicating about attachment relationships (and presumably within them) is more relationship specific than some earlier findings had led me to believe.

Also supporting the notion of relationship specificity is the significantly higher between-couple concordance on the CRI (which assesses their own relationship) than on the AAI (which is based on each partner's current view of family-of-origin relationships). It is not clear what to make of the gender differences on the past experience scales of the AAI and the CRI, although I note that the coherence scales are correlated across instruments for men and women. For both genders, coherence in discussing relationships is more consistent between the AAI and the CRI than evaluations of parents or partners as loving or rejecting.

Owens et al. conclude from their findings that individuals form distinct models of self in different attachment relationships, "however constrained or biased by early experiences" (p. 232). My main argument with this interpretation is that the direction of effects is not necessarily from AAI to

CRI. Given that the AAI presumes to assess an individual's current "state of mind" with respect to past childhood experiences in attachment relationships (Main et al., 1985), changes in AAI classifications induced by the experience of a supportive romantic relationship seem possible (for support of this interpretation, see Ricks, 1985).

Even if perfect concordance between the AAI and the CRI classifications had been found in terms of the secure, dismissing, preoccupied, and unresolved patterns, we should not expect internal working models of relationships with parents and with sex partners to be identical. At the most concrete level of dyadic interaction schemas, I would predict a secure individual to have well-differentiated working models of self and partner in different relationships, models that are well attuned to the particular attachment partner's individuality. The blind application of a single model across different relationships would reflect the opposite of mental health. However, at a more general or abstract level, these differentiated relationships might be construed as similar (e.g., well attuned to the particular partner; trusting and supportive). Thus, when Owens et al. talk about the "prototype hypothesis," they are referring to concordance only in terms of security/insecurity or secure-autonomous, dismissing, preoccupied, and unresolved patterns.

In the Owens et al. study, even the weak form of the prototype hypothesis does not hold for a very substantial minority of couples. This suggests that, whereas individuals may approach a close adult relationship with some general expectations (internal working models) derived from their current construction of past relationships, the ensuing relationship can be only incompletely predicted from AAI assessments. In some instances, two partners whose relationships with their own parents are classified as dismissing or preoccupied may nevertheless be able to discuss their mutual relationship with coherence and emotional openness.

Owens et al.'s comparisons of relationship interviews are premised on the assumption that infant-adult attachments and romantic relationships are "the same kind of relationship." For Bowlby, adult-adult and child-adult attachments were comparable because of convergent accounts of adults' and children's responses to bereavement, that is, similar responses to secure-base deprivation (Bowlby & Parkes, 1970; Marris, 1958; Weiss, 1973; and see the review in Bowlby, 1980). Attachment theory–based studies of divorce (Weiss, 1977) and wartime separations (Vormbrock, 1993) have also demonstrated that involuntary separations from adult partners are anxiety provoking and lead to proximity-seeking behavior, even when—as in the case of divorce—loving feelings have vanished. In a more recent paper, Weiss (1991) listed the following properties of childhood attachment to parents that characterize some adult relationships, particularly pair bonds: proximity seeking, secure-base effect, separation protest, elicitation of attachment behavior by threat, specificity of attachment figure, inaccessibility of attachment feelings to conscious control, duration of the relationship, and persistence of attachment even when the attachment figure is neglectful or abusive.

However, pair bonds also differ from child-parent attachment relationships in a number of important respects. In addition to the role of sexuality, a very important difference is the mutuality characteristic of adult attachment relationships wherein both partners seek and provide emotional support and physical protection/care and both serve as reciprocal secure bases for each other. Additionally, whereas in a child-parent relationship extensive caregiving behavior by the child toward the parent is regarded as indicative of emotional ill health, in an adult love relationship it would be regarded as problematic were one partner to provide care and support for the other without reciprocation. Mutually affirming and emotionally open but respectful communication patterns are likely to be helpful in maintaining a satisfactory attachment/autonomy balance in adult attachment relationships. Unlike Owens et al., I therefore see the communication skills fostered in marital therapy as closely related to partners' ability to serve as secure base and haven for each other.

Concluding Remarks

This *Monograph* provides a number of provocative new findings, conceptualizations, and measurement tools. Like most good research, it also raises many interesting new questions. On the one hand, almost all the investigators represented in this volume report statistically significant findings in support of their hypotheses. On the other hand, their findings also underscore that there is much about the effect of relationships on relationships, about the development of shared or disparate working models of self and attachment partner, and about the differences between marital and parent-child relationships that we do not yet understand.

An important emphasis in this *Monograph* is the focus on co-constructive processes. In this view, communication not only serves the purpose of mutual information and relationship maintenance but also creates a shared reality. When defensive processes come to play a predominant role in relationships, this process is hampered, and misunderstandings cannot easily be corrected, leading to further miscommunications. How these defensive processes operate in relationships and how they are mutually upheld are extremely important questions. Instruments such as the AAI and the CRI provide some insight, but these questions must be investigated in much greater depth.

From outside attachment theory comes evidence that supportive parent-child relationships are one significant contributor to an individual's constructive, relatively benign, and optimistic worldview. Epstein (1991) reports that individuals who hold such a view are more likely to evoke positive responses *from* others and thereby co-construct a more positive reality *with* others. The reverse was found for adverse parent-child relationships experienced in childhood—these appear to be associated with a view of the world as a dangerous, nontrustworthy place. The findings in this *Monograph* suggest that, at least within the range of relationships studied here, the conceptual links are more complex. Individuals' expectations of relationships remain open to influence by feedback from the partner. Some individuals who have not come to grips with adverse experiences in very important past relationships are able to co-construct more positive ways of relating with a reciprocating other. Conversely, positive internal working models (or positive meaning making) in one important relationship do not reliably protect individuals from co-constructing a dissatisfying relationship with another partner. Examining these ideas further offers challenging prospects for the study of attachment from the cradle to the grave.

References

Ainsworth, M. D. S. (1967). *Infancy in Uganda: Infant care and the growth of love.* Baltimore: Johns Hopkins University Press.

Ainsworth, M. D. S., & Bell, S. M. (1969). Some contemporary patterns in the feeding situation. In A. Ambrose (Ed.), *Stimulation in early infancy.* London: Academic.

Ainsworth, M. D. S., & Bell, S. M. (1970). Attachment, exploration, and separation: Illustrated by the behavior of one-year-olds in a strange situation. *Child Development,* **41,** 49–67.

Ainsworth, M. D. S., Bell, S. M., Blehar, M. C., & Main, M. (1971, April). *Physical contact: A study of infant responsiveness and its relation to maternal handling.* Paper presented at the meeting of the Society for Research in Child Development, Minneapolis.

Ainsworth, M. D. S., Bell, S. M., & Stayton, D. J. (1971). Individual differences in Strange Situation behaviour of one-year-olds. In H. R. Schaffer (Ed.), *The origins of human social relations.* London: Academic.

Ainsworth, M. D. S., Bell, S. M., & Stayton, D. J. (1974). Infant-mother attachment and social development. In M. P. Richards (Ed.), *The introduction of the child into a social world.* London: Cambridge University Press.

Ainsworth, M. D. S., Blehar, M. C., Waters, E., & Wall, S. (1978). *Patterns of attachment: A psychological study of the Strange Situation.* Hillsdale, NJ: Erlbaum.

Beeghly, M., & Cicchetti, D. (1994). Child maltreatment, attachment, and the self system: Emergence of an internal state lexicon in toddlers at high social risk. *Development and Psychopathology,* **6,** 5–30.

Bell, S. M., & Ainsworth, M. D. S. (1972). Infant crying and maternal responsiveness. *Child Development,* **43,** 1171–1190.

Blehar, M. C., Lieberman, A. F., & Ainsworth, M. D. S. (1977). Early face-to-face interaction and its relation to later infant-mother attachment. *Child Development,* **48,** 181–194.

Bowlby, J. (1951). *Maternal health and mental health* (Monograph Series, No. 2). Geneva: World Health Organization.

Bowlby, J. (1961). Processes of mourning. *International Journal of Psycho-Analysis,* **42,** 317–340.

Bowlby, J. (1973). *Attachment and loss: Vol. 2. Separation.* New York: Basic.

Bowlby, J. (1979). *The making and breaking of affectional bonds.* London: Tavistock.

Bowlby, J. (1980). *Attachment and loss: Vol. 3. Loss, sadness and depression.* New York: Basic.

Bowlby, J. (1982). *Attachment and loss: Vol. 1. Attachment* (2d rev. ed.). New York: Basic. (Original work published 1969)

Bowlby, J. (1988). *A secure base.* New York: Basic.

Bowlby, J., & Parkes, C. M. (1970). Separation and loss within the family. In E. J. Anthony & C. Koupernik (Eds.), *The child in his family* (International Yearbook of Child Psychiatry and Allied Professions). New York: Wiley.

Bretherton, I. (1985). Attachment theory and research: Retrospect and prospect. In I. Bretherton & E. Waters (Eds.), *Growing points in attachment theory and research. Monographs of the Society for Research in Child Development,* **50**(1–2, Serial No. 209).

Bretherton, I. (1990). Open communication and internal working models: Their role in the development of attachment relationships. In R. A. Thompson (Ed.), *Socioemotional development* (Nebraska Symposium on Motivation). Lincoln: University of Nebraska Press.

Bretherton, I. (1991). Pouring new wine into old bottles: The social self as internal working model. In M. Gunnar & L. A. Sroufe (Eds.), *Self processes in development* (Minnesota Symposia on Child Development, Vol. 23). Hillsdale, NJ: Erlbaum.

Bretherton, I. (1992). The origins of attachment theory: John Bowlby and Mary Ainsworth. *Developmental Psychology,* **28,** 759–755.

Bretherton, I. (1993). From dialogue to representation: The co-construction of self in relationships. In C. A. Nelson (Ed.), *Memory and affect in development* (Minnesota Symposia on Child Development, Vol. 26). Hillsdale, NJ: Erlbaum.

Bretherton, I., Prentiss, C., & Ridgeway, D. (1990). Family relations as represented in a story completion task at thirty-seven and fifty-four months of age. In I. Bretherton & M. Watson (Eds.), *Children's perspectives on the family* (New Directions in Child Development, vol. 48). San Francisco: Jossey-Bass.

Bretherton, I., & Waters, E. (Eds.). (1985). Growing points of attachment theory and research. *Monographs of the Society for Research in Child Development,* **50**(1–2, Serial No. 209).

Epstein, S. (1991). Cognitive-experiential self theory: Implications for developmental psychology. In M. R. Gunnar & L. A. Sroufe (Eds.), *Self processes in development* (Minnesota Symposia in Child Psychology, Vol. 23). Hillsdale, NJ: Erlbaum.

Escher-Graeub, D., & Grossmann, K. E. (1983). *Bindungssicherheit im zweiten Lebensjahr—die Regensburger Querschnittuntersuchung* [Attachment security in the second year of life—the Regensburg cross-sectional study] (Research Report). University of Regensburg.

Fogel, A. (1993). *Developing through relationships.* Chicago: University of Chicago Press.

Fonagy, P., Steele, H., & Steele, M. (1991). Intergenerational patterns of attachment: Maternal representations during pregnancy and subsequent infant-mother attachments. *Child Development,* **62,** 891–905.

Fox, N., Kimmerly, N. I., & Schafer, W. D. (1991). Attachment to mother/attachment to father: A meta-analysis. *Child Development,* **62,** 210–225.

Grossmann, K., Fremmer-Bombik, E., Rudolph, J., & Grossmann, K. E. (1988). Maternal attachment representations as related to patterns of infant-mother attachment and maternal care during the first year. In R. A. Hinde & J. Stevenson-Hinde (Eds.), *Relationships within families.* Oxford: Oxford University Press.

Grossmann, K., Grossmann, K. E., Spangler, G., Suess, G., & Unzner, L. (1985). Maternal sensitivity and newborns' orientation responses as related to quality of attachment in

Northern Germany. In I. Bretherton & E. Waters (Eds.), *Growing points of attachment theory and research. Monographs of the Society for Research in Child Development*, **50**(1–2, Serial No. 209).

James, W. (1890). *The principles of psychology* (Vol. **1**). New York: Holt.

Main, M., Kaplan, N., & Cassidy, J. (1985). Security in infancy, childhood, and adulthood: A move to the level of representation. In I. Bretherton & E. Waters (Eds.), *Growing points of attachment theory and research. Monographs of the Society for Research in Child Development*, **50**(1–2, Serial No. 209).

Marris, P. (1958). *Widows and their families*. London: Routledge.

Miller, P. J., Hoogstra, L., Mintz, J., Fung, H., & Williams, K. (1993). Troubles in the garden and how they get resolved: A young child's transformation of his favorite story. In C. A. Nelson (Ed.), *Memory and affect in development* (Minnesota Symposia on Child Psychology, Vol. 26). Hillsdale, NJ: Erlbaum.

Muir, R. C. (1994). *Transpersonal processes: A bridge between object relations and attachment theory in normal and psychopathological development*. Unpublished manuscript, C. M. Hincks Institute, University of Toronto.

Nelson, K. (1989). *Narratives from the crib*. Cambridge, MA: Harvard University Press.

Nelson, K. (1993). Events, narratives, memory: What develops? In C. A. Nelson (Ed.), *Memory and affect in development* (Minnesota Symposia on Child Psychology, Vol. 26). Hillsdale, NJ: Erlbaum.

Ricks, M. H. (1985). The social transmission of parental behavior: Attachment across generations. In I. Bretherton & E. Waters (Eds.), *Growing points of attachment theory and research. Monographs of the Society for Research in Child Development*, **50**(1–2, Serial No. 209).

Sagi, A., van IJzendoorn, M. H., Aviezer, O., Donnell, F., & Mayseless, O. (1994). Sleeping away from home in a kibbutz communal arrangement: It makes a difference for infant-mother attachment. *Child Development*, **65**, 988–1000.

Salter, M. D. (1940). *An evaluation of adjustment based upon the concept of security* (Child Development Series). Toronto: University of Toronto Press.

Slough, N., & Greenberg, M. (1990). 5-year-olds' representations of separation from parents: Responses for self and a hypothetical child. In I. Bretherton & M. Watson (Eds.), *Children's perspectives on the family* (New Directions for Child Development). San Francisco: Jossey-Bass.

Stayton, D., & Ainsworth, M. D. S. (1973). Individual differences in responses to everyday brief separations as related to other infant and maternal behaviors. *Developmental Psychology*, **9**, 226–235.

Stern, D. N. (1985). *The interpersonal world of the infant*. New York: Basic.

Steward, M. S. (1993). Understanding children's memories of medical procedures: "He didn't touch me and it didn't hurt." In C. A. Nelson (Ed.), *Memory and affect in development* (Minnesota Symposia on Child Psychology, Vol. 26). Hillsdale, NJ: Erlbaum.

Tracy, R. L., & Ainsworth, M. D. S. (1981). Maternal affectionate behavior and infant-mother attachment patterns. *Child Development*, **52**, 1341–1343.

Tracy, R. L., Lamb, M. E., & Ainsworth, M. D. S. (1976). Infant approach behavior as related to attachment. *Child Development*, **47**, 571–578.

Tronick, E. Z., Winn, S., & Morelli, G. A. (1985). Multiple caretaking in the context of human evolution: Why don't the Efe know the Western prescription to child care? In M. Reite & T. Field (Eds.), *The psychobiology of attachment and separation*. San Diego: Academic.

van IJzendoorn, M. H., & Bakermans-Kranenburg, M. J. (in press). Attachment representations in mothers, fathers, adolescents, and clinical groups: A meta-analytic search for normative data. *Journal of Consulting and Clinical Psychology*.

van IJzendoorn, M. H., Goldberg, S., Kroonenberg, P. M., & Frenkel, O. J. (1992). The relative effects of maternal and child problems on the quality of attachment: A meta-analysis of attachment in clinical samples. *Child Development*, **63**, 840–858.

van IJzendoorn, M. H., & Kroonenberg, P. M. (1988). Cross-cultural patterns of attachment: A meta-analysis of the Strange Situation. *Child Development*, **59**, 147–156.

Vormbrock, J. (1993). Attachment theory as applied to war-time and job-related marital separation. *Psychological Bulletin*, **114**, 122–144.

Washington, J., Minde, K., & Goldberg, S. (1986). Temperament in preterm infants: Style and stability. *Journal of the American Academy of Child Psychiatry*, **25**, 493–502.

Waters, E. (1987). *Attachment Behavior Q-Set* (Revision 3.0). Unpublished instrument, State University of New York at Stony Brook, Department of Psychology.

Waters, E., & Deane, K. E. (1985). Defining and assessing individual differences in attachment relationships: Q-methodology and the organization of behavior in infancy and early childhood. In I. Bretherton & E. Waters (Eds.), *Growing points of attachment theory and research. Monographs of the Society for Research in Child Development*, **50**(1–2, Serial No. 209).

Weiss, R. S. (1973). *Loneliness: The experience of emotional and social isolation.* Cambridge, MA: MIT Press.

Weiss, R. S. (1977). *Marital separation.* New York: Basic.

Weiss, R. S. (1991). The attachment bond in childhood and adulthood. In C. M. Parkes, J. Stevenson-Hinde, & P. Marris (Eds.), *Attachment across the life cycle.* London: Routledge.

CONTRIBUTORS

Mary D. S. Ainsworth (Ph.D. 1939, University of Toronto) is an emeritus professor of psychology at the University of Virginia. She has been a leading researcher in the area of parent-child attachments across the life span for over 40 years. She is the author of *Infancy in Uganda* and (with M. Blehar, E. Waters, and S. Wall) *Patterns of Attachment: A Psychological Study of the Strange Situation.* Mary Ainsworth is recognized as one of the founders of attachment theory.

Ora Aviezer (Ph.D. 1986, University of Chicago) is presently a lecturer of education at the School of Education of the Kibbutz Movement, Oranim, Israel. She is the co-author (with M. H. Van IJzendoorn, A. Sagi, and C. Shuengel) of "'Children of the Dream' Revisited: 70 Years of Collective Early Child-Care in Israeli Kibbutzim." Her research interests include socioemotional development across the life span.

Inge Bretherton (Ph.D. 1975, Johns Hopkins University) is a professor of child and family studies and an affiliate of the Waisman Center at the University of Wisconsin—Madison. She has served on the editorial boards of *Child Development* and the *Monographs of the Society for Research in Child Development* and currently serves on the editorial board of *Social Development.* Her research interests focus on child-parent and parent-child attachment from a representational perspective. Another major interest is the history and development of attachment theory. She is currently studying attachment issues in postdivorce families with preschoolers.

Judith A. Crowell (M.D. 1978, University of Vermont) is an associate professor of child psychiatry at the State University of New York at Stony Brook Health Sciences Center. A child psychiatrist, her primary research interests are in stability and change in attachment across the life span and relations between attachment behavior and other behavior in relationships.

Frank Donnell (M.A. 1991, University of Haifa) is currently lecturer of social work, Tel-Hai Regional College, University of Haifa. His research interests focus on socioemotional development across the life span.

Yuan Gao (Ph.D. 1995, State University of New York at Stony Brook) is a postdoctoral research associate in the Department of Psychology, State University of New York at Stony Brook. Her research concerns the cross-cultural generality of secure-base behavior in infants and the manifestations and functions of secure-base behavior in adult relationships.

Wenche Haaland (Ph.D. 1985, University of Bergen) is a professor of clinical psychology at Bergen University, Bergen, Norway. Her research has focused on psychotherapy and on parent-child attachment relationships.

Yael Harel (M.A. 1995, University of Haifa) is presently a social worker at Kupat Holim, Lin Medical Center, Haifa.

Christoph M. Heinicke (Ph.D. 1953, Harvard University) is a professor in the Department of Psychiatry and Biobehavioral Sciences and director of the Family Development Project at the University of California, Los Angeles. As a member of the Tavistock Child Development Research Unit, he collaborated with John Bowlby in the study of the effects of mother-child separation. This research led to the publication of *Brief Separations*. His current research interests focus on the prebirth determinants of family development and the conditions under which a home visiting intervention can modify that development.

Carollee Howes (Ph.D. 1979, Boston University) is a professor in the Graduate School of Education at the University of California, Los Angeles. Her research focuses on developmental outcomes associated with variability of child-care regimes, especially on the consequences for parent-child and child-adult relationships.

Tirtsa Joels (Ph.D. candidate 1994, University of Haifa) is a research associate in the Laboratory for the Study of Child Development, University of Haifa. She is conducting research on issues concerning socioemotional development across the life span.

Kiyomi Kondo-Ikemura (Ph.D. 1985 [Ethology], University of Osaka) is a researcher in the Faculty of Human Sciences at the University of Osaka. Her research interests include behavioral development in both free-ranging primates and human infants.

Nina Koren-Karie (Ph.D. candidate 1992, Hebrew University of Jerusalem) is presently a research associate in the Laboratory for the Study of Child Development, University of Haifa. Her research focuses on socioemotional development across the life span.

Keng-Ling Lay (Ph.D. 1991, State University of New York at Stony Brook) is an associate professor of psychology at the National Taiwan University. Her primary research interest is in relations between emotion and attachment in childhood.

Robert S. Marvin (Ph.D. 1972, University of Chicago) is on the faculty of the Department of Pediatrics, University of Virginia Medical School. His clinical and research interests focus on relationship difficulties in families who have young children with developmental disabilities and on young children who are experiencing disrupted bonds with their primary caregivers.

Greg Moran (Ph.D. 1978, Dalhousie University) is dean of the Faculty of Graduate Studies at the University of Western Ontario. He conducts research on the interaction antecedents of parent-child relationships and is keenly interested in the relations between evolution and development.

Elizabeth O'Connor (Ph.D. 1993, State University of New York at Stony Brook) is a postdoctoral research associate in the Department of Psychology, State University of New York at Stony Brook. Her research interests include relations of maternal attachment to parent-child interactions and child psychopathology and relations of adult attachment to marital discord, jealousy, and aggression.

David Oppenheim (Ph.D. 1990, University of Utah) is a lecturer in the Department of Psychology at the University of Haifa. His research interests include the development of parent-child relationships and the implications of individual differences in these relationships for child adaptation.

Gretchen Owens (Ph.D. 1994, State University of New York at Stony Brook) is an assistant professor in the Department of Child Study, St. Joseph's College. Her primary research focus is on attachment representations formed in the course of adult close relationships.

Helen Pan (Ph.D. 1985 [Neuroscience], University of Michigan) is an advanced graduate student in clinical psychology at the State University of New York at Stony Brook. Her research is focused on relating attachment theory to cognitive-behavioral marital therapy. She is especially interested in evolutionary perspectives and in secure-base behavior and aggression in marriages.

David R. Pederson (Ph.D. 1966, University of Iowa) is an associate professor of psychology at the University of Western Ontario. His research is focused on parent-child relationships and family processes in families with both high-risk and normally developing infants.

German Posada (Ph.D. 1989, State University of New York at Stony Brook) is an assistant professor of psychology at the University of Denver. He has research interests in parent-child attachment from infancy through childhood and in family processes bearing on the formation and maintenance of attachment relationships and on the development of secure-base behavior.

Roberto Posada (Psychologist 1991, Universidad Javeriana, Bogota) is an assistant professor of psychology, Department of Psychology, Universidad Javeriana, Bogata. His work focuses on the construction of knowledge in school-aged children.

Doreen Ridgeway (Ph.D. 1986, State University of New York at Stony Brook) was a postdoctoral fellow with the MacArthur Foundation Attachment Node from 1986 to 1990. She is a founding member of the Attachment Representations Research Group at the State University of New York at Stony Brook. Her research focuses on emotional development, the effects of mood on behavior, and the relations between cognitive representations of experience and emotional responses to complex stimuli.

Abraham Sagi (Ph.D. 1976, University of Michigan) is a professor of psychology, University of Haifa. He is a coauthor (with O. Aviezer, M. H. van IJzendoorn, and C. Shuengel) of the review " 'Children of the Dream' revisited: 70 Years of Collective Early Child-Care in Israeli Kibbutzim." His research focuses on socioemotional development across the life span.

Masha Schiller (Ph.D. 1994, University of Rhode Island) is a postdoctoral research fellow in the Department of Psychiatry and Human Behavior at the Brown University School of Medicine. Her current research focuses on parent-child interaction and attachment relationships.

Axel Schöelmerich (Dr. Rer. Nat. 1990, Universität Onsabrück) is a visiting Fogarty fellow at the National Institute of Child Health and Human

Development, Bethesda, Maryland. His research interests include observational methods for studying social and emotional development, curiosity, and exploration during early infancy.

Ronald Seifer (Ph.D. 1981, University of Rochester) is an associate professor in the Department of Psychiatry and Human Behavior at the Brown University School of Medicine, Bradley Hospital. His research interests include relationship processes in children at risk for psychopathology, the development of temperament, and attachment relationships.

F. Francis Strayer (Ph.D. 1974, Simon Fraser University) is a professeur of developmental psychology at the Université de Toulouse II. He is also director of the Laboratory of Human Ethology at the Université du Québec à Montréal and directeur d'études at the Institute de Formation des Maîtres in Toulouse. His primary research concerns the application of psychobiological models in the study of the social relations of young children.

Berit Synnevaag (Doctoral candidate in clinical psychology, University of Bergen) is a psychotherapist and research scientist at Bergen University, Bergen, Norway. Her research has focused on neuropsychology and attachment and on family relationships.

Margarita Tascon (Psychologist 1991, Universidad Javeriana, Bogota) is a psychologist of the Instituto Colombiano de Bienestar Familiar, Bogata. Her work has focused on adoption and the evaluation of children's living conditions.

Dominique Treboux (Ph.D. 1989, Fordham University) is a postdoctoral research associate in the Department of Psychology, State University of New York at Stony Brook. Her research interests include family and peer influences on adolescent sexual behavior, behavior problems, and family interaction. She is also investigating adult attachment in engaged and dating adults and in adolescent mothers.

Marinus H. van IJzendoorn (Ph.D. 1978, Free University of Berlin) is professor of child and family studies at Leiden University. He specializes in attachment and parenting across the life span. He is the coauthor (with R. Van der Veer and J. Valsiner) of *Reconstructing the Mind: Replicability in Research on Human Development* and the author of "Adult Attachment Representations, Parental Responsiveness, and Infant Attachment."

Brian E. Vaughn (Ph.D. 1979, University of Minnesota) is a professor of family and child development at Auburn University. His research interests include the antecedents and consequences of infant-parent attachments and the relations between family attachments and the successful construction of larger social networks.

Manuela Verissimo (M.A. 1991, Institute for Applied Psychology, Lisbon) is a doctoral candidate in developmental psychology at the Université du Québec à Montréal. Her dissertation research centers on sociocultural determinants of parent-child relationships and the modulation of developmental trajectories in different socioecological contexts.

Everett Waters (Ph.D. 1977, University of Minnesota) is a professor of psychology at the State University of New York at Stony Brook. His research interests include observational methods for evaluating attachment behavior and attachment relationships beyond infancy and the consequences of individual differences in the assembly of secure-base behavior for subsequent relationships. He is the coauthor (with M. Ainsworth, M. Blehar, and S. Wall) of *Patterns of Attachment: A Psychological Study of the Strange Situation*.

Harriet Salatas Waters (Ph.D. 1976, University of Minnesota) is an associate professor of psychology at the State University of New York at Stony Brook. An expert on cognitive development, her research has focused on memory development and the development of prose production skills in children, adolescents, and adults.

Fang Wu (Ph.D. 1992, University of California, Los Angeles) is an assistant professor of education at Hood College. Her research focuses on crosscultural approaches to the study of children's peer relationships and on parent-child interactions.

The *Monographs* series is intended as an outlet for major reports of developmental research that generate authoritative new findings and use these to foster a fresh and/or better-integrated perspective on some conceptually significant issue or controversy. Submissions from programmatic research projects are particularly welcome; these may consist of individually or group-authored reports of findings from some single large-scale investigation or of a sequence of experiments centering on some particular question. Multiauthored sets of independent studies that center on the same underlying question can also be appropriate; a critical requirement in such instances is that the various authors address common issues and that the contribution arising from the set as a whole be both unique and substantial. In essence, irrespective of how it may be framed, any work that contributes significant data and/or extends developmental thinking will be taken under editorial consideration.

Submissions should contain a minimum of 80 manuscript pages (including tables and references); the upper limit of 150–175 pages is much more flexible (please submit four copies; a copy of every submission and associated correspondence is deposited eventually in the archives of the SRCD). Neither membership in the Society for Research in Child Development nor affiliation with the academic discipline of psychology are relevant; the significance of the work in extending developmental theory and in contributing new empirical information is by far the most crucial consideration. Because the aim of the series is not only to advance knowledge on specialized topics but also to enhance cross-fertilization among disciplines or subfields, it is important that the links between the specific issues under study and larger questions relating to developmental processes emerge as clearly to the general reader as to specialists on the given topic.

Potential authors who may be unsure whether the manuscript they are planning would make an appropriate submission are invited to draft an outline of what they propose and send it to the Editor for assessment. This mechanism, as well as a more detailed description of all editorial policies, evaluation processes, and format requirements, is given in the "Guidelines for the Preparation of *Monographs* Submissions," which can be obtained by writing to the Editor, Rachel K. Clifton, Department of Psychology, University of Massachusetts, Amherst, MA 01003.